THE

AMERICAN REVOLUTION

Vol. I

By SIR G. O. TREVELYAN, Bart., O.M.

THE AMERICAN REVOLUTION
In Six Volumes.   Crown 8vo   .   .   .   .

Separately, as follows : —
THE AMERICAN REVOLUTION
Volume I., with Portrait and Map.   .   .   .
Volume II., with Two Maps .   .   .   .   .
Volume III., with Map and Complete Index to Volumes I.–III.
Crown 8vo   .   .   .   .
Volume IV., Saratoga and Brandywine, Valley
Forge, England and France at War.
Crown 8vo, with Three Maps and Index .
GEORGE THE THIRD AND CHARLES FOX
The Concluding Part of "The American Revolution."
In Two Volumes.   Crown 8vo.   Cloth, gilt top.
Volume I., with a Map .   .   .   .   .   .
Volume II., with Map and Index to both Volumes

NEW YORK : LONGMANS, GREEN, AND CO.

Frank Holl R.A. Sep.t 1886.   Walker & Cockerell. Ph.Sc.

George Otto Trevelyan

ÆT 48.

THE

AMERICAN REVOLUTION

BY THE RIGHT HON.

SIR GEORGE OTTO TREVELYAN, BART.

AUTHOR OF " THE LIFE AND LETTERS OF LORD MACAULAY "
AND " THE EARLY HISTORY OF CHARLES JAMES FOX "

NEW EDITION

VOLUME I

WITH FRONTISPIECE

NEW IMPRESSION

LONGMANS, GREEN, AND CO.
FOURTH AVENUE & 30TH STREET, NEW YORK
LONDON, BOMBAY, CALCUTTA, AND MADRAS
1921

First Edition (Part I.) printed January, 1899.
Reprinted October, 1899, and December, 1903.
New Edition (Volume I.), Revised and Rearranged, January, 1905.
Reprinted May, 1908, September, 1909, and January, 1915.
Reprinted, with Revisions, April, 1917; July, 1921.

Norwood Press
J. S. Cushing & Co. — Berwick & Smith Co.
Norwood, Mass., U.S.A.

THESE VOLUMES ARE DEDICATED

TO THE BELOVED MEMORY

OF

EDWARD ERNEST BOWEN

AND

HENRY SIDGWICK

" Animæ, quales neque candidiores
Terra tulit, neque queis me sit devinctior alter."

PREFACE

THE "History of the American Revolution" has
been received with a degree of favour greatly surpass-
ing the expectations of the writer. Americans, especially, have learned with pleasure the brotherly feelings
entertained towards the colonists, from the beginning
to the end of the controversy, by a very large section
of the British people. The author has received assurances to that effect from historical students and writers,
and from statesmen at Washington of the highest authority, in private letters which it would not be becoming to print; and the same view has been developed by
many leading newspapers in the States. One passage,
from a well-known New York journal, may be extracted
as a fair specimen of a very great number of these
opinions. "We have been able to reproduce only a
small part of the evidence brought forward by Sir
George Trevelyan to show that the majority of the
British people were opposed to the attempt to coerce
the American Colonies. In our opinion, all candid
readers of the two volumes will acknowledge that he
has proved his case. It would not be easy to overestimate the effect which such a demonstration ought
to have, and doubtless will have, on the feeling with

vii

which Americans will hereafter regard Great Britain. It is manifest that most of our school histories of the United States will have to be rewritten, for the major part of them fail to recognize the momentous truth which the work before us must be held to have established."

The only return for such indulgence, which the author can make, is to do his best to deserve it. He commenced the book mainly for the personal pleasure of writing about events which had always attracted and moved him; and he is conscious that the First Part, which was published in 1899, made its appearance originally in a defective form. That First Part has now been completely re-arranged and somewhat re-written, and henceforward will stand as the First Volume of the "History of the American Revolution." A small amount of irrelevant matter has been expunged, and some important, (and it is hoped not uninteresting,) touches have been added. The chapters are consecutively numbered throughout the volumes, which form a continuous and sustained history of the period whereof they treat.

Something has been said in both countries about the absence of a printed list of the authorities consulted; but reflection will show that the composition of such a list would be undesirable and, indeed, impossible. No one could aspire to write a history of the American Revolution who had not read, and re-read, many scores

of books from cover to cover; who had not examined
and indexed several hundreds of other volumes; and
who had not looked into, or through, an innumerable
multitude of memoirs, pamphlets, newspapers, magazines, poems, and collections of printed and unprinted
documents.   The material for such a work is everywhere; and the collection of that material has been
to the author at first the unconscious, and of late the
conscious, occupation and delight of a lifetime.   To
print a list of those books from which something has
been taken, — and those which have been turned over
with no result except to find the confirmation of what
had been learned already, — might well be regarded as
ostentatious; and most readers will excuse, and probably applaud, the omission.   Wherever specially important assistance has been derived from any author,
whether living or dead, full and grateful recognition
is expressed in the notes throughout the volumes.

WELCOMBE,
STRATFORD-ON-AVON.

CONTENTS

OF VOLUME I

CHAPTER I

CHAPTER II

CHAPTER V

CHAPTER VI

CHAPTER VII

CHAPTER VIII

CHAPTER IX

CHAPTER X

CHAPTER XI

APPENDICES

At the End of the Volume

Map of Boston with its Environs.

O thou, that sendest out the man
 To rule by land and sea,
Strong mother of a Lion-line,
Be proud of those strong sons of thine
 Who wrench'd their rights from thee !

TENNYSON.

THE AMERICAN REVOLUTION

CHAPTER I

THE TEA-DUTY. THE BRITISH POLICY TOWARDS AMER-
ICA. THE COLONIAL GOVERNORS. SOCIAL CONDITION
OF GREAT BRITAIN AND THE COLONIES

IN the spring of 1766 a new chapter of peace and
good-will, — the first, as it seemed, of many fair volumes,
— had opened before the delighted eyes of all true
fellow-countrymen on either side of the Atlantic. "We
should find it hard," so writes an excellent and learned
author, "to overstate the happiness which, for a few
weeks, filled the hearts of the American people at the
news that the detested Stamp Act had been repealed.
As, in 1765, through the bond of a common fear, the
thirteen colonies had been brought for the first time into
some sort of union, so, in 1766, that union was for a
while prolonged through the bond of a common joy.
Certainly, never before had all these American communities been so swept by one mighty wave of grateful
enthusiasm and delight." [1]

No citizen of America, who recollected anything, forgot how and where he heard the glad tidings. Her
history, for a year to come, reads like the golden age.
Philadelphia waited for the fourth of June in order to
celebrate the King's Birthday, and the repeal of the

[1] Professor Tyler's *Literary History of the American Revolution.* This
book is a remarkable specimen of the historical faculty, and the descriptive
power, which have been expended by Americans on particular features in
that great panorama.

Stamp Act, together. Toasts were drunk to the Royal Family, to Parliament, and to " our worthy and faithful agent, Dr. Franklin." Franklin, determined that his household should rejoice in real earnest, sent his wife and daughter a handsome present of satins and brocades, to replace the clothes of their own spinning which they had worn while the crisis lasted, and while all good patriots refused to buy anything that had come from British ports. John Adams kept the occasion sadly. " A duller day than last Monday, when the Province was in a rapture for the repeal of the Stamp Act, I do not remember to have passed. My wife, who had long depended on going to Boston, and my little babe, were both very ill of an whooping-cough." But, in his view, the great concession had done its work thoroughly and finally. In November 1766, after six months' observation of its effects, he wrote : " The people are as quiet and submissive to Government as any people under the sun ; as little inclined to tumults, riots, seditions, as they were ever known to be since the first foundation of the Government. The repeal of the Stamp Act has composed every wave of popular disorder into a smooth and peaceful calm."

The mother-country had erred, had suffered, had repented, and had now retrieved her fault. Parliament, at the instance of Lord Rockingham and his colleagues, embodied in a statute the assertion of its own right to make laws binding on the colonies in all cases whatsoever ; and then it repealed the Stamp Act, as a practical admission that the right in question should be exercised only in cases where the colonies did not object. The proceeding was intensely English ; but unfortunately it lacked the most important condition of a great English compromise, for it was not accepted by the beaten party. George Grenville, the parent of the Stamp-duty, and reputed to be the greatest living master of finance, bitterly resented the reversal of his policy; and he spoke the views of a very powerful minority of the Commons. In the other House a Protest was carefully drawn with

the purpose of defying, and insulting, what was then
the unanimous opinion of Americans. It was signed
by a body of lay peers, respectable at any rate in numbers, and by five bishops, who wrote their names between
those of Sandwich and Weymouth like men so sure of
their cause that there was no need to be nice about their
company. Warburton of Gloucester, the ablest and by
far the most distinguished among them, has left on
record his own view of the duty of a father of the Church
when dealing with affairs of State ; and the theory which
satisfied him was good enough for his brethren. " Let
us private men," he wrote, when already a bishop, " preserve and improve the little we have left of private virtue ; and, if one of those infected with the influenza of
politics should ask me, 'What then becomes of your
public virtue ?' I would answer him with an old Spanish
proverb : 'The King has enough for us all.'"

The King's idea of public virtue at this memorable
conjuncture was notorious everywhere, and talked about
freely by every one except by the Ministers, who, from
the unfortunate obligations of their position, were bound
to pretend to believe the Royal word. The course of
action which alone could secure peace and welfare to his
Empire had in him an opponent more resolute and
bitter even than Grenville. No Protest, phrased deco-
rously enough to be admitted upon the Journals of the
House of Lords, could have adequately expressed the
sentiments of George the Third towards his subjects
beyond the water. On their account the dislike which
he had all along entertained for his Ministers had deepened into busy and unscrupulous hostility. He looked
upon the conciliation of America, which those Ministers
had effected, as an act of inexpiable disloyalty to the
Crown. He thwarted them by an intrigue which has
acquired a shameful immortality from the literary ability
of a statesman who suffered from it, and of historians
who have recounted it. How the King, acting through
the King's Friends, harassed and hampered the King's
Ministers during the debates on the Stamp Act, is told

by Burke in the " Thoughts on the Discontents," and by Macaulay in the second Essay on Chatham ; and seldom or never did either of them write more pointedly and powerfully. The process is concisely described by Mr. Lecky, in the twelfth chapter of his History. "When the measure was first contemplated, two partisans of Bute came to the King, offering to resign their places, as they meant to oppose the repeal; but they were told that they might keep their places and vote as they pleased. The hint was taken, and the King's Friends were among the most active, though not the most conspicuous, opponents of the Ministers."

When, in spite of his efforts, the work of pacification was accomplished, George the Third never forgave his wise and faithful servants for having saved him from himself. Determined to punish, he fell diligently to the task of finding an instrument; and he soon was able to place his hand on a noble weapon, which he used with remarkable skill in a very bad cause. The love of Britain for Pitt was not stronger than the aversion with which, in life, and after death, he was regarded by Britain's sovereign. But at this crisis the great Commoner was recommended to the Royal notice by the circumstance, which was unhappily notorious, that he looked coldly upon the statesmen whom George the Third hated ; and, as soon as the King was sure of Pitt, he got quit of Rockingham. Under cover of a name which has elevated and adorned the annals of our Parliament, was formed a bad and foolish administration which woefully misdirected our national policy. That tissue of scrapes and scandals which marked their conduct of home affairs belongs to a period when Chatham was no longer in office ; but the most disastrous and gratuitous of their blunders abroad dates from the time when he still was nominally Prime Minister. On the second of June, 1767, a series of Resolutions were passed in Committee of Ways and Means, imposing duties upon a number of commodities admitted into the British colonies and plantations in America; and it was

the seventeenth of these Resolutions which provided
" That a duty of 3*d*. per pound-weight avoirdupois be
laid upon all tea imported into the said colonies and
plantations."

It is a measure of the greatness of Chatham that, citizen and subject as he was, his opinions and predilec-
tions, nay his very moods and prejudices, affected the
general course of events as deeply as it has, ever or anywhere, been affected by the character of the most powerful monarchs who have had an absolute hold on the
resources and policy of a State.   Just as the history of
Germany would have run in other channels if Frederic
the Great had not been King of Prussia at the death of
the Emperor Charles the Sixth; just as Spain would
have been spared untold calamities if any one but
Napoleon had been on the throne of France when
Ferdinand quarrelled with his father; so the fortunes
of the English-speaking world would have looked very
different in the retrospect if only Chatham had been in
the mind to act cordially with the right men at the right
moment.   With Rockingham as his second in command,
— with Lord John Cavendish, or Dowdeswell, or, (still
better,) with Burke as his Chancellor of the Exchequer,
— he might have lingered in the retirement, to which his
shattered health inclined him, without any damage to
the public interest or to his own fame.   But with Grafton dispensing the patronage, and holding Cabinets, in
his absence, and with Charles Townshend master of the
revels in the House of Commons, the step was taken,
and taken in the name of Chatham, which in one day
reversed the policy that he had nearest at heart, and
undid the work of which he was most justly proud.
The Boston Massacre; the horrors of the Indian warfare; the mutual cruelties of partisans in the Carolinas;
Saratoga and Yorktown; the French war; the Spanish
war; the wholesale ruin of the American loyalists; the
animosity towards Great Britain which for so long afterwards coloured the foreign policy of the United States;
— all flowed in direct and inevitable sequence from

that fatal escapade.   Among the bright possibilities of history, very few can be entertained with better show of reason than a belief that the two nations might have kept house together with comfort, and in the end might have parted friends, if the statesman whom both of them equally revered and trusted would have thrown in his lot with that English party which, almost to a man, shared his wise views in regard to the treatment of our colonies, and sympathised with the love which he bore their people.

The first cardinal mistake had now been made, and the next was not long in coming.   British politicians had much else to talk of ; and the hardworking, quiet-living British people, after the Stamp Act was repealed, had returned to their business, and put America out of their thoughts, as they supposed, for ever.   They were not prepared for the instant and bewildering sensation which the news of what had been done at Westminster produced across the ocean.   It was, indeed, a rude awakening for the colonists, one and all, irrespective of class, creed, and calling.   In the assurance that past scores were now clean wiped out, they had settled themselves down to the sober enjoyment of a victory which seemed the more secure because all concerned had their part in it ; for if America had carried her point, England had conquered herself.   And now, without warning, without fresh reason given, the question was reopened by the stronger of the two parties under circumstances which to the weaker portended ruin.   The situation was far more ominous than if the Stamp-duty had been left where it was.   Parliament, by repealing the Act, had publicly recognised and admitted that the claim to tax America was one to which America would never submit ; and yet, a twelvemonth afterwards, that claim was revived on a larger scale, and with a deliberation which showed that this time England meant business.   It was impossible for the colonists, — who were all, in a sort, politicians, one as much as another, — to understand that the great mass of Englishmen attended seldom and little to a matter which for themselves was everything; which had exclusively occupied their minds, and con- sumed their energies, during six and thirty busy and anxious months; and which, almost against their will, had taught them to feel as a nation, to meet in general council, and to plan combined action.

But, if America did not take sufficient account of the indifference and ignorance of England as a whole, her instinct told her, and told her rightly, that great men behind the scenes, before they raised the standard of British supremacy, had counted the cost, and were now fighting to win. Awed by the suddenness and magni- tude of the peril, the colonial leaders acted with circum- spection and rare self-control. Abstaining themselves, and with notable success restraining their followers, from the more violent courses which had marked the campaign against the Stamp Act, they undertook the task of appealing to the good sense and the friendliness of the British people. John Dickinson of Pennsylvania, so true to England that he lost all heart for politics as soon as a time came when he could no longer be true to England without being disloyal to America, put the case against the Revenue Acts with conclusive force, and in attractive shape. His " Farmer's Letters," having done their work at home, were published by Franklin in London, were translated into French, and were read by everybody in the two capitals of civilisation who read anything more serious than a play-bill. The members of the Massachusetts Assembly resolutely and soberly assumed the responsibility of giving an official voice to the grievances of America. They explained their con- tention in a letter which their agent in England was directed to lay before the British Cabinet; and they transmitted a Petition to the King, recounting the early struggles of their colony, its services to the Empire, the rights and privileges with which it had been rewarded, and its recent intolerable wrongs. The language used was manly, simple, and even touching, if anything could have touched him whom they still tried to regard as the father of his people. The documents were written in draft by Samuel Adams; and one of them, at least, was revised no less than seven times in full conclave with the object of excluding any harsh or intemperate expression. And then they prepared themselves for the very worst; because, though they fain would hope against hope, they only too well knew that the worst would come. They addressed a circular letter to the other representative Assemblies on the American continent, urging them to take such steps, within the limits of the Constitution, as would strengthen the hands of a sister colony which had done its duty, according to its light, in the presence of a great emergency, and which now ventured freely to make known its mind to them upon a common concern.

It was all to no purpose. Their Petition was thrown aside unanswered, much as if they had been a meeting of heritors in Scotland who had passed a resolution calling for the repeal of the Act of Union during the hours which ought to have been spent on parish business. But, as regards the circular letter, even that parallel could not hold; for no Minister would have treated the humblest local body in any of the three Kingdoms in the style which the Secretary of State employed in dealing with the senates of America.[1] Lord Hillsborough informed the Governor of Massachusetts that her representatives must rescind the resolution on which that audacious letter was based, or be sent back to their homes then and there. The Assemblies of the twelve other colonies were enjoined, in so many words, to take no notice of the appeal from Boston, and to treat it

---

[1] George the Third, and his Cabinet, were much less wise in their generation than Charles the Second, and his Commissioners of Trade and Plantations. John Evelyn, who was on the Board, gives an interesting account of their first meeting, which took place on the twenty-sixth of May, 1671. The King specially recommended them to consider the form in which to address the colony of New England, where the people were so rich, powerful, and independent. "Some of our Council," said Evelyn, "were for sending them a menacing letter, which those who better understood the peevish and touchy humour of that colony were utterly against."

with the contempt which it deserved, on pain, in their
case likewise, of an immediate prorogation or dissolution.
Such a message could bring only one answer from men
who had our blood in their veins, and in whose village
schools our history was taught as their own.   Junius,
no blind partisan of the Americans, wrote of them with
force and truth.   " They have been driven into excesses
little short of rebellion.   Petitions have been hindered
from reaching the Throne ; and the continuance of one
of the principal Assemblies rested upon an arbitrary
condition, which, considering the temper they were in,
it was impossible they should comply with."   At Boston, in the fullest House that had ever met, ninety-two
members, as against seventeen, flatly declined to withdraw the letter.   The Assemblies of the other colonies
stood stoutly by their fugleman, and faced, and in some
cases paid, the threatened penalty.

In one city and another, from New York to Charleston, the language which had been familiar under the
Stamp Act again was heard.   The Sons of Liberty began to stir.   The glorious majority was celebrated by
processions with ninety-two torches, and banquets with
an almost interminable list of toasts.   Above all, a combination against the use of British manufactures once more
was openly talked of ; and the young ladies looked out
their spinning-wheels, and the young gentlemen reflected
ruefully that the weather was already warm for home-
made linsey-wolsey.   Boston itself, all things considered,
was tranquil almost to tameness, until an unhappy incident ruffled the peaceful waters.   The captain of a frigate, which mounted guard over the town, had taken
advantage of his station at the mouth of the harbour to
intercept and impress New England sailors as they returned home from sea.   During the height of his unpopularity a boat's-crew from his ship, on an alleged breach
of the revenue laws, seized a sloop which, to make the
matter worse, was owned by a prominent patriot, and
was called " The Liberty."   A disturbance ensued, far
less serious than the magistrates of Sunderland and

Hartlepool, and every North of England port which possessed a custom-house and was visited by a press-gang, in those rough times were accustomed to deal with as part of the year's work. But the English Ministers were sore and nervous. The mildest whisper of a non-importation agreement, and the most distant echo of a revenue riot, so long as they came from beyond the Western waters, awoke reminiscences which were too much for their temper and their equanimity. The King, especially, had Boston on the brain. To this day there are some among her sons who can forgive his memory for anything rather than for the singular light in which he persisted in regarding their classic city. The capital of Massachusetts, in the eyes of its Sovereign, was nothing better than a centre of vulgar sedition, bristling with Trees of Liberty and strewn with brickbats and broken glass; where his enemies went about clothed in homespun, and his friends in tar and feathers.

Whatever his view might be, George the Third was now well able to impose it on the Ministry. Chatham had retired, and the Duke of Grafton, who was not master of his colleagues, held the office of First Lord of the Treasury. The Bedfords by this time had contrived to establish themselves solidly in the Government, and were always at hand to feed the flame of the King's displeasure. They eagerly represented to him that his authority had been trifled with long enough, and promised that five or six frigates and one strong brigade would soon bring not only Massachusetts, but the whole American continent, to reason. Lord Shelburne, to his infinite credit, fought the battle of sense and humanity singlehanded within the Cabinet, and stoutly declared that he would be no party to despatching to New England a cutter, or a company, in addition to the force that was there already. Franklin, whom Shelburne admired and believed in, had reminded the House of Commons that a regiment of infantry could not oblige a man to take stamps, or drink tea, if he chose to do without; and had expressed it as his opinion that, if troops were sent to America, they would not find a rebellion, although they would be only too likely to make one.[1]   But Franklin's wit had too much wisdom in it for George the Third, and for such of his counsellors as knew what advice was expected of them.   The Bedfords carried the day, and Shelburne resigned office.   Early in October 1768, eight ships of war lay in Boston harbour.   Their loaded broadsides commanded a line of wharves a great deal more peaceable than was the quay of North Shields during one of the periodical disputes between the keelmen and the coal-shippers.   Cannon and infantry were landed, and the men were marched on to the Common with drums beating and colours flying, and sixteen rounds of ball-cartridge in their pouches.   The first contingent consisted of two battalions, and the wing of another ; and subsequent reinforcements increased the garrison until Boston contained at least one red-coat for every five of the men, women, and children who made up the total of her seventeen thousand inhabitants.

Thus the second stage was reached in the downward course.   How serious a step it was, how absolutely irretrievable except on the condition of being retracted forthwith, is now a commonplace of history.   But its gravity was acknowledged at the time by few Englishmen ; and those who were specially responsible for the conduct of affairs were blind amidst the one-eyed.   It is not too much to say that, among our own people of every degree, the governing classes understood America the least.   One cause of ignorance they had in common with others of their countrymen.   We understand the Massachusetts of 1768 better than it was understood by most Englishmen who wrote that date at the head of their letters ; for, when the question is that of getting to

[1] Examination of Dr. Benjamin Franklin before the House in Committee. *The Parliamentary History of England*, vol. xiv., p. 147.   Burke said that, when Franklin appeared before Parliament to be examined on the condition of things in America, it was like a parcel of schoolboys interrogating the master.

know what the world outside Europe was like four generations ago, distance of time is less of an obstacle to us,
in an age when all read, than was distance of space to
our ancestors before the days of steam and telegraph.
A man bound for New York, as he sent his luggage on
board at Bristol, would willingly have compounded for
a voyage lasting as many weeks as it now lasts days.
When Franklin, still a youth, went to London to buy
the press and types by which he hoped to found his
fortune, he had to wait the best part of a twelvemonth
for the one ship which then made an annual trip between
Philadelphia and the Thames.   When, in 1762, already
a great man, he sailed for England in a convoy of merchantmen, he spent all September and October at sea,
enjoying the calm weather, as he always enjoyed everything; dining about on this vessel and the other; and
travelling "as in a moving village, with all one's neighbours about one."   Adams, during the height of the war,
hurrying to France in the finest frigate which Congress
could place at his disposal, — and with a captain who
knew that, if he encountered a superior force, his distinguished guest did not intend to be carried alive under
British hatches, — could make no better speed than five
and forty days between Boston and Bordeaux.   Lord
Carlisle, carrying an olive-branch the prompt delivery
of which seemed a matter of life and death to the Ministry that sent him out, was six weeks between port and
port, tossed by gales which inflicted on his brother
Commissioners agonies such as he forbore to make a
matter of joke even to George Selwyn.   General Ried-
esel, conducting the Brunswick auxiliaries to fight in a
quarrel which was none of theirs, counted three mortal
months from the day when he stepped on deck at Stade
in the Elbe to the day when he stepped off it at Quebec
in the St. Lawrence.   If such was the lot of plenipoten-
tiaries on mission, and of generals in command, it may
be imagined how humbler individuals fared, the duration
of whose voyage concerned no one but themselves.
Waiting weeks on the wrong side of the water for a full

complement of passengers, and weeks more for a fair
wind ; — and then beating across in a badly found tub,
with a cargo of millstones and old iron rolling about
below ; — they thought themselves lucky if they came
into harbour a month after their private stores had run
out, and carrying a budget of news as stale as the ship's
provisions.[1]

Whatever else got across the Atlantic under such conditions, fresh and accurate knowledge of what people on
the opposite coast thought, and how they lived, most
assuredly did not.   War is a great teacher of geography.
The ideas about men, laws, and localities in the United
States, which were current here until Lee's Virginian
campaigns and Sherman's March to Savannah, the Proclamation of Freedom, and the re-election of Lincoln,
came successively to enlighten us, were vague and distorted even in an era of ocean steamers ; but those
ideas were tame and true as compared to the images
which floated across the mental vision of our grandfather's grandfather whenever he took the trouble to
think about the colonies.   The hallucinations of the
British mind, practical even in its fantasies, assumed
the shape of fabulous statistics which went to show that
America, unless her commercial ambition was kept tight
in hand, would overset the intentions of Providence by
ceasing to supply her wants exclusively from Britain.
" The great defect here," Franklin wrote from London,
" is in all sorts of people a want of attention to what
passes in such remote countries as America ; an unwillingness to read anything about them if it appears a little
lengthy ; and a disposition to postpone the consideration
even of the things they know they must at last consider,
so that they may have time for what more immediately
concerns them, and withal enjoy their amusements, and
be undisturbed in the universal dissipation." [2]   They

[1] Among accounts of such voyages, none are more life-like than those
which may be found in Davis's *Travels in America*, published in 1803 ;
an exquisitely absurd book, which the world, to the diminution of its gaiety,
has forgotten.
[2] Letter to Samuel Cooper ; London, July 7, 1773.

read as little as they could help; and, when they did
read, they were informed by the debates in Parliament
that the farmers and backwoodsmen of the West, if
they were permitted to manufacture in iron, in cotton,
and in wool, and to export the produce of their labour
all the world over, would speedily kill the industries of
Leeds and Manchester and Sheffield. And they learned
from the newspapers, for whom Niagara and the
Rapids did not exist, that the interests of Newfoundland
were threatened by a scheme for the establishment of
a cod and whale fishery in Lake Erie and Lake On-
tario. That was the sort of stuff, said Franklin, which
was produced for the amusement of coffee-house students
in politics, and was the material for "all future Livys,
Rapins, Robertsons, Humes, and Macaulays who may
be inclined to furnish the world with that rara avis, a
true history."[1]

Over and above the misconceptions prevailing in
other quarters, Ministers of State were under a disadvantage peculiar to themselves. While other Englishmen were ignorant, they were habitually misinformed.
In recent years the nation has more than once learned
by bitter experience the evils which arise from bad
advice sent home by administrators on the spot, whether
they be dull people who cannot interpret what is passing around them, or clever people with a high-flying
policy of their own. But the Colonial Governors and
High Commissioners of our own times have been men
of good, and sometimes of lofty, character; whereas
the personages upon whose reports Lord Hillsborough
and Lord Dartmouth had to depend for forming their
notions of the American population, and in accordance
with whose suggestions the course taken at an emer-

[1] Letter of May 1765 to the editor of a newspaper, under the signature of "A Traveller." Mrs. Catharine Macaulay, author of *The History of England from the Accession of James the First to that of the
Brunswick Line*, was then much in vogue among the Whigs. They were
rather at a loss for an historian of their own, to set against the Jacobitism
of David Hume.

gency by the British Cabinet was necessarily shaped, were in many cases utterly unworthy of their trust Among them were needy politicians, and broken-down stockjobbers, who in better days had done a good turn to a Minister, and for whom a post had to be found at times when the English public departments were too full, or England itself was too hot, to hold them. There remained the resource of shipping them across the Atlantic to chaffer for an increase of salary with the Assembly of their colony, and to pester their friends at home with claims for a pension which would enable them to revisit London without fear of the Marshalsea. They took small account socially of the plain and shrewd people amongst whom their temporary lot was thrown; and they were the last to understand the nature and motives of that moral repugnance with which their superciliousness was repaid.

On the Secretary of State's list there were better men than these, who unfortunately were even worse governors. It so happened that in critical places, and at moments which were turning-points of history, the highest post in the colony was more often than not occupied by some man of energy and industry, who in personal conduct was respectable according to the standard then ruling in the most easy branch of a public service nowhere given to austerity. But they were not of an intellectual capacity equal to a situation which would have tried the qualities of a Turgot. They moved in an atmosphere such that perverted public spirit was more dangerous than no public spirit at all. A great man would have sympathised with the aspirations of the colonists; a lazy man would have laughed at and disregarded them; but, (by a tendency irresistible in times of unrest and popular discontent,) a narrow and plodding man is the predestined enemy of those whom it is his vocation to govern. Exactly in proportion as people are keen to detect their rights, and formidable to insist on having them, a governor of this type is certain to distrust their aims, to disapprove their methods, and bitterly to dislike their turn of character. In his eyes, the rough and ready incidents that accompany the spread of political excitement in a young community are so many acts of treason against his office, which he is always apt to magnify.   His self-respect is wounded; his sense of official tradition is honestly shocked ; and, while the people are intent upon what they regard as a public controversy, he is sure to treat the whole matter as a personal conflict between himself and them.

Such a man, in such a state of mind and temper, makes it his duty, and finds it his consolation, to pour out his griefs and resentments in the correspondence which he carries on with his official superiors.   It is the bare truth that his own Governors and Lieutenant-Governors wrote King George out of America.   The stages of the process are minutely recorded by an analytic philosopher who enjoyed every facility for conducting his observations.   "Their office," wrote Franklin, "makes them insolent; their insolence makes them odious ; and, being conscious that they are hated, they become malicious.   Their malice urges them to continual abuse of the inhabitants in their letters to Administration, representing them as disaffected and rebellious, and, (to encourage the use of severity,) as weak, divided, timid, and cowardly.   Government believes all; thinks it necessary to support and countenance its officers. Their quarrelling with the people is deemed a mark and consequence of their fidelity.   They are therefore more highly rewarded, and this makes their conduct still more insolent and provoking."

It was a picture painted from life, in strong but faithful colours.   The letters of Bernard, the Governor of Massachusetts, contained the germ of all the culpable and foolish proceedings which, at the long last, alienated America.   As far back as the year 1764 he wrote a memorandum in which he urged the Cabinet to quash the Charters of the colonies.   Throughout the agitation against the Stamp-duty he studiously exaggerated the turbulence of the popular party, and underrated their

courage and sincerity. "The people here," he wrote
in January 1766, "talk very high of their power to resist
Great Britain ; but it is all talk. New York and Boston
would both be defenceless to a royal fleet. I hope
that New York will have the honour of being subdued first." When, to his chagrin, the obnoxious tax
was abolished, Bernard set himself persistently to the
work of again troubling the quieted waters. He proposed, in cold blood, during the interval between the
repeal of the Stamp Act and the imposition of the Tea-
duty, that Massachusetts should be deprived of her Assembly. When the new quarrel arose, he lost no chance
of stimulating the fears of the Court, and flattering its
prejudices. He sent over lists of Royalists who might
be nominated to sit as councillors in the place of the
ejected representatives, and lists of Patriots who should
be deported to England, and there tried for their lives.
He called on the Bedfords for troops as often and as
importunately as ever the Bedfords themselves had
called for trumps when a great stake was on the card-
table. He advised that the judges, and the civil servants, of Massachusetts should be paid by the Crown
with money levied from the colony. He pleaded in
secret that the obnoxious taxes should never, and on no
account, be repealed or mitigated; while in a public
despatch he recommended that a petition from the Assembly, praying for relief from these very taxes, should
be favourably considered. For this plot against the
liberties of America was carried on out of the view of
her people. Amidst the surprise and dismay inspired
by each successive stroke of severity with which they
were visited, the colonists did not recognise, and in some
cases did not even suspect, the hand of their own paid
servants, who were for ever professing to mediate between them and their angry sovereign. Since Machia-
velli undertook to teach the Medici how principalities
might be governed and maintained, no such body of literature was put on paper as that in which Sir Francis
Bernard, (for his services procured him a baronetcy,)

instructed George the Third and his Ministers in the art
of throwing away a choice portion of a mighty Empire.

But in order to comprehend a policy which lay so
far outside the known and ordinary limits of human
infatuation, it must never be forgotten that there was a
deeper and a more impassable gulf than the Atlantic
between the colonists and their rulers.   If Cabinet
Ministers at home had known the Americans better,
they would only have loved them less.   The higher up
in the peerage an Englishman stood, and the nearer to
influence and power, the more unlikely it was that he
would be in sympathy with his brethren across the seas,
or that he would be capable of respecting their suscepti-
bilities, and of apprehending their virtues, which were
less to his taste even than their imperfections.   It is
unnecessary to recapitulate any portion of the copious
mass of evidence, drawn from their own mouths, and
those of their boon companions and confederates, by
aid of which a description, — and the accuracy of it no
one has thought fit to impugn, — has been given of the
personal habits and the public morality prevalent among
those statesmen whom the majority in Parliament supported, and in whom the King reposed his confidence.[1]
How they drank and gamed ; what scandalous modes
of life they led themselves, and joyously condoned in
others ; what they spent and owed, and whence they
drew the vast sums of money by which they fed their
profusion, may be found in a hundred histories and
memoirs, dramas, novels, and satires.   But the story is
nowhere recorded in such downright language, and with
so over-brimming an abundance of detail, as in the easy
mutual confidences of the principal actors ; if, indeed,
that can be called a confidence which the person concerned would have told with equal freedom and self-
complacency to any man, — and, it must be confessed,
to many women, — as long as the hearers were of **his**
own rank, and belonged to his own party.

[1] Chapter iii. of the *Early History of Charles James Fox.*

These folk were the product of their age, which, in its worst aspect, resembled nothing that England has known before or since. The stern heroes who waged the great civic contest of the seventeenth century, and who drew their strength from the highest of all sources, had been succeeded by a race who in private very generally lived for enjoyment, and in Parliament fought for their own hand. The fibre of our public men had long been growing dangerously lax; and at length temptation came in irresistible force. The sudden wealth, which poured into England after Chatham had secured her predominance in both hemispheres, brought in its train a flood of extravagance and corruption, and occasioned grave misgivings to those who were proud of her good name, and who understood her real interests. There was now, however, in store for our country a severe and searching lesson, the direct consequence of her faults, and proportioned to their magnitude, but by which as a nation she was capable of profiting. She escaped the fate of other world-wide empires by the noble spirit in which she accepted the teaching of disaster. From the later years of the American war onwards there set in a steady and genuine reformation in personal and political morals which carried her safe, strong, and pure through the supreme ordeal of the wrestle with Napoleon.

But nothing is more certain than that there was a period when Englishmen who had studied the past, and who watched the present, recognised a very close parallel between their own country and the capital of the ancient world at the time when the Provinces lay helpless and defenceless at the disposal of the Imperial Government. They read their Gibbon with uneasy presentiments, and were not disposed to quarrel with satirists who found in London and Bath much the same material as Rome and Baiæ had afforded to Juvenal. Smollett, though by preference he drew from ugly models, depicted things as he saw them, and not as he imagined them. Those scenes of coarseness and debauchery, of place-hunting and bribery, of mean tyranny and vulgar

c 2

favouritism, which make his town-stories little short ot
nauseous, and give to his sea-stories their unpleasing
but unquestionable power, were only the seamy side of
that tapestry on which more fashionable artists recorded
the sparkling follies and splendid jobbery of their era.
Great in describing the symptoms, Smollett had detected
the root of the disease, as is shown in his description of
the throng of visitors who came to drink the Bath waters.
"All these absurdities," he wrote, "arise from the general tide of luxury, which hath overpowered the nation,
and swept away all, even the dregs of the people. Clerks
and factors from the East Indies, loaded with the spoils
of plundered provinces; planters, negro-drivers, and
hucksters from our American plantations, enriched they
know not how; agents, commissaries, and contractors,
who have fattened in two successive wars on the blood
of the nation; usurers, brokers, and jobbers of every
kind; men of low birth and no breeding, have found themselves suddenly translated to a state of affluence unknown to former ages."[1]

Other writers, who were not professional cynics, and
who observed mankind with no inclination to make the
worst of what they saw, were all in the same story.
Horne Tooke pronounced that English manners had not
changed by degrees, but of a sudden; and he attributed
it chiefly to our connection with India that luxury and
corruption had flowed in, "not as in Greece, like a gentle
rivulet, but after the manner of a torrent."[2] On such
a point no more unimpeachable witnesses can be found
than those American Tories who sacrificed their homes,
their careers, and their properties for love of England,
and for the duty which they thought that they owed her.
These honest men were shocked and pained to find that
in passing from the colonies to the mother-country they
had exchanged an atmosphere of hardihood, simplicity,
and sobriety for what seemed to them a perpetual cy-
clone of prodigality and vice. Their earlier letters,

---

[1] *Humphrey Clinker;* the letter from Bath of April 23.
[2] *Memoirs of John Horne Tooke*, vol. ii., p. 488.

before they had grown accustomed to a state of manners
which they never could bring themselves to approve,
breathe in every paragraph disappointment and disillu-
sion.[1] The blemishes on the fair fame of England,
which these unhappy children of her adoption discovered
late in life, were familiar to her native sons from the
time when they first began to take account of what was
going on around them. Churchill's denunciations of
the rake, the gamester, and the duellist in high places
of trust and power read to us now like the conventional
invective of satire; but in his own generation they were
true to the life and the letter. And Cowper, whose
most halting verse had a dignity and sincerity which
must ever be wanting to Churchill's bouncing couplets,
made it a complaint against his country

> "That she is rigid in denouncing death
> On petty robbers, and indulges life
> And liberty, and oft-times honour too,
> To peculators of the public gold :
> That thieves at home must hang, but he that **puts**
> Into his overgorged and bloated purse
> The wealth of Indian provinces, escapes." [2]

By whatever channels money flowed into the country,
it was in the nature of things that those who were the
strongest should get the most. The people of birth
and fashion, who as a class were always in power, had
no mind to be outbid and outshone by any nabob, or
army contractor, or West Indian planter who was push-

---

[1] Samuel Curwen, for instance, who left Salem in Massachusetts for London in May 1775, writes in July of the same year : "The dissipation, self-
forgetfulness, and vicious indulgences of every kind which characterise this
metropolis are not to be wondered at. The unbounded riches of many
afford the means of every species of luxury, which, (thank God,) our part
of America is ignorant of." And again in the following August : "You
will not wonder at the luxury, dissipation, and profligacy of manners said
to reign in this capital, when you consider that the temptations to indulgence, from the lowest haunts to the most elegant and expensive rendez-
vous of the noble and polished world, are almost beyond the power of
number to reckon up."

[2] Book I. of *The Task*.

ing himself to the front in Parliament and in society.   In order to hold their own against the new men in wealth, and in all that wealth brings, they had one resource, and one only.   The opinion of their set forbade them to engage in trade; and, apart from any question of sentiment, their self-indulgent habits unfitted them for the demands of a genuine business life, which were more severe then than now.   The spurious business which a gentleman may do in his off hours with no commercial training, no capital, and no risk except to honour, was unknown in those primitive days.   In the eighteenth century the City did not care to beg or to buy any man's name, unless he gave with it the whole of his time and the whole of his credit.   But a great peer had small cause to regret that the gates of commerce were barred to him and his, as long as he could help himself out of the taxes, and help himself royally; for, in that paradise of privilege, what an individual received from the public was in proportion to the means which he possessed already.   Horace Walpole, who lived very long and very well on sinecures which were waiting for him when he came of age, said that there was no living in England under twenty thousand a year. "Not that that suffices; but it enables one to ask for a pension for two or three lives."

A nobleman with a large supply of influence to sell, who watched the turn of the market, and struck in at the right moment, might make the fortune of his family in the course of a single week.   "To-morrow," Rigby wrote to the Duke of Bedford in September 1766, "Lord Hertford kisses hands for Master of the Horse. Lord Beauchamp is made Constable of Dublin Castle for life in the room of an old Mr. Hatton.   Lord Hertford gives Mr. Hatton a thousand pounds to quit his employment, which was five hundred a year.   A thousand more is added, and Lord Beauchamp has got it for his life.   There is another job done for another son in a Custom-house place, which will be a thousand a year more.   In short, what with sons and daughters,

and boroughs, and employments of all kinds, I never
heard of such a trading voyage as his Lordship's has
proved." Rigby himself, — whose stock-in-trade was an
effrontery superior to the terrors of debate, a head of
proof in a drinking bout, and an undeniable popularity
with all circles whose good-will was no compliment, —
was Master of the Rolls in Ireland, or rather out of Ireland, for life. In addition, he enjoyed for the space of
fourteen years the vast and more than questionable
emoluments of a Paymaster of the Forces who was
without a conscience, and with a good friend at the
Treasury. A balance of eleven hundred thousand
pounds of public money stood in his name at the bank,
the interest on which went to him, or rather to his
creditors; for he lived and died insolvent. To this day
the nation has against him a bad debt of a large
amount, — in the sense, that is, in which a traveller
whose purse has been taken has a bad debt against a
highwayman.

The increasing luxury, and the rise in the standard of
living, which drove great men into these raids on the
Exchequer, at the same time provided the means of
gratifying, if not of satisfying, their rapacity. New
offices were created out of the superfluities of the
revenue; and, as each year went round, those which
already existed became better worth having. The
receipts of the Customs and the Excise together under
Lord North were double what they had been under Sir
Robert Walpole. The profits of patent places, received
in the shape of fees or percentages, mounted steadily
upwards as the business which passed through the
hands of the holder, or of his humble and poorly paid
subordinates, grew in importance and in volume. The
Usher of the Exchequer saw his gains, in the course of
one generation, grow from nine hundred to eighteen
hundred, and from eighteen hundred to four thousand
two hundred pounds a year. The spread of commerce,
the rush of enterprise, brought causes into the Courts,
and private Bills on to the table of Parliament, in

numbers such that many a post, which twenty years
before had been regarded as a moderate competence for
life, now enabled its occupier to entertain the ambition
of founding a family out of the tribute which he levied
from litigants and promoters.[1]

The domestic history of the epoch clearly shows that
every noble, and even gentle, household in the kingdom
claimed as the birthright of its members that they should
live by salary. The eldest son succeeded to the estate;
the most valuable part of which, more productive than
a coal-mine or a slate-quarry, was some dirty village
which returned a member for each half-score of its
twenty cottages. The second son was in the Guards.
The third took a family living, and looked forward to
holding at least a Canonry as well. The fourth entered
the Royal Navy ; and those that came after, (for fathers
of all ranks did their duty by the State, whose need of
men was then at the greatest,) joined a marching regiment as soon as they were strong enough to carry the
colours. And as soldiers and sailors, whatever might
be the case in other departments, our ancestors gave
full value for their wages. From the day when Rodney
broke the line off Dominica, back to the day when de
Grammont did not break the line at Dettingen, a commission in the British army or navy was no sinecure.
Our aristocracy took the lion's share; but they played
the lion's part. The sons and grandsons of the houses
of Manners and Keppel did not do their work in the
trenches and on the quarter-deck by proxy. Killed in
Germany, killed in America, killed in the Carnatic with
Lawrence, killed on the high seas in an action of frigates,

[1] The case was well put by Dr. Watson, afterwards Bishop of Llandaff,
in a letter to the Duke of Manchester in the year 1780. Writing, (for so
staunch a Whig,) with great moderation, Watson said : " The influence of
the Crown, — which has acquired its present strength more, perhaps, from
the additional increase of empire, commerce, and national wealth, than
from any criminal desire to subvert the Constitution, — has pervaded, I
fear, the whole mass of the people. Every man of consequence almost in
the kingdom has a son, relation, friend, or dependant, whom he wishes to
provide for ; and, unfortunately for the liberty of this country, the Crown
has the means of gratifying the expectation of them all."

drowned in a transport, died of wounds on his way home from the West Indies, — such entries, coming thick and fast over a period of forty years, during which we were fighting for five and twenty, make the baldest record of our great families a true roll of honour.

Whether they lived on their country or died for her, the members of our ruling class were an aristocracy, State-paid, as far as they earned money at all; seldom entering the open professions; and still further removed from the homely and laborious occupations on which the existence of society is founded. But they governed the Empire, and, among other parts of the Empire, those great provinces in North America which were inhabited by a race of men with whom, except their blood and language, they had little in common. Burke, who told the House of Commons that he had taken for some years a good deal of pains to inform himself on the matter, put the white population in the colonies at not less than two millions, which was something between a fourth and a fifth of the population of Great Britain. The outposts of that army of pioneers were doing battle with the wilderness along an ever-advancing frontier of eighteen hundred miles from end to end. In the Southern States, where life was cruelly rough for the poorer settlers, and where the more wealthy landowners depended on the labour of negroes, society was already constituted after a fashion which differed from anything that was to be seen in New England, or in Old England either. But the great majority of the colonists were gathered together, though not very near together, in settled districts, with a civilisation and a type of character of their own such as the world had never before witnessed.

The French nobles, who brought their swords and fortunes to the assistance of the Revolution in America, opened their eyes on the morning after their arrival upon a state of things which closely resembled the romantic ideal then fashionable in Parisian circles. But

for a certain toughness and roughness, of undoubted
English origin, which the young fellows began to notice
more when they had learned to speak English better,
the community in which they found themselves seemed,
in their lively and hopeful eyes, to have been made to
order out of the imagination of Rousseau or of Fénelon.
They were equally delighted with the external aspect,
and the interior meaning, of the things around them.
The Comte de Ségur, in all his long and chequered
existence, met with nothing which so pleased him as
what he espied along the high roads of Delaware, New
Jersey, and Pennsylvania.   "Sometimes," he wrote, "in
the midst of vast forests, with majestic trees which the
axe had never touched, I was transported in idea to the
remote times when the first navigators set their feet on
that unknown hemisphere.   Sometimes I was admiring
a lovely valley, carefully tilled, with the meadows full of
cattle; the houses clean, elegant, painted in bright and
varied colours, and standing in little gardens behind
pretty fences.   And then, further on, after other masses
of woods, I came to populous hamlets, and towns where
everything betokened the perfection of civilisation, —
schools, churches, universities.   Indigence and vulgarity
nowhere; abundance, comfort, and urbanity everywhere.
The inhabitants, each and all, exhibited the unassuming
and quiet pride of men who have no master, who see
nothing above them except the law, and who are free
from the vanity, the servility, and the prejudices of our
European societies.   That is the picture which, throughout my whole journey, never ceased to interest and
surprise me."

De Ségur and his comrades in arms were young and
enthusiastic when they first visited America; but they
recorded, or re-published, their impressions of it after an
experience of men and cities such as falls to the lot of
few.   Lafayette, whatever might be the misfortunes of
his middle life, had sooner or later seen a great deal
of the world under the pleasant guise which it presents
to the hero of a perpetual ovation.   Mathieu Dumas, —

who, before he was Lieutenant-General of the armies of
King Louis the Eighteenth, served Napoleon long and
faithfully, — had marched, and fought, and administered
all Europe over in the train of the most ubiquitous of
conquerors.   And yet, after so much had been tried and
tasted, the remote and ever-receding picture of their
earliest campaign stood out as their favourite page in
the book of memory.   They liked the country, and they
never ceased to love the people.   They could not forget
how, in " one of those towns which were soon to be cities,
or villages which already were little towns," they would
alight from horseback in a street bright with flowers
and foliage.   They would lift the knocker of shining
brass, and behind the door, gay with paint which never
was allowed to lose its gloss, they were sure to meet
with a hospitality that knew no respect of persons.
" Simplicity of manners," said Lafayette, "the desire to
oblige, and a mild and quiet equality are the rule everywhere.   The inns are very different from those of Europe.
The master and mistress sit down with you, and do the
honours of an excellent dinner ; and, when you depart,
there is no bargaining over the bill.   If you are not in
the mind to go to a tavern, you can soon find a country-
house where it is enough to be a good American in order
to be entertained as in Europe we entertain a friend."

Mathieu Dumas detected a visible difference between
English and American manners.   "In spite," he said,
"of the resemblance in language, in costume, in customs,
in religion, and in the principles of government, a distinct national character is forming itself.   The colonists
are milder and more tolerant, more hospitable, and in
general more communicative than the English.   The
English, in their turn, reproach them with levity and too
keen a taste for pleasure."   But the contrast was not
with England alone among European nations ; and the
cause lay deep in the favourable conditions of life
which prevailed in the New World, and were wanting
to the Old.   "An observer," wrote de Ségur, "fresh
from our magnificent cities, and the airs of our young

men of fashion, — who has compared the luxury of our upper classes with the coarse dress of our peasants, and the rags of our innumerable poor, — is surprised, on reaching the United States, by the entire absence of the extremes both of opulence and misery. All Americans whom we met wore clothes of good material. Their free, frank, and familiar address, equally removed from uncouth discourtesy and from artificial politeness, betokened men who were proud of their own rights and respected those of others."

That national character, which the young French colonels admired, was home-grown; but it bore transportation well. The American qualities of that plain and strong generation did not require American surroundings to set them off to advantage. John Adams began life as a rural schoolmaster, and continued it as a rural lawyer. He never saw anything which Lord Chesterfield or Madame du Deffand would have recognised as society until he dined with Turgot to meet a member of the family of de Rochefoucauld. He learned French as he went along, and at the bottom of his heart had no great love or respect for Frenchmen. But, soon after he began his sojourn in France, he became at home in the diplomatic world; and before long he had acquired there a commanding influence, which proved to be of inestimable value to his country. Franklin in London had no official position above that of agent for a colonial Assembly, and no previous knowledge of English society except what he had picked up as a youth, working for a printer, and lodging in Little Britain at three and sixpence a week. And yet he was welcomed by all, of every rank, whom he cared to meet; and by some great people with whose attentions, and with a good deal of whose wine, he would have willingly dispensed.[1] When he took up his abode in Paris, he con-

[1] " We have lost Lord Clare from the Board of Trade," Franklin wrote in July 1768. " He took me home from Court the Sunday before his removal, that I might dine with him, as he said, alone, and talk over American affairs. He gave me a great deal of flummery ; saying that

tinued to live as he had lived in Philadelphia till the age
of seventy, — talking his usual talk, and dressed in sober
broadcloth. But even so he became the rage, and set
the fashion, in circles which gave undisputed law to the
whole of polite Europe in matters where taste and behaviour were concerned.

The fact is that intelligent travellers from the countries of continental Europe found in America exactly
what they had been searching after eagerly, and with
some sense of disappointment, in England. Anglo-
mania was then at its height in Parisian society; and
the noblest form of that passion led men to look for,
and imitate, the mode of life which must surely, (so
they hoped and argued,) be the product of such laws
and such freedom as ours. Of simplicity and frugality,
of manliness and independence, of religious conviction
and sense of duty, there was abundance in our island,
if they had known where to seek it. In every commercial town from Aberdeen to Falmouth, and on many a
countryside, the day's work was being done by men of
the right stamp, with something of old manners, but of
solid modern knowledge; close attendants at church, or,
in more cases still, at chapel; writing without effort and
pretension a singularly clear and vigorous English, and
making the money which they spent, and a good deal
more, by their own labour and their own enterprise.
From them came Howard and Raikes, Arkwright and
Wedgwood, Watt and Brindley. For them Wesley and
John Newton preached, and Adam Smith and Arthur
Young wrote. Intent on their business, they yet had
time to spare for schemes of benevolence and general
utility; and they watched the conduct of State affairs
with deep and growing interest, and with indignation
which was mostly silent. For their opportunity was

though at my Examination I answered some of his questions a little pertly,
yet he liked me for the spirit I showed in defence of my country. At parting, after we had drunk a bottle and a half of claret each, he hugged and
kissed me, protesting that he had never in his life met with a man he was
so much in love with."

not yet; and they were creating and maturing quietly, and as it were unconsciously, that public opinion of their class which grew in strength during the coming fifty years, and then for another fifty years was destined to rule the country. They were the salt of the earth in those days of corruption; but they were not the people whom a gentleman from Versailles, visiting London with letters of introduction from the Duc de Choiseul or the Chevalier de Boufflers, would be very likely to meet. They lived apart from high society, and did not copy its habits or try to catch its tone; nor did they profess the theory of an equality which, as their strong sense told them, they could not successfully assert in practice. Preserving their self-respect, and keeping within their own borders, they recognised that the best of the world, whether they liked it or not, was made for others. However little they might care to put the confession into words, they acted, and wrote, and spoke as men aware that the government of their nation was in the hands of an aristocracy to which they themselves did not belong.

It was far otherwise in America. The people in the settled districts had emerged from a condition of cruel hardship to comfort, security, and as much leisure as their temperament, already the same as now, would permit them to take. Their predecessors had fought and won their battle against hunger and cold and pestilence, against savage beasts and savage men. As time went on, they had confronted and baffled a subtler and more deadly adversary in the power of the later Stuarts; for, as soon as the exiles had conquered from the wilderness a country which was worth possessing, the statesmen of the Restoration unsuccessfully tried to destroy their liberties, to appropriate their substance, and to impose on them the form of Church government to escape which they had crossed the ocean. Those varied and protracted struggles had left a mark in the virile and resolute temper of the existing generation, in their readiness to turn a hand to any sort of work on however sudden an emergency, and in their plain and unpretentious habits. But there was nothing uncivilised or unlettered about them. In their most bitter straits, while the existence of the community was still at hazard, the founders of the colony had taken measures for securing those supreme benefits to the individual which in their eyes were the true end and object of all combined human effort. By the time they had reaped their fifth harvest on the shores of the Massachusetts Bay, they had established a public school at Cambridge; and the next year it was raised to the dignity of a college, with a library and something of an endowment. Again a twelve-month, and the first sheet was drawn from beneath a New England printing-press; and eight years later on, in 1647, it was ordered that every township, " after the Lord hath increased them to the number of fifty house-holders, shall appoint one within their towns to teach all such children as shall resort to him to write and read; and, where any town shall increase to the number of one hundred families, they shall set up a grammar school, the masters thereof being able to instruct youth so far as they may be fitted for the university."

Not otherwise did the Scottish statesmen of 1696 read their duty, with great results to the future of their people, ancient and immovable as were the limits by which that future was circumscribed and confined. But the lawgivers of the Puritan colonies had a blank parchment before them; and they were equal to the task of ruling the lines along which the national character was to run. The full fruit of their work was seen four generations afterwards in the noble equality of universal industry, and of mutual respect, which prevailed among a population of whom none were idle and none were ignorant. "There," wrote de Ségur, "no useful profession is the subject of ridicule or contempt. Idleness alone is a disgrace. Military rank and public employment do not prevent a person from having a calling of his own. Every one there is a tradesman, a farmer, or an artisan. Those who are less well off, — the servants, labourers, and sailors, — unlike men of the lower classes in Europe, are treated with a consideration which they merit by the propriety of their conduct and their behaviour. At first I was surprised, on entering a tavern, to find it kept by a captain, a major, or a colonel, who was equally ready to talk, and to talk well, about his campaigns, his farming operations, or the market he had got for his produce or his wares. And I was still more taken aback when, — after I had answered the questions put to me about my family, and had informed the company that my father was a General and a Minister of State, — they went on to inquire what was his profession or his business."

There could be no personal sympathy, and no identity of public views, between the governors in Downing Street and the governed in Pennsylvania and New England. On the one hand was a commonwealth containing no class to which a man was bound to look up, and none on which he was tempted to look down; where there was no source of dignity except labour, and no luxury but a plenty which was shared by all. On the other hand was a ruling caste, each member of which, unless by some rare good fortune, was taught by precept and example, from his schooldays onwards, that the greatest good was to live for show and pleasure; that the whole duty of senatorial man was to draw as much salary as could be got, in return for as little work as might be given for it; and that, socially and politically, the many were not to be reckoned as standing on a level with the few.

The great English public schools, to which the aristocracy then resorted, were described by Cowper in a poem of striking power, which is far too earnest, and too scrupulously truthful, to be classed as a satire.[1] At Eton, especially, the stern and often cruel education of the seventeenth century was obsolete, and had been succeeded by a laxity of manners which was due, in large measure, to the ill-considered action of Lord Holland.

---

[1] Cowper's *Tirocinium, or a Review of Schools*, was published in 1784. He had been educated at Westminster, and he left school in 1749.

Charles Fox had been withdrawn from his studies to accompany his father on a long Continental tour, in the course of which he was plunged prematurely into the temptations of the great and idle world. He went back to Eton with unlimited money, and the taste and habit of dissipation. Nature had endowed the boy with qualities which dazzled and bewitched his comrades, and excused him in the eyes of his superiors; and his influence in the school was unbounded. Lord Shelburne gave it as his opinion that the great change for the worse, which had taken place among the youth of the upper classes, dated from the time that the Foxes were predominant at Eton. It was the exaggerated statement of one who was no friend to the family; for it left out of sight the consideration that, bad as Lord Holland's conduct was, others than he were responsible for the morality of the school. Charles Fox would have followed a better path if it had been pointed out by instructors whom he loved and reverenced; and, at the very worst, a few private interviews with a strong-willed and stout-armed headmaster should have convinced the most precocious scapegrace that Eton was not Spa or Paris. But discipline, in any true sense of the word, in the middle of that century did not exist at Eton.[1] Clever boys there wrote Latin, as it was written nowhere else. That, to the end of his days, was the persuasion of Charles Fox; and his own productions go to prove it; for his schoolboy exercises were often marked by a rare facility of handling, and a lively and most fascinating sense of personal enjoyment on the part of the writer. Nor did Latin verse comprise all that was to be learned at Eton. The authorities gave careful lessons in the art of elocution to lads many of whom inherited, as part of their patrimony, the right of sitting for a borough, or the obligation of standing for a county. But there the duty of a teacher towards his pupils, as

[1] Some extracts relating to the Eton of those days, taken from the Twelfth Report of the *Historical Manuscripts Commission*, are given in the First Appendix to this volume.

he himself read it, ended.   The boys feared the masters less than the masters feared the boys, and with good cause ; for the doctrine of non-resistance was not popular among these Whigs of sixteen, and an Eton rebellion was a very serious matter indeed.[1]

The senators of the future, when they left school for college, found themselves in a place where boundless indulgence was shown towards the frailties of the powerful and the high born.   The Duke of Grafton, in 1768, was in the very depths of a scandal of which Junius took care that all the world should be cognisant ; and in the course of that very year his Grace was unanimously chosen by the Cambridge senate as Chancellor of the University.   The Earl of Sandwich ran a dead heat for the High Stewardship of the same educational body ; and Cambridge owed its salvation from the ineffaceable disgrace which would have attended his success to the votes of the country clergy, among whom his opponent Lord Hardwicke, a nobleman of blameless character, most fortunately had, as we are told, "much connection."[2]   Gibbon, in three out of his six autobiographies, has related how the fourteen months which he spent at Oxford were totally lost for every purpose of study and improvement, at a college where "the dull and deep potations of the fellows excused the brisk intemperance of youth, and the velvet cap of a Gentleman Commoner was the cap of liberty"; and his account of Magdalen is illustrated by the experience of Lord Malmesbury, who states in less finished phrases that the life among his own set at Merton was a close imitation of high life in London.   After having undergone such a preliminary training at the famous centres of national education,

[1] A picturesque account of a school riot, which occurred there just after the close of the American war, is given in the Fourteenth Report, Appendix, Part 1, of the *Historical Manuscripts Commission*.

[2] Sandwich likewise, in the course of time, established a connection with the clergy of a sort peculiar to himself.   The Rev. Mr. Hackman, who wanted to marry one of his mistresses, was hanged for murdering her; and the Rev. Dr. Dodd, who was hanged for forgery, according to Walpole had married another.

a young man of fortune was started on the grand tour,
to be initiated in the free-masonry of luxury and levity
which then embraced the whole fashionable society of
Europe. If he was his own master he travelled alone,
or with a band of congenial companions. If his father
was alive, he made his voyage under the ostensible superintendence of a tutor, whom he had either subjugated
or quarrelled with by the time the pair had traversed
one or two foreign capitals. A youth so spent was a
bad apprenticeship for the vocation of governing with
insight and sympathy remote colonies inhabited by a
hardy, an industrious, and a religious people.

CHAPTER II

THAT the pictures drawn in these pages are not over-
coloured will be admitted by those who compare the
correspondence of George the Third and Lord North
with Washington's confidential letters, or the Last Journals of Horace Walpole with the diary of John Adams ;
— by those who contrast the old age of Lord Holland
and of Franklin, or turn from the boyhood and youth
of Charles Fox and Lord Carlisle to the strait and stern
upbringing of the future liberators, creators, and rulers
of America. Any reader, who belongs to the English
race, may well take pride in the account which the
founders of the great Republic have given of themselves in documents not written for publication, and
marked by a sincerity which attracts sympathy, and
commands belief. There he may see the records of
their birth, their nurture, and their early wrestling with
the world. There he may admire the avidity with which,
while they worked for their daily bread, they were
snatching on every side at scraps of a higher education,
and piecing them together into a culture admirably suited
for the high affairs of administration, and diplomacy, and
war to which their destiny was of a sudden, and unex-
pectedly, to call them. But though they had larger
minds and stronger wills than the common, their lot was
the same as that of the majority among their countrymen in the Northern colonies ; and their story, as far as
their circumstances and chances in life were concerned,
is the story of all.

The father of John Adams was a labouring farmer,
who wrought hard to live, and who did much public

work for nothing. His eminent son put on record that
" he was an officer of militia, afterwards a deacon of the
church, and a Selectman of the town ; almost all the
business of the town being managed by him in that
department for twenty years together ; a man of strict
piety, and great integrity ; much esteemed and beloved,
wherever he was known, which was not far, his sphere
of life not being extensive." He left behind him property valued at thirteen hundred pounds, and he had
made it a prime object to give the most promising of
his children that college education which he himself had
missed. In those last particulars, and in much else, he
was just such another as the father of Thomas Carlyle ;
but there was this difference, that the elder John Adams,
with his hard hands and his few score pounds a year,
lived in a society where a man knew his own worth, and
claimed and took the place which was due to him.[1] Pro-
genitor of a long line of Presidents and Ambassadors,
the old Selectman of Braintree town held his head as
erect in every presence as did any of his descendants.
His son, a generation further removed from the depressing influences of the old world, and driven by the irresistible instinct of a strong man born on the eve of
stirring times, prepared himself diligently for a high
career with a noble indifference to the million and one
chances that were against his attaining it. While teaching in a grammar school, for the wages of a day labourer,
he bound himself to an attorney, and studied hard in his
remnants of leisure. For a while his prospects seemed
to him doleful enough. " I long," he wrote, " to be a
master of Greek and Latin. I long to prosecute the

[1] " Even for the mere clothes-screens of rank my father testified no
contempt. Their inward claim to regard was a thing which concerned
them, not him. I love to figure him addressing those men with bared
head by the title of 'Your Honour,' with a manner respectful but unem-
barrassed ; a certain manful dignity looking through his own fine face,
with his noble grey head bent patiently to the alas! unworthy." —
Reminiscences of James Carlyle, p. 16. The beautiful passage, (towards
the end of the little biography,) which begins " he was born and brought
up the poorest " might, even to the figure of old Mr. Carlyle's fortune,
have been written word for word about the father of John Adams.

mathematical and philosophical sciences. I long to know a little of ethics and moral philosophy. But I have no books, no time, no friends. I must therefore be contented to live and die an ignorant obscure fellow."

A man who rails in that strain against his own deficiencies is seldom long in mending them. John Adams read greedily, whenever he could lay his hand on those literary works which possessed sufficient weight and momentum to have carried them across the seas and into Massachusetts, — Bacon and Bolingbroke, Bentley and Tillotson and Butler; as well as Sydenham and Boerhaave, and a whole course of medical and surgical authorities which were lent him by a physician in whose house he was lodging. After two years of this training he became a lawyer, settled himself at Braintree, and the very next morning fell to work upon his Justinian. In 1759, while still three and twenty, he rewrote for his own guidance the fable of the choice of Hercules, with girls, guns, cards, and violins on the one side, and Montesquieu and Lord Hale's "History of the Common Law" on the other. A list of the books which he had mastered, and which he planned to master, proves that his thoughts travelled far above the petty litigation of county and township. The field of study most congenial to him lay amidst those great treatises on natural law and civil law which were the proper nourishment for men who had the constitution of an empire latent in their brains. According to his own estimate he was a visionary and a trifler, — too proud to court the leaders of the local Bar, and too fine to gossip himself into the good graces of local clients. But his comrades, who knew him as the young know the young, had to seek beyond eighteen hundred years of time, and twice as many miles of space, for an historical character with whom to compare him. Jonathan Sewall, the close ally and generous rival of his early days, — who in later years justified his Christian name by an affection and fidelity proof against the strain of a difference of opinion concerning that Revolution which ruined the one friend, and raised the other to the first place in the State, — consoled John Adams in his obscurity by a parallel with no less a jurist than Cicero. "Who knows," Sewall wrote, "but in future ages, when New England shall have risen to its intended grandeur, it shall be as carefully recorded that Adams flourished in the second century after the exodus of its first settlers from Great Britain, as it now is that Cicero was born in the six hundred and forty-seventh year after the building of Rome?"[1]

Such are the day-dreams of five and twenty; and seldom have they resulted in as notable a fulfilment. John Adams was the first who reached his goal of those young Americans whose aspirations, trivial only to the ignoble, have afforded to a great master the theme for some of his most musical sentences. "The youth, intoxicated with his admiration of a hero, fails to see that it is only a projection of his own soul which he admires. In solitude, in a remote village, the ardent youth loiters and mourns. With inflamed eye, in this sleeping wilderness, he has read the story of the Emperor Charles the Fifth, until his fancy has brought home to the surrounding woods the faint roar of cannonades in the Milanese, and marches in Germany. He is curious concerning that man's day. What filled it? The crowded orders, the stern decisions, the foreign despatches, the Castilian etiquette. The soul answers: 'Behold his day here! In the sighing of these woods, in the quiet of these grey fields, in the cool breeze that sings out of these northern mountains; in the hopes of the morning, the ennui of noon, and sauntering of the afternoon; in the disquieting comparisons; in the regrets at want of vigour; in the great idea, and the puny execution; — behold Charles the Fifth's day; another yet the same; behold Chatham's, Hampden's, Bayard's, Alfred's, Scipio's, Pericles's day — day of all that are born of women.'"[2]

[1] Sewall to Adams; 13th Feb., 1760.
[2] Emerson's oration at Dartmouth College; July, 1838.

The young man's outward environment was in strange contrast to the ideas on which his fancy fed. For many years to come his life was like a sonnet by Wordsworth done into dry and rugged prose. Slowly, with immense exertions of mind and body, he built up a leading practice in the scattered and remote court-houses of the rural districts. He pursued his livelihood through a continuous course of rudest travel. Side by side with passages of keen political disquisition, and high-minded personal introspection, his journal tells the plain honourable narrative of his humble adventures ; — how he was soaked in the rain, and pinched by cold, and sent miles out of his way by a swollen ford, and lost for hours amidst the interminable forests ; where he slept, or tried to sleep, after a hard day's journey, and with what tiresome company he had to share his bedroom ; where he "oated," and where the best he could do for his little mare was to set her loose, up to her shoulders in grass, in a roadside meadow ; and how he reached a friend's house at a quarter after twelve in the day, just as they had got their Indian pudding, and their pork and greens, upon the table. Occupied as he was in maintaining his family, Adams never shrank from his turn of public duty. He was surveyor of the highways of Braintree, and a very good surveyor; and, rising in due course through the official hierarchy, he became assessor and overseer of the poor, and Selectman, as his father before him. In 1768 he removed to Boston, which then was just of a size with the Boston in Lincolnshire of the present day. To his younger eyes it had seemed a mighty capital, full of distractions and temptations; and the time never came when he felt at home in a town, or indeed anywhere except among the sea-breezes and the pine-forests of "still, calm, happy Braintree." "Who can study," he wrote, "in Boston streets? I cannot raise my mind above this crowd of men, women, beasts, and carriages, to think steadily. My attention is solicited every moment by some new object of sight, or some new sound. A coach, cart, a lady, or a priest may at any time disconcert a whole page of excellent thoughts." But his position as a lawyer, and the grave aspect of national affairs,—on which his opinions, rarely and modestly expressed, were universally known, and carried unusual weight,—made it his duty to establish himself in the neighbourhood of the superior courts, and in the political centre of the colony which was soon to become, for years together, the political battle-ground of the Empire.

Jonathan Sewall, who already was Attorney-General of Massachusetts, was commissioned by the Governor to offer Adams the post of Advocate-General in the Court of Admiralty. It was, as he records, a well-paid employment, a sure introduction to the most profitable business in the province, and a first step on the ladder of favour and promotion. But Charles Townshend's new custom duties were by this time in operation; and Adams, in firm but respectful terms, replied that in the unsettled state of the country he could not place himself under an obligation of gratitude to the Government. Four years afterwards he computed his worldly wealth, and found that, after paying two hundred and fifty pounds towards the purchase of his house in town, and after acquiring twenty acres of salt-marsh in the country, he was worth three hundred pounds in money. He was seven and thirty. It was the age at which Thurlow and Wedderburn reached the rank of Solicitor-General; and at which Charles Yorke thought himself ill-used because he had been nothing higher than Attorney-General. "This," Adams wrote, "is all that my most intense application to study and business has been able to accomplish; an application that has more than once been very near costing me my life, and that has so greatly impaired my health. Thirty-seven years, more than half the life of man, are run out. The remainder of my days I shall rather decline in sense, spirit, and activity. My season for acquiring knowledge is past, and yet I have my own and my children's fortunes to make." That was the reward which hitherto

had fallen to the share of one who became the ruler of
the United States long before George the Third had
ceased to rule the United Kingdom, and who survived
until his own son asked for his blessing on the day
when he, in his turn, was chosen to fill the same exalted
office.

There was another celebrated colonist whose youth
had been fostered at a greater distance still from the
lap of luxury.   The inventory of the effects owned by
the great-great-grandfather of John Adams showed
that there had been a silver spoon in the family four
generations back.   But Franklin ate his breakfast with
pewter out of earthenware until, when he was already
a mature householder, his wife bought him a china
bowl and a silver spoon, on the ground that her husband deserved to live as handsomely as any of his
neighbours.[1] If he inherited no plate, he derived a
more valuable legacy from his ancestors, who in their
history and their qualities were worthy forerunners of
the most typical American that ever lived.   England
in the seventeenth century gave, or rather thrust upon,
the New World much of what was staunch and true,
and much also of what was quick-witted and enterprising, in her population.   The Franklins, a Northamptonshire clan of very small freeholders, among whom the
trade of blacksmith was as hereditary as in an Indian
caste, were good Protestants in the worst of times.
During the reign of Queen Mary the head of the household kept his English Bible fastened with tapes beneath
the seat of a stool, and read it aloud with the stool reversed between his knees, while a child stood in the
doorway to give the alarm in case an apparitor from
the Spiritual Court was seen in the street.   Benjamin
Franklin's father was a stout and zealous noncon-

---

[1] "I am," Franklin wrote, "the youngest Son, of the youngest Son, of
the youngest Son, of the youngest Son for five generations ; whereby I find
that, had there originally been any Estate in the Family, none could have
stood a worse chance of it."

formist; and, when conventicles were forbidden in England by laws cruelly conceived and rigorously enforced, he carried his wife and children to Massachusetts in order that they might enjoy the exercise of their religion in freedom. He set up at Boston first as a dyer, and then as a maker of soap and candles. The family character was marked by native ingenuity and homely public spirit. One of Franklin's uncles invented a shorthand of his own. Another, who remained at home in Northamptonshire, taught himself law; filled local offices of importance; was prime mover in all useful undertakings in town and county; and was long remembered in his village as a benefactor, an adviser, and (by the more ignorant) as a reputed conjurer. He set on foot a subscription to provide a set of chimes, which his nephew heard with satisfaction three-quarters of a century afterwards; and he discovered a simple, effective method of saving the common lands from being drowned by the river. "If Franklin says he knows how to do it, it will be done," was a phrase which had passed into a proverb for the neighbourhood. He died four years to a day before his brother's famous child was born. "Had he died four years later," it was said, "one might have supposed a transmigration."

Benjamin Franklin had a right to be proud of the mental gifts which were born within him, when he looked back from the height of his fame to the material circumstances which surrounded him on his entrance into this world. Seldom did any man who started with as little accomplish so much, if we except certain of the august self-seekers in history whose career was carved out at a great cost of human life and human freedom. He had a year at a grammar-school, and a year at a commercial school; and then he was taken into the family business, and set to serve at the counter and run on errands. He disliked the life; and his father, who feared that he would break loose and go to sea, gravely took him a round of the shops in Boston, and showed him joiners, bricklayers, turners, braziers, and cutlers at their work, in order that, with knowledge of what he was about, he might choose his calling for himself. The boy, who was twelve years old, everywhere learned something which he never forgot, and which he turned to account in one or another of the seventy years that were before him. The combined good sense of parent and child led them to decide on the trade of a printer. He was bound apprentice, and from this time forward he read the books which passed under his hand. Others, which he loved better, he purchased to keep; dining, a joyful anchorite, on a biscuit or a handful of raisins, in order that he might spend his savings on his infant library. He gave himself a classical education out of an odd volume of the "Spectator," rewriting the papers from memory, and correcting them by the original; or turning the tales into verse, and back again into prose. He taught himself arithmetic thoroughly, and learned a little geometry and a little navigation; both of which in after days he made to go a long way, and put to great uses.

But, above all, he trained himself as a logician; making trial of many successive systems with amazing zest, until he founded an unpretentious school of his own in which his pre-eminence has never been questioned. He traversed with rapidity all the stages in the art of reasoning, from the earliest phase, when a man only succeeds in being disagreeable to his fellows, up to the period when he has become a proficient in the science of persuading them. He began by arguing to confute, "souring and spoiling the conversation," and making enemies, instead of disciples, at every turn. "I had caught this," he wrote, "by reading my father's books of dispute on religion. Persons of good sense, I have since observed, seldom fall into it, except lawyers, university men, and generally men of all sorts who have been bred at Edinburgh." He next lighted upon a translation of Xenophon's "Memorabilia," and, captivated by the charms of the Socratic dialogue, he dropped the weapons of abrupt contradiction and positive as-

sertion, and put on the humble inquirer. He grew
very expert in drawing people into concessions, the
consequences of which they did not foresee, — especially people who were not familiar with Shaftesbury's
"Characteristics" and Collins's "Discourse on Free
Thinking." From his own study of those works he had
derived conclusions which made it safer for him to
proselytise the Boston of that day by a process of suggestion and induction rather than by dogmatic exposition. At length he found that his friends grew wary,
and would hardly reply to the most common question
without asking first what he intended to infer from the
answer. Then he once more changed his style of conversation; and this time for good. Keeping nothing of
his former method except the habit of expressing himself "with modest diffidence," he refrained altogether
from the words "certainly," and "undoubtedly," and
from the air of aggressive superiority which generally
accompanies them. The phrases with which he urged
his point, and seldom failed to carry it, were "I conceive," or "I apprehend," or "It appears to me," or
"It is so, if I am not mistaken." He made it a practice,
likewise, to encourage his interlocutors to think that
the opinion which he aimed at instilling into them was
theirs already. If, as he pleased himself with believing,
he had learned these arts from Socrates, the teaching
of the Academy had for once borne an abundant crop
of Baconian fruit; for it would be hard to name a man
who, over so long a space of time as Franklin, ever
talked so many people into doing that which was for
their own improvement and advantage.

The theatre of his beneficent operations was not his
native city. Boston, in common with the world at large,
gathered in due time some of the crumbs which fell
from the table of his inventiveness; but she very soon
lost the first claim upon one who was as clever a son
as even *she* ever produced. At the age of seventeen
Franklin walked into the capital of Pennsylvania, his
pockets stuffed with shirts and stockings, but empty of

money; carrying a roll under each arm, and eating as he went along. The expansive possibilities of an American's career may be traced in every page of his early story. The intimate companions of his poverty, young as he, made their way in the world soon and far. One, who went to England, got himself into a couplet of the "Dunciad"; wrote a History of William the Third which was praised by Charles Fox; and extracted from the Earl of Bute a pension twice as large as Dr. Johnson's. Another became an eminent lawyer, and died rich while he and Franklin were still below middle age. The two friends had agreed that the one who left the earth first should afterwards pay a visit to the other; but the ghost had yet to be found which had the courage to present itself to Franklin.

He worked hard, and lived very hardly indeed in Philadelphia, and in London for a while, and in Philadelphia again. At the end of ten years he was securely settled in business as a stationer and master-printer, and the owner of a newspaper which soon became an excellent property, and which bore the trace of his hand in every corner of its columns.[1] By a miracle of industry and thrift, he had paid out his first partners, and paid off his borrowed capital. It was no longer necessary for him to breakfast on gruel, and sup on half an anchovy and a slice of bread; to be at work when his neighbours returned at night from the club, and at work again before they rose in the morning; to wheel the paper for his Gazette home through the streets on a barrow, and to take neither rest nor recreation except when a book "debauched" him from his labours. From the moment that he had set his foot firmly on the path

---

[1] The following advertisement appears in the *Pennsylvanian Gazette*, for June 23rd, 1737: "Taken out of a pew in the church, some months since, a Common Prayer Book, bound in red, gilt, and lettered D. F. on each cover. The person who took it is desired to open it and read the eighth Commandment, and afterwards return it into the same pew again; upon which no further notice will be taken." D. F. stands for Deborah Franklin.

of fortune, he threw his vast energy, his audacious crea-
tiveness, his dexterity in the management of his fellow-
creatures, and a good portion of his increased though
still slender substance, into the service of his adopted
city. One scheme followed hard upon another; each
of them exactly suited to local wants which Franklin
was quick to discern, and to a national taste with which
he was entirely in sympathy. By the end of a quarter
of a century Philadelphia lacked nothing that was possessed by any city in England, except a close corporation and a bull-ring, and enjoyed in addition a complete outfit of institutions which were eagerly imitated
throughout the Northern colonies.

Franklin's first project was a book-club; the mother,
to use his own words, of those subscription libraries
which perceptibly raised the standard of American conversation, "and made tradesmen and farmers as intelligent as the gentry of other countries." Then came,
in rapid succession, a volunteer fire company; a paid
police-force; a public hospital; a Philosophical Society;
an Academy, which he lived to see develop itself into
the University of Pennsylvania; and a paper currency
which, with his stern views on private and public credit,
he, fortunately for him, did not live to see at the height
of its notoriety in the shape of the memorable Pennsylvanian Bonds. He turned his attention successfully to
the paving and scavenging of the highways. When
the city was first lighted, he designed the form of street-
lamp which has long been in universal use wherever
Anglo-Saxons now burn gas, or once burned oil. He
invented a hot-stove for sitting-rooms, and refused a
patent for it, on the ground that he himself had profited
so much by the discoveries of others that he was only
too glad of an opportunity to repay his debt, and to
repay it in a shape so peculiarly acceptable to his
country-women. Whitefield, whom everybody except
the clergy wished to hear, had been refused the use
of the existing pulpits. Franklin, as his contribution to
the cause of religion, promoted the building of a spacious

meetinghouse, vested in trustees, expressly for the use
of any preacher of any denomination who might desire
to say something to the people of Philadelphia.

In 1744, on the breaking out of war with France,
Franklin excited the patriotism of Pennsylvania by
voice and pen, and directed it into the practical channel
of enrolling a State militia, and constructing a battery
for the protection of the river. He raised the requisite
funds by a lottery in which he was artful enough to
induce the members of the Society of Friends to take
tickets, knowing well that, without their support, no
scheme appealing to the purse would be very productive in Philadelphia. In order to arm his embrasures,
he applied to Governor Clinton of New York for cannon, who met him with a flat refusal. But Franklin
sate with him over his Madeira until, as the bumpers
went round, his Excellency consented to give six guns,
then rose to ten, and ended by contributing to the defence of the Delaware no less than eighteen fine pieces,
with carriages included. Eleven years afterwards, when
Braddock marched to the attack of Fort Duquesne,
Franklin, by the earnest request of the general, and at
formidable risk to his own private fortune, organised
the transport and commissariat with an ability and a
foresight in marked contrast to the military conduct of
the ill-fated expedition. In the terrible panic which
ensued when the news of the disaster reached Philadelphia, the authorities of the colony, — catching at the
hope that, as he understood everything else, there was
at least a chance of his understanding how to fight, —
entrusted him with the defence of the North-West
frontier against the imminent peril of an Indian invasion. He levied and commanded a respectable force,
and threw up a line of forts, the planning and building
of which gave him the most exquisite satisfaction; and,
on his return home, he accepted the highest title of a
true American by becoming a Colonel of Militia, and
was greeted by his regiment with a salvo of artillery
which broke several glasses of the electrical apparatus

that had already made his name famous throughout the entire scientific world.

There were few military posts with regard to which Franklin, if he was not competent to fill them himself, could not give a useful hint to their holder. The chaplain of his troops complained that the men would not attend public worship. The commanding officer accordingly suggested that the chaplain should himself serve out the rum when prayers were over; "and never," said Franklin, "were prayers more generally and punctually attended. I think this method preferable to the punishment inflicted by some military laws for non-attendance on divine service." Wherever he went, and whatever he was engaged upon, he was always calculating, and never guessing. When he built his forts, he soon noticed that two men cut down a pine of fourteen inches in diameter in six minutes, and that each pine made three palisades eighteen feet in length. When he was collecting money for his Battery, he satisfied himself, by means of an intricate computation, that, out of every twenty-two Quakers, only one sincerely disapproved of participation in a war of defence. And, on an evening when Whitefield was delivering a sermon from the top of the Court-House steps, Franklin moved about in the crowd, and measured distances, until he had ascertained that the human voice, or at any rate Whitefield's voice, could be heard by more than thirty thousand people. "This," he said, "reconciled me to the newspaper accounts of his having preached to twenty-five thousand people in the fields, and to the history of generals haranguing whole armies, of which I had sometimes doubted."

His growing reputation brought him important public employment, though not any great amount of direct public remuneration. He was chosen Clerk of the Pennsylvanian Assembly in 1736; and next year he was placed at the head of the Pennsylvanian Post Office. As time went on, the British Government, finding that the postal revenue of the colonies had fallen to less than nothing, appointed Franklin Joint Postmaster-General of

America, with a colleague to help him. The pair were to have six hundred pounds a year between them, if they could make that sum out of the profits of the office. For four years the balance was against them ; but at the end of that time the department, managed according to the precepts of " The Way to Wealth" in Poor Richard's Almanac, began to pay, and paid ever better yearly, until it yielded the Crown a net receipt three times as large as that of the Post Office in Ireland. So much he did for himself, and so much more he was enabled to do for others, by a strict obedience to the promptings of a mother-wit which, in great things as in small, was all but infallible, and by a knowledge of human nature diplomatic even to the verge of wiliness. When he had a project on foot, he would put his vanity in the back-ground, and would represent the matter as the plan of a number of friends, who had requested him to go about and recommend it to public favour and support. To conciliate an enemy, if all other means failed, he would beg of him a trifling service, which in decency could not be refused ; relying on the maxim that " He who has once done you a kindness will be more ready to do you another than he whom you have yourself obliged." For the furtherance of all his undertakings, he had a powerful instrument in a newspaper as respectable as it was readable ; which, with a fine prescience of the possible dangers of a free press to America, and not to America alone, he steadily refused to make the vehicle of scurrilous gossip and personal detraction. By such arts as these he fulfilled to the letter the augury of his good old father, who in past days loved to remind him that a man diligent in his calling should stand before Kings, and not before mean men. " I did not think," said Franklin, " that I should ever literally stand before Kings, which, however, has since happened ; for I have stood before five, and even had the honour of sitting down with one, the King of Denmark, to dinner." Franklin had the habit, which was the basis of his originality, of practising himself what he preached to

others. He kept his accounts in morals as minutely as
in business matters. He drew up a catalogue of twelve
virtues which it was essential to cultivate, commencing
with Temperance and ending with Chastity; to which
at a subsequent period a Quaker friend, who knew him
well, advised him to add Humility. " My intention," he
wrote, " being to acquire the *habitude* of those virtues,
I judged it would be well not to distract my attention
by attempting the whole at once, but to fix it on one of
them at a time ; and, when I should be master of that,
then to proceed to another, till I should have gone
through the thirteen. And, as the previous acquisition
of some might facilitate the acquisition of certain others,
I arranged them with that view." By the time he became Joint Postmaster-General of America, he had
made his ground sure enough to justify him in relaxing
his vigilance, though he carried his little book on all his
voyages as a precaution and a reminder. The Joint
Postmaster-General of England, who was no other than
the Earl of Sandwich, would not have got very far along
the list of virtues, at whichever end he had begun.

The leaders of thought in America, and those who in
coming days were the leaders of war, had all been bred
in one class or another of the same severe school.
Samuel Adams, who started and guided New England
in its resistance to the Stamp Act, was a Calvinist by
conviction. The austere purity of his household recalled
an English home in the Eastern Counties during the
early half of the seventeenth century. He held the
political creed of the fathers of the colony ; and it was a
faith as real and sacred to him as it had been to them.
His fortune was small. Even in that city of plain living, men blamed him because he did not take sufficient
thought for the morrow; but he had a pride which knew
no shame in poverty, and an integrity far superior to its
temptations. Alexander Hamilton, serving well and
faithfully, but sorely against the grain, as a clerk in a
merchant's office, had earned and saved the means of

E 2

putting himself, late in the day, to college. Jefferson, who inherited wealth, used it to obtain the highest education which his native country could then provide; entered a profession; and worked at it after such a fashion that by thirty he was the leading lawyer of his colony, and that no less a colony than Virginia. The future warriors of the Revolution had a still harder apprenticeship. Israel Putnam had fought the Indians and the French for a score of years, and in a score of battles; leading his men in the dress of a woodman, with firelock on shoulder and hatchet at side; a powder horn under his right arm, and a bag of bullets at his waist, and, (as the distinctive equipment of an officer,) a pocket compass to guide their marches through the forest. He had known what it was to have his comrades scalped before his eyes, and to stand gashed in the face with a tomahawk, and bound to the trunk of a tree, with a torture-fire crackling about him. From adventures which, in the back settlements, were regarded merely as the harder side of a farmer's work, he would go home to build fences with no consciousness of heroism, and still less with any anticipation of the world-famous scenes for his part in which these experiences of the wilderness were training him. Nathanael Greene, the ablest of Washington's lieutenants, — of those at any rate who remained true to their cause from first to last, — was one of eight sons, born in a house of a single story. His father combined certain humble trades with the care of a small farm, and, none the less or the worse on account of his week-day avocations, was a preacher of the gospel. "The son," Mr. Bancroft tells us, "excelled in diligence and manly sports. None of his age could wrestle, or skate, or run better than he, or stand before him as a neat ploughman and skilful mechanic." Under such literary and scientific guidance as he could find among his neighbours, he learned geometry, and its application to the practical work of a new country. He read poetry and philosophy, as they are read by a man of many and great thoughts, whose books are few but good. Above all, he made a special study of Plutarch and of Cæsar, — authors who, whether in a translation, or in the original Greek and Latin, never give out their innermost meaning except to brave hearts on the eve of grave events.[1]

Meantime the military chief upon whom the main weight of responsibility was to rest had been disciplined for his career betimes. At an age when a youth of his rank in England would have been shirking a lecture in order to visit Newmarket, or settling the colour of his first lace coat, Washington was surveying the valleys of the Alleghany Mountains. He slept in all weathers under the open sky ; he swam his horses across rivers swollen with melted snow ; and he learned, as sooner or later a soldier must, to guess what was on the other side of the hill, and to judge how far the hill itself was distant. At nineteen he was in charge of a district on the frontier ; and at twenty-two he fought his first battle, with forty men against five and thirty, and won a victory, on its own small scale, as complete as that of Quebec. The leader of the French was killed, and all his party shot down or taken. It was an affair which, coming at one of the rare intervals when the world was at peace, made a noise as far off as Europe, and gained for the young officer in London circles a tribute of hearty praise, with its due accompaniment of envy and misrepresentation. Horace Walpole gravely records in his Memoirs of George the Second that Major Washington had concluded the letter announcing his success with the words : "I heard the bullets whistle, and, believe me, there is something charming in the sound." Of course there was nothing of the sort in the despatch, which in its business-like simplicity might have been written by Wellington at six and forty. Many years afterwards a clergyman,

---

[1] Those who read or write about the American Revolution owe great obligations to Mr. Bancroft. His *History of the United States of America* supplies a vast mass of detail, illuminated by a fine spirit of liberty, which is inspired indeed by patriotism, but is not bounded in its scope by any limitations of country or of century.

braver even than Washington, asked him if the story **was** true. " If I said so," replied the General, "it was when I was young."

But his was a fame which struck its roots deepest in discouragement, and even in defeat; and that unwelcome feature in his destiny he soon had cause to recognise. In July, 1755, he came from the ambuscade in front of Fort Duquesne with thirty men alive out of his three companies of Virginians; with four shot-holes in his coat; and a name for coolness and conduct which made him the talk of the whole empire, and the pride of the colony that bore him.[1]   During the three coming years, as Commander-in-Chief of her forces, he did his utmost to keep her borders safe and her honour high.   For himself it was a season of trial, sore to bear, but rich in lessons. The Governor of Virginia grudged him rank and pay, and stinted him in men and means; lost no opportunity of reminding him that he was a provincial and not a royal officer; and made himself the centre of military intrigues which gave Washington a foretaste of what he was to endure at the hands of Charles Lee, and Gates, and Benedict Arnold, in the darkest hours of his country's history. But a time came when William Pitt, who understood America, was in a position to insist on fair play and equal treatment to the colonists who were supporting so large a share in the burdens and dangers of the war.   Under his auspices Washington directed the advanced party of an expedition which placed the British flag on Fort Duquesne, and performed the last offices to the mortal remains of those British soldiers who had perished in the woods which covered the approaches to the fatal stronghold.   After this success, which made his native province as secure from invasion as Warwickshire, the young man

[1] Long before Washington reached the age of thirty, his fame was solidly established on both sides of the Atlantic. He was born in 1732 ; and in 1759 the Rev. Andrew Burnaby, Archdeacon of Leicester and Vicar of Greenwich, visited Mount Vernon during the first year of Washington's proprietorship, and saw it with admiration and approval. "This place," the traveller wrote, "is the property of Colonel Washington, and truly deserving of its owner."

retired into private life, with no recompense for his services except the confidence and gratitude of his fellow-
citizens. He had received a practical education in the
science of generalship such as few except born princes
have ever acquired by six and twenty, combined with a
mental and moral drilling more indispensable still to one
whose military difficulties, however exceptionally arduous,
were the smallest part of the ordeal laid up for him in
the future.

Such were the men who had been reluctantly drawn
by their own sense of duty, and by the urgent appeals of
friends and neighbours, into the front rank of a conflict
which was none of their planning. Some of them were
bred in poverty, and all of them lived in tranquil and
modest homes. They made small gains by their private
occupations, and did much public service for very little
or for nothing, and in many cases out of their own
charges. They knew of pensions and sinecures only by
distant hearsay; and ribands or titles were so much outside their scope that they had not even to ask themselves
what those distinctions were worth. Their antecedents
and their type of character were very different from those
of any leading Minister in the British Cabinet; and they
were likely to prove dangerous customers when the one
class of men and of ideas was brought into collision with
the other. While Washington and the Adamses led
laborious days, the English statesmen who moulded the
destinies of America into such an unlooked-for shape
were coming to the front by very different methods.
They had for the most part trod an easier though a more
tortuous path to place and power; or rather to the power
of doing as their monarch bade them. George the
Third's system of personal government had long become
an established fact, and the career of an aspirant to office under that system was now quite an old story. "A
young man is inflamed with love of his country. Liberty
charms him. He speaks, writes, and drinks for her. He
searches records, draws remonstrances, fears Preroga-

tive. A secretary of the Treasury waits on him in the evening. He appears next morning at a minister's levee. He goes to Court, is captivated by the King's affability, moves an address, drops a censure on the liberty of the press, kisses hands for a place, bespeaks a Birthday coat, votes against Magna Charta, builds a house in town, lays his farms into pleasure-grounds under the inspection of Mr. Brown, pays nobody, games, is undone, asks a reversion for three lives, is refused, finds the constitution in danger, and becomes a patriot once more." [1] That passage would be no libel if applied to all except a few members of the Government; — a Government which was controlled by the Bedfords, and advised on legal questions by Wedderburn, whose creed was self-interest; and which was soon to be advised on military questions by Lord George Germaine, who had forfeited his reputation by refusing to bring forward the cavalry at Minden. It was a cruel fate for a country possessing statesmen like Chatham and Burke, a jurist like Camden, and soldiers with the unstained honour and solid professional attainments of Conway and Barré. With such talents lying unemployed, and such voices crying unheeded, the nation was precipitated into a gratuitous and deplorable policy by men who did not so much as believe in the expediency of the course which they were pursuing. To the worse, and unfortunately the abler, section of the Ministry, the right and wrong of the question mattered not one of the straws in which their champagne bottles were packed; while the better of them, knowing perfectly well that the undertaking on which they had embarked was a crime and a folly, with sad hearts and sore consciences went into the business, and some of them through the business, because the King wished it.

And yet, of all the political forces then in existence, the King's influence was the very last which ought to have been exerted against the cause of concord. He

[1] *The Spectator. Number None, written by Nobody.* Sunday, January 19th, 1772.

might well have been touched by the persistence with
which his American subjects continued to regard him
as standing towards them in that relation which a sovereign "born and bred a Briton" should of all others
prefer. A law-respecting people, who did not care to
encroach on the privileges of others, and liked still less
to have their own rights invaded, they were slow to detect the tricks which of recent years had been played
with the essential doctrines of the English Constitution.
When the home Government ill-used them, they blamed
the Ministry, and pleased themselves by believing that
the King, if he ever could contemplate the notion of
stretching his prerogative, would be tempted to do so
for the purpose of protecting them. George the Third
was the object of hope and warm devotion in America
at the moment when, in the City of London, and among
the freeholders of the English counties, he was in the
depths of his unpopularity. In the April of 1768 the
King, if he had listened to any adviser except his own
stout heart, would not have ventured to show himself
outside his palace. His Lord Steward was exchanging
blows with the angry Liverymen at the doors of the
Presence Chamber; the Grand Jury of Middlesex was
refusing to return the rioters for trial; and Junius
could not attack the Crown too ferociously, or flatter
Wilkes too grossly, to please the public taste. But in
that very month Franklin, writing to a Pennsylvanian
correspondent a sentiment with which almost every
Pennsylvanian would have concurred, expressed his
conviction that some punishment must be preparing
for a people who were ungratefully abusing the best
constitution, and the best monarch, any nation was ever
blessed with. A year afterwards, in the letter which
conveyed to his employers in America the unwelcome
intelligence that the House of Commons had refused
to repeal Townshend's custom-duties, Franklin carefully
discriminated between the known ill-will entertained
by Parliament towards the colonies, and the presumed
personal inclinations of the King. "I hope nothing

that has happened, or may happen, will diminish in the least our loyalty to our sovereign or affection for this nation in general.   I can scarcely conceive a King of better dispositions, or more exemplary virtues, or more truly desirous of promoting the welfare of all his subjects.   The body of this people, too, is of a noble and generous nature, loving and honouring the spirit of liberty, and hating arbitrary power of all sorts.   We have many, very many, friends among them." Six years afterwards, when the first blood had been shed, — when George the Third was writing to his Minister to express his delight at the cruel laws that were passed against the colonists, and his discontent with every English public man who still regarded his brethren across the water with friendly, or even tolerant, feelings, — this letter, with others from the same hand, was seized by a British officer in Boston, and sent to London to be submitted to his Majesty's inspection.   With what sensations must he then have read the evidence of a love and a loyalty which by that time were dead for ever !

Franklin, in the passage which has been quoted, did well to give the British people their share in the good-will which America felt towards the British sovereign. The colonists were favourably disposed to George the Third not only for himself, or for his supposed self, but because he was the great representative of the mother-country, — the figurehead of the stately ship which so long had carried the undivided fortunes of their race. They loved the King because they dearly loved the name, the associations, the literature, the religious faith, the habits, the sports, the art, the architecture, the scenery, the very soil, of his kingdom.   That love was acknowledged in pathetic language by men who had drawn their swords against us because, willing to owe everything else to England, they did not recognise her claim to measure them out their portion of liberty. The feeling entertained towards her by some of the best of those who were forced by events to enroll themselves among her adversaries is well exemplified by the career and the writings of Alexander Garden. Born in South Carolina, he had been sent to Europe for his education; and when he came to man's estate, he defied a Loyalist father in order to fight for the Revolution under Nathanael Greene and Henry Lee. In his later years he collected an enormous multitude of personal anecdotes relating to the great struggle, told with transparent fidelity, but infused with no common dose of that bombastic element which in our generation has died out from American literature, but not before it has made for itself an imperishable name. "One truth," (so Garden wrote in his better and less ornate style,) "comes home to the recollection of every man who lived in those days. The attachment to England was such that to whatever the colonists wished to affix the stamp of excellence the title of 'English' was always given. To reside in England was the object of universal desire, the cherished hope of every bosom. It was considered as the delightful haven, where peace and happiness were alone to be looked for. A parent sending his sons to Eton or Westminster would say : 'I am sending my sons home for their education.' If he himself should cross the Atlantic, though but for a summer season, to witness their progress, he would say, 'I am going home to visit my children.'"

The esteem and veneration of America had been concentrated all the more upon the throne itself, because there were very few British statesmen who were famous and popular in the colonies. The difficulties of locomotion were still so great that not one rural constituent, out of a hundred, in England had ever heard his member speak in the House of Commons. It was hard enough even for a Yorkshireman, or a Cornishman, to feel much enthusiasm for orators meagrely reported after the whimsical methods then in fashion ;[1] and to an average New Englander the most celebrated personalities in the West-

---

[1] The Parliamentary Reports in the *Gentleman's Magazine* were, for a long while together, composed in the language of *Gulliver's Travels*. The reader was informed how the Nardac Poltrand had moved an Address in

minster Parliament were mere names, and nothing more. About any individual Right Honourable gentleman, or Lord Temporal, the colonists knew little, and cared less ; and their only concern with Lords Spiritual was to insist, obstinately and most successfully, that they should keep themselves on their own side of the Atlantic. But at last a man arose whose deeds spoke for him, and the fragments of whose eloquence were passed far and wide from mouth to ear, and did not lose the stamp of their quality in the carrying. With his broad heart, his swift perception, and his capacious intellect, Chatham knew America, and he loved her ; and he was known and loved by her in return. He had done more for her than any ruler had done for any country since William the Silent saved and made Holland; and she repaid him with a true loyalty. When the evil day came, it was to Chatham that she looked for the good offices which might avert an appeal to arms. When hostilities had broken out, she fixed on him her hopes of an honourable peace. And when he died, — in the very act of confessing her wrongs, though of repudiating and condemning the establishment of that national independence on which her own mind was by that time irrevocably set, — she refused to allow that she had anything to forgive him, and mourned him as a father of her people.

His name recalled proud memories, in whatever part of the colonies it was spoken. Under his guidance, throughout a war fertile in splendid results, Americans had fought side by side with Englishmen as compatriots rather than as auxiliaries. They had given him cheerfully, in men, in money, and in supplies, whatever he had asked to aid the national cause and secure the common safety. On one single expedition nine thousand provincials had marched from the Northern dis-

the House of Hurgoes, complaining of the injuries sustained by Lilliputian subjects trading in Columbia ; and how the Hurgo Ghewor had replied that "ungrounded jealousy of Blefuscu had already cost the Treasury of Lilliput no less than five hundred thousand sprugs." An editor was driven to such devices in the hope of baffling or conciliating the government censors.

tricts alone. The little colony of Connecticut had five thousand of her citizens under arms. Massachusetts raised seven thousand militia-men, and taxed herself at the rate of thirteen shillings and fourpence in the pound of personal income. New Jersey expended, during every year of the war, at the rate of a pound a head for each of her inhabitants. That was how the French were cleared from the Great Lakes, and from the valley and the tributaries of the Ohio. That was how Ticonderoga and Crown Point fell, and the way was opened for the siege of Quebec and the conquest of the Canadian Dominion. What they had done before, the colonists were willing and ready to do again, if they were allowed to do it in their own fashion. In every successive collision with a foreign enemy England would have found America's power to assist the mother-country doubled, and her will as keen as ever. The colonies which, for three livelong years between the spring of 1775 and the spring of 1778, held their own against the unbroken and undiverted strength of Britain, would have made short work of any army of invasion that the Court of Versailles, with its hands full in Europe, could have detached to recover Canada or to subdue New England. Armed vessels in great number would have been fitted out by a patriotism which never has been averse to that enticing form of speculation, and would have been manned by swarms of handy and hardy seamen, who in war-time found privateering safer work than the fisheries, and vastly more exciting. The seas would have been made so hot by the colonial corsairs that no French or Spanish trader would have shown her nose outside the ports of St. Domingo or Cuba except under an escort numerous enough to invite the grim attentions of a British squadron. But it was a very different matter that America should be called upon to maintain a standing army of royal troops, at a moment when not a grain of our powder was being burned in anger on the surface of the globe ; and that those troops should be quartered permanently within her borders, and paid out of American taxes which the British Parliament had imposed, exacted by tax-gatherers commissioned by the British Ministry. It is hard to understand how any set of statesmen, who knew the methods which Chatham had employed with brilliant success, should have conceived the design of using German mercenaries and Indian savages to coerce English colonists into defending the Empire in exact accordance with the ideas which happened to find favour in Downing Street.

So great was the value of America for fighting purposes. But, in peace and war alike, her contribution to the wealth, the power, the true renown of England, exceeded anything which hitherto had marked the mutual relations of a parent State with a colony; and that contribution was growing fast. Already the best of customers, she took for her share more than a fourth part of the sixteen million pounds' worth in annual value at which the British exports were then computed; and no limit could be named to the expansion of a trade founded on the wants of a population which had doubled itself within a quarter of a century, and whose standard of comfort was rising even more rapidly than its numbers. But the glory which was reflected on our country by her great colony was not to be measured by tons of goods or thousands of dollars. All who loved England wisely, dwelt with satisfaction upon the prosperity of America. It was to them a proud thought that so great a mass of industry, such universally diffused comfort, so much public disinterestedness and private virtue, should have derived its origin from our firesides, and have grown up under our ægis.

It is impossible to avoid regretting that American society, and the American character, were not allowed to develop themselves in a natural and unbroken growth from the point which they had reached at the close of the first century and a half of their history. The Revolutionary war which began in 1775 changed many things and troubled many waters; as a civil war always has done, and always must. The mutual hatred felt, and the

barbarities inflicted and suffered, by partisans of either
side in Georgia and the Carolinas between 1776 and 1782
left behind them in those regions habits of lawlessness
and violence, evil traces of which lasted into our life-
time; and as for the Northern States, it was a pity that
the wholesome and happy conditions of existence prevailing there before the struggle for Independence were
ever disturbed; for no change was likely to improve
them. If the King, as a good shepherd, was thinking
of his flock and not of himself, it is hard to see what he
hoped to do for the benefit of the colonists. All they
asked of him was to be let alone; and with reason; for
they had as just cause for contentment as any population on the surface of the globe. "I have lately," wrote
Franklin, "made a tour through Ireland and Scotland.
In those countries a small part of the society are land-
lords, great noblemen, and gentlemen, extremely opu-
lent, living in the highest affluence and magnificence.
The bulk of the people are tenants, extremely poor,
living in the most sordid wretchedness, in dirty hovels
of mud and straw, and clothed only in rags. I thought
often of the happiness of New England, where every
man is a freeholder, has a vote in public affairs, lives in
a tidy warm house, has plenty of good food and fuel,
with whole clothes from head to foot, the manufacture
perhaps of his own family." [1]

It was no wonder that they were freeholders; inasmuch as real property could be bought for little in the
cultivated parts of New England, and for next to nothing in the outlying districts. Land was no dearer as the
purchaser travelled southwards. There is in existence
an amusing series of letters from a certain Alexander
Mackrabie in America to his brother-in-law in England:
and that brother-in-law knew a good letter from a dull
one, inasmuch as he was Philip Francis. In 1770 Mackrabie wrote from Philadelphia to ask what possessed
Junius to address the King in a letter "past all endurance," and to inquire who the devil Junius was. He

[1] Benjamin Franklin to Joshua Badcock; London, 13 January, 1772.

sweetened the alarm which he unconsciously gave to his
eminent correspondent by offering him a thousand good
acres in Maryland for a hundred and thirty pounds, and
assuring him that farms on the Ohio would be "as cheap
as stinking mackerel." [1] Colonists whose capital consisted in their four limbs, especially if they were skilled
mechanics, had no occasion to envy people who could
buy land, or who had inherited it. Social existence in
America was profoundly influenced by the very small
variation of income, and still smaller of expenditure, at
every grade of the scale. The Governor of a great
province could live in style in his city house and his
country house, and could keep his coach and what his
guests called a genteel table, on five hundred pounds a
year, or something like thirty shillings for each of his
working days. A ship's carpenter, in what was for
America a great city, received five and sixpence a day,
including the value of his pint of rum, the amount of
alcohol contained in which was about an equivalent to
the Governor's daily allowance of Madeira. The Rector
of Philadelphia Academy, who taught Greek and Latin,
received two hundred pounds a year; the Mathematical
Professor a hundred and twenty-five pounds; and the
three Assistant Tutors sixty pounds apiece; — all in
local currency, from which about forty per cent. would
have to be deducted in order to express the sums in
English money. In currency of much the same value a
house carpenter or a bricklayer earned eight shillings
a day, which was as much as a Mathematical Professor,
and twice as much as an Assistant Tutor.[2]

All lived well. All had a share in the best that was
going; and the best was far from bad.[3] The hot buck-

[1] *Memoirs of Sir Philip Francis;* vol. i., p. 439.

[2] The salaries are mentioned in various letters of Franklin. The wages
he quotes from Adam Smith, who, says his biographer, "had been in the
constant habit of hearing much about the American colonies and their
affairs, during his thirteen years in Glasgow, from the intelligent merchants
and returned planters of the city." — Rae's *Life of Adam Smith*, p. 266.

[3] The bills of fare of a Philadelphian angling club, for the year 1762,
have been published by the Historical Society of Pennsylvania. On June 1

wheat cakes, the peaches, the great apples, the turkey
or wild-goose on the spit, and the cranberry sauce stew-
ing in the skillet, were familiar luxuries in every household. Authoritative testimony has been given on this
point by Brillat Savarin, in his " Physiologie de Goût," —
the most brilliant book extant on that which, if mankind
were candid, would be acknowledged as the most universally interesting of all the arts. When he was driven
from his country by the French Revolution, he dined
with a Connecticut yeoman on the produce of the garden, the farmyard, and the orchard. There was "a
superb piece of corned beef, a stewed goose, and a magnificent leg of mutton, with vegetables of every description, two jugs of cider, and a tea-service," on the table
round which the illustrious epicure, the host, and the
host's four handsome daughters were sitting. For
twenty years and thirty years past such had been the
Sunday and holiday fare of a New England freeholder ;
except that in 1774 a pretty patriot would as soon have
offered a guest a cup of vitriol as a cup of tea. A member of what in Europe was called the lower class had in
America fewer cares, and often more money, than those
who, in less favoured lands, would have passed for his
betters. His children were taught at the expense of the
township ; while a neighbour who aspired to give his
son a higher education was liable to be called on to pay
a yearly fee of no less than a couple of guineas. And
the earner of wages was emancipated from the special
form of slavery which from very early days had established itself in the Northern States, — the tyranny exercised over the heads of a domestic establishment by
those whom they had occasion to employ.[1]

the members had " Beefsteaks, six chickens, one ham, one breast of veal,
two tongues, two chicken-pies, one quarter of lamb, two sheeps' heads,
peas, salad, radishes, cream-cheese, gooseberry-pies, strawberries, two
gallons of spirits, and twenty-five lemons ; " and they sate down to no
worse a dinner in the course of the whole season.

[1] " You can have no idea," Mackrabie wrote to Francis in 1769, " of the
plague we have with servants on this side the water. If you bring over a
good one he is spoilt in a month. Those from the country are insolent

Equality of means, and the total absence of privilege, brought about their natural result in the ease, the simplicity, the complete freedom from pretension, which marked the intercourse of society. The great had once been as the least of their neighbours, and the small looked forward some day to be as the best of them. James Putnam, the ablest lawyer in all America, loved to walk in the lane where, as a child of seven years old, he drove the cows to pasture. Franklin, while still a poor boy living on eighteen pence a week, was sought, and almost courted, by the Governor of Pennsylvania and the Governor of New York. Confidence in a future, which never deceived the industrious, showed itself in early marriages; and early marriages brought numerous, healthy, and welcome children. There was no searching of heart in an American household when a new pair of hands was born into the world. The first Adams who was a colonist had eight sons, with whatever daughters Heaven sent him; his eldest son had a family of twelve, and his eldest son a family of twelve again. Franklin had seen thirteen of his own father's children sitting together round the table, who all grew up, and who all in their turn were married. "With us," he wrote, "marriages are in the morning of life; our children are educated and settled in the world by noon; and thus, our own business being done, we have an afternoon and evening of cheerful leisure to ourselves."

The jolly relative of Philip Francis took a less roseate view of the same phenomenon. "The good people," he wrote, "are marrying one another as if they had not a day to live. I allege it to be a plot that the ladies, (who are all politicians in America,) are determined to raise young rebels to fight against old England." Throughout the colonies the unmarried state was held

and extravagant. The imported Dutch are to the last degree ignorant and awkward." The observations made by this rather narrow-minded Briton upon the other nationalities which supplied the household service of America had better be read in the original book, if they are read at all. — *Memoirs of Sir Philip Francis;* vol. i., p. 435.

in scanty honour. Bachelors, whether in the cities or villages, were poorly supplied with consolations and distractions. The social resources of New York, even for a hospitably treated stranger, were not inexhaustible. "With regard," Mackrabie complained, "to the people, manner, living, and conversation, one day shows you as much as fifty. Here are no diversions at all at present. I have gone dining about from house to house, but meet with the same dull round of topics everywhere : — lands, Madeira wine, fishing parties, or politics. They have a vile practice here of playing back-gammon, a noise which I detest, which is going forward in the public coffee-houses from morning till night, frequently ten or a dozen tables at a time. I think a single man in America is one of the most wretched beings I can conceive." The taverns in country districts were uncomfortable, and, as centres of relaxation and sociable discourse, unlovely. Adams, who had put up at a hundred of them, complained that a traveller often found more dirt than entertainment and accommodation in a house crowded with people drinking flip and toddy, and plotting to get the landlord elected to a local office at the next town's meeting.

In a new country the graces and amenities, — and all the provisions for material, intellectual, and what little there may be of artistic, pleasure, — are within the home, and not outside it. Women in America were already treated with a deference which was a sign of the part they played in the serious affairs of life. They had not to put up with the conventional and over-acted homage which in most European countries was then the substitute for their due influence and their true liberty. Married before twenty, and generally long before twenty, they received in the schoolroom an education of the shortest, and something of the flimsiest. To work cornucopias and Birds of Paradise in coloured wools, to construct baskets of ornamental shells, and to accompany a song on the virginal, the spinet, or the harpsichord, were the accomplishments which an American girl had time to learn, and could find instructors to teach her.

But, like the best women in every generation before our own, their most valuable attainments were those which, in the intervals of domestic cares, they taught themselves with a favourite author in their hand, and their feet on the fender. In their literary preferences they were behindhand in point of time; but it was not to their loss. John Quincy Adams, the second President of his race, relates how lovingly and thoroughly his mother knew her Shakespeare and her Milton, her Dryden, her Pope, and her Addison; and how, when she was in need of a quotation tinctured with modern ideas of liberty, she had recourse to Young and Thomson. He well remembered the evening when the cannon had fallen silent on Bunker's Hill, and Massachusetts began to count her losses. A child of eight, he heard Mrs. Adams apply to Joseph Warren, their family friend and family physician, the lines, — mannered indeed, and stilted, but not devoid of solemn and sincere feeling, — which Collins addressed to the memory of a young officer who had been killed at Fontenoy.

We need not go to sons and husbands for our knowledge of what the matrons of the Revolution were. The gentlemen of France, who came to the help of America, were quick to discern the qualities which dignified and distinguished her women; and it is to the credit of the young fellows that they eagerly admired an ideal of conduct which might have been supposed to be less to the taste of a soldier of passage than that which they had left behind them at Paris. It is difficult to believe that the Knight-errants of the war of American Independence, each of them the soul of chivalry, belonged to the same nation as certain swashbucklers of Napoleon who, after trailing their sabres over Europe, confided to the chance reader of their autobiographies their personal successes, real or pretended, among beautiful and unpatriotic women in the countries which they had visited as invaders. After their return home Lafayette and De Ségur, courageous in the drawing-room as in the field, openly proclaimed and steadfastly maintained that in the beauty, elegance, and talent of its ladies Boston could hold its own with any capital city, that of France included. De Ségur, in particular, astonished and charmed his hearers by his description of a community where what passed as gallantry in Paris was called by a very plain name indeed; where women of station rode, drove, and walked unattended both in town and country; where girls of sixteen trusted themselves to the escort of a guest who yesterday had been a stranger, and talked to him as frankly and as fast as if he had been a cousin or a brother; and, above all, where a young Quakeress who, in her white dress and close muslin cap, looked, (though he did not tell her so,) like a nymph rather than a mortal, lectured him on having deserted his wife and children to pursue the wicked calling of a soldier, and sternly rejected the plea that he had severed himself from all that he held most dear in order to fight for the liberty of her country. After the war was over, De Ségur embodied his experience and his observations in a series of predictions concerning the future of the United States. He clearly foresaw that the question whether the South and North were to part company would one day arise in a formidable shape; he foretold that wealth would bring luxury, and luxury corruption; but with regard to that private morality which, of all that he found in America, he approved the most, he did not venture on a specific prophecy. " I shall be told," he wrote, " that America will not always preserve these simple virtues and these pure manners; but if she preserves them only for a century, that at any rate will be a century gained."[1]

---

[1] Voltaire, an old friend of De Ségur's mother, in half a dozen sentences full of wisdom and good feeling, and turned as only he could turn them, had given him his literary blessing, and the advice to keep to prose. That advice was religiously followed by a family which handed down through three generations, in unbroken succession from father to son, the good traditions of the memoir-writer. There is an extraordinary likeness, in form and substance, between the writing of the father, who served in the American war, and afterwards became French ambassador to Russia; of the son, who told the story of Austerlitz, and the retreat from Moscow; and of the grandson, author of the Life of Count Rostopchine. Which of the three wrote best is a problem of the sort that to those, who love books, will always remain the idlest of questions.

CHAPTER III

CHANGE OF VENUE TO ENGLAND OF TRIALS FOR TREA-
SON. MILITARY OCCUPATION OF BOSTON. DIFFICUL-
TIES CONNECTED WITH TRADE AND REVENUE BECOME
ACUTE

SUCH was the country, and such the people, on which
the British Cabinet now tried the experiment of carrying through a political policy by the pressure of an
armed force. They were blind to the truth which Byron,
a genuine statesman, expressed in the sentence, "The
best prophet of the future is the past;" for that experiment had never succeeded when an English-speaking
population was made the subject of it. It had been
tried under the Commonwealth when the Major-Generals
administered England; and the Journal of George Fox,
read side by side with Hudibras, proves that the saints
liked being ruled by saints in red coats almost as little
as did the sinners. It had been tried after the Restoration, when the Stuarts espoused the cause of the Bishops
as against the Scotch Covenanters; and the result was,
over the whole of the south of Scotland, to kill the cause
of the Bishops and of the Stuarts too. And in 1688 the
wrath and terror which the mere threat of coercion by
an Irish army excited throughout the kingdom did much
to ruin James the Second, as it had ruined his father before him.

Now the same remedy, fatal always to the physician,
was applied to a case that differed from those which
preceded it only in being more hopelessly unsuited to
such a treatment. The character, the circumstances,
and the history of the inhabitants of New England made
it certain that they would feel the insult bitterly and

70

resent it fiercely. It was a measure out of which, from the very nature of it, no good could be anticipated; and it may well be doubted whether the authors of it, in their heart of hearts, expected or desired that any good should come. The crime of Massachusetts was that she refrained from buying British goods, and that she had petitioned the Crown in respectful terms. Fifty regiments could not oblige her to do the one, or make her think that she had been wrong in having done the other. And, in truth, the action of the British Government was intended to punish, and not to persuade. It was a device essentially of the same sinister class as the Dragonnades which preceded the Revocation of the Edict of Nantes; less trenchant, indeed, in its operation, owing to the difference in type of the instruments employed; for British soldiers were too good to be set to such work, and far too manly and kind-hearted to do it efficaciously. But the motives that suggested and brought about the military occupation of Boston showed poorly, in one important respect, even by the side of those which actuated Louis the Fourteenth and his clerical advisers. In both cases there was ruffled pride, the determination at all costs to get the upper hand, and want of sympathy which had deepened down into estrangement and positive ill-will. But the French monarch at least believed that, by making his subjects miserable in this world, he would possibly save their souls in the next, and would undoubtedly cleanse his dominions from the stain of heresy; whereas the quarrel between George the Third and his people beyond the sea was of the earth, earthy. As an Elizabethan poet had said in good prose: "Some would think the souls of princes were brought forth by some more weighty cause than those of meaner persons. They are deceived; there's the same hand to them; the like passions sway them. The same reason that makes a vicar go to law for a tithe-pig, and undo his neighbours, makes them spoil a whole province, and batter down goodly cities with the cannon." [1]

[1] Webster's *Duchess of Malfi*, Act ii., Scene I.

The King was determined to stand on his extreme rights; and he met his match in the Americans. In their case he had to do with people accurately and minutely acquainted with what was due to them and from them, and little likely to miss, or refrain from pressing to the utmost, any single point which told in their favour. Burke was informed by an eminent bookseller that in no branch of his business, after tracts of popular devotion, were so many volumes exported to the colonies as those which related to the law. Nearly as many copies of Blackstone's Commentaries had been sold in America as in England. So eager were the colonists to read our treatises on jurisprudence that they had fallen into the way of reprinting them across the Atlantic; a habit, it must be allowed, which they soon applied on a generous scale to more attractive classes of literature. Burke, who observed and investigated America with the same passionate curiosity that he subsequently bestowed upon India, had arrived at the conclusion that a circumstance which made against peace, unless the British Government reverted to the paths of caution, was to be found in the addiction of the colonists to the study of the law. "This study," he said, "renders men acute, inquisitive, dexterous, prompt in attack, ready in defence, full of resources. In other countries the people, more simple, and of a less mercurial cast, judge of an ill principle in government only by an actual grievance; there they anticipate the evil, and judge of the pressure of the grievance by the badness of the principle. They augur misgovernment at a distance, and snuff the approach of tyranny in every tainted breeze." [1]

The times were such that the lawyers in America, like all other men there, had to choose their party. In the Government camp were those favoured persons whom the Crown regularly employed in court, and those who held, or looked to hold, the posts of distinc tion and emolument with which the colonies abounded;

[1] Mr. Burke's Speech on moving his Resolution for Conciliation with the Colonies.

for the Bar in America, as in Ireland and Scotland to this day, was a public service as well as a profession. But, with these exceptions, most lawyers were patriots; for the same reason that, (as the royal Governors complained), every patriot was, or thought himself, a lawyer. The rights and liberties of the province had long been the all-pervading topic of conversation in Massachusetts. There were few briefs for a learned gentleman who, in General Putnam's tavern or over Mr. Hancock's dining-table, took the unpopular side in an argument; especially if he did not know how to keep those who came to him for advice on the safe side of a penal statute. " Look into these papers," said an English Attorney-General in 1768, "and see how well these Americans are versed in the Crown law. I doubt whether they have been guilty of an overt act of treason, but I am sure that they have come within a hair's breadth of it." [1] Leading merchants, who were likewise eminently respectable smugglers on an enormous scale, were the best clients of a Boston advocate. Their quarrels with the Commissioners of Revenue brought him large fees, and coveted opportunities for a display of eloquence. His wits as a casuist were sharpened by a life-time of nice steering among the intricacies of the commercial code; and the experience which he thence gained taught him as a politician to assume higher ground, and to demand that trade should be as free and open to British subjects in the New World as it was to those in the Old.[2] His public attitude was stiffened by the recollection of a threat which had been levelled against his private interests. A secondary, but an evident and even confessed, object of the Stamp Act had been to impose an all but prohibitory tax upon the manufacture of legal documents, and thereby to injure the practice, and to pare

[1] Bancroft's History, Epoch III., chapter 37.
[2] These are the words of Mr. Sabine in his Historical Essay at the commencement of his two volumes on the American Loyalists. His description of the opinions prevalent in the several professions at the commencement of the Revolution is amusing and instructive.

away the gains, of those unofficial lawyers among whom were to be found the most skilful and stubborn opponents of the Government.

Already the commercial prosperity of the mother-country was grievously impaired. The colonists had met Charles Townshend's policy by an agreement not to consume British goods; and the value of such goods exported to New England, New York, and Pennsylvania fell in a single year from 1,330,000*l.* to 400,000*l.* Washington, when he sent his annual order for a supply of European commodities to London, enjoined his correspondent to forward none of the articles unless the offensive Act of Parliament was in the meantime repealed. Less scrupulous patriots found reason to wish that they had followed his example. Mackrabie relates how two Philadelphians had sent over for a Cheshire cheese, and a hogshead of English Entire Butt. "These delicacies happened unfortunately to have been shipped from Europe after the Resolutions on this side had transpired, and in consequence the Committee took the liberty to interfere. The purchasers made a gallant stand, but their opposition was in vain. They cursed and swore, kicked, and cuffed, and pulled noses; but the catastrophe was that the prisoners were regaled with the cheese and porter. They have sent away a ship loaded with malt to-day. Nobody could either buy or store it." The phraseology of the movement against taxation without representation appeared in odd places. A mechanic, whose shop had been broken open, advertised a reward for the apprehension of the thief, and reminded his fellow-citizens how hard it was for a man to part with his own property without his own consent. It is curious to note that Grenville, as the father of the Stamp Act, till his death, and long after it, came in for much of the discredit which properly belonged to Charles Townshend. "I would not as a friend," Mackrabie wrote from Philadelphia, "advise Mr. George Grenville to come and pass a summer in North America. It might be unsafe." This was in

1768. But as late as 1773 Edmund Burke, who, of all people, had been asked by a friend in Virginia to send him out a clever lad accustomed to ride light weights, wrote to Lord Rockingham : " If poor George Grenville was alive, he would not suffer English jockeys to be entered outwards without bond and certificate : or at least he would have them stamped or excised, to bear the burdens of this poor oppressed country, and to relieve the landed interest." Ten years later the poets of Brooks's Club were still singing of

> "Grenville's fondness for Hesperian gold;
> And Grenville's friends, conspicuous from afar,
> In mossy down incased, and bitter tar."

All the British regiments which had ever sailed from Cork or Portsmouth could not force Americans to purchase British merchandise. Nor was it possible that the presence of troops, under a free constitution such as Massachusetts still enjoyed, should do anything towards the better government of the colony, or the solution of the difficulties which had arisen between the Assembly and the Crown. One function the soldiers might be called upon to discharge ; and it was evidently in the minds of the Cabinet which sent them out. As soon as the news of their arrival at Boston had reached London, the supporters of the Ministry, in manifest concert with the Treasury Bench, moved an address to the King praying that persons who, in the view of the Governor of Massachusetts, had committed, or had failed to disclose, acts of treason might be brought over to England and tried under a statute of Henry the Eighth. The Ministers themselves moved Resolutions framed with the object of indicating for the Governor's guidance that, in the action which the Assembly of the colony had taken, and in the votes which it had passed, treason had already been committed.

Such a proposal was shocking to many independent members of Parliament, and most of all to those who knew by experience what a serious matter a voyage from

America was, even in a case where there would be little prospect indeed of a return journey.   Thomas Pownall, who had governed Massachusetts strongly and discreetly during Pitt's great war, was earnest in his remonstrances; and his views were enforced by Captain Phipps, afterwards Lord Mulgrave, a competent and experienced navigator.   They commented forcibly on the cruelty and injustice of dragging an individual three thousand miles from his family, his friends, and his business, "from every assistance, countenance, comfort, and counsel necessary to support a man under such trying circumstances," in order that, with the Atlantic between him and his own witnesses, he might be put to peril of his life before a panel of twelve Englishmen, in no true sense of the word his peers.   Of those jurymen the accused colonist would not possess the personal knowledge which alone could enable him to avail himself of his right to challenge; while they on their side would infallibly regard themselves as brought together to vindicate the law against a criminal of whose guilt the responsible authorities were fully assured, but who would have been dishonestly acquitted by a Boston jury. All this was said in the House of Commons, and listened to most unwillingly by the adherents of the Ministry, who after a while drowned argument by clamour.   A large majority voted to establish what was, for all intents and purposes, a new tribunal, to take cognisance of an act which, since it had been committed, had been made a crime by an *ex post facto* decree.   Parliament had done this in a single evening, without hearing a tittle of evidence, and, (after a not very advanced stage in the proceedings,) without consenting to hear anything or anybody at all.   But a House of Commons, which had so often dealt with Wilkes and the Middlesex electors, had got far beyond the point of caring to maintain a judicial temper over matters affecting the rights, the liberty, and now at last the lives, of men.[1]

[1] The Government were in a bad House of Commons mess.   They could not produce a copy of the alleged treasonable Resolution of the

That which was the sport of a night at Westminster was something very different to those whom it most concerned at Boston. The chiefs of the popular party saw the full extent of their danger in a moment. They already had done what placed their fortunes, and in all probability their very existence, at the mercy of the Governor; and, whether the blow fell soon, or late, or not at all, their peace of mind was gone. To poor men, as most of them were, transportation to England at the best meant ruin. Their one protection, the sympathy of their fellow-citizens, was now powerless to save them. Time was when Governor Bernard would have thought twice before he laid hands on the leaders of public opinion in a country where the arm of authority was strong only when it had public opinion with it. He was not likely to forget how, when the populace were hanging the Boston stamp distributer in effigy, the civil power requested that the Militia might be called out by beat of drum, and how the colonel replied that his drummers were in the mob. To arrest Samuel Adams and John Hancock, even with their own concurrence, by the aid of such peace officers as cared to respond to a summons, was in the view of the Governor a sufficiently arduous undertaking. And when the time for their deportation came, it would have been a more serious business still to march them, through streets crowded with angry patriots, down to a wharf over the edge of which the crews of half a hundred coasting vessels would have tossed the constables, and the sheriff too, with as little scruple as they would have run a cargo of sugar on a dark night into a creek of Rhode Island. But the troops had come, and the ships which had brought them

Massachusetts Assembly, on which their own proposals were founded. Governor Pownall, backed by Burke, denied that such a Resolution was in existence. "The chorus-men, who at proper times call for the question, helped them out at this dead lift, by an incessant recitative of the words, 'Question, question, question.' At length, at four o'clock in the morning, the whole House in confusion and laughing, the Resolutions and addresses were agreed to." Such is the account given, in expressive, but not very official language, in the *Parliamentary History* for the 26th of January, 1769.

were never again likely to be far away; and that difficulty was a thing of the past.   With a quay commanded
by the cannon of men-of-war, and a harbour alive with
their armed boats, and with a forest of bayonets on
land, there would be no fear of a rescue, or even of a
riot.   All prominent opponents of the Government henceforward lived in the knowledge that their fate was at
the arbitrary disposal of one whom, as an officer of the
State, they had braved and baffled ; and who insisted on
regarding them, each and all, as his private enemies.
The revival of the old Tudor statute, which kept a hal-
ter suspended over the neck of every public man whom
the people of Massachusetts followed and trusted, was
a device as provocative, and in the end proved to be as
foolish and as futile, as the operation which in the story
of our great civil contest is called, not very accurately,
the Arrest of the Five Members.

From the day that the troops landed all chance of a
quiet life, for those who valued it, was over and done
with.   John Adams, who was intent on making a livelihood, — and who, to use his own words, had very little
connection with public affairs, and hoped to have less, —
observed with disapproval that endeavours were being
systematically pursued " by certain busy characters to
kindle an immortal hatred between the inhabitants of
the lower class and the soldiers."   But the fact was
that every class, without any prompting from above or
below, had its own reasons for disliking the military
occupation of their city.   Boston was a non-official
community, where no man was under orders, and where
every man worked every day and all day to get his
bread by supplying, in one shape or another, the
natural wants and requirements of the society in which
he lived.   But now the whole place was invaded by
officialism in its most uncompromising and obtrusive
form.   For every two civilians there was at least one
wearer of a uniform, whose only occupations were to
draw his pay, to perform his routine duties, and to obey

some one who was placed above him. Boston was Whig; and the army, from top to bottom, with few exceptions, was ultra-Tory. Charles Lee, who had served with distinction up to the rank of colonel in a royal regiment, — and with whom royal officers lived, and generally continued to live, on free and equal terms, — remembered an occasion when a clever and spirited subaltern inveighed against David Hume as a champion of divine right and absolute monarchy. The young man was taken to task by a veteran who rebuked him for speaking with irreverence of Charles the First, and, with more loyalty than logic, pronounced that such sentiments were indecent and ungrateful in those who ate the King's bread.[1] That was the creed of the mess-room; ominous enough in the days of a sovereign who, now that the Stuarts were no longer a danger to himself, was only too ready to take them for his model.

The social tone of military circles was even more uncongenial to the atmosphere of Boston than their political opinions. That tone has been changing for the better ever since, and never so quickly and so steadily as during the period which covers the career of those who now command our brigades. The British officer of this generation is a picked man to begin with. He enters the army at an age when he has already laid the ground of a liberal education, and in after life he never misses an opportunity of perfecting his professional acquirements. In Indian and colonial service he gains a large, and even cosmopolitan, view of affairs and men, while he has always present to his mind the obligation to maintain the credit of the country abroad by his personal conduct and demeanour. And, when employed at home, he is accustomed to act with the Militia and Volunteers; to take a share in the work of their organisation and their discipline; to recognise their merits; and to make full allowance for deficiences from which citizen soldiers can never be exempt in peace, or in the first campaign of a war.

It was a different story with an officer whose lot was

[1] *Memoirs of Major-General Lee;* Dublin, 1792: page 101.

cast in the third quarter of the eighteenth century. When on active service in Germany every one, against whom, or by whose side, he fought, was a regular soldier ; and, in the case of our Prussian allies, a regular of the regulars.   When he returned to England, to quarters in a Cathedral town, (or, if a guardsman, to his lodging in St. James's Street,) he moved in social circles where no single person pursued any one of those work-a-day trades and callings which in New England ranked as high as the very best.   With such a training and such associations, a man who possessed no more than the average share of good sense and good feeling cared little for colonial opinion, whether civil or military, and seldom went the right way to conciliate it.   Pitt did his utmost to correct what was amiss ; and, when he could lay his hand on a general of the right sort, he did much.   Young Lord Howe, who led the advance against Ticonderoga in 1758, — and who in truth, as long as he was alive, commanded the expedition, — tried hard to break down the barrier between the two sections of his army by precept, and by his fine example.   But when he was shot dead, skirmishing with Israel Putnam's Rangers in front of his own regiment, the Fifty-fifth of the line, he left no one behind him, south of the St. Lawrence, who had the capacity or inclination to carry out the great Minister's wise and large policy.   The relations of royal and provincial officers became anything but fraternal, and the rank and file of the American companies were only too ready to espouse the quarrel of their leaders.   American colonels, during the Ticonderoga campaign, complained that they were hardly ever summoned to a council of war, and that, until the orders came out, they knew no more of what was to be done than the sergeants.   The men of an American regiment, which was stationed on the Hudson, conceived themselves affronted by an English captain, and nearly half the corps disbanded itself and marched off home.   An English Quartermaster-General, great in nothing but oaths, — whom his own Commander-in-Chief described as a very odd man, with whom he was sorry to have any concern, — was told by a Virginian colonel that he would rather break his sword than serve with him any longer. These incidents, when brooded over in winter quarters, engendered a dissatisfaction which found vent in a heated newspaper controversy between London and Boston.

Mr. Parkman, in his fascinating story of "Montcalm and Wolfe," as elsewhere throughout his writings, preserves a carefully measured impartiality of praise and blame towards English and French, regular soldiers and colonial levies, and even Indians; though it cannot be said that these last gain, either as men or warriors, by an unvarnished description. He thus speaks about British officers: "Most of them were men of family, exceedingly prejudiced and insular, whose knowledge of the world was limited to certain classes of their own countrymen, and who looked down on all others, whether foreign or domestic. Towards the provincials their attitude was one of tranquil superiority, though its tranquillity was occasionally disturbed by what they regarded as absurd pretensions on the part of the colony officers. The provincial officers, on the other hand, and especially those of New England, being no less narrow and prejudiced, filled with a sensitive pride and a jealous local patriotism, and bred up in a lofty appreciation of the merits and importance of their country, regarded British superciliousness with a resentment which their strong love for England could not overcome." [1] There were faults on both sides. But the British officers had the most to give; and, if they had cordially and cheerfully taken their cue from spirits as finely touched as those of Wolfe and Howe, their advances towards intimacy with their American comrades would have been eagerly met and their friendship warmly valued.

If there was so little sense of fellowship between the regular army and the colonists during the Seven Years' War, when they were serving together in the field against a common adversary, it may well be believed that in 1772

[1] Parkman's *Montcalm and Wolfe*, chapter xxi.

and 1773 things did not go pleasantly in the streets of Boston. The garrison was there, in order to remind the city that Britain's arm was long and heavy, and that her patience was exhausted. It was a situation without hope from the very first; for it gave no opportunity for the play of kindly impulses, and was only too certain to bring into prominence the least estimable persons on either side. There were men of refinement and good education in the British regiments, and on the staff, more especially among those of older standing, who would gladly have employed their social gifts to mitigate the asperity of politics. There were, as the sequel proved, some of all ranks and ages who had studied the case of the colonists closely enough to question and condemn the action of their own Government. And there were veterans who had fought the enemies of their country bravely all the world over, without being able to hate them, and who were still less inclined to be harsh towards those whom they regarded as her erring children. But the winter of discontent was so severe that Uncle Toby himself could not have melted the ice in a Boston parlour. The men of the popular party, and the women quite as rigidly, set their faces like flint against any show of civility, or the most remote approach to familiarity. The best among the officers, forbidden by self-respect to intrude where they were not welcome, retired into the background, and left the field clear for the operations of certain black-sheep of the mess-room, whom the citizens, in the humour which then prevailed, came not unnaturally to look upon as representatives of British character and conduct.

That sort of military man, as readers of the English classics know, appeared frequently in the dramas and novels of the eighteenth century; where his self-sufficiency and impertinence were unsparingly castigated, although he was sometimes endowed with a sprightliness of which in real life little trace could be found.[1] The

[1] Mrs. Grant of Laggan, who was a strong Loyalist, as a young lady was well acquainted with the officers quartered in a neighbouring provincial

recruiting officer who travelled with Mr. Spectator on his
return from the visit to Sir Roger de Coverley ; the ensign who insulted Tom Jones ; the captain whom Rod-
erick Random met in the Bath coach, — were of a type
which has now become extinct in our army.   But of old
days that type was much in evidence, as many a quiet
and inoffensive person everywhere, but especially in the
colonies, knew to his cost.   For, when these gentlemen
disported themselves in American society, they were in
the habit of parading a supreme disdain for every one
who did not wear a uniform.   To all such they applied
indiscriminately the name of "Mohairs," an epithet
which still rankled in the mind of many a brave man
after he had worn to tatters more than one uniform
while fighting against the cause to which the services of
these reprobates were so great a discredit, and so small
a gain.[1]   In undisturbed times, and in cities against
which the Government that employed them did not bear
a grudge, their contempt for civilians found expression
in acts of buffoonery, the victims of which were cautiously
but not always judiciously chosen.   A Philadelphian
writer of the period relates the feats of a pair of officers
who made themselves notorious by a series of practical
jokes, marked with scanty fun and great impudence, and
directed against citizens of pacific appearance and occupations.   At length the worst of the two happened to
mistake his man, and received a lesson which he was
not likely soon to forget.

The nature of such pranks, when their perpetrators

town. "The Royal Americans," she writes, "had been in garrison.
They were persons of decent morals and a judicious and moderate way
of thinking, who, though they did not court the society of the natives,
expressed no contempt for their manners or opinion."

After a while the place of the Royal Americans was taken by another
battalion.   The officers of the new regiment "turned the plain burghers
into the highest ridicule, and yet used every artifice to get acquainted
with them.   They wished to act the part of very fine gentlemen ; and the
gay and superficial in those days were but too apt to take for their model
the fine gentlemen of the detestable old comedies, which good taste has
now very properly exploded."

[1] Garden's *Revolutionary Anecdotes.*

were sober, gives some faint indication of what they permitted themselves in their hours of conviviality ; for those were days when to drink more than was good for him, — or indeed more than would have been good for himself and his neighbours on either side of him, — was a duty which no one could decline except a man of unusual resolution, or of a grade in the army higher than any which these worthies were ever likely to attain. Mackrabie, who between 1768 and 1770 was made much at home in the garrisons of America, was very candid in keeping his brother-in-law informed of the price which he paid for the privilege. " We have been most hospitably and genteelly entertained," he writes from Fort Pitt, (as Fort Duquesne had been styled ever since it fell into British hands,) " and allowing for the *politesse à la militaire* which obliges us to compound for being *un peu enivrés* at least once a day, we pass our time most agreeably." On the fourth of June at New York he anticipates that the General, as a matter of course, will make all the officers in the town drunk at his house in honour of the King's birthday. In another letter he gives a description of serenading, as practised in Philadelphia. " The manner is as follows. We with four or five young officers of the regiment in barracks drink as hard as we can, to keep out the cold, and about midnight sally forth, attended by the band, — horns, clarinets, hautboys, and bassoons, — march through the streets, and play under the window of any lady you choose to distinguish, which they esteem a high compliment." In 1770, when feeling was already so hot that a good Englishman should have been careful to evince his loyalty to the King by courtesy and forbearance towards the King's subjects, he was invited to join in celebrating St. George's Day at a banquet attended by all the native-born Englishmen in the city. " We should have had," he writes, "the Governor at our head, but that the party was only proposed two days before. However, we met at a tavern, stuffed roast beef and plum pudding, and got drunk, *pour l'honneur de St.*

George ; wore crosses, and finished the evening at the play-house, where we made the people all chorus 'God save the King,' and 'Rule Britannia,' and 'Britons strike home,' and such like nonsense, and, in short, conducted ourselves with all the decency and confusion usual on such occasions." [1]

Those manners, unrebuked and even tacitly encouraged in high military quarters, were not likely to win back the affections of a community which still walked in the footsteps of its early founders. Mr. Thomas Hollis, — a learned English antiquary, and an enterprising art-collector, who met with the success which falls to him who is early in that field, — had been a munificent benefactor to American colleges, and most of all to Harvard. He maintained with the leading scholars and divines of America very close relations of friendship, of good offices, and, (whenever the opportunity offered itself,) of hospitality. Indeed, his position in reference to New England was very much that of the Proxenus of a foreign State in the cities of ancient Greece. He knew the colonists of old ; and, if the Ministry had consulted him, he could have put them into communication with informants and advisers of a higher stamp than the broken-down office-holders and subsidised newswriters who were their confidential correspondents across the ocean. "The people of Boston and Massachusetts Bay," so Hollis wrote within a month of the day that the troops sailed for America, "are, I suppose, take them as a body, the soberest, most knowing, virtuous people at this time upon earth. All of them hold Revolution principles, and were to a man, till disgusted by the Stamp Act, the staunchest friends to the house of Hanover." There was a seriousness, he went on to say, in their conversation and deportment which in the more ribald public prints had obtained for them the appellation of Boston Saints ; and, like the saints of old, they now had a taste of persecution. Although physical

[1] Mackrabie to Francis, Fort Pitt, 14th July, 1770 ; New York, 4th June 1768 ; Philadelphia, 9th March, 1768 ; Philadelphia, 24th April, 1770.

cruelty was absent, they endured something of martyrdom in the moral repugnance created by the license and
the rioting with which their much-enduring town was
thenceforward flooded. It is not difficult to imagine the
feelings of a quiet family, who had never heard music
outside the church of their own denomination, when they
were treated to a military serenade after the style of
Philadelphia; knowing only too well that, if the ladies
of the house were suspected by their Whig neighbours
of liking the entertainment, they might wake up some
morning to find their front door tarred and feathered.

For they were not all saints in Boston. In the alleys
which ran down to the water-side there were as rough
men of their hands as in any seaport in the world;
ardent patriots all of them, (with the exception of a very
few who took excellent care to keep their sentiments to
themselves,) and vigilant censors and guardians, after
their own fashion, of the patriotism of others. Unfortunately these were the inhabitants of Boston who came
most closely and frequently in contact with the rank
and file of the British army. It was a pity that there
should have been so deep and impassable a gulf of mis-
understanding between two sets of people who had
much in common, whose interests were in no point ad-
verse, and whose attitude of reciprocal enmity was imposed upon them from above. None who are widely
read in military memoirs, — and there is no nation more
rich in the journals of privates and non-commissioned
officers than our own, — can doubt that the men of Minden, like the men of Talavera and Salamanca, were as
honest, humane, and (under the ordinary temptations
and trials of military life) as well-conducted soldiers as
ever carried a sick comrade's knapsack or shared their
rations with a starving peasant. But they knew very
well that their presence in Boston was not meant as a
delicate attention to the city, and that to make themselves disagreeable to its citizens was part of the un-
written order of the day. Any compunction that they
might have harboured was soon extinguished by the

inexorable hostility which met them at every step, and hemmed them in from every quarter. If they had been a legion of angels under Gabriel and Michael they would have been just as much, and as little, beloved in Fish Street, or in Battery Marsh. Their good qualities were denied or travestied, their faults spied out and magnified. Men who during Pitt's war never tired of standing treat with soldiers, now talked of them as idle drunkards. If they civilly passed the time of day to a woman, she drew herself aside with a shudder. The very colour of the cloth in which, in order that America might be safe and great, Englishmen had struggled through the surf at Louisburg, and clambered up the heights of Abraham, was made for them a by-word and a reproach. No single circumstance was employed with such great injustice, but so much effect, to excite disgust and derision as one condition in their professional existence which, poor fellows, was no fault of theirs. The custom of flogging, (and that punishment, in the case of a heavy sentence, might well mean death by the most horrible of tortures,) revolted, sometimes beyond all power of repression, the humanity of the populations among whom our troops were quartered, and of the allies with whom they served. This feeling was strong in America, where the sense of personal dignity and inviolability was more deeply rooted than in Europe; and it found expression in a savage nickname which, as the event showed, a man with a loaded musket in his hand, all the more because he was respectable, might find himself unable tamely to endure.[1]

[1] During the later period of the war a young colonist, hardly more than a boy, deserted from Colonel Tarleton's corps in the royal army. He was sentenced to a thousand lashes, and died under them. On one occasion an American sentinel saw a red coat on the opposite bank of a river, and gave the alarm. On closer inspection it was discovered to be the cast-off uniform of a British soldier, who had been flogged with such severity that " his lacerated back would admit of no covering."

The shock to the popular sentiment became more intense, as time went on, both at home and on the Continent. During the war with Napoleon a battalion which had suffered terribly from illness in the West Indies, and was going out to suffer terribly at Walcheren, was quartered at Ripon in

Boston, through its constituted authorities, met the
invasion with passive, but most effective and irritating,
resistance. The Colonels called upon the Council to
house and feed their men. They were reminded that
under the statute the city was not bound to provide
quarters or supplies until the barracks in the Castle
were full; and the Council and the Colonels alike knew
that the regiments had been sent, not to defend the
Castle, (which stood on an island in the Bay,) but to
occupy and annoy the city. General Gage, the Commander-in-Chief in America, came on from New York
to find his soldiers sleeping in tents on the Common,
with a New England winter rapidly approaching. He
tried his best to insist that billets should be found for
them; but the law was against him, in a country where,
as he sulkily remarked, the law was studied by everybody. There was nothing for it but to hire private
houses at exorbitant rates, and supply the wants of the
troops through the agency of the Commissariat, and at
the expense of the British Treasury.

The soldiers were now in the heart of the town, with
nothing to do except to clean their accoutrements; to
mount guard in public places which, before they came,
had been as peaceful as Berkeley Square; and to pick
quarrels with the townsmen, who on their side were not
slow to take up the challenge. Every man fought his

Yorkshire. A soldier was severely flogged. Several of his comrades fainted
in the ranks ; and the inhabitants, who had with difficulty been restrained
by a cordon of sentries from rushing in upon the scene of execution, pelted
the regiment on the way back to barracks. After Salamanca, as an episode
of our triumphal entry into Madrid, a culprit received eight hundred lashes,
inflicted by the strongest drummers and buglers in the brigade. The people of the city crowded about the sufferer, and would have loaded him with
money if he had been allowed to take it. A German rifleman in the British service has left an account of the operations near Alicante in 1813.
"The inhabitants," he says, "had never had an opportunity of witnessing
an English military punishment, and the flogging of an artilleryman made
a considerable impression on them. They cut down the fig-tree to which
he had been tied, and even grubbed up the roots." *American Anecdotes*,
vol. i., pp. 74 and 399. *The Vicissitudes of a Soldier's Life*, by John Green,
late of the 68th Durham Light Infantry, chapters ii. and x. *Adventures of
a Young Rifleman;* London, 1826 ; chapter viii.

hardest with the weapons which were most familiar to
him. Samuel Adams argued, in a series of published
letters, that it was illegal in time of peace, without the
consent of Parliament, to keep up a standing army;
and that Americans, who were not represented in Parliament, were therefore suffering under a military tyranny.
British officers spoke and wrote their minds about the
treatment to which they had been subjected in consequence of the hostility of the citizens; and the Grand
Jury found bills against them for slandering the city of
Boston. A captain, who bade his men remember, if a
hand were laid on them, that they wore side-arms, and
that side-arms were meant for use, was called upon to
answer before the tribunals for the words which he had
uttered. Humbler and ruder people in either camp followed the lead of their superiors; and during eighteen
months insult and provocation were rife in the air, and
the street was seldom free, for long together, from rough
play which at any moment might turn into bloody work.
On the evening of the 5th of March, 1770, there came
a short and sharp encounter between a handful of soldiers and a small crowd, voluble in abuse, and too free
with clubs and snowballs. There was a sputter of musketry, and five or six civilians dropped down dead or dying.
That was the Boston massacre. The number of killed
was the same as, half a century afterwards, fell in St.
Peter's Fields at Manchester. It was not less certain
that American Independence must result from the one
catastrophe than that English Parliamentary Reform
would result from the other; and in each case the inevitable consequence took just the same period of time
to become an accomplished fact of history.

It would be as idle to apportion the shares of blame
among the immediate actors in the miserable business as
to speculate on the amount of the responsibility for an
explosion which attached itself to an artilleryman whose
officer had sent him into a magazine to fill cartridges
by the light of an open candle. Of the high parties
concerned, the popular leaders hastened to put them-

selves in the right, and to prove that the extemporised statesmanship of plain folk might be better than anything which Privy Councillors, and Lord Chancellors present and expectant, had to show. Their first care was to get the soldiers out of the town; and for this humane and public-spirited object they availed themselves deftly, and most justifiably, of the apprehension aroused in the minds of the British authorities by an outburst of wrath such as no American city had hitherto witnessed. All that night the drums were rolling, and the bells clashing, and the streets resounding with the cry of "Town-born, turn out, turn out!" The population was on foot, armed and angry; and no one went home to bed until the troops had been ordered back to barracks, and the captain who had commanded the party of soldiers in the fatal affray was in custody of the Sheriff, and under examination before the magistrates. Next morning there was a public meeting, attended by almost every able-bodied man in Boston, and by the first comers of the multitudes which all day long streamed in from the surrounding country. There was no bloodshed, no outrage, no violence even of language. After a prayer for the divine blessing, at which any opponent who liked was at liberty to laugh, a committee of citizens was gravely chosen, and charged with the duty of providing, according to the best of their judgement, for the common safety. Samuel Adams, Warren, and Hancock, with their colleagues, on the one side, and the Lieutenant-Governor surrounded by his Council and the chief officers of the Army and Navy on the other, talked it out through the livelong day. There were adjournments for the purpose of affording the representatives of the Crown an opportunity to confer privately among themselves, and of enabling the delegates to make their report to the people, who sate in continuous session, or stood over the whole space between their own hall of meeting and the State-house in vast and ever-increasing numbers. It was a hard tussle; but fresh arguments, which required no marshalling or commenting, were coming in from the neighbouring townships by hundreds every hour. The ominous prospect of the night, which was likely to follow such a day, clenched the discussion; and just before dark a promise was given that the whole military force should be removed to the Castle, and three miles of salt water should be placed between the troops and the townspeople.

Danger to public peace was for the moment averted; but there still remained a matter which touched the public reputation. The soldiers who had pulled the triggers were to be tried for their lives; and Captain Preston, who had ordered them to fire without the sanction of a civil magistrate, would have been in peril even if local opinion had been neutral or quiescent. Moved by a happy inspiration, he applied to John Adams and Josiah Quincy to defend him. Quincy was a young man, eloquent for liberty, who had begun to play a great part when his career was cut short by death at the exact point when the war of words passed into the war of bullets.[1] His father, whom he loved and respected, wrote to dissuade him from accepting the brief, in terms of vehement remonstrance. The reply, it has been truly said, was in the vein which sometimes raises the early annals of the American Revolution above the ordinary level of history. "To inquire my duty," the son wrote, "and to do it, is my aim. I dare affirm that you and this whole people will one day rejoice that I became an advocate for the aforesaid criminals, charged with the murder of our fellow-citizens." Adams, some years the older, and with more to lose, had the watchful and jealous eyes of an exasperated people fixed on him with concentrated intensity. Long afterwards, at the age of eighty-two, he wrote in answer to the inquiry of a friend: "Nothing but want of interest and patronage prevented me from enlisting in the army. Could I have obtained a troop of horse or a company of foot, I should infallibly have been a soldier. It is a problem in my

---

[1] Adams heard the news of Josiah Quincy's death on the 30th April, 1775, eleven days after Lexington.

mind, to this day, whether I should have been a coward or a hero." As far as physical danger went he showed, on more than one occasion, that he could not resist the temptation of a fight even at times when his first duty towards his country was to keep himself alive and whole. And as regards moral courage, no finer proof was ever given than when he undertook the defence of Captain Preston, and secured a verdict of acquittal by the exercise of an enormous industry and the display of splendid ability.[1]

A trial so conducted, and with such a result, was a graceful and a loyal act on the part of the colony; and the mother-country should not have been behindhand to meet it in the same spirit. The moment was eminently favourable for an entire and permanent reconciliation. On the very day that the shots were fired at Boston, Lord North, as Chancellor of the Exchequer, rose in the House of Commons to move the repeal of the duties levied in America under Charles Townshend's Act, with the solitary exception of the duty upon tea. The maintenance of that impost had caused a division of opinion in the Cabinet, as acute and defined as ever took place without then and there breaking up a Ministry. The Duke of Grafton, who still was the titular Head of the Government, had only just arrived at the age when the modern world begins to look for political discretion in a public man. His fatal luck had made him Prime Minister at thirty, with the training of a London rake; and he was married most unhappily, though not worse than he at the time deserved. He had been a novice in statecraft under a royal master who had a policy, while he himself had none. For the crown of his misfortune, his

[1] John Adams was very poorly repaid either by his professional gains, or in the shape of gratitude from the Royalist party. "Nineteen guineas," he wrote, "were all the fees I ever received for a whole year of distressing anxiety, and for thirteen or fourteen days of the hardest labour in the trials that I ever went through. Add to all this the taunts, and scoffs, and bitter reproaches of the Whigs; and the giggling and tittering of the Tories, which was more provoking than all the rest."

faults and follies were denounced to his contemporaries, and blazoned forth for the wonder of posterity, by two past masters in the art of invective. Grafton's critic in Parliament was Edmund Burke, the greatest man of letters who has given all his best literary powers to politics. And in the public press he was assailed by Junius, as keen a politician as ever employed literature for the instrument of his righteous indignation.

The lesson was sharp. Grafton had taken it to heart, and was now intent on shaking off his old self, and doing what he could to redeem his unhappy past. His reputation in the eyes of history was already beyond mending. Burke and Junius had seen to that. But it was open for him to clear his conscience; and he now took the first step towards that end, the importance of which he was man enough to estimate at its true value. He earnestly recommended the Cabinet to sacrifice a trumpery tax which brought into the Treasury a net yearly income of three hundred pounds. The retention of it cost the country, directly, at least five thousand times as much money on account of the refusal on the part of the colonies to purchase British products; and indirectly, — in the shape of distrust and ill-will, scandals and disturbances, military preparations and national dangers, — an account was being run up on the wrong side of the ledger, the ultimate total of which no man could calculate. He was supported by every member of the Cabinet whose character stood high, or who had served with distinction in civil life, in the field, or on deep water. Lord Camden was with Grafton; and so were General Conway and Lord Granby. The famous admiral, Sir Edward Hawke, kept away by illness, would otherwise have voted on the same side. Against him were the Lords Rochford, and Gower, and Weymouth, and Hillsborough, — a list of personages who, (except that some of them were noted as hard-livers in a generation when such pre-eminence was not easily achieved,) have been preserved from oblivion by the mischief which on this unique occasion they had the opportunity of doing.

Shelburne had already been driven from the Ministry, or Grafton would have carried the day; but the casting vote now lay with the Chancellor of the Exchequer, and he gave his voice for retaining the tax out of deference to the King, and against his own view of his own duty.

George the Third had dictated North's line of action; but North had to explain it himself in Parliament. On the necessity of reconciling America he spoke cogently, and with a depth of feeling which impressed his audience. Then he approached the ungracious part of his task, and defended the continuation of the Tea-duty perfunctorily, and far from persuasively. Conway argued for the repeal of the entire Act, as did Barré and Sir William Meredith. All men of sense were united in thinking that it was the occasion for a complete and final settlement, and not for a compromise. George Grenville exposed, in trenchant terms, the folly and inconsequence of a course for which, though he was regarded on both sides of the ocean as the apostle of colonial taxation, he flatly refused to stultify himself by voting. At one moment it looked as if the House of Commons would take the matter into its own hands, and would inflict on the Ministers a defeat most acceptable to all members of the government who had any notion how to govern; but, when the division came, the Tea-duty was retained by a majority of sixty-two. The King's Friends had been duly warned, and primed, and mustered to do the King's work; and never did they more richly earn the unanimity of condemnation which has been awarded to them by historians whose verdict has weight and whose names are held in honour.

The concession was partial and grudging; but the good effect which, even so, it produced showed that a frank and unstinted renunciation of claims which were hateful to America, and worse than unprofitable to England, would have reunited the two countries in sincere and lasting friendship. New York, which had observed her engagement to exclude British goods more faithfully than any other colony, and whose trade had suffered in proportion, now withdrew from the agreement, and sent orders home for all sorts of merchandise, except tea. On New Year's day, 1771, Dr. Cooper wrote to Franklin from Boston: "You will hear, before this reaches you, of the acquittal of Captain Preston and the soldiers concerned in the action of the 5th of March. Instead of meeting with any unfair or harsh treatment, they had every advantage that could possibly be given them in a court of justice. The agreement of the merchants is broken. Administration has a fair opportunity of adopting the mildest and most prudent measures respecting the colonies, without the appearance of being threatened and drove." At home the Ministry would have been cordially supported in a policy of indulgence and consideration by the commercial men of the entire Kingdom; and with good reason; for the very best which possibly could be done for British commerce was to leave well alone. Jealousy of America was the sentiment of politicians who thought that they understood trade better than the traders themselves, and was not shared by men who knew business from the inside, and who lived by the pursuit of it. Burke was a man of business in every respect, except that he applied his knowledge and insight to the profit of the nation instead of his own. It had been finely said that he worked as hard and as continuously at commercial questions as if he was to receive a handsome percentage on the commerce of the whole Empire. He now replied, with crushing force, to the chief of the amateur economists whose happiness was poisoned by the fear of American competition.[1] "He tells us that their seas are covered with ships, and their rivers floating with commerce.

---

[1] *Observations on a late publication intitled " The Present State of the Nation,"* 1769. The motto to Burke's pamphlet, taken from Ennius, was happily chosen.

> "O Tite, si quid ego adjuvero, curamque levasso,
>   Quæ nunc te coquit, et versat sub pectore fixa,
>   Ecquid erit pretii?"

Titus was Mr. George Grenville.

This is true; but it is with *our* ships that the seas are covered, and their rivers float with British commerce. The American merchants are our factors ; all, in reality ; most, even in name." According to Burke, the Americans traded, navigated, and cultivated with English capital, working for the profit of Englishmen, and taking nothing for themselves, "except the *peculium*, without which even slaves will not labour."

In the production and fabrication of goods it was not a question of rivalry, but of a practical monopoly for British mills and foundries which nothing could break down ; unless the meddling of British public men should irritate the colonists into taking measures to supply their own wants by their own industry. The colonies, according to Franklin, possessed no manufactures of any consequence. "In Massachusetts a little coarse woollen only, made in families for their own wear. Glass and linen have been tried, and failed. Rhode Island, Connecticut, and New York much the same. Pennsylvania has tried a linen manufactory, but it is dropped, it being imported cheaper. There is a glass house in Lancaster County, but it makes only a little coarse ware for the country neighbours. Maryland is clothed all with English manufactures. Virginia the same, except that in their families they spin a little cotton of their own growing. South Carolina and Georgia none. All speak of the dearness of labour, that makes manufactures impracticable." That was the state of things before the non-importation agreement. After it had been in force a year, a single town in Massachusetts had made eighty thousand pairs of women's shoes, and was sending them to the Southern colonies, and even to the West Indies.[1] Franklin never wearied of preaching that advantageous circumstances will always secure and locate manufactures, so long as things are allowed to take and keep their natural course. "Sheffield," he exclaimed, "against all Europe these hundred years past!" And it would have been Sheffield, and Man-

[1] *Franklin Correspondence;* March 13, 1768, and August 3, 1769.

chester, and Burslem, and Birmingham against all
Europe, and against all America too, long enough for
every living manufacturer, who had his wits about him,
to make his fortune, if only George the Third and his
Ministers had known when and where it was wise to do
nothing. The satisfaction with which Englishmen, who
had a business connection with America, regarded a situation which, as far as their own interests were concerned, nothing could improve, was clearly indicated by
the dead silence into which, on this side of the Atlantic,
the American controversy had fallen. During the whole
of 1771, and the two following years, no debate on any
matter connected with that question is reported in the
Parliamentary History of England.[1] The Historical
Summary in the "Annual Register" for 1773 gives to
America less than a single column of printed matter.
In the Historical Summary for 1775 American affairs
fill a hundred and forty-two out of a hundred and fifty-
eight pages.

It was not otherwise beyond the water. The colonies
generally acquiesced in an arrangement under which
they enjoyed present tranquillity, even though it was
founded on the admission of a principle containing the
germ of future discord. New England was no exception.
"The people," wrote Mr. Johnson of Connecticut, a
trustworthy and cool-headed servant of the public,
"appear to be weary of their altercations with the
mother-country. A little discreet conduct on both sides
would perfectly re-establish that warm affection and respect towards Great Britain for which this country was
once so remarkable." Even with regard to Massachusetts the Governor, who made the worst of everything, reported in September 1771 that there was a
disposition to let the quarrel subside.

But one perennial source of discomfort and disorder
remained in full operation. The Revenue laws were in

---

[1] In the session of 1772, (to be quite accurate,) during the progress of
the Annual Mutiny Bill through the House of Commons a few words were
said about Courts-martial in America.

those days ill obeyed, and worse liked, all the Empire over; and it was extremely difficult to enforce them. Communication by land and sea was not on system; and traffic and travel were conducted along numerous and ever-varying channels by the agency of rough and ready men. The police was insufficient, and badly organised; and, above all, the State, when demanding its dues, had the mass of the community against it. From the peers and members of Parliament who walked ashore at Dover, with three embroidered suits of silk and satin worn one inside another, down to the poor wives in the Kent and Sussex villages who drank their smuggled Dutch tea laced with smuggled French brandy, the Custom-house had no partisans, and few contributors except under stern compulsion. Nobody had a good word for it except honest or timid traders whose market was spoiled by illicit dealing; or moralists who preached abstinence from smuggling as a counsel of perfection, the observance of which placed a man out of the reach of temptation to graver crimes. The position is clearly laid down by Franklin. "There are those in the world who would not wrong a neighbour, but make no scruple of cheating the King. The reverse, however, does not hold; for whoever scruples cheating the King will certainly not wrong his neighbour."

In the three kingdoms practice was everywhere lax; while in many districts the population lived by smuggling as generally, and almost as openly, as Lancashire lived by spinning. The Mr. Holroyd, who was afterwards Lord Sheffield, complained to Arthur Young in 1771 that want of hands cramped the agriculture of Sussex. "All the lively able young men are employed in smuggling. They can have a guinea a week as riders and carriers without any risk. Therefore it is not to be expected that they will labour for eight shillings." Lord Holland's country seat lay between Broadstairs and Margate, across the top of a pathway which led from the beach of a convenient inlet between two chalk headlands. A party of coastguardsmen inhabit the house, now that they are less wanted. According to George Selwyn, all Lord Holland's servants were professed smugglers; and Selwyn's own servant made a profit by taking contraband goods off their hands. Lord Carlisle sate on a special Commission as the representative of his country at a moment when she was going into war with half the civilized world because the Americans would not pay the Tea-duty. Not many years before his Lordship's town-mansion had been beset by Custom-house officers. It appeared that Lady Carlisle's chairman, like the rest of his fraternity, used to employ his leisure, when the London season was over and he was no longer on duty between the poles, in landing tea surreptitiously from the ships in the river.[1] Lord Dartmouth had a correspondent in Cornwall who from time to time gave him information about what was going on in a part of the world which lay a great deal nearer home than the shores of Maine and New Hampshire. "I am concerned in the wine trade," this gentleman wrote, "and between myself and partners we have a considerable capital in the trade; but on account of the smuggling on every side of us, and our rivals in trade doing such things as I trust our consciences ever will start back from with abhorrence, we hardly make common interest of our money." Lisbon wine, he goes on to say, which no honest merchant could import at less than four shillings a gallon, was sold throughout the county for half a crown. Rum, which had paid duty, did not reimburse the importer at less than nine shillings; but everybody who wanted to drink it was able to buy it at five. The tobacconists would purchase, with circumstances of great ostentation, one pound of duty-paid tobacco, and under cover of that transaction would sell twenty pounds which had been smuggled over from Guernsey.

The officers of the Revenue were overmatched by sea and land. Sixty horses, each carrying a hundredweight and a half of tea, had been seen traversing Cornwall

---

[1] *Historical Manuscripts Commission;* Fifteenth Report, Appendix, Part VI.; pp. 273 and 297 of the *Carlisle Papers.*

in bright moonlight to supply the wants of Devonshire. When conveying their goods across country the contraband traders did the law so much compliment as to confine their operations to the night; but any hour of the day was a business hour for the large Irish wherries, (as they then were called,) which infested the Cornish coast. A Revenue cutter stationed to the south of Tintagel Head was chased by one of these smugglers. The King's vessel took refuge in Padstow harbour, and her adversary hung out a flag, and fired a salvo of seven guns in honour of the victory. That was the condition of an English county which had forty-four representatives in Parliament to look after its interests and its proprieties. It was almost pharisaical for Ministers, with such a state of things at their own doors, to maintain that public morality demanded of them to set fleets and armies in motion because the Revenue was defrauded, and its officers flouted, in half-settled regions on the outskirts of the Empire.[1]

It cannot of course be denied that in America, and most of all in New England, enmity to the claims of the Revenue was active and universal. The origin of that enmity lay far back in history. It has been observed by a writer, who knew his subject well, that the part which the merchants and shipowners of the Northern colonies played in the contest with the home Government has been understated both as regards the importance of their action, and the breadth and justice of the motives by which it was inspired.[2] They had been born into the inheritance of a cruel wrong, which was more deeply felt as the forces that govern trade came to be better understood, and in some cases were for the first time discovered. Cromwell, with an insight beyond his

[1] William Rawlins to the Earl of Dartmouth, August 26, 1765, from St. Columb. Again, from the same to the same, April 24, 1775, from Padstow. *Historical Manuscripts Commission;* Fifteenth Report, Appendix, Part I.

[2] *Loyalists of the American Revolution,* by Lorenzo Sabine, vol. i., pp. 3 to 14.

age, had refused to fetter and discourage the infant commerce of America ; and under the Commonwealth that commerce grew fast towards prosperous maturity. But a Stuart was no sooner on the throne than the British Parliament entered on a course of selfish legislation which killed the direct maritime trade between our dependencies and foreign ports, and, (to borrow the words of an eminent historian,) deliberately crushed every form of colonial manufacture which could possibly compete with the manufactures of England.[1]

The traditional resentment against such injustice, kept alive by the continuing and ever-increasing material injury which it inflicted, arrayed men of all classes, creeds, and parties in opposition to the interests of the Exchequer, and to the officers by whom those interests were guarded. A gentleman of New York says, in a letter written shortly after the American Revolution broke out : " I fix all the blame of these proceedings on the Presbyterians. You would ask whether no Church of England people were among them. Yes, there were; to their eternal shame be it spoken. But in general they were interested either as smugglers of tea, or as being overburdened with dry goods they knew not how to pay for." [2] Thomas Hancock, — the uncle of John Hancock, to whom, oblivious of political divergences, he left most of his property, — was an ardent royalist and a declared Tory. He was reputed to be worth that comfortable amount of money which his contemporaries, in the phrase used by Pope and Arbuthnot, still called a plum. Hancock had made the better part of his fortune by importing contraband tea from Holland, and supplying it to the mess-tables of the army and navy. Considering that it was to people holding his political opinions that

---

[1] Mr. Lecky, in the twelfth chapter of his History, treats of the commercial relations between England and the American colonies. Within the compass of four pages he gives a description of their character and consequences which is clear, full, and unanswerable.

[2] *American Archives, prepared and published under authority of an Act of Congress.* The letter is dated May 31, 1774.

the Crown lawyers would resort if they had occasion to pack a jury, it is not difficult to compute their chances of securing a conviction on a charge of evading the Revenue. Whenever a gauger or tide-waiter was found tripping, the Court-house overflowed in every quarter with triumphant emotion. About the period of Preston's trial, John Adams argued a suit for a penalty against a Custom-house officer for taking greater fees than those allowed by law : and, in his own estimation, he argued it very indifferently. He won his case; and in the enthusiasm of the moment, somewhat to his amusement and yet more to his disgust, he was overwhelmed with assurances that he had outdone all his own previous efforts, and would thenceforward rank as an equal of the greatest orator that ever spoke in Rome or Athens.

For ten years past, ever since George Grenville's influence began to be felt in the distant parts of the Empire, the claims of the Revenue had been enforced with unwonted rigour, which in the summer of 1771 assumed an aggressive and exasperating character. Sandwich, who had succeeded Hawke at the Admiralty, had appointed an officer with his own surname, and, (as it is superfluous to state,) of his own party, to command the powerful squadron now stationed in American waters. Admiral Montagu, who came fresh from hearing the inner mind of the Bedfords as expressed in the confidence of the punch-bowl, was always ready to make known his opinion of New England and its inhabitants in epithets which, on a well-ordered man-of-war, were seldom heard abaft the mast. In comparison with him, (so it was said,) an American freeholder, living in a log-house twenty feet square, was a well-bred and polite man. To make matters worse, the Admiral's lady was as much too fine as the Admiral himself was coarse. "She is very full," wrote Adams, "of her remarks at the assembly and the concert. 'Can this lady afford the jewels and dresses she wears?' 'Oh, that my son should come to dance with a mantua-maker!'" Between them they encouraged, in those officers whom their example swayed, a tone of arrogance and incivility foreign indeed to a noble service.[1]

The Navy, like every profession, has its bad bargains; and the lieutenant in command of the schooner Gaspee, which was watching the coast of Rhode Island, set himself to the task of translating the language used on the quarter-deck of the flagship into overt acts. He stopped and searched vessels without adequate pretext, seized goods illegally, and fired at the market boats as they entered Newport harbour. He treated the farmers on the islands much as the Saracens in the Middle Ages treated the coast population of Italy, cutting down their trees for fuel, and taking their sheep when his crew ran short of fresh meat. The injured parties made their voices heard; and the case was laid before the Admiral, who approved the conduct of his subordinate officer, and announced that, as sure as any people from Newport attempted to rescue a vessel, he would hang them as pirates. It was a foolish answer as addressed to men who were not long-suffering, nor particular as to their methods of righting a grievance; and they resolved that, if it came to a hanging matter, it should be for a sheep, and not for a lamb. At the first convenient opportunity they boarded the royal schooner, set the crew on shore, and burned the vessel to the water's edge. A terrible commotion followed. Thurlow, in his capacity as Attorney-General, denounced the crime as

---

[1] The Admiral's appearance was milder than his language. Philip Freneau, in a satirical Litany, prayed to be delivered

> " From groups at St. James's, who slight our petitions,
> And fools that are waiting for further submissions;
> From a nation whose manners are rough and abrupt;
> From scoundrels and rascals whom gold can corrupt;
> From pirates sent out by command of the King
> To murder and plunder, but never to swing;
> From hot-headed Montagu, mighty to swear,
> The little fat man with his pretty white hair."

It was believed in America that Sandwich and the Admiral were brothers; and the story, in that shape, has got into history.

of a deeper dye than piracy, and reported that the whole business was of five times the magnitude of the Stamp Act. By a Royal order in Council the authorities of Rhode Island were commanded to deliver the culprits into the hands of the Admiral, with a view of their being tried in London. But before the crew of a Providence fishing-boat could be arraigned at the Old Bailey, and hanged in chains in the Essex marshes, they had first to be got out of Narragansett Bay; and Stephen Hopkins, the old Chief Justice of Rhode Island, refused to lend his sanction to their arrest in face of the destiny which awaited them. Admiral Montagu himself, right for once, acknowledged that British Acts of Parliament, — at any rate such Acts as the revived statute of Henry the Eighth, — would never go down in America unless forced by the point of the sword. And the estimable and amiable Dartmouth, who now was Secretary of the Colonies, contrived to hush up a difficulty which, as he was told by a wise and friendly correspondent, if it had been pressed to an extreme issue, "would have set the continent into a fresh flame."[1]

It was too much to expect that Sandwich and Thurlow would sit quiet under their defeat. There was no use in having the law, good or bad, on their side if those who interpreted and administered it in America were independent of their influence and dictation. The members of that Cabinet were never slow to make up a prescription for anything which they regarded as a disease in the body politic; and, as usual, they tried it first on Massachusetts. It was arranged that her judges should henceforward have their salaries paid by the Crown, and not by the Colony. Samuel Adams discerned the threatening nature of the proposal itself, and foresaw the grave perils involved in the principle which lay beneath it. At his instigation the patriots of Boston

[1] *Dartmouth Correspondence;* August 29, 1772, and June 16, 1773. *Historical Manuscripts Commission;* Fourteenth Report, Appendix, Part X.

invited all the townships of the province to establish Committees of Correspondence for the purpose of guarding their chartered rights, and adjured every legislative body throughout America to aid them in repelling an invasion which, if it succeeded in their own case, undoubtedly would be directed in turn against all their neighbours. Massachusetts rose to the call; and the Assembly of Virginia, with the political instinct which seldom misled it, took prompt and courageous action; but in other quarters the response was neither hearty nor universal. The spirit which had defeated the Stamp Act could not be aroused at short notice and on a partial issue; and friends and adversaries alike knew that the threatened colony, if things came to the worst, must be prepared to rely mainly upon herself.

There was, however, good reason to doubt whether the mother-country was in the temper to fight so paltry a matter to such a bitter end. England, outside Parliament and within it, was tired of bullying and coercing men who after all were Englishmen, whose case rested on honoured English precedents, and was asserted and maintained by honest English methods. Never was a community, (as the men of Massachusetts pathetically complained,) so long and so pitilessly assailed with malicious abuse as theirs had been during the past two years by enemies in London and within their own borders. The reaction now set in; and a large and increasing section of the English nation watched with respect, and often with sympathy, a resistance conducted on strict constitutional lines to that which, even as seen from England, looked very like a deliberate system of small-minded and vexatious tyranny. In July 1773, Franklin addressed a letter from London to Thomas Cushing, then Speaker of the Massachusetts Assembly. "With regard," he said, "to the sentiments of people in general here concerning America, I must say that we have among them many friends and well-wishers. The Dissenters are all for us, and many of the merchants and manufacturers. There seems to

be, even among the country gentlemen, a growing sense
of our importance, a disapprobation of the harsh measures with which we have been treated, and a wish that
some means might be found of perfect reconciliation."

Under such circumstances it would have seemed impossible that a Ministry could rise to such a height of
perverted ingenuity as to deliver Massachusetts from
her isolation ; to unite all the colonies in sudden, hot,
and implacable disaffection towards the Crown ; and to
drive them into courses which would shock the pride
and alienate the good-will of England.   But even that
feat proved to be within the resources of statesmanship.
Foremost among the questions of the day at Westminster was the condition of the East India Company, which
now stood on the verge of bankruptcy.   The home Government came forward handsomely with a large loan on
easy terms, and a pledge not to insist on an annual tribute of four hundred thousand pounds which India had
somehow contrived to pay, in spite of her deficits, into the
British exchequer.   But, over and above these palliatives,
the Cabinet had at its disposal the means of relieving the
famous Corporation from all its embarrassments.   There
lay stored in the warehouses tea and other Indian goods
to the value of four millions, which had been in course
of accumulation ever since the Company, not by its own
fault, had lost a most promising customer.   The American colonies, making a protest against their fiscal wrongs
in a form which had its attractions for a thrifty people,
had supplied themselves with smuggled tea from France,
Denmark, Sweden, and especially from Holland ; and
those foreign merchants who had been tempted into the
trade soon learned to accompany their consignments of
tea with other sorts of Oriental produce.   The Custom-
house officers reckoned that Indian goods, which paid
nothing to the Treasury and brought no profit to the
Company, found their way into America to the amount
of half a million in money every twelvemonth.

The opportunity was golden, and without alloy.   If
Ministers could bring themselves to adopt the sugges-

tion made by the East Indian Directors, and advise a willing House of Commons to repeal the Tea-duty, they would, by one and the same straightforward and easy operation, choke up the underground channels along which commerce had begun to flow, pacify the colonies, and save the East India Company. The demand of the American market for tea was already enormous. The most portable and easily prepared of beverages, it was then used in the backwoods of the West as lavishly as now in the Australian bush. In more settled districts the quantity absorbed on all occasions of ceremony is incredible to a generation which has ceased to rejoice and to mourn in large companies, and at great cost. The legislative assembly of more than one colony had passed sumptuary laws to keep the friends of the deceased from drinking his widow and orphans out of house and home; and whatever the gentlemen, who drove and rode in to a funeral from thirty miles round, were in the habit of drinking, the ladies drank tea. The very Indians, in default of something stronger, took it twice a day;[1] and however much attached they might be to their Great Father beyond the water, it must not be supposed that they made special arrangements in order to ensure that he had been paid his dues on the article which they consumed. If only the Chancellor of the Exchequer, with a few heartfelt sentences of frank retractation and cordial welcome, had thrown completely open the door of the Custom-house which already was ajar, all would have been well, then and thereafter. Before Parliament was many sessions older, America, (after a less questionable fashion than the expression, when used in an English budget speech, usually implies,) would have drunk the East India Company out of all its difficulties.

A course which went direct to the right point was not of a nature to find favour with George the Third and his Ministers. They adopted by preference a plan under which the East India Company was allowed a

---

[1] *Dartmouth Correspondence;* January 19, 1773.

drawback of the whole Tea-duty then payable in England, while the Exchequer continued to claim the threepence on the pound which was paid, (or, to speak more
exactly, left unpaid,) in America.   Their object was
such as every one who ran a boatload of smuggled
goods between Penobscot Bay, and the mouth of the
Savannah River, could read.   This wise scheme, (so
Franklin put it,) was to take off as much duty in England as would make the Company's tea cheaper in
America than any which foreigners could supply; and
at the same time to maintain the duty in America, and
thus keep alive the right of Parliament to tax the colonies.   "They have no idea," he wrote, "that any people
can act from any other principle but that of interest;
and they believe that threepence in a pound of tea, of
which one does not perhaps drink ten pounds in a
year, is sufficient to overcome all the patriotism of an
American."

They were not long in finding out their mistake.   The
King, (so North stated,) meant to try the question with
America;   and arrangements were accordingly made
which, whatever else may be said of them, undoubtedly
accomplished that end.   In the autumn of 1773 ships
laden with tea sailed for the four principal ports on the
Atlantic seaboard; and agents or consignees of the
East India Company were appointed by letter to attend
their arrival in each of the four towns.   The captain of
the vessel despatched to Philadelphia found such a reception awaiting him that he sailed straight back to
England.   Boston, under circumstances which have
been too frequently described to admit of their ever
again being related in detail, gratified the curiosity of
an energetic patriot who expressed a wish to see whether
tea could be made with salt water.   At Charleston the
cargo was deposited in a damp cellar, where it was
spoiled as effectually as if it had been floating on the
tide up and down the channel between James Island
and Sullivan's Island; and, when New York learned
that the tea-ships allotted to it had been driven by a gale

off the coast, men scanned the horizon, like the garrison of Londonderry watching for the English fleet in Lough Foyle, in their fear lest fate should rob them of their opportunity of proving themselves not inferior in mettle to the Bostonians. The great cities, — to which all the colonies looked as laboratories of public opinion, and theatres of political action, — had now deliberately committed themselves to a policy of illegal violence which could not fail to wound the self-respect of the English people, and make Parliament, for many a long and sad year to come, an obedient instrument in the hands of men who were resolved, at all hazards, to chastise and humble America.

CHAPTER IV

THE news from Boston came upon the mother-country
in the provoking shape of a disagreeable surprise. For
the ordinary English citizen it was news indeed. He
had heard how at Philadelphia, on the 4th of June, 1766,
— the first King's birthday which followed the repeal of
the Stamp Act, — the healths of George the Third and
Doctor Franklin had been drunk in public at the same
table; and from that moment he had reposed in a serene
conviction that the American difficulty, for his own life-
time at all events, was over and done with. He took it
for granted that the mob in New England was in the
habit of hunting Custom-house officers, just as a Lon-
doner, in the days before railroads, lived in the belief
that the mob in the manufacturing districts of Lancashire was always breaking frames. He was aware
that the troops had shot some townspeople in the streets
of Boston; but he was equally aware that, not many
months before, the Footguards had shot some Wilkites
in the Borough of Southwark; and the one occurrence
had to his mind no deeper and more permanent signifi-
cance than the other. The last serious fact connected
with America, which had come to his knowledge, was
that Parliament had gone a great deal more than half
way to meet the wishes of the colonies, had removed all
but a mere fraction of the unpopular duties, and had
made an arrangement with the East India Company by
which the colonists would thenceforward drink tea much
cheaper than he could drink it himself. And now, as
a recognition of her patience and self-control, and as a

reply to her friendly advances, England was slapped in
her smiling face with a zest and vigour which sent a
thrill of exultation through all, in any quarter of the
world, who envied her and wished her ill. It was true
that close and dispassionate investigation would show
that, for the treatment which she had received, she had
herself, or rather her chosen governors, to thank. But
the first effect of an insult is not to set Englishmen com-
puting and weighing what they have done to deserve it;
and the national indignation, in heat and unanimity,
hardly fell short of that which was in our own time
aroused throughout the Northern States of America by
the bombardment of Fort Sumter.

The country was in a temper for any folly which its
rulers would allow it to commit; and unfortunately the
crisis had come just when the system of Personal Government had reached the culminating point of success
towards which the King had long been working. Every
particle of independence, and of wisdom which dared to
assert itself, had at last been effectually eliminated from
the Cabinet. Administrative experience was to be found
there, and some forethought and circumspection, and
plenty of timidity; but those Ministers who were afraid
of strong courses stood in much greater terror of their
strong monarch. The men who, in March 1770, had
pronounced themselves against the retention of the Tea-
duty were no longer in a position to warn or to advise
him. The Duke of Grafton, after the humiliating defeat which on that occasion he suffered, lost no time in
surrendering to Lord North the first place in the Government. He consented indeed, at the instance of the
King, to keep the Privy Seal; but he consulted his own
dignity by refusing to sit as a subordinate in a Cabinet
which, while he was still Prime Minister, had overruled
him in the case of a decision second in importance to
none which any Cabinet was ever called on to take.

Conway and Sir Edward Hawke had retired from
office; and Granby had met, in mournful fashion, death
which he had gaily confronted on many a disputed field.

Though four generations have come and gone, an English reader learns with something of a personal shock
that there was a dark side to that brilliant career. Posterity remembers him as the Master-General of the
Ordnance, and Commander-in-Chief of the army, whom
no officer envied; the statesman whom every ally, and
every opponent, loved; the leader of horse who was
named with Ziethen and Seidlitz in all the cavalry barracks of Europe; the idol of the people in days when
the people seldom troubled themselves to distinguish between one politician and another. But, with all this,
Granby behind the scenes was an erring, an overburdened, and at last a most unhappy man. He was a
jovial companion to high and humble; a profuse and
often unwise benefactor; a soldier of the camp in
foreign lands, with little time, and less inclination, to
look closely into his private affairs at home; and, above
all, an elderly heir-apparent to an immense estate; —
and it cannot be denied that he had the faults of his
qualities and of his position. Like some greater men,
and with more excuse, at fifty years of age he had a
broken constitution, and he was deep in debt. None
the less, at the bidding of duty, he resisted the entrea-
ties of George the Third, who was sincerely desirous not
to lose him from the Ministry. Resigning his employments and emoluments, he retired into pecuniary em-
barrassment unrelieved by occupation and uncheered by
health. A year afterwards he died at Scarborough,
where he had gone in the hope of a cure, only to find
himself involved in the worry and tumult of a contested
Yorkshire election. "You are no stranger," a friend of
the family writes, "to the spirit of procrastination. The
noblest mind that ever existed, the amiable man whom
we lament, was not free from it. I have lived to see
the first heir, of a subject, in the Kingdom, lead a miserable shifting life, attended by a levee of duns, and at
last die broken-hearted, — for so he really was, — rather
than say, 'I will arise and go to my father.' It is impossible to describe the distress of the whole country.

Every place you passed through in tears, and the Castle was the head-quarters of misery and dejection. The Duke rose up to meet me with an appearance of cheerfulness, but soon relapsed into a sullen melancholy, and for three weeks he appeared to me petrified." [1]

The departure of Conway, Hawke, and Granby, three men of the sword who feared nothing except an unrighteous quarrel, left the honour of England in the keeping of the Bedfords. For them it must be said that, when urging their views in council, they had all the advantage which proceeds from sincerity of conviction. Their ideas of ministerial discretion permitted them, whether sober, drunk, or half-seas over, to rail at the colonists as rebels and traitors before any company in London ; and it may well be believed that they did not pick their words within the walls of that chamber where they had a right to speak their entire mind in as plain terms as their colleagues would endure. What is known about the tractability of those colleagues is among the miracles of history ; though the full extent of it can only be conjectured by a comparison of the partial revelations which have seen the light of day. In 1779 Lord North confessed to the King that, for at least three years, he had held in his heart an opinion that the system which the Government had pursued would end in the ruin of his Majesty and the country. Yet during three more years he continued to pursue that system, and would never have desisted from it if Washington had not been too strong for him abroad, and Charles Fox and his friends too many for him at home. Lord Gower, the President

---

[1] *Historical Manuscripts Commission.* Twelfth Report, Appendix, Part V. The letter is in sad contrast with another in the same volume written nine years before to Granby, then a recalcitrant invalid, by Lord Ligonier, — one of the few men who had a right to criticise or to compliment him. " I am to thank you for the remedy you have discovered for a fever. It has ever been unknown till your time ; but now it is manifest that, if a man is ordered to his bed with this disorder, he has nothing more to do than to jump out of it, get upon his horse, and fight away. But however prevailing that remedy has been on a late occasion, I do not recommend it for the future." Granby had just come victorious out of the last and fiercest of his German battles.

of the Council, supported in public North's policy, although he loved it no better than did North himself; but five years so spent were enough for him, and at the end of that period he appeased his conscience by a resignation which, for a member of that Ministry, may be called prompt, and even premature. Strangest of all was the letter in which Lord Barrington, before ever a cannon had been fired or a sabre stained, had laid down in black and white his inward judgement on what had been the origin of the dispute, and on what should be the conduct of the war. He argued that it was madness on the part of any Ministry to impose a tax which no Ministry had the strength to levy; that the attempt to fight the colonists on land could only result in disaster and disgrace; that a judicious employment of our naval force was the least unpromising method of combating the rebellion; and that, so far from reinforcing the army in Massachusetts, the garrison should at once be withdrawn from Boston, leaving that undutiful city to its own devices. Those were his views, deliberately entertained and never abandoned; and nevertheless, as Secretary at War, he despatched to America every soldier who fought between the day of Bunker's Hill and the day of Monmouth Court House.

The theory of ministerial responsibility which then prevailed in high official circles was carefully laid down by Lord Barrington's brother, the Bishop of Durham, in a passage of biography agreeably redolent of fraternal pride. "In conjunction," the Bishop wrote, "with the other members of Administration, Lord Barrington bore the censures which were now very generally directed against the supporters of the American War: yet no person less deserved those censures. There is the clearest and most decisive evidence that Lord Barrington disapproved the adopted mode of coercion, and that he submitted, both to the King and his Ministers, his sentiments on the subject in the most unequivocal terms. His opinion was that, though it became his duty to remonstrate with his colleagues in office, it was neither honourable nor proper for him to appeal to the uninformed judgements of others, and to play a game of popularity at the expense of the public."

The colleague to whom Lord Barrington more particularly addressed his remonstrances was Lord Dartmouth, the Secretary of State in charge of America. His selection for that post had been an act of true wisdom. With an empire such as ours, a judicious ruler, who has an appointment to make, takes due account of local tastes and preferences. He will flatter one colony by sending to it as Governor a public man who is supposed to have studied agriculture, and will please another by appointing a nobleman who undoubtedly understands horses. Bringing the same knowledge of mankind into higher regions, George the Third and Lord North paid America a marked and acceptable compliment when they committed the care of her interests to the most distinguished member of a school of thought and practice which was already beginning to be called Evangelical.

The fame of Lord Dartmouth had been carried far and wide throughout the English-speaking world by that association of brave and sincere men who were in hard conflict with the vices of the age, and in earnest protest against the lukewarmness of its religious faith. He was a Churchman; and the claims of the Establishment were in small favour with the colonists. But he belonged to that section of Churchmen who looked outside, as well as within, their own borders for allies to aid them in their lifelong warfare against ignorance and indifference, misery, cruelty, and sin. Lord Halifax, accounted a rake and spendthrift even by that lax generation, had gone as far as he dared, and much farther than was safe, into a scheme for planting bishops in America. But Dartmouth, the light of whose goodness would have shone in the brightest days of Christianity, recognised only one spiritual banner beneath which men should fight, and cared little or nothing to what regiment belonged the arm that sustained it, if only it

was carried worthily. He had long ago applied himself
to the sage and praiseworthy task of turning to account
the spirit of enthusiasm which had grown strong within
the Church itself, under the fostering care of John
Wesley. The great preacher in his letters to the Secretary of State, occasionally pushed somewhat far
a friend's privilege of criticism and remonstrance; but
Dartmouth had no notion of throwing away the advantage of such an intimacy on account of a few frank
and rough words. "Have you a person," asked
Wesley, "in all England who speaks to your lordship
so plain and downright as I do; who considers not the
peer, but the man; who rarely commends, but often
blames, and perhaps would do it oftener if you desired
it?"   More than once, as will be seen in the course of
this narrative, Wesley made good his promise at a time
when honest advice was of priceless value.

Dartmouth assisted Lady Huntingdon with his means
and influence, and the still more needed contribution of
his sound sense and knowledge of the world, in her
endeavours to provide English pulpits with a supply of
preachers who believed what they said, and were trained
in the art of saying it. He found a wiser, and not less
open-handed, auxiliary than her Ladyship in John Thornton, the true founder of the Evangelicalism which was
prevalent and prominent in the Established Church
during the period when that Church took a forward part
in courageous and unpopular movements for the general
benefit of mankind. The two friends quietly and steadily
applied themselves to mend the income of poor livings
held by good men, to purchase advowsons, and to confer
them upon clergymen who expounded the Gospel as
they themselves had learned it. While pursuing this
work they had the rare privilege of establishing a permanent claim on the gratitude of very many who have
little sympathy with their specific creed. Lord Dartmouth made interest in high episcopal quarters to obtain
the ordination of John Newton, who was too much in
earnest about religion to be readily entrusted with a

commission to teach it, except as a matter of favour to a great man. The statesman placed the divine in the curacy of Olney ; and Mr. Thornton added an allowance of two hundred pounds a year. " Be hospitable," he wrote to Newton, "and keep an open house for such as are worthy of entertainment. Help the poor and needy." That roof soon sheltered a guest than whom few had been worthier of entertainment since Abraham's tent was pitched on the plains of Mamre, and none had been more in need of it since this world began. For William Cowper spent the period of gloom and depression which fell upon him in middle life under Newton's care, and as a member of his family. It was at Dartmouth's cost that the house had been fitted and furnished, and decorated in a manner to suit the taste of the inmates. And to Dartmouth Newton made periodical reports of his friend's condition in phraseology now long out of date, but alive with sentiments of tenderness and delicacy which were to the honour of him who wrote, and of him who read.[1]

Cowper, and Newton, and Lady Huntingdon, and the Wesleys were Church people, or laboured stoutly to be accounted so. But Dartmouth's breadth of charity and ardour of conviction were bounded by no ecclesiastical barriers ; and in this respect he was in full sympathy with his friend John Thornton, who seldom enjoyed an excursion to the mountains or the sea-coast unless he was accompanied by some Nonconformist minister who wanted, but could not afford, a holiday. Already, long before official position had made it worth his while to court popularity in the colonies, the peer had taken most effective interest in a school established on the

---

[1] As soon as a favourable change arrived in Cowper's health, Dartmouth was the first to be informed by John Newton that the Lord was " on his way to turn mourning into joy." When Cowper came once more to himself, he found his shelves bare of the books, which had been sold during the period of his sickness and poverty. Dartmouth's library then supplied him with the volumes of travels over the study of which his mind regained its strength, and acquired a cheerfulness that endured long enough to depict itself for our delight in indelible colours before it once again was overclouded.

New Hampshire frontier for the conversion and civilisation of the Indians: a school which, as time went on,
and his benefactions multiplied, received the name of
Dartmouth College. In 1771 he invited the co-operation of the Bishop of London, and received a reply of a
nature which goes further to illustrate the inward
causes of the American troubles than many ponderous
volumes of minutes and reports. The Bishop, (so the
answer ran,) had received no intimation that the Head
of the College was to belong to the Church of England,
or that the prayers to be used were those of the Liturgy.
The other members of the Board, his Lordship further
remarked, appeared to be Dissenters, and he therefore
could not see how a bishop could be of use among them,
and accordingly begged to decline the honour which
the trustees had done him. The Bishop altogether ignored the circumstance that members of the Church of
England were the Dissenters in Massachusetts; and
that, at the very outside, they numbered only one-fif-
teenth of the population. Dartmouth, however, was well
aware that a religious undertaking in New England, if
Congregationalists and Presbyterians were kept out of it,
could not be expected to overflow with vitality; and, in
face of the Bishop of London's disapproval, he continued
to be President of the Board.

The colonists saw that Dartmouth understood their
ways, and was at one with them on matters which he
regarded as infinitely higher and more important than
any political differences. Whether he was in or out of
office, — when he was advocating their cause, and when,
in obedience to worse and stronger men than himself,
he was doing his utmost to ruin it, — they persisted in
looking on him as a friend at heart. Virginia and New
York addressed to him their felicitations on the repeal
of the Stamp Act, accompanied, among other less
romantic presents, by a young eaglet; at whose full-
grown claws and beak, in coming years, he must have
looked with mingled feelings when he paid a visit to his
aviary. On the occasion of the Boston massacre of

March 1770 the popular leaders transmitted to Dartmouth a full account of their proceedings, as to an honest man who would take care that their statement of the case should be known at Court. When, in August, 1772, he was appointed Secretary of the Colonies, the news was hailed with satisfaction throughout America by people of all parties; and as months rolled on, and the plot thickened, every post brought him more valuable testimonies of affection and confidence in the shape of letters of counsel from the most unlikely quarters. Good men, even from among the ranks of those whom he never without a twinge could call rebels, dared to write him their true thoughts, and cared to do it. When he allowed himself to become the instrument of an hostility which was foreign to his nature, — and, it is to be feared, not consonant with his opinions, — they diminished something from their respect, but he always retained their love. Two generations afterwards, in the July of 1829, the citizens of New York asked leave to detain his portrait, then on its way from England to the College which bore his name. The request was granted; and they placed the picture in their Hall of Justice, next those of Washington and Franklin, on the day of the Celebration of Independence. If Dartmouth could have ruled the colonies according to the dictates of his own judgement and his own conscience, that Independence would have been postponed till he had ceased to be Secretary of State; and, whenever it arrived, it would have excited very different feelings and recollections from those with which it was destined to be associated.

Among men of our race, in every quarter of the globe, and under every form of government, as soon as a public danger is clearly recognised, some one will be found to face it. The undisguised tyranny of the Stuarts in the seventeenth century had worked its own cure by the sturdy opposition which it evoked from all classes, and almost every creed. By the time George the Third had

been on the throne ten years, there were no two opinions
among politicians about the righteousness and wisdom
of the Revolution of 1688.   To hear them talk, they
were all Whigs together; but meanwhile, under their
eyes, and with their concurrence, a despotism of a subtle
and insidious texture was being swiftly and deftly inter-
woven into the entire fabric of the Constitution.   The
strong will, the imperious character, and the patient,
unresting industry of the King, working through subservient Ministers upon a corrupt Parliament, had made
him master of the State as effectively, and far more securely, than if his authority had rested on the support
of an army of foreign mercenaries.   The purpose to
which he was capable of putting his all but unlimited
authority was soon to be written in blood and fire over
the face of the globe; but already there was a man who,
from his reading of history, his knowledge of human
nature, and his experience of what politics had become
since the new policy began to be inaugurated, foresaw
the consequences which could not fail to result from the
establishment of absolute power.

That man was Edmund Burke, who for some time
past had been looking about him in search of forces able
to make good a resistance which he himself, at any personal hazard whatever, was resolved to offer.   He hoped
little from the people.   Even if the public at large had
been awake to what was going on, and had cared to stop
it, all effort in that direction would have been sorely
hampered by the trammels of the system under which
Parliament was then chosen.   Free electoral bodies existed in most of the counties of England, and in some
of her great cities; but those bodies could do little, however strongly they might desire to make their influence
felt.   They were overweighted and overborne by the
three hundred and sixty members for boroughs in the
hands of private patrons or of the Treasury itself, and
by Scotland, which was one close constituency returning
fifty so-called representatives.   In truth, however, the
opinion of the country was asleep; and those who were

most anxious to arouse it, in despondent moments, were inclined to pronounce it dead. " As to the good people of England," said Burke, " they seem to partake every day, more and more, of the character of that administration which they have been induced to tolerate. I am satisfied that, within a few years, there has been a great change in the national character. We seem no longer that eager, inquisitive, jealous, fiery people which we have been formerly, and which we have been a very short time ago. No man commends the measures which have been pursued, or expects any good from those which are in preparation; but it is a cold, languid opinion, like what men discover in affairs that do not concern them. It excites to no passion. It prompts to no action."[1]

Despairing of the mass, Burke turned to individuals; and he found his recruits for the party of independence and purity among the most exalted and wealthy of the land. He argued, (and there was reason for it,) that a sense of public duty must be founded on a consciousness of public responsibility. Thousands of honest votes, cast in the polling booths of Yorkshire and Somersetshire, went for no more than the voice of a constituency the whole of which could sit round one table within reach of the same haunch of venison. The average elector, when once that knowledge had been brought home to him, did not care to inform himself minutely about affairs of State, a share in the control of which was so capriciously and unequally distributed. But it was another matter with those who were born to govern. The peer with an hereditary seat in that House which then afforded almost as good a platform for an orator as the other, and a still more advantageous starting-point for an administrator; the young man of fortune, who had only to choose the borough for his money, as his brother in orders would choose a living, or his brother in the army a regiment; the great landowner, whom the freeholders trusted and liked as a country neighbour,

[1] Letter to Lord Rockingham; August 23, 1775.

without very close inquiry into the side which he took in the squabbles and intrigues among which he had to shape his course at Westminster ; — these were men who had leisure for public affairs, who could influence their direction and their issue, and who had the deepest interest in understanding them.   The nature and extent of that interest Burke explained in a fine lesson, couched under the form of flattery, and addressed to a disciple who was soon to improve upon the teaching of his master.   "Persons in your station of life," he wrote to the Duke of Richmond, "ought to have long views. You, if you are what you ought to be, are in my eyes the great oaks that shade a country and perpetuate your benefits from generation to generation.   The immediate power of a Duke of Richmond, or a Marquis of Rockingham, is not so much of moment; but if their conduct and example hand down their principles to their successors, then their houses become the public repositories and offices of record for the Constitution : not like the Tower, or Rolls Chapel, where it is searched for, and sometimes in vain, in rotten parchments under dripping and perishing walls; but in full vigour, and acting with vital energy and power, in the character of the leading men and natural interests of the country."   Such, and so very far from democratic, was the origin of the party which from that time onward fought the battle of liberal principles in Parliament.

When tidings of popular violence, most exasperating to the English mind, arrived from America, a grave responsibility devolved upon statesmen who were out of office ; for, — with all who were prudent in the Ministry cowed and silent, and its reckless members dominant and noisy, — the nation, at this supreme moment, was likely to be ill piloted.   More often than appears on the face of history, a Cabinet has been saved from the full consequences of its own policy by an Opposition which did not shrink from the labour, and the odium, of preventing the men in power from effecting all the mischief upon which their minds were set; but such a task, the most invidious which can fall within the sphere of public duty, requires something more for its successful performance than patriotic impulses and good intentions. Unfortunately those honourable and seemly political commodities now constituted nearly the whole stock in trade of the peers and county members who watched and criticised the Government. As Ministers, eight years before, they had done their duty faithfully and well during the brief period which elapsed between the moment when the King had no choice but to accept their services, and the moment when he first could find a pretext for dispensing with them. Burke's "Short Account of a Short Administration" set forth, with the unadorned fidelity of an inventory, the catalogue of performances which Lord Rockingham and his colleagues had packed into the compass of one year and twenty days. In tastes, in character, and in worldly position these men were suited to use power well, and to abandon it cheerfully as soon as they were unable any longer to employ it for the advantage of the country; but they were not equally inclined to conduct, year in and year out, the thankless and hopeless battle against able and unscrupulous opponents who were fighting like irritated bulldogs in defence of their salaries. For true gentlemen, (and such the Rockinghams were,) the prospect before them was not enticing. The best they could anticipate was to spend years in being bantered by Rigby, and brow-beaten by Thurlow, and denounced as traitors by Wedderburn for expressing in mild terms their sympathy with a cause which in former days he had almost contrived to bring into disrepute by the violence with which he had advocated it. And at the end of those years they might, as the crown of success, be able to force themselves into the counsels of a monarch who hated them, and who treated them as none among them would have treated the humblest of their dependents and retainers.

The Whig magnates, while they had little to gain from a political career, had in their own opinion almost

everything to lose.   In that age of enjoyment they held
the best seats in the theatre of life ; and their notions
of pleasure squared, even less than those of most men,
with the conditions under which hard public work is
done.   There were politicians for whom the sweetest
hours of the twenty-four began when the rattle of the
coaches up St. James Street told that the House of
Commons was no longer sitting, and ended when they
were helped into their beds by daylight ; — in whose
eyes Ranelagh surpassed all the gardens of Chatsworth,
and the trees in the Mall were more excellent than the
elms at Althorp or the oaks of Welbeck.   But Rockingham and his followers loved the country ; and there
were few amongst them who did not possess plenty of
it to love.   Assembling for business in a November fog,
and wrangling on until a June sun shone reproachfully
through the windows, seemed a doubtful form of happiness even to Gibbon, whose conceptions of rustic solitude did not go beyond a cottage at Hampton Court
during the summer months.   But to haunt London
when the thorns were red and white, and the syringas
fragrant, or when the hounds were running over the
Yorkshire pastures, and the woodcocks were gathering
in the Norfolk copses ; to debate amidst clamour, and
vote in a lobby where there was hardly space to stand,
with the hope that at some unknown point in the future
he might draw salary for a few quarter days, — was not
a career to the mind of a great landowner who seldom
got as much sport and fresh air as he could wish, and
who, since he had outgrown the temptations of the
card-table, had never known what it was to spend half
his income.

In the spring of 1774 the Opposition retained very
little hold on Parliament, and still less on the country.
Their impotence was the constant theme of every one
who was their well-wisher, and who would have been
their supporter if they had provided him with anything
to support.   Their supine attitude was noticed with delight and exultation in the private letters of their adver-

saries, who were however far too judicious to taunt them
with it in public; and among themselves it formed an
unfailing subject of mutual confession and expostulation.
For years together, both before and after the outbreak
of the American War, the comments of Londoners who
kept their friends at a distance informed of what was
doing at Westminster are all in the same strain. " I
wish I could send you some news," wrote Lord Townshend in 1772; "but all is dull and the town thin. The
Opposition, poor souls who can do no harm, (the Dukes
of Richmond, Devonshire, and Portland excepted,) seem
to have left the nation entirely to this wicked Ministry."
"Lord North," said Sir George Macartney in 1773,
"has had a wonderful tide of success, and there does
not seem anything likely to interrupt it. Opposition is
growing ridiculous and contemptible, and 'tis now said
that after this Session Lord Rockingham will give it
up."

The colonial difficulty, instead of bracing the sinews
of the Opposition, only made them more conscious of
their own helplessness. The Duke of Richmond, who
was the fighting man of the party in the Lords, admitted
in March 1775 that he felt very languid about the
American business; that he saw no use in renewing
efforts which invariably failed; and that, in his view,
nothing would restore common-sense to the country
except the dreadful consequences which must follow
from what he called the diabolical policy on which it
was embarked.[1] Horace Walpole, an honest and anxious patriot beneath all his fashionable gossip and anti-
quarian frippery, thus wound up a long series of passages
reflecting on the degeneracy of the party which professed to withstand the Court. " I would lay a wager
that if a parcel of schoolboys were to play at politicians,

[1] Samuel Curwen, a Tory exile who had fled across the Atlantic in what
may be described as the First Emigration, comforted his fellow-Loyalists,
whom he had left behind him in America, with assurances that the Opposition in the British Parliament was too inconsiderable in numbers, influence, and activity to hinder the plans of the Administration for restoring
order in New England.

the children that should take the part of the Opposition
would discover more spirit and sense. The cruellest
thing that has been said of the Americans by the Court
is that they were encouraged by the Opposition. You
might as soon light a fire with a wet dishclout."

Epithet for epithet, the retrospective loyalty due from
Liberals to a former chief of their party would incline
them to compare Lord Rockingham to a nobler article
of domestic use than that which suggested itself to Horace Walpole; but a wet blanket he certainly must be
called. He was the most exalted instance in Parliamentary history of the force of Burke's maxim that a
habit of not speaking at all grows upon men as fast as
a habit of speaking ill, and is as great a misfortune.
To the end of his days, whenever Rockingham had
mustered courage to open his mouth in public, he was
congratulated as if he had been a young County Member who had moved the Address, without breaking down,
on the first day of his first Parliament.   " It gave me
great pleasure," wrote the Duke of Richmond in 1769,
"to hear that you had exerted yourself to speak in the
House; and I am particularly pleased that you returned
to the charge on the second day, and replied : for it
gives me hopes that you will get rid of that ill-placed
timidity which has hitherto checked you. Be assured,
you cannot speak too often. Practice will make it easy
to you."   It was a curious way of writing to a man who
had already been Prime Minister.

If in the Lords the Opposition had a leader whose
heart sank within him whenever he gave the word of
command, the Opposition in the Commons had to do as
they best.could without any leader whatsoever. They
came to the House, as Burke ruefully expressed it, to
dispute among themselves, to divert the Ministry, and
to divide eight and twenty. There was indeed always
Burke, who during a quarter of a century adorned and
illustrated the cause of freedom ; and who, when in his
declining years he exerted his eloquence against the
French Revolution, led, or rather drove, the House of

Commons and the Government, and the country too. But his merits and his failings alike disqualified him to be the titular head of one of the great parties in the fastidious and aristocratic Parliaments of the eighteenth century. He had some of the faults of his time, and some of the defects which are popularly imputed to his place of birth. He wanted self-control in debate; and he seldom observed a sense of proportion either in the length of his speeches, or in the size and colour of his rhetorical figures. There are passages in Burke, rich to gaudiness and audacious almost to crudity, which are equally astonishing when we reflect that a human im- agination was capable of producing them without pre- vious study, and when we remember that they were spoken, in the actual words which we now read, to a House of Commons waiting for its dinner or, (more inconceivable still,) to a House of Commons that had dined.[1] He lived beyond his means, and was far too much in the company of relatives who were not particu- lar as to the methods by which they endeavoured to fill their empty purses; but that circumstance in itself should have been no bar to the favour of an Assembly where the receipt for mending an impaired fortune was to sell votes for allotments in government loans, and for shares in government contracts. The unpardonable sin of Edmund Burke was that he owed his position in the political world to nothing except his industry and his genius.

He knew his place; and if he ever forgot it, there were those at hand who made it a matter of conscience

[1] In 1770, when arguing for an inquiry into the administration of the law of libel, Burke thus expressed his want of confidence in the Judges : "The lightning has pierced their sanctuary, and rent the veil of their temple from the top even to the bottom. Nothing is whole, nothing is sound. The ten tables of the law are shattered and splintered. The Ark of the Covenant is lost, and passed into the hands of the uncircumcised. Both they and ye are become an abomination unto the Lord. In order to wash away your sins, let Moses and the prophets ascend Mount Sinai, and bring us down the second table of the law in thunders and lightnings ; for in thunders and lightnings the Constitution was first, and must now, be established."

to deal with him faithfully. He left among his papers a noble composition which, if it had been a fifth of the length that it is, would have been as widely admired as Dr. Johnson's reply to Lord Chesterfield. It was the draft answer to a letter from Dr. Markham, the Bishop of Chester, and tutor to the Prince of Wales. Markham had taken upon himself to reprove Edmund Burke for his public conduct; and on that occasion he sadly forgot what was due to an old friendship, and to the personal claims of the man whom he was addressing. Even at this distance of time it is impossible to read without indignation the contemptuous terms in which a successful formalist, who had risen by worldly arts into a great ecclesiastical position,[1] ventured to upbraid an exalted thinker, who had missed wealth and prosperity, for his presumption in expressing an opinion on matters which were too high for him, and on people of a station above his own. The Churchman expressed surprise that the member of Parliament resented the advice to bring down the aim of his ambition to a lower level, and reminded him that arrogance in a man of his condition was intolerable. Burke's conduct was ridiculous folly, and his house, "a hole of adders"; and, being what he was, he had the insolence to ill-treat the first men of the kingdom; — those first men being Rigby and Lord Barrington, whose names are now chiefly remembered because they occasionally appear to disadvantage in a corner of one of his scathing sentences. "My Lord," was the reply, "I think very poorly of Ned Burke or his pretensions; but, by the blessing of God, the just claims of active members of Parliament shall never be lowered in the estimation of mankind by my personal or official insignificance. . . . If ever things should entitle me to

[1] In 1764 Markham entreated the Duke of Bedford to procure him "one of the inferior bishoprics." "Whatever preferment," the Reverend Doctor wrote, "I may chance to rise to, I shall not set a higher value on any of its emoluments than on the ability it may possibly give me of being useful to some of your Grace's friends." — *The Bedford Correspondence;* vol. iii., p. 275.

look for office, it is my friends who must discover the place I hold in Parliament. I shall never explain it. I protest most solemnly that, in my eye, thinking as I do of the intrinsic dignity of a member of Parliament, I should look upon the highest office the subject could aspire to as an object rather of humiliation than of pride. It would very much arrange me in point of convenience. It would do nothing for me in point of honour." [1]

Burke needed no candid friend to bid him take a lower seat. The iron had entered into his soul, never to leave it; and, far from aspiring to the first place, he was well aware that he could not afford even to be conspicuous. "I saw and spoke to several," he writes on one occasion. "Possibly I might have done service to the cause, but I did none to myself. This method of going hither and thither, and agitating things personally, when it is not done in chief, lowers the estimation of whoever is engaged in such transactions; especially as they judge in the House of Commons that a man's intentions are pure in proportion to his languor in endeavouring to carry them into execution." [1] So deeply impressed was he with the preponderating influence which birth and rank then exercised in the transactions of politics that he seriously thought of inviting Lord George Germaine to marshal and command the party. At a very early moment, however, it became evident that, for people who wanted to be taken under fire, it was not enough to get Lord George Germaine into the saddle; for a division in Parliament answers to a charge in the field, and Lord George had as little eye or heart for the one as for the other. It soon got to Burke's saying plainly and bluntly that, whether his Lordship concurred or not, no human consideration would hinder himself, for one, from dividing the House; and the paths of the two men thenceforward finally diverged. The nobleman took the road which led to place, and salary, and a perceptible addition to the heavy account which already

[1] Burke to Rockingham; January 10, 1773. *Correspondence of Edmund Burke;* vol. i., pp. 276 to 338.

stood against him in a ledger of Britain's glory. The commoner returned to his continuous, and at length victorious, wrestle with corruption in high places, and to his honourable and indispensable, but obscure, labours behind the scenes of the senatorial theatre.

"Burke," said the Duke of Richmond, "you have more merit than any man in keeping us together;" and none knew better than his Grace how hard the task was. The exertions of the great orator were by no means confined to the Chamber in which he himself sate. He counted the peers as a part of the flock which he tended with so small a prospective share in the profits, and so exclusive a monopoly of the toil and the anxiety. He wrote their Protests; he drew their Resolutions; he told them when they were to speak, and sketched, not always in outline, what they were to say. From Rockingham downwards he urged on them the duty of attendance at Westminster, putting aside the plea of weak health with decorous but unambiguous incredulity. His desk was full of pathetic epistles in which the fathers of the Whig party, in both Houses, begged to be allowed a little longer holiday from the public debates, and, (what in that season of discouragement and depression they liked even less,) from the private consultations of the party. "Indeed, Burke," wrote the Duke of Richmond from Goodwood, "you are too unreasonable to desire me to be in town some time before the Meeting of Parliament. You see how very desperate I think the game is. You know how little weight my opinion is of with our friends in the lump; and to what purpose can I then meet them? No; let me enjoy myself here till the Meeting, and then, at your desire, I will go to town and look about me for a few days." Even Savile stopped at home, for reasons sufficiently elevated and disinterested to have commended themselves to John Hampden, but which none the less kept him out of the way when he was most wanted. Lord John Cavendish, never good at excuses, and lightest among the light weights who could afford to be well

mounted, was reduced to admit that he stayed in the
country to hunt; and Burke's sentiment with regard to
him was divided between respect for his frankness, and
regret for the absence of the keenest politician in a
family group who required no watching or stimulating
when once he had collected them in London.[1]

The Whigs defended themselves to each other, — and,
when they dared, tried to pacify their taskmaster, — by the
allegation that public action was useless in the House
because public feeling was asleep in the country. But
this, as Burke did not hesitate to inform them, was their
own fault. They were selfishly indifferent about what
he regarded as a statesman's primary function, that of
instructing the people to discern and pursue their own
highest interests. When it was a question of preventing a rival family from securing the representation of
the Shire in which he lived, any one of them was ready
to spend his last guinea; to mortgage his home-farm; to
cut down his avenue; to rise from a sick bed, (like poor
Granby,) in order to vote, and canvass, and dine in a
stuffy tavern, at an unheard-of hour, in a company with
whom, outside politics, he had not a taste in common.
And yet the same man would take no trouble, and sacrifice none of his leisure, in order to teach his countrymen
what they ought to think about their own grievances,
and the dangers and duties of the nation. If the Opposition, (so Burke told them,) were to electioneer with the
same want of spirit as they displayed over the advocacy

---

[1] The state of things was described by Mason in a satire written just
before the change for the better came.

> "For, know, poor Opposition wants a head.
> With hound and horn her truant schoolboys roam
> And for a fox-chase quit Saint Stephen's dome,
> Forgetful of their grandsire Nimrod's plan,
> 'A mighty hunter, but his prey was man.'"

Even in his rebukes Mason drew a distinction, creditable to the Rockinghams, between their favourite pursuits and the recreations in vogue among
their political adversaries, who, according to the poet,

> "At crowded Almack's nightly bet,
> To stretch their own beyond the nation's debt."

K 2

of those great principles which were the end and object
for which elections exist, there would not be a Whig
member left in Yorkshire or in Derbyshire.   "The people," he wrote, "are not answerable for their present
supine acquiescence: indeed they are not.   God and
nature never made them to think or act without guidance and direction."

But guidance was impossible when the guides themselves were uncertain about the quarter towards which
they should advance, and, in any case, were in no hurry
to start.   As far as the supply of public questions was
concerned, the party was living from hand to mouth,
and fared very sparingly.   Wilkes, if it is not profane
to say so, had in his day been nothing short of a God-
send; and, to do them justice, the Whigs had made the
most of him.[1]   But by this time the country was tired of
Wilkes; and Wilkes was still more heartily tired of himself as a public character, and an idol for popular enthusiasm.   Nor could anything be hoped from a movement
in favour of Parliamentary Reform.   Although the
Middlesex election had brought strongly into notice the
glaring defects of our representative system, it was
impossible to unite the Rockinghams over any proposal by which those defects might be remedied; for on
that point Burke himself was a Tory of the Tories.
Several Whig statesmen had Reform bills of their own;
but whenever they showed any disposition to agree upon
a plan, and to array themselves in support of it, Burke
threw himself across their path as an opponent; and,
like the conquering brigade at Albuera, his dreadful
volleys swept away the head of every formation.   It
was useless for Savile to recommend the shortening of
parliaments, or for Richmond to suggest the extension
of the franchise.   As soon as their proposals had taken

[1] "The people were very much, and very generally, touched with the
question on Middlesex.   We never had, and we never shall have, a matter
every way so well calculated to engage them.   The scantiness of the
ground makes it the more necessary to cultivate it with vigour and diligence ; else the rule of *exiguum colito* will neither be good farming, nor
good politics." — Burke to Lord Rockingham ; September 8, 1770.

shape, and attracted notice, Burke appealed to all sober
thinkers to say whether England was not the happiest
of communities in its exemption from the horrible disorders of frequent elections ; and whether it would not
be more in the spirit of our constitution, and more agreeable to the pattern of our best laws, rather to lessen the
number, and so add to the weight and independency, of
our voters.

At last the Whigs were confronted by a question
which aroused them as their forefathers were stirred by
the imposition of Ship-money. It became known that
the Irish Parliament meditated a bill laying a tax of two
shillings in the pound on the estates of absentee landowners, and that the Irish Government, in sore straits
for funds, would assist the measure to become law. The
rich Whig proprietors were deeply moved ; and on this
occasion they showed no want of vigour and alacrity.
They addressed to the Prime Minister a memorial praying that the Privy Council would refuse to pass the bill ;
and no abler and more artful state-paper had been signed
by the great names of the party since the invitation to
William of Orange. The letter to Lord North was even
better worded than that historical document of the past,
for it was drafted by Burke himself ; but all the considerations put forth in condensed and formidable array by
the most skilful of Irish pens, employed on a strange
office, will not avail against a couple of sentences which
described the attitude of the first among living Englishmen. "I could not," said Chatham, "as a peer of England, advise the King to reject a tax sent over here as
the genuine desire of the Commons of Ireland, acting in
their proper and peculiar sphere, and exercising their
inherent exclusive right, by raising supplies in the manner they judge best. This great principle of the constitution is so fundamental, and with me so sacred and
indispensable, that it outweighs all other considerations."
In the end, the proposal was defeated in the Irish Parliament. The noblemen who had broad acres in both
countries commanded a greater influence in Dublin even

than that which they exercised at Westminster. The Irish Ministry, who by this time had learned that the King, for once agreeing with the Rockinghams, had condemned the tax as "very objectionable," [1] fought to lose, and with some difficulty got themselves beaten by a narrow majority. But, narrow as it was, it saved the Whigs from the calamity of a debate in the British Parliament; a prospect which Sir George Savile contemplated with the repugnance of a sensible man who had no fancy for losing his sleep in a cause so damaging to his party. Little credit, (so he wrote to Rockingham,) was to be obtained out of a question in which it was notorious that they were all personally interested. "Having a day of it, as the phrase is, will not get us much laurels. I am sure having a night of it will be worse to me than a land-tax." [2]

The exhibition to which Savile looked forward with just apprehension was happily averted; but none the less the Whigs were out of touch with the country, out of heart with their parliamentary work, and of small account among a class whose adhesion no party, which looks to office, can afford to lose. Pushing men, whose prime object is to make their way in life, whether they aspire to be Lord Chancellors or tide-waiters, are apt to grow cool in their loyalty, and, (after a more or less decent interval,) hot in their antagonism, to statesmen who cannot fight their own battles. Philip Francis was only one of thousands who, to employ his own words, had seen plainly that "no solid advantage would come from

[1] The King to Lord North; November 23, 1773.
[2] A London newspaper of 1776 related how, a few years before that date, — when Irish landowners, and especially the absentees, were screwing up their estates to the utmost pitch, — Sir George Savile received an offer of £4000 a year from a middleman for the rents of an estate which brought him in only half that revenue. Savile went over to Ireland, had the land valued, enquired into the situation of his tenants and cottagers, and found that they could, without oppression, pay £2500 a year. He added that £500 to the rental; but ordered it not to be remitted to him, but spent upon the estate in building cottages and farm-houses, and in giving lime, and otherwise assisting the industrious, without receiving a shilling for himself.

connection with a party which had almost all the wit,
and popularity, and abilities in the kingdom to support
them, but never could carry a question in either House
of Parliament." England had seldom been in a worse
case. The tornado was approaching fast, and, according to Horace Walpole, her public men were at their
wit's end; which, he added, was no long journey. There
were some, he said, who still put their faith in Lord
Chatham's crutch, as a wand which might wave the
darkness and the demons away together; though his
Lordship, in Walpole's opinion, was better at raising a
storm than at laying one. But it was natural enough
that men should turn in their despair to the imposing
figure of the old magician, who had made the name of
their country supreme abroad, and who had always stood
for freedom and justice whenever and wherever they
were in peril. Chatham had broadened and ennobled
the discussion of the Middlesex election. He had surveyed the problem of the Absentee Tax from the point
of view of a true statesman. He had watched the growing greatness of the American colonies with an affectionate pride which he, of all men, had a right to feel; and
for years past he had been in favour of Parliamentary
Reform. "Allow a speculator in a great chair," he
wrote in 1771, "to add that a plan for more equal representation, by additional Knights of the Shire, seems
highly reasonable."

However much, in his habitual strain of stately humility, Chatham might affect to disparage his own importance, he was far removed from the modern notion
of an arm-chair politician; for, when he felt strongly,
he was still ready to place himself where hard blows
were being taken and given. But years had begun to
tell upon him; and, when the occasion came, he was no
longer certain of being equal to his former self.[1] His

[1] Mr. Joseph Cradock relates in his memoirs how, on a day when the
King opened Parliament, there was crowding, and something like rioting, at the very door of the House of Lords. "Lord Carlisle," said Cradock, "seeing my distress, most kindly recognised me, and made room for

health was worse than fitful; and he sate in the wrong House of Parliament for forming and leading a national party.   Nor must it be forgotten that the only existing nucleus for such a party was the group which owed allegiance to Lord Rockingham; and against Rockingham and his associates Chatham was bitterly prejudiced.   He taught himself to believe that his quarrel with them was on account of their moderation; a fault which, if he had cared to take them in the right way, he would have been the very man to cure.   But instead of trying to infuse into them the fire and resolution which they lacked, his mind was bent on outbidding and discrediting them.   " I am resolved," he said, " to be in earnest for the public, and shall be a scare-crow of violence to the gentle warblers of the grove, the moderate Whigs and temperate statesmen."   That was not the tone which Charles Fox, as fierce a fighter as Chatham himself had been in his most strenuous days, ever permitted himself to adopt towards men whose abilities and virtues he respected, and whose inertness and unconcern were soon exchanged for very opposite qualities when once he had filled them with his own spirit; and the hour was now approaching for the entry on the scene of that Whig leader whose exhortation and example kept bench and lobby packed with an animated,

me between himself and another nobleman.   That nobleman got up to speak ; and then I perceived that it was the great Lord Chatham, whom I had never seen but as Mr. Pitt.   He spoke only for a short time, was confused, and seemed greatly disconcerted ; and then, suddenly turning to me, asked whether I had ever heard him speak before.   'Not in this House, my Lord,' was my reply.   'In no House, Sir,' says he, 'I hope, have I ever so disgraced myself.   I feel ill, and I have been alarmed and annoyed this morning before I arrived.   I scarce know what I have been talking about.' "   Later on in the debate a peer made an uncomplimentary reference to Chatham.   " He suddenly arose, and poured forth a torrent of eloquence that utterly astonished.   The change was inconceivable; the fire had been kindled, and we were all electrified with his energy and excellence.   At length he seemed quite exhausted, and, as he sat down, with great frankness shook me by the hand, and seemed personally to recollect me ; and I then ventured to say, ' I hope your Lordship is satisfied.'   'Yes, Sir,' replied he, with a smile, ' I think I have now redeemed my credit.' "

a devoted, and an ever-increasing, throng of followers throughout all the closing sessions of the great dispute.

When Charles Fox left office in the February of 1774, the first marked period of his political life came to its close. From that time forward he moved across the stage a far wiser man, pursuing higher ends by worthier methods. An epicure in history will regret the moment when he must begin to take seriously the young aristocrat who hitherto had kept the world of London as much alive as ever was the Athens of Alcibiades; and the early career of Lord Holland's favourite son will always remain an amazing, if not an exemplary, chapter in the annals of the House of Commons and of the town. That career has been recounted in a former book without disguise or palliation; and an historian who wishes to do his best by Charles Fox will preserve the same system to the last. He thought so clearly, spoke so forcibly, and acted so fearlessly that what was good in him does not need to be set off by favourable comment; and what was wrong could not be concealed by reticence, or mended by excuses which he himself would have scorned to give.

When measuring the extent of a change for the better in any given individual, it is necessary to take into account how much there had been that needed amending; and in the case of Fox there was spacious room for improvement. Enough, and more than enough, of his old self remained. It required all the discipline of a long interval filled with toil, disaster, and disappointment, before the free-lance of the Wilkes controversy had settled down into the much-enduring champion who stood for liberty through the dreary years of political reaction which closed the eighteenth, and ushered in the nineteenth, century. But the grave and fatal error of Charles Fox's career belonged to a period later than the years of which these volumes treat; and his public action between 1774 and 1782 will, in its character and its fruits, bear favourable comparison with an equal period in the life of any statesman who in the prosecution of his policy enjoyed no power or influence except such as his tongue gave him. The contrast between Fox during the eight years before he was five and twenty, (for he began life early,) and the eight years after, exceeds anything recorded outside religious autobiography. That is a province of literature in which, from Saint Augustine to Bunyan, the effect of such a contrast is apt to be heightened by the author's overestimate of his own early wickedness; but Charles Fox was the last man who cared to exaggerate his past delinquencies, — if, indeed, they would have admitted of it. The difference between what he had been, and what he became, was so great, and the transformation so sudden, that it could never have occurred but for a series of events which, treading with startling rapidity in each other's steps, in their combined effect were singularly calculated to chasten and inspire such a nature and such an intellect.

His political career, so far as it could lead to anything which in the eyes of his contemporaries seemed worth having, was ruined. With his own hands, to make sport for himself, he had pulled down the pillars of his temple, and had crushed none of his adversaries or, (what then meant much the same to him,) his leaders. When just turned three and twenty he had resigned his first place, on what, by a very friendly interpretation, might be construed as public grounds. Before the year was out he had been brought back again by a ministerial rearrangement costing much trouble and money, and more scandal, which had been undertaken solely with a view to his re-enlistment in office. Such a tribute to the terror of his eloquence might well have turned an older and steadier head; and Lord North soon learned that Charles Fox, however far down he might sit at the Board of Treasury, took his own view of his own position in Parliament. Among the three recognised functions of subordinate officials, — to make a House, to keep a House, and to cheer ministers, — Fox never failed of the first when he was known to be going to speak, or of the second as long as he was on his legs; but the only comfort and encouragement which his more exalted colleagues got from him was to find themselves planted in an inextricable, and sometimes an absurd, situation whenever it suited his passing humour, or that queer conglomeration of prejudices and sentiments which he then called his immutable principles. There could be but one end to such a connection. Fox was dismissed from office, without the consolation of having sacrificed himself to a cause; without a following; with no tribute of sympathy other than the ironical congratulations of an enormous circle of friends and acquaintances, who were only surprised that the event had not taken place weeks before; and, (what was the most serious,) with nothing which the world around him would call a hope. He had sinned against the light, — such light as illuminated the path of the Wedderburns and the Welbore Ellises from one overpaid post to another. He had not learned even from personal experience, (what wise men took for granted,) how bitter it was to have shut oneself out in the cold. He had shown that salary could not tempt him to surrender a whim. What sort of a colleague would he be if he ever came to indulge himself in a conscience? Above all, he had proved that he could not follow. There was that about him which made it certain that no party should admit him into its ranks unless it was prepared to be led by him; and in a House of Commons where, during his career of joyous knight-errantry, he had tilted successively into the middle of every group and section, there were none who would not scout the notion of placing themselves under his banner. His political prospect was now an avenue which opened on the desert of life-long opposition; and if he did not know what that meant, Lord Holland was there to tell him. It was a cruel thought for the old statesman that a son of such hopes should already, and all for nothing, have made himself as complete a political outlaw as was the father at the close of a long career, during which, at any rate, he had acquired vast wealth, and had reached the height of power.

The blow was the more crushing because it came at the moment when the family fortunes paid a signal penalty for the family failings. Lord Holland had just brought to a conclusion the gigantic operations by means of which he rescued his two eldest sons from the most pressing consequences of his indulgence and their own folly. Stephen's debts were very large; but, with the best will in the world, he had not the genius for prodigality of his younger brother. Charles, before he came to man's estate, was the prince of spendthrifts in that heroic age of dissipation. He sate later than others at the faro table; he staked higher; and he shut his eyes more tightly against what was suspicious in a run of ill-luck which to the mind of the bystanders required explanation. He ordered larger consignments of silk and gold lace from across the Channel than any of his rivals in the game of fashion; he kept a longer string of worse horses at Newmarket; and, above all, he raised money with more magnificent indifference to the laws which govern that department of industry. Indeed, with regard to those laws he had his own theory, which for the time being fully satisfied him. "I remember," so Horace Walpole wrote in 1793, "that when Mr. Charles Fox and one or two more youths of brilliant genius first came to light, and into vast debts at play, they imparted to the world an important secret which they had discovered. It was, that nobody needed to want money if they would pay enough for it. But, as they had made an incomplete calculation, the interest so soon exceeded the principal that the system did not maintain its ground for above two or three years."

The last of those years ended with the Christmas of 1773; and, on or about that date, Lord Holland had brought to a close a minute and wide-reaching investigation of the all but innumerable claims upon his children's honour and his own sense of paternal obligation.

The chief culprit assisted in the task with a dutiful
eagerness which would have been more helpful if he
had kept a stricter account of his multifarious transactions. It stands on something like record that, when
Charles had given in what he regarded as a complete
list of his liabilities, somebody else brought to light the
existence of deferred annuities amounting to five thousand a year, which the grantees, on *their* part, had not
forgotten. One hundred and forty thousand pounds
had to be forthcoming before he was free from debt,
and his friends from the bitter anxieties in which their
affection for him had involved them. The young fellows, who had helped the two brothers to raise money,
were regarded by Lord Holland, for doing that which
fathers in all ages of the world have found it the hardest to forgive, with a gratitude characteristic of the man.[1]
He made the immense sacrifice which the situation demanded without hesitation and without complaint. But
the shaft had gone home; and Charles awoke to the
knowledge that he had distressed and darkened the
failing years, or rather months, of a father who had
never wronged him unless by the extravagances of a
love which could not be surpassed. His sorrow bore
fruit in amended, though far from perfect, conduct, and
in self-reproach which, though not obtrusive, was never

---

[1] There still exists a paper such as only one father, that ever lived,
would have dictated without a thought of anger. The signature is that
of a broken man.

"I do hereby order direct and require you to sell and dispose of my
Long Annuitys, and so much of my other Stock Estates and Effects, as
will be sufficient to pay and discharge the debts of my son The Honble
Charles James Fox not exceeding the sum of one hundred thousand
pounds. And I do hereby authorize and empower you to pay and discharge such Debts to the amount aforesaid upon takeing an assignment, not
only of the judgments Bonds and other securitys so to be paid and discharged, but allso of all such Bonds Judgments and other securitys wherein
any other person or persons is or are bound or concerned, with or for my
said son, to and for my own use and benefit.

" HOLLAND.

" Dated this 26th Novr. 1773
　　To John Powell Esqr.
　　　　at the Pay Office."

and nowhere disavowed. A year or two afterwards, during hot and grave debate, he was taunted in a full House of Commons with having ruined himself by the most scandalous vices. His assailant was a man of his own standing, a soldier, and, (what did not perhaps make the rebuke more acceptable,) a cousin. But Charles Fox, — a master of retort, and to whom a duel was a joke, as far as his own danger was concerned, — quietly and sadly replied that he confessed his errors, and wished from his heart that he could atone for them.

Everything about Fox, whether it partook of good or evil, was on a scale so extensive that he was regarded rather as a portent, than an ordinary personage, even by the contemporaries who might meet him in the flesh, (and there was enough of it,) any day in the week, if they did not look for him too early in the morning. It is not to be wondered at that this generation — with its more rational habits, and its less marked individuality — should read of his early prodigality, his vehement penitence, his eloquence and energy, and the extraordinary strength of the friendship which through life he inspired and felt, as if they were the fictitious attributes of some mythical hero. But no one who has studied the letters which he wrote and received, from his boyhood onward to his premature old age, can doubt that popular tradition, whatever it has done for or against Charles Fox, has not run in the direction of exaggeration. That he should have wasted an enormous fortune at four and twenty, and at thirty have been contending on equal terms with as masterful a sovereign as any who had ruled in England since the Tudors, seems perfectly natural and accountable to those who follow his correspondence through all the stages of his moral and intellectual development. The sprawling boyish hand gradually acquired form and consistency, while the matter grew in weight and worth. But from first to last every sentence was straightforward, honest, and perfectly clear in its meaning; and the character of the penmanship, so legible and flowing, and so instinct with good-humour, was enough to put the most dejected friend, (and he had always a supply of such,) in high spirits by the very sight of it.   His early vices and follies, and in after days the frequent excesses of his public spirit, and the occasional perversity of his political conduct, are all told with the joyous, unconsciona- ble frankness of one who never knew what it was to be ashamed of that which at the time he was engaged in; for when Charles Fox became ashamed of any- thing, he left off doing it.

The communications which passed between him and his cronies, during the period when the oldest among them was five and twenty, are such as, it is to be feared, have often been indited and relished by clever young men of fashion bred in London and in Paris; especially if, like Charles Fox, they were conversant with the temptations of both capitals.   Letters of this class, when they have been written, as a rule have mercifully perished; but his celebrity was already such, when he might still have been at Eton, and certainly ought to have been at Oxford, that every scrap of paper which proceeded from his pen was treasured like the familiar epistles of a prime minister.   The most free and lively of the letters were addressed to the Richard Fitzpatrick who is celebrated as the friend of Fox, and who merited on his own account more fame than has befallen him.

In one important respect the memory of Fox and Fitzpatrick rather gains than loses from the outspoken tone of these youthful disclosures.   They prove, be- yond any manner of question, that the writers were the last people in the world to assume a virtue when they had it not.   For that very reason, when we come to the later letters which, for many and many a long year to come, passed between the pair of kinsmen, we have an assurance that their views on state policy and public duty were heartfelt and genuine; and they were views which, if ascertained to be sincere, are to the immortal honour of those who held them.   The best comment on the character of the Fox papers as a whole is the

effect which they produced on the only two men who
are certainly known to have seen them in their entirety.
What Lord Holland felt is briefly, but most sufficiently,
recorded in bronze on the railing which separates
the Kensington Road from the grounds of Holland
House : —

> " Nephew of Fox and friend of Grey,
>   Be this my deed of fame
> That those who know me best may say,
>   ' He tarnished neither name.' "

These lines, almost as they stand in the inscription,
were found after Lord Holland's death on his dress-
ing table, and in his handwriting. Charles Fox, however, was his uncle, and such an uncle as falls to
the lot of few ; and the world may suspect the impartiality of a nephew who resembled him in his noble
and amiable nature, and held, to the full and beyond,
his political creed. But Lord Holland made over the
Fox manuscripts to the late Earl Russell, whose standard of private and public virtue was as high as that
which any man has ever maintained in practice throughout a long and honoured life.[1] And Earl Russell
revered Fox as a statesman, admired him and respected
him as an individual, and entertained for him a personal
affection which is rare indeed in a case where the grave
has forbidden the opportunity of personal intercourse
and knowledge.

The correspondence of Charles Fox may be divided

---

[1] The quotations in this chapter, and in the Second of the Appen-
dices, are almost entirely from unpublished letters. I am unable adequately to express the gratitude which I felt when the late Dowager
Countess Russell placed the Fox manuscripts at my disposal for the purposes of this book, and my pride at the confidence which, in so doing,
she thought fit to repose in me. Lady Agatha Russell has done me the
great honour of continuing the kindness which her mother showed me.
The letters referring to the period covered by the American Revolution,
though interesting and important, are few in comparison with those
which commence when Fox became Secretary of State in 1782 ; which
succeed each other thenceforward in continuous order ; and which supply
the matter for three out of the four volumes of Earl Russell's *Memorials
and Correspondence of Charles James Fox.*

into three very unequal portions. First came that of his scapegrace epoch, which began earlier than is easily credible, and ended far sooner than is generally supposed. Then, when his own ruin, and still more the sorrow which he had brought upon others, had taught him to look life gravely in the face, there succeeded the period of eager and anxious repentance. That period was a short one, for two reasons. First, because he was a man who, when he was minded to do right, did it, and did not talk about it; and next, because those whom he most warmly loved, and had most deeply pained, passed beyond the reach of his protestations. And, afterwards, until his life and his public career were terminated together, there followed an enormous mass of letters, dealing openly and copiously with many subjects, but with none in which he did not take a keen and unaffected interest; — letters clear and easy in style; lofty in tone where the matter demanded it; and animated everywhere by the same fire which, in his early correspondence, was expended in vivifying less valuable and much more questionable material.

In that early correspondence not the least amusing, and very far from the most unedifying, passages throw a light upon the otherwise inconceivable process by which a parcel of boys contrived to get rid of several hundred thousand pounds in a few years, without any of it remaining in their own circle to enrich some of them at the expense of the others. Charles and Stephen Fox, Richard Fitzpatrick and his brother Lord Ossory, Lord Carlisle, Uvedale Price and Mr. Crawford, were one and all men of strict honour according to the code which was then professed in aristocratic circles more universally than it was practised. His own enemy, in a warfare which knew no truce, each of them robbed and injured himself, and himself only. It is true that, if money had to be raised, and a name was wanted on a bill, none of them would scruple to make a request which, for a friend to refuse a friend, was an idea that their imagination could not even contemplate. But they would no more have cheated at cards, or ordered a horse to be pulled on the racecourse, than they would have declined a challenge, or slunk away from the table when the wine was passing and the punch brewing. They had, however, titled and be-ribboned associates around them to whom the laws of honour were even less binding than the Ten Commandments. Older men, who had diced and drunk with their fathers in the days of Carteret, and who now liked the lads for their own sake, were indignant at the treatment of which they were the victims, and astonished at the blindness which prevented them from detecting it. But there are traces in his correspondence that even Charles Fox was not so simple as he appeared. There is a very perceptible distinction between the tone in which he and his coævals referred to those whom they trusted as gentlemen, and that which they reserved for certain high-born sharpers whom they made no pretence of liking or respecting; and whose title to be paid, when they themselves were in cash, they ranked far below the claims of a loyal gamester or a true sportsman, and only just above those of an honest shop-keeper.

The time had come, soon, but none too soon, when this comedy of manners ended, and the historical drama began. It opened with a scene of filial contrition like that which took place in the room adjoining the Jerusalem Chamber of the Palace at Westminster.[1] The letters from Charles Fox to his mother Lady Holland, during the winter of 1773-4, breathe the spirit of the penitence which does exhale itself in words; but it was already fully late to redeem his past in the quarter

---

[1] "If I do feign,
O let me in my present wildness die,
And never live to show th' incredulous world
The noble change that I have purposed!"

Some passages from letters written by Charles Fox to his mother, after his debts had been paid by Lord Holland, and at the time when her own health had visibly begun to fail, are given in the Second Appendix to this volume.

where he cared most to make reparation. That which, in spite of all that could be said about the standard of conduct prevailing among its members, had been among the happiest of homes, was on the eve of being broken up for ever. Lord Holland was dying, with even less reluctance than he had anticipated. He had long been pleasing himself with the reflection that his departure would leave his children richer, or, (as now was the best which could be hoped,) less embarrassed than in his lifetime; although he had shrunk from death for the sake of the wife who could not live without him. But now the long romance, whose earlier chapters, thirty years before, had brightened Downing Street with a glimpse of Arcadia, and had forced the entire fashionable world to take sides in the most fascinating, but by no means the least perilous, of controversies, was drawing to an appropriate close.[1] The lovers who had braved the Court and the Prime Minister, and disobeyed angry parents in days when the anger of parents, who were a Duke and Duchess, went for much, had set forth on their common journey through life in the spirit of true fellow-travellers. A whole generation of warm friends and implacable enemies united in admiring and envying their devotion and their constancy.

> "We'll spring together, and we'll bear one fruit;
> One joy shall make us smile, and one grief mourn;
> One age go with us, and one hour of death
> Shall close our eyes, and one grave make us happy."

As far as lay with themselves, they kept that pledge to the letter; and what was beyond their power Heaven did for them. On the first day of July, 1774, Lord Holland passed away painlessly and calmly, as one tired out in mind and body; and Lady Holland, who had long suffered terribly from an internal cancer, did not outlive the month.

Their eldest son, who had all along been regarded as the worst of lives by those who had a professional

---

[1] Chapter i. of the *Early History of Charles James Fox.*

interest in ascertaining the chances of longevity, died before the year was out. He left a young widow, daughter of the Earl of Upper Ossory, and sister to Richard Fitzpatrick. Singularly sweet and refined, young Lady Holland is never mentioned by the audacious cynics, who were the chroniclers of the day, without a genuine expression of liking and esteem. Her little son, whose appearance in the world terrified Charles's creditors out of their forbearance, and set rolling the financial avalanche which nearly overwhelmed the family, grew up into the Lord Holland whose connection with Fox presents an example of what the relations between nephew and uncle at the very best may be.[1] In the meantime, however, the loss which had befallen him was a crowning sorrow to the young statesman. Stephen had stood by the brother, of whom he was so proud, in fair weather and in foul; in the Commons he had always zealously adopted, even at the risk of caricaturing it, the policy which pleased Charles at the moment; and by his death he now left him without a party in the Lords. There was something absurd about the poor fellow who was dead; but Fox, (as his married life so curiously showed,) did not insist on perfection in those whom he loved. Now that Stephen had gone, the home of his boyhood was desolate; and he went forth into the world in a mood of stern and melancholy purpose of which a twelvemonth before none who knew him would have believed him capable.

Good resolutions are ill to keep in bad company; and it would have gone hard with the young man's aspirations after better things if he had not cut himself adrift from the reckless official crew who were enjoying themselves at their comfortable moorings before they started on the most disastrous enterprise on which a British Government ever deliberately embarked. Of

---

[1] It did not take Charles long to forgive the parents for the sex of their baby. "My love to Lady Mary, who I am glad to hear is so well, as well as her son ; to whom, now he is come, I wish as well as if he had been a daughter." — Charles Fox to Stephen ; December 24, 1773.

the Ministers who had force, wit, and spirit, the best
made no professions of virtue, and had a very easy
standard of practice; and not a few were as competent
preceptors in evil as ever called a main or pushed a
bottle. The most decent and respectable of their colleagues were not of a mental calibre to exercise any
influence, except that of repulsion, over one who still
was at an age when the taste is only too fastidious with
regard to anything dull and strait-laced. It was useless
to expect that a youth, who had taken his first lessons
in the art and aims of politics from the inimitable table-
talk of Lord Holland, should seek an antidote to such
pleasant poison by sitting at the feet of Lord Bathurst,
a very feeble figure in our line of strong Chancellors,[1]
or by doing that which George Selwyn would have described as singing psalms with Lord Dartmouth. Fox,
being just what he was, could have learned nothing but
harm from those whom he had left behind him in office;
and fortunate it was for him that the manner of his
parting from them gave no room for repentance and
reconciliation.

Over and above the negative advantage of being forbidden henceforward to look up to Rigby and Sandwich
as his models and his mentors, there was awaiting him
a privilege which it only required that he should stretch
out his hand to take; the acceptance of which, (for he
was not blind to his opportunities,) became the source of
most that was gracious in his life, and of all that is
enduring in his fame. That privilege was the personal
friendship of Lord Rockingham and his followers.
Aristocrats in the best sense of the word, these men
were worthy of their high position; and the more prom-

---

[1] Lord Campbell had a kindly feeling for the memory of Lord Bathurst,
and made out as fair a case for him as the conscience of a biographer,
versed in the traditions of the Inns of Court, would permit. "It should be
borne in mind," Lord Campbell wrote, "that, as far as the public could
observe, he performed almost decently the duties of the offices in which, to
the surprise of mankind, he was placed; affording a memorable example
of what may be accomplished by a dull discretion." — *Lives of the Lord
Chancellors,* chapter clii.

inent among them were marked out from self-seeking and dissolute contemporaries by their disinterested political action, and their blameless private habits. They had no taste for the amusements to which the bolder and more important among the Ministers, even as elderly people, were addicted; and their repugnance to such a course of life had almost as much to do with their estrangement from those Ministers as any divergence in policy and opinions.[1]

More desirable companions than the Rockinghams, for a young man of Charles Fox's character and aspirations, could not possibly be found. Horace Walpole, whose testimony as a witness for character was conclusive, whatever it might be when he spoke against it, thus wrote of the Duke of Richmond, at a time when he was at variance with that nobleman on the two burning questions of the hour. "I worship his thousand virtues beyond any man's. He is intrepid and tender, inflexible and humane, beyond example. I do not know which is most amiable, his heart or conscience. He ought to be the great model of all our factions. No difference in sentiments between him and his friends makes the slightest impression on his attachment to them." Of Lord John Cavendish Walpole says: "I have often disagreed with him, but always honoured his integrity. Surely that is the fountain of principles. Whatever has grown on his margin, the source has remained limpid and undefiled." Sir George Savile has been justly described as the model to all time of a country gentleman in Parliament; and Lord Rockingham's career marks the highest point to which the respect and affection of those among whom he lived and worked

---

[1] Rigby, earlier in his life, was at the pains to describe his nightly round ; how he drank till past three in the morning, when, — finding that no one cared to sit any longer, except one man who could not sit upright, — he went to the Ridotto, and at length, most reluctantly, to his bed; and how he was abroad again in time for a cock-fight, where he won forty pounds in ready money. That was the life which Rigby formerly led ; and in 1775 he, and Sandwich, and Rochford led very much such a life still.

ever carried a man whose health, tastes, and disposition
were the opposite of all that the requirements of politics
demand. It was inscribed under his statue by a friendly,
but not a flattering, hand, that his virtues were his arts.
To be one of such a fraternity was an honour and an
advantage from which Charles Fox had hitherto been
excluded. He had struck too hard on the wrong side
to please men who contended for principle where he
was only seeking an excuse for forcing his way into the
centre of a faction fight. But when he had finally left
the ranks of that Ministry against whose example their
own attitude was a living protest; — when he stood
alone, unhappy and in earnest, among the ruins of his
joyous and careless past; — then the Rockinghams began to watch his course with interest, and soon with
sympathy. At the earliest indication which he gave of
a desire to enroll himself in their band, they received
him with open arms. He became first the comrade, then
the close ally, and at length the adored and undisputed
leader of men from whom, in whatever relation he might
act with them, there was nothing but good to learn.

The immediate change in his habits, it must be admitted, stopped many degrees below the mark of perfection. He still lived on credit; which he could not very
well help if he was to live at all. He still entered in the
book at Brooks's Club his fifty-guinea bets that war with
France would not break out for two years; that Lord
North would have ceased to be Prime Minister within
the twelvemonth; and that he himself would be called
to the Bar before four given peers were all either dead
or married. He still played high, and long, and often.
He still attended race-meetings with a sort of religious
regularity, and gradually built up for himself a reputation of being the best handicapper in England. He
liked going to his bed as little as ever, though he con-
formed so far to the received theories regarding the
necessity of sleep that, when once there, he left it later
than had been his wont. He continued to spend his
waking hours with those who enjoyed existence; but he

did not distinguish, as rigidly as might have been desired, between the forms of enjoyment favoured by the widely different circles in all of which he was ever and equally welcome.   His habitual associates were men of honour, and men of culture, after the school of St. James's Street; and as time went on, and faction waxed hotter, he consorted more and more by preference with Whigs.   It would be impossible for a student of the exuberant literature which periodically issued from Brooks's to deny that that haunt of wit and fashion was no monastery. Among the younger members of the party, which after a time monopolised the Club, there were plenty of jovial blades whose notions on a most essential point of morality were not merely defective, but positively inverted. It has been said, without any great malice or exaggeration, that the political creed of some of them began and ended in the preference for a stout man, who admired women, to a thin man, who was insensible to their charms.

But the leaders of established fame and authority with whom Charles Fox consulted behind the scenes on the strategy of the session, and by whose side in the House of Commons he carried on the arduous and thankless work of opposition, were men whose companionship was an education in all that was right and becoming. Advising with Richmond on the draft of a protest in the Lords; arranging with Savile the list of Resolutions to be submitted to a county meeting; corresponding with Burke about the line to be taken on the hustings; and then going northwards to Soho for an evening with Johnson and Gibbon, Garrick and Reynolds, at the immortal Club into which the kings of art and of letters had elected the young fellow at a moment when his fortunes were at their very lowest; — such was now the course of Charles Fox's day, when he spent it well; and, as he grew in years, the time which he employed bore ever a larger proportion to the time which he wasted. His elders loved him none the less because he was a learner in the intercourse of society, and never intentionally a teacher; for what he had to tell mankind he was quite satisfied with imparting to them five times a week in the House of Commons. He tended steadily and perceptibly throughout his life towards higher views and quieter ways, until his sweet and lofty nature had lost all trace of what had been disastrous, and nearly fatal, to him in his early circumstances and training. Before he was old, or even elderly, a moralist would have been hard to please who would not allow him to be a good man ; and assuredly the most imaginative of novelists could not have invented a better fellow.

Of those forces which work for the improvement of character the most powerful is the pursuit of an object of a nature to tax all the faculties, and fix them over a long period in one continuous strain of exertion. Such an object awaited Charles Fox outside the gates of office ; and it was the best present that Fortune ever made him. It was full time for him, — and for every one, high or humble, who had in him the making of a true citizen, — that some work worth the doing should be set before them. The apathy of the people, which Burke deplored, was largely due to the transient and personal character of even the most serious among the questions which of recent years had divided the State. The furious popular excitement, and the vast amount of Parliamentary time, which had been expended on the seating and unseating of Wilkes, had in the end lowered the tone and relaxed the springs of politics. Members of the Opposition had been forced, by no fault of their own, to make a champion of one about whom the best which could be said was that he represented, — what he did not possess or profess, — a principle. Even the multitude were weary of staring at, and almost ashamed of having helped to feed, the conflagration which for eleven livelong years had blazed and flickered in the train of that graceless hero. The party hostile to the Court was now passing through a reaction akin to that which the Reformers half a century afterwards experienced, when the passions which raged over the rights and wrongs of Queen Caroline had died away, and had left no solid gain to liberty behind them.

But in the spring of 1774 events were at hand which broke the slumbers, and tried the mettle, of all true patriots in the kingdom. A controversy was at their door, unlimited in its scope, inexorable in its demands on their attention; and of all men, inside Parliament and out, to none did it come pregnant with greater issues than to Fox. It was fortunate for him now that, during his apprenticeship in debate, the topics of his choice had been trivial and ephemeral; and that, possibly by a wholesome instinct, he had left graver problems alone. It mattered little which side he had espoused on the question whether an unlucky printer was to be sent to jail, or committed to the charge of the Serjeant-at-Arms; but it mattered very much indeed that, on the transcendent decision whether America was to be enslaved or pacified, Fox should have nothing to unsay. He came to the great argument fresh and unhampered, his mind and body full of elasticity and strength. Without misgiving, without flagging, and with small thought of self, he devoted an eloquence already mature, and an intellect daily and visibly ripening, to a cause which more than any one else he contributed to make intelligible, attractive, and at length irresistible. That cause at its commencement found him with a broken career. Its triumph placed him in the position of the first subject, and even, (considering that his principal antagonist had been the King himself,) of the first man, in the country.

CHAPTER V

FRANKLIN AND THE LETTERS. THE PENAL LAWS. THE
ACTION OF MASSACHUSETTS. THE COLONIES MAKE
COMMON CAUSE

THERE was one man who possessed the talents, the
turn of character, the official position, and the intimate
personal acquaintance both with England and America
which qualified him to be mediator between the public
opinion of the two countries; and he had all the will in
the world to perform the office. Out of the last seventeen years Franklin had spent fourteen in London as
agent for Pennsylvania; and of late he had been agent
for Georgia and Massachusetts as well. The ambassadors accredited to St. James's from foreign Courts
treated him like an esteemed member of their own
body. He was at home in the best society in town and
country, awing every company by his great age and
pleasing them by his immortal youth. The ministers
of state, with whom he had business, minded their behaviour in the presence of one who had talked with Sir
William Wyndham before they themselves had been
born or thought of. Men of letters, and men of science,
could not have enough of the reminiscences of a veteran who fifty years before had heard Mandeville discourse at his club, and had been shown by Sir Hans
Sloane over his collection of curiosities at a time when
the British Museum was yet in the future. People
hardly remembered that he was a colonist, and were as
proud of his European reputation as if he had been the
native of an English county, and the scholar of an English university. He returned the feeling. He loved
our country, and all parts of it. At Dublin he had

been greeted with the irresistible welcome which Irishmen bestow upon those to whom they wish to do the
honours of Ireland.   He had spent in Scotland the six
happiest weeks of his life; and there, if circumstances
had permitted, he would gladly have passed the rest
of it.   And as for England, — "Of all the enviable
things," he said, " I envy it most its people.   Why
should that pretty island, which is but like a stepping-
stone in a brook, scarce enough of it above water to
keep one's shoes dry, enjoy in almost every neighbourhood more sensible, virtuous, and elegant minds than
we can collect in ranging a hundred leagues of our vast
forests?" [1]

He had long looked forward to the evening of life,
the last hours of which, in his cheerful view, were sure
to be the most joyous; and he had pleased himself with
the anticipation of dying, as he had been born and had
always lived, in "the King's dominions."   But now he
foresaw storms and troubles, and, at near seventy years
of age, he did not expect to see the end of them; as the
Ministers might read in a letter which they had thought
it worth their while to detain and violate.   That apprehension lent force and earnestness to the efforts which
he made in every quarter where his influence could
penetrate.   On the one hand he adjured the New Eng-

---

[1] In our own time, as in Franklin's, Americans are apt to express their
kindly sentiments towards England in diminutives, like a Russian who calls
the Empress his Little Mother.

> "An islet is a world," she said,
>   " When glory with its dust has blended,
> And Britain keeps her noble dead
>   Till earth and sea and skies are rended."
>
> .   .   .   .   .   .
>
> Nay, let our brothers of the West
>   Write smiling in their florid pages ;
> ' One-half her soil has walked the rest
>   In poets, heroes, martyrs, sages.' "

The verses are by Wendell Holmes ;   and the idea, or something like it,
has passed across the fancy of many a one of his countrymen beneath the
limes of Stratford-on-Avon churchyard, or in the transepts of Westminster
Abbey.

landers to reflect that, just as among friends every affront was not worth a duel, so between the mother-country and the colonies every mistake in government, and every encroachment on right, was not worth a rebellion. On the other hand, he took care that any British statesman to whose ears he could obtain access should hear the words of reason and soberness; and the best of them regarded him as a valuable coadjutor in preserving the peace of the Empire. Chatham, in the House of Lords, openly said that, if he were first minister, he should not scruple publicly to call to his assistance a man whom all Europe held in high estimation for his knowledge and wisdom, and classed with Boyle and Newton as an honour, not to the English nation only, but to human nature.

Most unfortunately, at this exact moment, Franklin became the centre of one of those unhappy scandals which in a season of political perturbation are certain to occur; and which are made the very most of by able men who mean mischief, and by the multitude, who do not understand the deeper issues, but can be voluble on a personal question. There had reached his hands a mass of correspondence which proved beyond any manner of doubt that Hutchinson and Oliver, the Governor and Lieutenant-Governor of Massachusetts, had persistently applied themselves to inflame the minds of the home authorities against the colony, and had been profuse in the suggestion of schemes framed with the object of destroying its liberties. The letters were private; but Franklin, as agent for Massachusetts, thought it incumbent upon him to send them to the Speaker of her Assembly; and he continued to think so until his life's end, though it was not a subject on which he loved to talk. It is a sound rule that confidential correspondence should, under no circumstances whatever, be used for the purpose of damaging a political adversary. In our own day, private letters attributed to a celebrated public man were printed in a great newspaper; and the step was defended on the ground that the writer was a public enemy, whose exposure was demanded by the interests of the State. That argument must have presented itself in its utmost force to the agent of a colony, when he lighted on the discovery that men, — born and reared within its confines, eating its bread and charged with its welfare, — had done their utmost to misrepresent its people, to destroy its chartered rights, and to bring upon it the insult, the hardship, and the fearful perils of a penal military occupation.

And, again, it must be remembered that the sanctity of the Post Office was then a transparent fiction. No man's correspondence was safe ; and those who suffered the most were tempted, when the occasion offered, to repay their persecutors in kind. The confidential clerks of the Postmaster-General were sometimes engaged twelve hours on a stretch in rifling private letters. The King, to judge by the endorsements in his own hand, — which marked the hour and minute when he received each packet of intercepted documents, and the hour and minute when he returned it to the Office, — must have passed a great deal of his time in reading them. A politician, when his turn came to be out in the cold, recognised the liability to have his letters opened as one of the incidents of Opposition, and did not expect even the poor compliment of having them reclosed with any decent appearance of concealing the treatment to which they had been subjected. "To avoid the impertinence of a Post Office," wrote Lord Charlemont to Edmund Burke, "I take the opportunity of sending this by a private hand;" and Hans Stanley, a public servant of considerable note in his day, complained to Mr. Grenville that all his correspondence, important or trivial, "had been opened in a very awkward and bungling manner."

Bold men, with a secure social position and a touch of humour, made use of the opportunity in order to give their opponents in the Cabinet a piece of their mind under circumstances such that it could not be resented. A friend of George Selwyn regaled him with a personal

anecdote, rather abstruse in itself, and rendered hopelessly unintelligible by being couched in bad Latin. " I
wrote this," he says, "to perplex Lord Grantham, who
may probably open the letter." " I don't know," Rigby
told the Duke of Bedford, "who is to read this letter,
whether French ministers or English ministers; but I
am not guarded in what I write, as I choose the latter
should know through every possible channel the utter
contempt I bear them." [1] But a system which was no
worse than a tiresome and offensive joke to men of the
world, who wore swords, and met the Postmaster-General on equal terms every other evening at White's or
Almack's, had its real terrors for humble people. A
gentleman wrote from London to New York, with nothing more treasonous to say than that he was concerned
at the alarming and critical situation. He expressed
himself, however, as fearing that his American letters,
to judge by the red wax over a black wafer, were
opened in the Post Office; and he justly observed that
intercourse between friend and friend was rendered pre-
carious by such conduct on the part of the authorities.
Franklin himself had the same grievance against the
British Government, and took it very coolly. Many
months before the war broke out he had occasion thus
to warn his sister in Boston: " I am apprehensive that
the letters between us, though very innocent ones, are
intercepted. They might restore to me yours at least,
after reading them; especially as I never complain of
broken, patched-up seals." " I am told," he said on
another occasion, "that Administration is possessed of
most of my letters sent, or received, on public affairs for
some years past; copies of them having been obtained
from the files of the several Assemblies, or as they
passed through the Post Office. I do not condemn
their ministerial industry, or complain of it."

[1] The letter, good reading like everything of Rigby's, referred to the
composition of Rockingham's first Government. "Their Board of Trade,"
he wrote, "is not yet fixed, except Lord Dartmouth for its head, who I
don't hear has yet recommended Whitefield for the bishopric of Quebec."

Whether Franklin was justified in his own sight by high considerations of policy, or by the bad example of the British Post Office, his conduct required no defence in the view of his employers beyond the water. He had intended the letters to be seen by about as many pairs of eyes as those which, in London official circles, had the privilege of prying into his own correspondence; and his object was to enlighten certain leading men of the colony, belonging to both parties, with regard to the character of the Governor, and to put them on their guard against his machinations. But such secrets are hard to keep when men's minds are in a ferment, and when great events are in the air. The Massachusetts Assembly insisted on having the letters. On the second of June, 1773, the House, sitting within closed doors, heard them read by Samuel Adams, and voted, by a hundred and one to five, that their tendency and design was to subvert the constitution of the Government, and to introduce arbitrary power into the Province. Before another month was out they had been discussed in all the farmhouses, and denounced from almost all the pulpits. They came upon the community as a revelation from the nether world, and everywhere aroused unaffected astonishment and regret, which soon gave place to resentment and alarm. "These men," (it was said with a unanimity which the majority of twenty to one in the Assembly inadequately represented,) "no strangers or foreigners, but bone of our bone, flesh of our flesh, born and educated among us," have alienated from us the affections of our sovereign, have destroyed the harmony and good-will which existed between Great Britain and Massachusetts, and, having already caused bloodshed in our streets, will, if unchecked, plunge our country into all the horrors of civil war.

The sentiments of the colony were embodied by the Assembly in an address to the King, stating the case against Hutchinson and Oliver in terms which cannot be described as immoderate, and still less as disrespectful; and humbly, but most pointedly, praying for their removal from office. Franklin placed the petition in the hands of the Secretary of State, for presentation to his Majesty at the first convenient opportunity; and Dartmouth, in return, expressed his pleasure that a sincere disposition prevailed in the people of Massachusetts to be on good terms with the mother-country, and his earnest hope that the time was at no great distance when every ground of uneasiness would cease, and tranquillity and happiness would be restored.

Dartmouth's intuitions, as usual, were good and wise. The opportunity had come for the mother-country to assume an attitude of true superiority. An ancient and powerful State, in its dealings with dependencies whose social system is still primitive, and whose public men are as yet untrained, can afford to make allowance for faults of taste, or even for breaches of official custom and propriety. But dignified self-restraint was not then the order of the day in high places. The complaint of Massachusetts against her Governors was referred to the Privy Council, and the Solicitor-General appeared on behalf of Hutchinson and Oliver to oppose the prayer of the petition. That Solicitor-General was Wedderburn, who, before he joined the Government, had told them in debate that their policy would inevitably ruin the country by the total loss of its American dominions; and that, if for reasons which could not be made public such a policy must be continued, Lord North would have to remain in office, as no man of honour or respectability would undertake to do the duties of his situation.

It was put about town that the famous advocate intended to handle Dr. Franklin in a style which would be worth the hearing. Privy Councillors attended in such numbers that they would almost have made a quorum in the House of Commons. At the bar stood rows of distinguished strangers, more worthy of the title than those who are ordinarily designated by it on such occasions, for Burke, and Priestley, and Jeremy Bentham were among them. The ante-room and passages were

thronged with people who had to content themselves
with learning, from the tones of his voice, that a great
orator was speaking contemptuously of some one.   For
the Solicitor was as good as his word.   Leaving aside
the merits of the question, he directed against Franklin
a personal attack which was a masterpiece of invective.
The judges in the case, encouraged by the undisguised
delight of their Lord President, rolled in their seats and
roared with laughter.   Lord North, alone among the
five and thirty, listened with gravity in his features and,
(it may be believed,) with something like death in his
heart.   Franklin, as a friend who closely observed his
bearing relates, "stood conspicuously erect, without the
smallest movement of any part of his body.   The
muscles of his face had been previously composed, so
as to afford a tranquil expression of countenance, and
he did not suffer the slightest alteration of it to appear
during the continuance of the speech."   He wore a full
dress suit of spotted Manchester velvet, which that
evening retired into the recesses of his wardrobe.   It
reappeared on the sixth of February, 1778, when he
affixed his signature to that treaty with France by
which the United States took rank as an independent
nation, and obtained a powerful ally.   So smart a coat
attracted the notice of his brother Commissioners, accustomed to see him in the staid and almost patriarchal
costume which all Paris knew.   They conjectured, and
rightly, that it was the first day, since the scene at the
Privy Council Office, on which he cared to be reminded
of what had occurred there.[1]

The immediate effect of Wedderburn's harangue, as
an appeal to men sitting in a judicial capacity, has in
our country never been surpassed ; and its ultimate consequences went far beyond the special issue towards
which it was directed.   Twenty years afterwards, when
Franklin's pamphlet entitled "Rules for Reducing a
great Empire to a small one" was republished in London, the editor paid to Lord Loughborough a compli-

[1] Attention is invited to the Third Appendix at the end of the volume.

ment which, as Alexander Wedderburn, he had justly earned. "When I reflect," such were the words of the Dedication, " on your Lordship's magnanimous conduct towards the author of the following Rules, there is a peculiar propriety in dedicating this new edition of them to a nobleman whose talents were so eminently useful in procuring the emancipation of our American brethren." [1]

In such a temper, and with such an example to guide them, the Houses of Parliament applied themselves to the question of the hour. When Privy Councillors, duly appointed to try an issue in their judicial capacity, had laughed the colonists out of court, it was not to be expected that the rank and file of a political assembly would grant them a patient, or even so much as a decent, hearing. England had open before her one policy which was prudent, and another which, at the worst, was not ignoble. Clemency and forbearance were her true wisdom; but, if she resolved to punish, she should have done so in a manner worthy of a great nation. The crime, since a crime it was adjudged to be, was common to the four chief cities of America. Phila-delphia had led the way in voting for resistance; Charleston had followed suit; and it was not till weeks had elapsed that Boston, on the same day as New York, adopted the Resolutions which had been passed in Philadelphia. Those Resolutions had been made good in action, by each of the places concerned, with just as

[1] Nearly thirty years afterwards Charles Fox reminded the House of Commons that fine speeches sometimes cost the country more than the gratification of listening to them was worth. "I remember a time," (he said,) "when the whole of the Privy Council came away, throwing up their caps, and exulting in an extraordinary manner at a speech made by the present Lord Rosslyn, (then Mr. Wedderburn;) and an examina-tion of Doctor Franklin, in which that respectable character was most uncommonly badgered. But we paid very dear for that splendid speci-men of eloquence, and all its attendant tropes, figures, metaphors, and hyperboles; for then came the bill; and in the end we lost all our American colonies, a hundred millions of money, and a hundred thousand of our brave fellow-subjects."

much, or as little, violence as under the circumstances of the special case was needed in order to do the work thoroughly. The British Ministry should have resorted to forgiveness and concession, or to a general and impartial severity. But neither of those two courses pleased the King and his advisers; and the opportunity was taken for exacting a vindictive penalty from one small, exposed, and, (as it was believed,) unwarlike and defenceless community.

Boston had done the same as the others, and had done it under the provocation of having been dragooned, in time of universal peace, for faults to which not one member of Parliament in ten could have put a name, if he had set his mind to think them over. But, where antipathy exists, men soon find reasons to justify it; and the drop-scene of the impending American drama, as presented to British eyes, was a picture of the New England character daubed in colours which resembled the original as little as they matched each other. The men of Massachusetts were sly and turbulent, puritans and scoundrels, pugnacious ruffians and arrant cowards. That was the constant theme of the newspapers, and the favourite topic with those officers of the army of occupation whose letters had gone the round of London clubs and English country houses. The archives of the Secretary of State were full of trite calumnies and foolish prophecies. Bostonians, (so Lord Dartmouth was informed by an officious correspondent,) were not only the worst of subjects, but the most immoral of men. "If large and loud professions of the Gospel be an exact criterion of vital religion, they are the best people on earth. But if meekness, gentleness, and patience constitute any part, those qualities are not found there. If they could maintain a state of independence, they would soon be at war among themselves."[1] Such was the forecast with regard to a city whose inhabitants were destined through a long future to enjoy in quite exceptional measure the blessings of mutual esteem, and

[1] *Dartmouth Manuscripts;* vol. ii., Letter of February, 1774.

of the internal peace which ensues from it. It was a specimen of the predictions which at that moment obtained belief in Parliament and in the country.[1]

The cue was given from above. On the seventh of March, 1774, Lord North communicated to the House of Commons a royal message, referring to the unwarrantable practices concerted and carried on in North America, and dwelling more particularly on the violent proceedings at the town and port of Boston in the province of Massachusetts Bay. The fact was that George the Third had seen General Gage, fresh from America; one of those mischievous public servants who know a colony so much better than the colonists know it themselves. " His language," said the King, " was very consonant to his character of an honest determined man. He says they will be lyons, whilst we are lambs; but, if we take the resolute part, they will undoubtedly prove very weak." His Majesty therefore desired Lord North not to repeat what he described as " the fatal compliance in 1766," — that repeal of the Stamp Act to which, in the royal view, all the difficulties of the present situation were owing. The Minister was directed to send for the General, and hear his ideas on the mode of compelling the Bostonians to acquiesce submissively in whatever fate might be reserved for them.

---

[1] Public writers, who supported the Ministry, endeavoured to affix the sole responsibility on Boston. Jonas Hanway replied to Paine's celebrated pamphlet by a Volume entitled "Common Sense ; in nine Conferences between a British Merchant, and a candid Merchant of America, in their private capacities as friends." The book included a conversation which had been overheard between a Shopman and a Mechanic.

" *Mechanic.* It is the New Englanders who make all the pother ? "

" *Shopman.* They are at the bottom of it. I do not see what any of the other colonies have to do with the punishment of an offence which they are not accused of. Their lawful trade is left as free as ever ; and of Boston the punishment was soft and merciful."

Hanway knew everything about tea, against which he was perpetually railing in print as the most pernicious of all human discoveries. He must have heard how the East India Company's ships had been treated at New York and Charleston, Philadelphia and Annapolis ; and he could not have believed that Boston stood alone in her iniquity. But such is political controversy.

The world soon learned what was in store for the unhappy city. On the fourteenth of March Lord North
introduced a bill for closing its harbour, and transferring
the business of the Custom-house to the port of Salem.
If the measure became law, (so he foretold in the affected
lightness of his heart), the presence of four or five frigates in Massachusetts Bay, without an additional regiment on Massachusetts soil, would at once place the
guilty municipality for purposes of foreign trade at a
distance of seventeen miles from the sea. Parliament
might well be flattered by the assurance that, in the
evenings of a week, it could do for the detriment of Boston four times that which the forces of nature had taken
eighteen centuries to do for Ravenna. The Government
majority was in a mood to believe anything. One of
their number, to whom the House listened while those
who spoke on behalf of the incriminated town were interrupted or silenced, declared that, if every dwelling in
it was knocked about the ears of its townsmen, they
would get no more than their deserts. He urged that
that nest of locusts should be extirpated, and enforced
his appeal by the famous sentence in which Cato adjured
the Roman Senate to demolish Carthage. A poor little
Carthage where every child attended school, and no man
was a professional soldier ; with its open streets, its unprotected quays, and a powerful force of legionaries
already quartered in its citadel !

That was the first blow; and others fell in rapid succession. On the twenty-eighth of March the Prime
Minister explained the plan of a measure by which he
purposed to extinguish self-government in Massachusetts. The bill, stringent in the earlier draft, was
altered for the harsher and the worse before it was laid
on the table. Lord George Germaine, in whom, not so
very long before, the Rockinghams had been fond
enough to discern their possible parliamentary leader,
commented upon the proposal of the Government as
well meant, but far too weak. He cordially approved
the provisions by which a town meeting might only be

held under permission from the Governor. Why, he asked, should men of a mercantile cast collect together, and debate on political matters, when they ought to be minding their private business? But the bill would only cover half the ground, and the least important half, so long as the central Council of the Colony was a tumultuous rabble, meddling with affairs of State which they were unable to understand. That Council, in his opinion, should be reconstructed on the model of the House of Peers. Lord North thanked the orator, (and a real orator even his former friends admitted that on this occasion he had proved himself to be,) for a suggestion "worthy of his great mind." On the fifteenth of April the bill was presented to the House with the addition of words enacting that the Council, in whose selection the Assembly under the existing constitution had a voice, should be nominated exclusively by the Crown.[1]

Governor Pownall, who had learned the institutions and geography of Massachusetts by ruling it on the spot, reminded the House that it was not a question of Boston only. If the measure was carried, local business could not be transacted in the furthest corner of Maine, unless special leave to hold a Town-meeting had been obtained from a Governor resident at the other end of three hundred miles of bad roads and forest tracks. Burke, very ill heard by an assembly which professed to regard a colonial Council as a riotous rabble, called in vain for the exercise of care and deliberation. They were engaged, he said, on nothing lighter than the proscription of a province : an undertaking which, whether they desired it or not, would expand itself ere long into the proscription of a nation. And Savile, begging that attention might be granted him during the length of a single sentence, exclaimed that a charter, which conveyed a sacred right, should not be broken without first

---

[1] "It was a year," wrote Horace Walpole, "of fine harangues ; " and he instanced especially Wedderburn against Franklin, Burke on the Tea-duty, and Lord George Germaine on the government of Massachusetts. — *Last Journals*, April, 1774.

hearing what might be put forward in defence of it by
those who lived beneath its safeguard. But such considerations were not to the purpose of the audience. It
was one of those moments when the talk and tone of
society have greater influence than the arguments of
debate; and a squire, who had recently been made a
baronet, gave the House a sample of what passed current in the lobby as a valuable contribution towards the
right understanding of the American question. Level-
ling principles, this gentleman affirmed, prevailed in New
England, and he had the best of reasons for stating it.
He had an acquaintance who called at a merchant's
house in Boston, and asked the servant if his master
was at home. "My master!" the man replied. "I
have no master but Jesus Christ."

The bill for annulling the charter was accompanied
by another for the Impartial Administration of Justice
in Massachusetts Bay : which was a fine name for a law
empowering the Governor, if any magistrate, revenue
officer, or military man was indicted for murder, to send
him to England for trial in the King's Bench. Barré
and Conway challenged Lord North to produce a single
example of a government servant who, having been
charged with a capital offence, had suffered from the
injustice of an American tribunal. They recalled to
the memory of Parliament, (so short if the good deeds
of those whom it disliked were in question,) how, at a
time when public feeling in the colony was at a height
which in the future never could be over-passed, Captain
Preston and his soldiers, after the fairest of fair trials,
had been acquitted by "an American jury, a New
England jury, a Boston jury." And now it was proposed to remove the cognisance of grave political
offences from a court without fear and without favour,
to one which was notoriously ready, — as Wilkes had
experienced, — to subserve the vengeance of Ministers,
and which, if the occasion arose, would be even more
willing to make itself the instrument of their misplaced
lenity. The Government supporters took no notice

whatsoever of Captain Preston's acquittal, though it was a concrete instance so recent, and so much in point, that it ought to have coloured and permeated the entire discussion. After the usual fashion of a party which has plenty of votes, and no case, they wandered far and wide over the whole colonial controversy. The most admired speech was that of young Lord Caermarthen, who denied the right of Americans to complain that they were taxed without being represented, when such places as Manchester, — and, he might have added, Leeds, and Sheffield, and Birmingham, — had no members of their own in the British Parliament. It was indeed a magnificent anticipation of the calling in of the New World to balance the inequalities of the old. The debate was wound up by the gentleman who had compared Boston to Carthage. Speaking this time in English, he recommended the Government, if the people of Massachusetts did not take their chastisement kindly, to burn their woods, and leave their country open to the operations of the military. It was better, he said, that those regions should be ruined by our own soldiers than wrested from us by our rebellious children.

The effect of Lord Caermarthen's allusion to unrepresented Manchester, as justifying the taxation of unrepresented America, was so great that four days afterwards Burke thought it worthy of a refutation. " So then," he said, " because some towns in England are not represented, America is to have no representative at all. They are our children ; but, when children ask for bread, we are not to give them a stone. When this child of ours wishes to assimilate to its parent, and to reflect with true filial resemblance the beauteous countenance of British liberty, are we to turn to them the shameful parts of our constitution ? Are we to give them our weakness for their strength, our opprobrium for their glory ? "

Even after the lapse of a century and a quarter these debates are not pleasant reading for an Englishman. They went far to justify Turgot in his wonder that a country, which had cultivated with so much success all the branches of natural science, should remain so completely below itself in the science the most interesting of all, that of public happiness.[1] The best which could be said for the policy adopted by Parliament was that a great country should stand upon its rights against everybody, and at all hazards. But kindred States, like the members of a family, sometimes do well to refrain from insisting on advantages which the law, if strictly read, allows them to take. "There was a time," (wrote Philip Francis, putting into five lines the moral of the whole story,) "when I could reason as logically and passionately as anybody against the Americans; but, since I have been obliged to study the book of wisdom, I have dismissed logic out of my library. The fate of nations must not be tried by forms." Passion had more to do than logic with the undertaking which occupied the two Houses during the spring of 1774. If preambles spoke the truth, it should have been stated broadly and plainly at the head of each of those fatal bills that, whereas the inhabitants of the capital city of Massachusetts Bay had incurred the displeasure of his Majesty and this present Parliament, it was adjudged necessary and expedient to pay the colony out. That was the object aimed at; and it was pursued with all the disregard of appearances which had marked the proceedings of the same House of Commons in its crusade against the electors of Middlesex, and with still greater indifference to consequences. The members of the majority forgot that in the long run it did not lie with them to decide that Boston, and Boston alone, should have to answer for a course of conduct in which four colonies had taken part, and which commanded the sympathy of all the others. They credited communities of their own race and blood with the baseness of consenting to sit quiet while one of their number was ruined for having done its share loyally, if somewhat boisterously, in an enterprise to which all were pledged. In

[1] Letter from Turgot to Dr. Price; March 22, 1778.

the optimism of their resentment they ignored human
nature, and put out of their recollection the unanimity
of America in her resistance to the Stamp Act; and in
their heat and haste they thrust out of sight the dignity
of debate, the rights of a parliamentary minority, and
even a show of fair play towards the people whose
freedom and prosperity they were intent on destroying.

The Americans who resided in London, or who found
themselves there in the course of travel, petitioned that
one of their cities should not be visited with unexampled
rigour before it was so much as apprised that any accu-
sation had been brought against it. Their prayer was
treated with silent contempt; but something more than
silent contempt was required to stifle the voice of the
true friends of England and of America within the
walls of St. Stephen's. Insolence and intolerance not
often before ran so high, or were directed against statesmen of such established character and standing. Barré
had to sit down before he had finished his say. Conway, for the crime of imploring the House, in a very
familiar Latin phrase, to hear the other side, was
shouted down by men who had listened to a fool when
he treated them to the quotation of " Delenda est Car-
thago." General Burgoyne expressed a wish, (and he
had better reason than he then knew for wishing it,) to see
America convinced by persuasion rather than the sword;
and the sentiment raised as great a storm as if it had
been a piece of impudent disloyalty. Johnstone, a dash-
ing sailor, who had been governor of Florida, contrived
to tell the House that the work on which they were
engaged would produce a confederacy of the colonies,
and would end in a general revolt; but the roisterers on
the benches opposite soon taught him that he had
brought his knowledge of America to the wrong
market.

Such was the treatment of men each of whom had
used a pistol in battle, and was ready for one on very
short notice in the ring of Hyde Park; for Johnstone
was a noted fire-eater, and Burgoyne, though good-

natured, never allowed a joke to go too far.[1] It may well be believed that things were still worse for civilians who had no better title to a respectful hearing than an acquaintance with the subject of debate, and a desire to place their views fairly and briefly before their colleagues. The speeches of ex-Governor Pownall, of Alderman Sawbridge, and the other more persistent opponents of the ministerial policy, were seldom allowed to die a natural death.   Burke himself, though he held the House while addressing it on bye-issues, had to contend against noise and ostentatious impertinence when he applied himself to the main question of the Government legislation. High-handed tactics are often at the time successful; and the whole batch of measures — including a bill for removing the legal difficulties which hitherto had preserved the American householder from the infliction of having soldiers quartered under his private roof — were placed on the Statute-book without abridgement or essential alteration.

The third great blunder had now been committed; and, as in the two former cases, the effect was soon visible in a shape very different from what had been expected.   The despatch of the troops led to the Boston massacre; the imposition and retention of the Tea-duty produced the world-famed scene in Boston harbour; and the result of the four penal Acts was to involve Great Britain in an unnecessary and unprofitable war with exactly as many powerful nations.   The main

[1] During a contested election in Lancashire a party of Burgoyne's political opponents met in a bar-room, and devised a scheme for what they described as "trotting the General."   A certain James Elton pulled out a valuable watch, and handed it to Burgoyne's servant, with the injunction that he should take it to his master, and request him to say whether he could tell the time of day.   Burgoyne placed the watch on a tray together with a pair of pistols, and desired his man to bring it after him to the inn where the party was assembled.   He went round the circle asking each of them whether he was the owner of the watch.   When no one claimed it, Burgoyne turned to his servant and said : "Since the watch belongs to none of these gentlemen, you may take it, and fob it, in remembrance of the Swan Inn at Bolton."   As any one who knew old Lancashire might readily believe, the real owner went by the name of Jemmy Trotter to his dying hour.

responsibility rested with the Government and their followers; but the Opposition were not free from blame. They allowed the Address in reply to the royal message to pass unchallenged, and they let the Boston Port bill go through all its stages without calling for a division. They voted against the two other principal bills on the third reading, with about as much effect as if the governor of a fortress was to reserve the fire of his batteries until the enemy had carried their sap beyond the counterscarp. Cowed by the aspect of the benches in front of them, uncertain as to the feeling in the country, and afraid to put it to the test by giving a vigorous lead to those wiser tendencies which largely prevailed in the great commercial centres,[1] they made a very poor fight in the Commons. The House of Lords almost shone by comparison. Rockingham, who wanted self-confidence but not conviction, put force enough upon himself to take a prominent part in the debate; and in private he spared no remonstrances in order to keep in the path of duty those among his friends who showed hesitation. Lord Chatham was despondent, and most unhappy. "America," he wrote, "sits heavy on my mind. India is a perpetual source of regrets. There, where I have garnered up my heart, where our strength lay, and our happiest resources presented themselves, it is all changed into danger, weakness, distraction, and vulnerability." He was not well enough to take a share in the earlier discussions; and his speech, when at length he broke silence, was rather a funeral oration over the departed peace and security of the Empire than a summons to political conflict.

But men do not look to the Upper House for the delay and mitigation of a coercion bill; and the Ministers won all along the line with an ease which surprised themselves, and even their Royal master, who knew the

---

[1] "The landed property, except some of the most sensible, are, as natural, for violent measures. The interest of the commercial part is very decidedly on the other side, and their passions are taking that turn." Shelburne wrote thus to Chatham as early as April the Fourth, 1774.

probabilities of politics as well as any man alive. His jubilation had no bounds. In four separate letters he could not find an adjective short of "infinite" to express the measure of his satisfaction over every fresh proof of the irresolution displayed by the Opposition. But in his own view he owed them no thanks. Their feebleness and futility, (such were the epithets which he applied to them,) were an involuntary tribute to the irresistible excellence of the ministerial legislation, and only procured them his disdain without detracting anything from his displeasure. So far from being touched by their submissive conduct, he was all the more indignant if ever they showed a spark of spirit. When they spoke and voted in favour of receiving a petition from an American gentleman in London, a former agent for Massachusetts, who prayed that the fate of the colony might not be finally decided until letters had travelled to and fro across the water, the King pronounced that the Opposition had violated the laws of decency, but that nothing better was to be expected from men who were reduced to such low shifts. He had a right to enjoy his triumph. By sheer strength of purpose he had imposed his favourite measures on the Cabinet; and the Cabinet had carried them through Parliament as smoothly as, — before Fox's day and after it, though not during it, — bills for the restraint or the suppression of liberty so often passed.

Fox's day was not yet. Everybody was talking about him; and behind his back little was said that was complimentary, and a great deal that was abundantly silly. But some veterans of public life, who remembered their own mistakes and excesses at an age more advanced than his, regarded his future with hope, and his past with amused indulgence. Chatham had his notice called to the tattle which represented the ex-Lord of the Treasury as a premature intriguer, encouraged in his mutiny by certain members of the Cabinet, who in their turn had acted on a hint from the exalted quarter which was then called the Closet. "The part of Mr. Fox," wrote the old statesman, "must naturally beget speculations. It may however be all resolved, without going deeper, into youth and warm blood. " At this point in his career, (said one who watched him narrowly and not unkindly,) it was no longer a question of shining by speeches, for he could scarce outdo what he had done already. The work which lay before him was to retrieve his character by reforming it, to practise industry and application, and to court instead of to defy mankind.[1]

If Fox was to be of use to his generation, his position in the House of Commons had still to be made ; and of that no one was more conscious than himself. Sorrow had caused him to think, and reflection had brought self-knowledge. He set no undue store on the gifts which came to him by nature, and he was acutely aware of the defects which were in full proportion to his extraordinary qualities. Strong in the unwonted sensation of being on his guard and his good behaviour, he at once adopted an independent but not a pretentious attitude, and maintained it with diligence, forethought, moderation, and even modesty. Leaving, as he safely could, the form of his speaking to take care of itself, he devoted his exclusive attention to the substance of it, and to the practical effect of the policy which he recommended. He began by a protest against the determination of the Speaker to exclude strangers from the gallery; so that a series of debates, which were to fix the destinies of the English-speaking world, might not be conducted in secret conclave. He stoutly objected to the clause which vested the responsibility of reopening Boston harbour, whenever the time came for it, with the Crown instead of with Parliament. When, by way of answer, he was accused of desiring to rob the King of his most valued prerogative, the opportunity of showing mercy, he allowed the courtly argument to pass without satirical comment. He contented himself with insisting that his motion to omit that clause, together with another which was more questionable still, should be put and nega-

[1] Chatham to Shelburne ; March 6, 1774. *Last Journals of Walpole ;* February, 1774.

tived ; in order that it might stand on record in the journals how, amidst the general panic, at least one member
of Parliament had objected to something which the
Government had demanded.

Fox spoke briefly, but not infrequently, on the other
bills relating to America; more especially when their
details were being arranged in Committee. On the
nineteenth of April the House of Commons considered a
motion to repeal the Tea-duty, which was brought forward by a private member. Burke signalised the evening by a splendid oration. Assisted by a comparison of
the notes furtively taken by various Honourable Gentlemen in the crown of their hats, he subsequently wrote
it out from memory, and saved it for a world which must
otherwise have been the poorer. The Government supporters would have refused to listen to Cicero denouncing Antony, if the performance had trenched upon the
Government time ; but, as it was an off-night, they gave
themselves up with a clear conscience for two livelong
hours to the enjoyment of the speech, which, among
other notable passages, contained a biographical account
of Charles Townshend as copious as the discourse of
an incoming French Academician over his deceased
predecessor. Even after such a feast of rhetoric they
were willing to hear Charles Fox, though they would
hear no one else on the same side. The latest words
of reason which the House accepted before it went
to a division, (and both Barré and Burgoyne tried to
address it,) were those in which the young man defined
the case in language as plain as his exposition of it was
accurate and adequate. A tax, he said, could only be
laid for three purposes : as a commercial regulation, for
the raising of revenue, or in order to assert a right. As
to the first two purposes, the Minister denied that he
had them even in mind ; while the so-called right of
taxation was asserted to justify an armed interference
on the part of Great Britain, and that interference would
have the inevitable consequence of irritating the American colonies into open rebellion.

For the first time in his life Fox looked only to what
was just and prudent in speech and action ; and he did
not endeavour, or expect, to attract a personal following.
One sworn partisan he always was sure of having.
Poor Stephen's heart was in the right place in his great
body. He stood by his brother through the darkest hour
of his fortunes, and attended him gallantly and jauntily
in his wise endeavours, as he had so often done in his
hare-brained courses. In the House, which was almost
identical with the fashionable world, Stephen was something of a favourite in spite of his faults, and even, it is
to be feared, on account of them. He took his share in
the uphill conflict ; and on the second of May, when
the Charter of Massachusetts was under consideration,
he delivered himself in phrases which were worthy of his
father's son in their manly common sense, and of his
son's father in their broad humanity. " I rise, sir," he
said. "with an utter detestation and abhorrence of the
present measures. We are either to treat the Americans
as subjects or as rebels. If we treat them as subjects,
the bill goes too far ; if as rebels, it does not go far
enough. We have refused to hear the parties in their
defence ; and we are going to destroy their charter without knowing the constitution of their Government."

Those were the last sentences which Stephen Fox is
known to have uttered in public ; for in two months he
was a peer, and within seven months he died. By that
time Charles had made good his ground in public estimation, and had secured a solid base of operations from
which he was soon to advance fast and far. Parliament
was very ready to forget and forgive in the case of a scion
of an old and famous parliamentary family. He had not
tried to shine ; he had placed to his account no transcendent effort ; and his colleagues liked him all the
better for his self-suppression, and admired him none
the less. But, whenever he addressed the House, he
had proved himself its potential master. Amidst a
tempest of violence and prejudice he alone among the
opponents of the Government never condescended to

begin with an apology, and never sate down without
having driven home all that he wished to say. He had
vindicated his right to argue a coercion bill as he would
have argued anything else, refusing to recognise the
hackneyed plea of public safety as an excuse for hurry
and slovenliness, and sturdily declining to mend his
pace under the pressure of public anger. Having
espoused the right cause, and fought for it like one who
was not ashamed of it, he brought an increased reputation, and an established authority, out of as sorry a business as Parliament had ever been engaged in. But he
was powerless to amend the Government measures.
The whole of the baleful harvest was safely garnered;
and, — amidst the Acts for paving and lighting streets,
and for widening and repairing county roads, with
which the Statute-book of 1774, like any other, is
crowded, — we still may read, in faded black and dingy
white, the dry and conventional text of those famous
laws that in their day set half the world on fire.

For the matter did not end when the bills had received
the Royal Assent. There was an Opposition beyond the
seas which was not kept from speaking out by the fear
of being called factious. The same ships that took over
copies of the Port Act, carried a parcel of Bibles and
prayer-books which Dartmouth entrusted for distribution
to a clergyman of Philadelphia, who wrote to report
the effect produced upon public opinion by the two
consignments. Personally, the good man expressed
nothing but gratitude towards his Lordship. The books
had been bestowed on those for whom they were intended, and there was every sign that they would be
blessed to the congregation ; but consternation prevailed
in Boston on hearing that their harbour was to be
blocked up, and all the colonies seemed to be united in
opposing the authority of Parliament.[1]

The worthy divine was correct in his reading of the
situation. But though a Pennsylvanian, whose judge-

[1] The Revd. William Stringer to Lord Dartmouth ; May 14, 1774.

ment was unclouded by the imminence of a terrible and incalculable danger, might already regard it as certain that the whole of America would make common cause, the future presented itself under a more dubious aspect to dwellers in the threatened city. "We have not men fit for the times," said John Adams in his private diary. "We are deficient in genius, in education, in travel, in fortune, in everything. I feel unutterable anxiety. God grant us wisdom and fortitude! Should this country submit, what infamy and ruin! Death, in any form, is less terrible." That was written for his own eyes alone; but the hour was too grave, and the men, and the women, around him too clear-sighted and resolute, for him to mince the truth even when writing to others. He reminded James Warren of Plymouth, who was as deep in the troubled waters as himself, of the ugly historical fact that people circumstanced like them had seldom grown old, or died in their beds. And to his wife he wrote : "We live, my dear soul, in an age of trial. What will be the consequence I know not. The town of Boston, for aught I can see, must suffer martyrdom. Our principal consolation is that it dies in a noble cause." That was the spirit in which the cowards of Boston met the announcement that they must bow their heads to the yoke, or fight against such odds as the world had never seen. The last time that Great Britain had exerted her full strength, she had beaten the French by land on three continents ; had established over France and Spain together an immeasurable superiority at sea ; and had secured for herself everything in both hemispheres which was best worth taking. Boston, on the other hand, contained five and thirty hundred ablebodied citizens ; and, in the view of her enemies, no population was ever composed of worse men and poorer creatures. So George the Third, his Ministers, and his army firmly believed ; and they engaged in the struggle armed with all the moral advantage which such a conviction gives.

Before America could be loyal to the people of Bos-

ton, it had first to be shown whether the people of Boston were true to themselves.   On the tenth of May the
intelligence arrived that the Assembly was henceforward
to sit, and the business of administration to be carried
on, in the town of Salem; and that the Custom-house
was to be removed to Marblehead, the principal landing
place in Salem harbour.   Three days afterwards General Gage arrived in Massachusetts Bay, with full powers
as Civil Governor of the colony, and as Commander-in-
Chief for the whole continent.   During those three days
the Committees of Correspondence which represented
Boston, and eight neighbouring villages, had quietly, and
rather sadly, taken up the glove which the giant Empire
had contemptuously flung to them.   They had got ready
their appeal to all the Assemblies of the continent, inviting a universal suspension of exports and imports;
promising to suffer for America with a becoming fortitude; confessing that singly they might find their trial
too severe; and entreating that they might not be left
to struggle alone, when the very existence of every
colony, as a free people, depended upon the event.
Brave words they were, and the inditing of them at such
a moment was in itself a deed; but something more
than pen and ink was required to parry the blows which
were now showered upon the town, and upon the State
of which it had already ceased to be the capital.

On the first of June the blockade of the harbour was
proclaimed, and the ruin and starvation of Boston at once
began.   The industry of a place which lived by building,
sailing, freighting, and unloading ships was annihilated
in a single moment.   The population, which had fed itself from the sea, would now have to subsist on the
bounty of others, conveyed across great distances by a
hastily devised system of land-carriage in a district
where the means of locomotion were unequal to such a
burden.   A city which conducted its internal communications by boat almost as much as Venice, and quite as
much as Stockholm, was henceforward divided into as
many isolated quarters as there were suburbs with salt

or brackish water lying between them. "The law,"
Mr. Bancroft writes in his History, "was executed with
a rigour that went beyond the intentions of its authors.
Not a scow could be manned by oars to bring an ox, or
a sheep, or a bundle of hay, from the islands. All water
carriage from pier to pier, though but of lumber, or
bricks, or kine, was forbidden. The boats that plied between Boston and Charlestown could not ferry a parcel
of goods across Charles River. The fishermen of
Marblehead, when they bestowed quintals of dried fish
on the poor of Boston, were obliged to transport their
offerings in waggons by a circuit of thirty miles." [1]
Lord North, when he pledged himself to place Boston
at a distance of seventeen miles from the sea, had been
almost twice as good as his word.

In a fortnight's time, as soon as the pinch began to be
felt, the troops came back into the town, sore and surly;
and a standing camp for two battalions was established
on Boston Common. Relief, or hope of relief, there was
none. Long before the summer was over the Constitution would be abolished; the old Councillors would be
displaced by Government nominees; and criminal and
civil cases would be tried by judges whose salaries the
Crown paid, and by juries which the Crown had packed.
The right of petition remained; but it was worth less
than nothing. A respectful statement of abuses, and a
humble prayer for their redress, was regarded by the
King and the Cabinet as a form of treason all the more
offensive because it could not be punished by law.
"When I see," said Franklin, "that complaints of grievances are so odious to Government that even the mere
pipe which conveys them becomes obnoxious, I am at
a loss to know how peace and union are to be maintained
or restored." A few weeks, or days, remained in which
the free voice of the country could still be heard; and
there were those who intended to take good care that its
latest accents should mean something. Early in June

[1] Bancroft's *History of the United States of America;* Epoch Third,
chapter iv.

the Assembly met at Salem.   On the seventeenth of the
month the House, behind locked doors, and with an attendance larger by a score than any that had yet been
known, took into consideration the question of inviting
the Thirteen Colonies to a general Congress.   The
Governor's secretary, on the wrong side of the keyhole,
read a message proclaiming that the Assembly was dissolved; but, when those, who had entered the room as
senators, filed out in their character of private citizens,
the work was past undoing.   The place named for the
Congress was Philadelphia; the date was to be the first
of September; and the five delegates for Massachusetts
had all been duly elected, including the pair of statesmen
whom Massachusetts Tories, by way of depreciation,
pleased themselves by calling the brace of Adamses.[1]

The note had been sounded sharp and clear, and the
response followed like an echo.   The first to rally were
those who had the most to gain by standing aloof.
James the Second, in the matter of the Declaration of
Indulgence, had failed to discover a bribe which would
tempt the English Nonconformists to assist him in per-
secuting even those who had persecuted *them ;* and their
descendants across the seas had not degenerated.   In
Marblehead and Salem together there were not found
eighty individuals, all told, who cared to play the part of
wreckers in the disaster which had befallen the good
ship Boston.   A much larger number of their fellow-
townsmen, in an address to General Gage, repudiated
any intention of being seduced by the prospect of their
own advantage into complicity with a course of action

---

[1] The name was started by an old ex-Governor in 1770, in a sentence
which began with the flavour of a Biblical reminiscence, but ran off into
another strain.   " Mr. Cushing I know, and Mr. Hancock I know ; but
where the devil this brace of Adamses came from I know not. "

In his Birthday Ode of the Fourth June William Whitehead, the poet
laureate, had drawn a much more pleasing picture of the attitude of
Massachusetts.

"The prodigal again returns,
    And on his parent's neck reclines.
With honest shame his bosom burns,
    And in his eye affection shines."

which, whether unjust or not from the point of view of
the Government, would on their own part be to the last
degree ungracious and unfriendly. "We must," they
said, "be lost to all feelings of humanity, could we indulge one thought to raise our fortunes on the ruin of
our suffering neighbours." To the Boston merchants
they offered the gratuitous use of their wharves and
warehouses, and promised to lade and unlade Boston
goods for nothing. And indeed they very soon took
the opportunity of the arrival from London of a bark,
with chests of tea on board, to treat the cargo in Boston
fashion, and so disqualify themselves for any further
marks of Royal and Ministerial favour.

Salem and Marblehead were forced by their circumstances to declare themselves at once; and, as the
provisions of the Act for regulating the government of
Massachusetts were successively put in force, the Townships of the colony, one after another, eagerly followed
suit. The new councillors were appointed on the King's
writ of mandamus, and twenty-five among them accepted
the office. It was the worst day's work they had ever
done for themselves, for their cause, and for the peace,
(and, in some unfortunate cases, for the fair reputation,)
of the neighbourhoods in which they severally resided.
For popular feeling ran high and fierce; and their
countrymen were determined that they should not serve,
to whatever lengths it might be necessary to go in
order to prevent them. Two thousand men marched
in companies on to the Common at Worcester, escort-
ing one of their townsmen whose abilities and personal
popularity had recommended him to the notice of the
Government, and formed a hollow square around him
while, with uncovered head, he read the resignation of
his seat at the Council Board. George Watson of Plymouth, who, in the stately language of the day, "possessed almost every virtue that can adorn and dignify
the human character," made known his intention of
assuming the proffered function. On the next Sunday
forenoon, when he took his accustomed place in the

meeting-house, his friends and familiar associates put on their hats and walked out beneath the eyes of the congregation. As they passed him he bent his head over the handle of his cane ; and, when the time arrived, he declined the oath of qualification. More violent methods, which in certain cases did not stop short of grotesque and even brutal horseplay,[1] were employed against less respected or more determined men. Of thirty-six who had received the King's summons, the majority either refused obedience from the first, or were persuaded or intimidated into withdrawing their consent to join the Council. The rest took sanctuary with the garrison in Boston ; and the tidings which came from their homes in the country districts made it certain that they would do very well to stay there.

The immediate vicinity of the soldiers was a preventive against outrages of which the best of the patriots were heartily ashamed ; but no body of troops could be large enough, or near enough, to deter New Englanders from acting as if they still possessed those municipal rights of which they had been deprived without a hearing. General Gage issued a proclamation warning all persons against attending Town-meetings ; and Town-meetings were held regularly, and were attended by larger numbers than ever. The men of Salem, towards whom he had special reasons for being unwilling to proceed to extremities, walked into the Town-house under his eyes, and between footways lined with his soldiers. Boston, whose character in official quarters had long been gone, was obliged to be more cautious. When called to account by the Governor, the Selectmen ad-

---

[1] Some rather cruel manifestations of popular wrath, employed during the American tumults, are new to history ; but the stock punishment of riding the rail was of old English County origin. In the Records of Worcestershire, for the year 1614, there is a memorandum that certain persons were bound over to appear at Sessions. "These three, with divers others, on Sunday the 4th October between 9 and 10 in the night, took Thomas Smith, Curate of Milton, and by violence put him upon a staffe, and carried him up and down the towne, and caused fiddlers to playe by him."

mitted that a meeting had been held; but it was a meeting, (so they argued,) which had been adjourned from a date anterior to the time when the Act came into force. Gage, who saw that, if this theory was accepted, the same meeting, by means of repeated adjournments, might be kept alive till the end of the century, reported the matter to his Council. The new Councillors pronounced themselves unable to advise him on a point of law, — that law which already had ceased to have force beyond the reach of a British bayonet; — but they took occasion to lay before his consideration the disordered state of the province, and the cruel plight to which his policy had reduced themselves.

When the day came round for the Courts of Justice to sit in their remodelled shape, the Judges were treated more tenderly as regarded their persons than the Mandamus Councillors, but with quite as little reverence for their office. They took their seats at Boston only to learn that those citizens, who had been returned as jurors, one and all refused the oath. A great multitude marched into Springfield, with drums and trumpets, and hoisted a black flag over the Court-house, as a sign of what any one might expect who entered it in an official capacity. At Worcester the members of the tribunal with all their staff walked in procession, safe and sorry, through a quarter of a mile of street lined on each side by people drawn up six deep. These militia-men, (for such they were,) had their Company officers to command them, and wanted nothing to make them a military force except the fire-arms which were standing ready at home, and which two out of every three amongst them could handle more effectively than an average European soldier. Wherever the Judges went, if once they were fairly inside a town, they were not allowed to leave it until they had plighted their honour that they would depart without transacting any legal business. After a succession of such experiences the Chief Justice and his colleagues waited upon the Governor, and represented to him that they must abandon the pretence of exercising their functions in a Province where there were no jurymen to listen to their charges, and where they could not even sit in court to do nothing unless the approaches were guarded by the best part of a brigade of British infantry.

The process of bringing Massachusetts into line with the Revolution was harsh, and sometimes ruthless. So far as any public opinion opposed to their own was in question, the patriots went on the principle of making the Province a solitude, and calling it unanimity. The earliest sufferers were Government servants. Clark Chandler, the Registrar of Probate at Worcester, had entered on the local records a remonstrance against action taken by the more advanced politicians among the citizens. He was called upon in open Town-meeting to erase the inscription from the books; and, when he showed signs of reluctance, his fingers were dipped in ink, and drawn to and fro across the page. The chaise of Benjamin Hallowell, a Commissioner of Customs, was pursued into Boston at a gallop by more than a hundred and fifty mounted men. Jonathan Sewall is known in the school histories of America as the recipient of a famous confidence. It was to him that John Adams, after they had travelled together as far as the parting of the ways, used those words of spirited tautology : "Swim or sink, live or die, survive or perish with my country, is my unalterable determination." Unfortunately for himself, Sewall was a law officer of the Crown as well as a bosom friend of the Crown's adversary. His elegant house in Cambridge was attacked by the mob. He was forced to retire to Boston, and subsequently to Europe, where, after long struggles and many sorrows, he died of a broken heart.

These were official people ; but their fate was shared by private gentlemen whose sins against liberty did not go beyond some rather violent and foolish ebullitions of speech. This one had hoped that the rebels would swing for it. That one had said that he should be glad to see the blood streaming from the hearts of the popular leaders ; and, in a milder mood, had contented himself with wishing that they might become turnspits in the kitchens of the English nobility. Another, while it was still a question whether Massachusetts should resist, or accept her punishment tractably, had a child baptized by the name of " Submit." Angry and idle, — for their life was now and henceforward one of enforced and unwelcome leisure, — they talked recklessly ; though most of them would not of their own accord have hurt a fly, let alone a fellow-citizen. They crowded the inns and boarding-houses of Boston, and the spare chambers of their city friends ; lingering on the very edge of the ocean before they started on a much longer flight, from which for most of them there was no returning.

Among those who had been expelled from their homes were some of the richest landowners in the province, — men who would have added respectability and distinction to any aristocracy in the world. Colonel Saltonstall was a good soldier, a just magistrate, and a kind neighbour ; but the mob of his district would not allow him to stay, and he went first to Boston, and then into exile. He refused to bear arms for the Crown, against so many old friends who would gladly have marched and fought under him if he had found it in his conscience to take service with the Continental army. He felt to the full such consolation as was afforded by the thought that he had done nothing with which to reproach himself. " I have had more satisfaction," he wrote from England, " in a private life here than I should have had in being next in command to General Washington." The Vassalls were a family of worth and honour, one of whom was grandfather of the Lady Holland who kept a salon and a dining-table for the Whigs of the great Reform Bill. John Vassall of Cambridge had no choice but to cross the seas with his kindred. His great property in Massachusetts was ultimately confiscated, after having been subjected to a course of systematised spoliation. His mansion-house at Cambridge became the headquarters of the Amer-

ican army. The Committee of Safety published a succession of orders, carefully regulating the distribution
of the produce on his estate ; and the Provincial Congress solemnly voted half a pint of rum a day to the
persons employed on cutting his crops, and those of his
fellow-refugees. Isaac Royall of Medford, to whom
hospitality was a passion, and the affection of all
around him, high and low, the prize which he coveted,
did not escape banishment and proscription. It was
lightly, but cruelly, said by his political opponents that
to carry on his farms in his absence was not an easy
matter; "for the honest man's scythe refused to cut
Tory grass, and his oxen to turn a Tory furrow." During the dreary years which lay before him, his cherished
wish was to be buried in Massachusetts; but that boon
was denied him. He died in England, before the war
was over, bequeathing two thousand acres of his neglected soil to endow a Chair in the famous university of
his native province which he himself was never permitted to revisit.

Women, whatever might be their opinions, were not
uncivilly treated. The habitual chivalry of Americans
was extended to every applicant for the benefit of it,
even if she might not always have been the most estimable of her sex. There was in Massachusetts a dame
of quality, who once had a face which contemporaries
described as of "matchless beauty," and a story very
closely resembling that of the notorious Lady Hamilton.
She had been the companion of a wealthy baronet,
Collector of the Customs for the Port of Boston. Those
Customs, with the license accorded to favoured place-
holders before the Revolution, he had contrived to collect while residing at his ease in the South of Europe.
He was frightened into marriage by the earthquake of
Lisbon; and after his death the widow returned to
America, to her late husband's country house, where
he had maintained what, for the New England of that
day, was a grand and lavish establishment. When the
troubles grew serious she was alarmed by the attitude

of the rural population, and asked leave to retire to Boston. The Provincial Congress furnished her with an escort, and passed a special Resolution permitting her to take into the city her horses, carriages, live-stock, trunks, bedding, and provisions. They detained nothing of hers except arms and ammunition, for which the lady had little use, and the patriots much. She got safe into Boston, and safe out of it to England, where she closed her career as the wife of a county banker.

Amenities such as these were not for every day or every person. There was one class of Government partisans which, in particular, fared very badly. It was frequently the case that a clergyman, accustomed to deal out instruction, held it incumbent upon him to inform laymen about matters in which they did not desire his guidance. Old Doctor Byles of Boston, though a stout Loyalist, had the good sense never to bring affairs of state inside the porch of his church. " In the first place," he told his people, " I do not understand politics. In the second place you all do, every man and mother's son of you. In the third place you have politics all the week; so pray let one day in the seven be devoted to religion. In the fourth place I am engaged on infinitely higher work. Name to me any subject of more consequence than the truth I bring to you, and I will preach on it the next Sabbath." That was his theory of duty; and it carried him unhurt, though not unthreatened, over the worst of the bad times. He continued to reside, through the war and for years after, in his native city; and he kept it alive by excellent jokes which no one relished more than the Whig officials who were usually the subjects of them. But others of his cloth were less prudent. Every minister of religion, who opposed the Crown, was inciting his congregation to armed revolt in the vein, and often with the very phrases, of the Old Testament Prophets; and for the ministers who supported the Crown to keep unbroken silence was more than human or clerical nature could endure. They delivered their souls, and were not long in discovering that those to whom they preached had no attribute of a flock about them except the name. One outspoken clergyman had bullets fired into his house. The pulpit of another was nailed up, and with some excuse, for he had announced from it that colonists who were shot by the royal soldiers would find that their punishment did not end in this life. A third, whose hearers complained that "his Toryism was most offensive," was put into the village pound, and had herrings thrown over for him to eat. The physicians as a rule adhered to the Crown; but, whatever might be the case with the spiritual needs of parishioners, the bodily health of citizens, actual and prospective, was not to be trifled with. The person of a medical man was very generally respected, and his property spared. The most dutiful Son of Liberty was willing to excuse his own forbearance by the explanation that doctors were indebted for their immunity from disciplinary treatment to "the exigencies of the ladies."

Massachusetts had stood by Boston; and it was soon evident that all the other colonies would stand by Massachusetts. The Port Act was carried through the American townships as swiftly as the rumour of a great disaster pervades the bazaars of India. It was printed on mourning paper, with a black border; it was cried about the streets as a Barbarous Murder; it was solemnly burned in the presence of vast crowds of people. The first of June was kept in Philadelphia with peals of muffled bells, and colours half-mast high on ships in the river, and with the shutters up from dawn to dark in ninety houses out of a hundred. The Assembly of Virginia set the day apart for humiliation and fasting; but the colonies found more effectual means of relieving Boston than by sharing her abstinence. South Carolina sent two hundred barrels of rice, with eight hundred more to follow. In North Carolina, Wilmington raised two thousand pounds in a few days; the sum which much about the same time a fashionable Club was spending at

Ranelagh on a Masquerade that was the wonder of the London season.[1] To convey the contributions of the little seaport a ship was offered freight free, and a crew volunteered to make the voyage without wages. The less remote districts of New England kept Boston supplied with portable and perishable victuals; and the class of food which could travel on foot came over many leagues of road, and not seldom from places which could badly spare it. Two hundred and fifty-eight sheep were driven in from one town in Connecticut, and two hundred and ninety from another. Israel Putnam brought a flock of six or seven score from his remote parish, and did not fail to show himself on the Common, where he could enjoy the sight of more soldiers together than he had seen since he fought by the side of Lord Howe at Ticonderoga. The British officers, who liked him well, suggested that they must owe the pleasure of his visit to his having sniffed powder in the air. They told him that he very soon might have it to his heart's content, as they were expecting twenty ships of the line, and as many regiments, from England. "If they come," said the old fellow gravely, "I am prepared to treat them as enemies."[2]

Indeed, Putnam's colony was full of fight. Besides bringing in sheep and bullocks, the men of Connecticut brought themselves and their cudgels in even greater numbers whenever it was known that the Massachusetts Judges were going to hold a Court within a long day's

---

[1] "Last night was the triumph of Boodle's. Our Masquerade cost two thousand guineas. A sum which might have fertilised a Province vanished in a few hours." So Gibbon wrote on May the Fourth, 1774, while he was still to all outward appearance a fine gentleman, and nothing more. "For my own part," he said, "I subscribe, but am very indifferent about it. A few friends, and a great many books, entertain me; but I think fifteen hundred people the worst company in the world."

[2] The first five chapters of Bancroft's Third Epoch relate, comprehensively and minutely, the uprising of the American colonies in consequence of the Penal Acts of 1774. The severities exercised against the friends of Government, which form the unpleasing side of the story, are most fairly and effectively told by Mr. Lorenzo Sabine in his *Biographical Sketches of the Loyalists of the Revolution.*

walk of the border-line between the two provinces. The clearest eye in America already discerned that the time was at hand when men would be wanted as much as money or provisions, and a great deal more than votes of sympathy. Patriotic circles were discoursing freely about the excellence of the oratory in the Colonial Convention of Virginia. Enthusiastic members of that Convention had assured John Adams, (who was accustomed to hear the same about himself from his own fellow-townsmen,) that Richard Henry Lee, and Patrick Henry, would respectively bear comparison with Cicero and with Demosthenes. But a shrewd delegate from South Carolina, who, on his way to Congress, had looked in at Williamsburg to see what they were doing in the Old Dominion, gave it as his opinion that the most eloquent speech had been made by Colonel Washington. "I will raise," that officer had said, "one thousand men towards the relief of Boston, and subsist them at my own expense." It was a sound Anglo-Saxon version of the march of the Marseillais. If they knew how to die, he would see that in the meanwhile they should know where they could get something to eat.

But above all, and before all, the proposal of a Congress met with eager acceptance on the part of twelve out of the thirteen colonies. They took care to make convenient for themselves both the day and the locality which Massachusetts had indicated. On the tenth of August the delegates, who had been chosen at Salem, set forth on their journey from Boston. The spaces which they had to traverse, and the welcome which everywhere greeted them, brought home to their minds, for the first time, a comfortable assurance that the task of subjugating so large a country, inhabited by such a people, would possibly require more months, and a great many more regiments, than had been allotted to it in the anticipations of the British War Office. Everywhere on their passage bells were ringing, cannons firing, and men, women, and children crowding "as if to a coronation." When John Adams was a very old gentleman, it took much to make him angry; but he never allowed any doubt to be thrown, in his presence, on the enthusiasm which attended himself and his colleagues during their progress to Philadelphia in the summer of 1774. The only time that his grandson ever incurred the indignation of the ex-President "was by his expression of surprise at the extent of those ceremonies, which he happened to find set forth in high colours in an old newspaper. He was then a boy, and knew no better. But he never forgot the reproof."

The material comforts which awaited the Bostonians, in ever greater profusion as they journeyed southwards, were matter for constantly renewed surprise and satisfaction, tempered by an inward sense of stern superiority at the recollection of the plain but invigorating fare which they had left behind them. New York, freehearted as now, would not let them go forward on their way until they had devoted six evenings to rest and refreshment, and as many days to seeing the sights;— the view from the steeple of the New Dutch church; St. Paul's, with its piazza and pillars, which had cost eighteen thousand pounds, in York money; and the statue of his Majesty on horseback in the Bowling Green, of solid lead gilded with gold, which had still two years to stand on the marble pedestal before it was pulled down to be run into bullets. They rode on through New Jersey, which they thought a paradise; as indeed it was, and as it remained until the Hessians had been allowed their will on it. They halted for a Sunday at Princeton College, where the scholars studied very hard, but sang very badly in chapel; and where the inmates, from the president downwards, were as high sons of liberty as any in America. They went on their course from town to city, honouring toasts; hearing sermons; recording the text from which the clergyman preached, and observing whether he spoke from notes; admiring the public buildings, and carefully writing down what they cost in the currency of the colony. At the "pretty village" of Trenton they were ferried over the Delaware, in the opposite direction from that in which it was to be crossed on the December night when the tide of war showed the first faint sign of turning.

On the nineteenth afternoon they entered Philadelphia, where they were housed and feasted with a cordiality which in those early days of the Revolution had the air of being universal, and with a luxury which threw even the glories of New York into the shade. They had known what it was to breakfast in a villa on the Hudson River with "a very large silver coffee pot, a very large silver tea pot, napkins of the finest materials, plates full of choice fruit, and toast and bread-and-butter in great perfection." But in Philadelphia, — whether it was at the residence of a Roman Catholic gentleman, with ten thousand a year in sterling money, "reputed the first fortune in America"; or the Chief Justice of the Province; or a young Quaker lawyer and his pretty wife, — there was magnificence, and, above all, abundance, under many roofs. "A most sinful feast again," John Adams wrote. "Everything which could delight the eye or allure the taste. Curds and creams, jellies, sweetmeats of various sorts, twenty sorts of tarts, fools, trifles, floating islands, and whipped sillabubs." These dainties were washed down by floods of Madeira, more undeniable than the political principles of some among their hosts; for, (as was proved just three years later, when red-coats were seated round the same tables,) Philadelphia loved to place her best before her visitors, quite irrespective of whether or not they were trusty patriots. But for the present the opinions of the entertainers seemed as sound as their wine, and gushed as freely. At elegant suppers, where the company drank sentiments till near midnight, might be heard such unexceptionable aspirations as : "May Britain be wise, and America be free!" "May the fair dove of liberty, in this deluge of despotism, find rest to the sole of her foot on the soil of America!" "May the collision of British flint and American steel produce that spark of liberty which shall illuminate the latest posterity!"

Philadelphia was destined in the course of the war to play the important, if not very noble, part of serving as a Capua to the British army; but the men of the first Congress were of a political fibre which was proof against any enervating influences. They fell to work forthwith, and their labours were continuous, severe, and admirably adapted to the particularities of the situation. Possessed of no constitutional authority to legislate or govern, they passed, after searching debate and minute revision, Resolutions which had the moral force of laws, and the practical effect of administrative decrees. On the eighth of October they put on record "that this Congress approve the opposition of the Massachusetts Bay to the late Acts of Parliament; and, if the same shall be attempted to be carried into execution by force, all America ought to support them in their opposition." They then proceeded to draw up a Declaration of Rights, claiming for the American people in their provincial assemblies a free and exclusive power of legislation on all matters of taxation and internal policy, and calling for the repeal, in whole or in part, of eleven Acts of Parliament by which that claim was infringed. They unanimously agreed not to import any merchandise from the mother-country; but, like wary men of business, they gave themselves another twelve-month during which American goods might be exported to Great Britain, if Great Britain chose to take them.

One class of imports was prohibited specifically, unconditionally, and apart from all considerations of politics. "We will," so Congress proclaimed, "neither import, nor purchase any slave imported, after the first day of December next; after which time we will wholly discontinue the slave trade." The pledge was binding upon all; but it bore the special stamp of Virginia. The Assembly of that colony had, over and over again, framed and carried, in condemnation of the slave trade, laws which had, over and over again, been disallowed by the Royal veto, enforced on one occasion by a personal and emphatic expression of the Royal anger. It is melan-

choly to reflect what the social condition and the political history of Virginia might have been if the Home Government had allowed free play to the generous impulses
which actuated her public men before the Revolutionary
war.   They liked to be told high and hard truths, and
were prepared to act them out in practice.   "Every
gentleman here is born a petty tyrant.   Taught to regard a part of our own species in the most abject and
contemptible degree below us, we lose that idea of the
dignity of man which the hand of Nature hath planted
in us for great and useful purposes.   Habituated from
our infancy to trample upon the rights of human nature,
every liberal sentiment is enfeebled in our minds; and
in such an infernal school are to be educated our future
legislators and rulers."   That was how, in 1773, a Virginian representative discoursed openly to his fellows.   No
such speech could have been made with impunity in the
State Legislature during the generation which preceded
the Secession of 1861.

And finally, knowing by repeated experience that for
Americans to petition Parliament was only to court their
own humiliation, Congress laid formality aside, and published a direct appeal to all true and kindly Englishmen.
The people of Great Britain, (so the document ran,) had
been led to greatness by the hand of liberty; and therefore the people of America, in all confidence, invoked
their sense of justice, prayed for permission to share their
freedom, and anxiously protested against the calumny
that the colonies were aiming at separation under the
pretence of asserting the right of self-government.
Chatham, after confiding to the House of Lords that his
favourite study had been the political literature of "the
master-countries of the world," declared and avowed
that the Resolutions and Addresses put forth by the Congress at Philadelphia, "for solidity of reasoning, force of
sagacity, and wisdom of conclusion, under such a com-
plication of difficult circumstances," were surpassed by
no body of men, of any age and nation, who had ever issued a state paper.   A contemporary Scotch journalist

described these productions as written with so much spirit, sound reason, and true knowledge of the constitution, that they had given more uneasiness than all the other proceedings of the Congress.[1]

The rate of speed at which compositions of that excellence were devised, drafted, criticised, amended, and sanctioned appears enviable to the member of a modern representative assembly ; but it fell short of what satisfied men accustomed to the succinct methods of a New England Town-meeting, and for whom Philadelphia was a place of honourable but, as it seemed to them, almost interminable exile. As early as the tenth of October John Adams wrote : " The deliberations of the Congress are spun out to an immeasurable length. There is so much wit, sense, learning, acuteness, subtlety, and eloquence among fifty gentlemen, each of whom has been habituated to lead and guide in his own Province, that an immensity of time is spent unnecessarily." The end was not far off. On the twentieth of the month the Pennsylvanian Assembly entertained Congress at a dinner in the City Tavern. The whole table rose to the sentiment, " May the sword of the parent never be stained with the blood of her children ! " Even the Quakers who were present drained their glasses on the ground that it was not a toast, but a prayer ; and a prayer which was much to their own liking. Six days afterwards Congress dissolved itself. The tenth of May was appointed for the meeting of its successor ; and the Canadian colonies, and the Floridas, were invited to send representatives. Two days more, and the Massachusetts delegates mounted for their homeward journey. " We took our departure," said Adams, " in a very great rain, from the happy, the peaceful, the elegant, the hospitable and polite city of Philadelphia. It is not very likely that I shall ever visit this part of the world again ; but I shall ever retain a most grateful sense of the many civilities I have received in it, and shall think

[1] The passage referred to in the text is quoted by Professor Tyler in chapter xv. of his *Literary History*.

myself happy to have an opportunity of returning them. " Events were at hand of such a nature that to set a limit to what was likely needed more than human foresight. John Adams had not seen Philadelphia for the last time, by many ; and the return dinners with which he requited her hospitality were given by him as President of seventeen States, and six millions of people.

CHAPTER VI

THE GENERAL ELECTION OF 1774. THE WINTER SESSION

WHILE the House of Commons was scheming the ruin of Boston, its own days were already being numbered; and those who speculated on the exact date of its disappearance had a very narrow margin within which their calculations could range. Charles Fox experienced the fortune which frequently awaited him where money was to be lost or won. He laid Sir George Macartney ten guineas to five that the Dissolution would not take place before Christmas, 1774; and on the last day of September sixty messengers passed through one single turnpike, in a hurry to inform the country that the writs were being prepared for immediate issue.

When dealing with so long, and so eventful, a national history as ours, it is never safe to speak in superlatives; but it may confidently be asserted that the burden of proof rests with those who maintain that a worse Parliament ever sate than that which was elected in the spring of 1768. Chosen amidst an orgy of corruption, its title to remembrance rests on two performances. By a great and sustained exertion of misdirected energy it succeeded in depriving the Middlesex electors of their rights for half a dozen sessions; and it threw away the loyalty of America. One good deed stands to its account. In a better moment, inspired by the inflexible integrity of George Grenville, it had enacted a law framed in the interest of electoral morality with sincere intention, and not a little skill. The trial of an election petition, which had hitherto been determined by a party-vote in a Committee of the whole House, was now transferred to a small number of selected members, who were bound to listen to the whole evidence, and decide the case according to its rights. The proceeding became henceforward something of a judicial reality, instead of a mere opportunity for the people in power to increase their existing majority by substituting a friend in the place of an opponent. Great things were expected from the new Act by honest men of all political opinions. Samuel Johnson congratulated the electors of Great Britain on the circumstance that a claim to a seat in Parliament would now be examined with the same scrupulousness and solemnity as any other title. Under the old state of things, (so he most truly said,) to have friends in a borough was of little use to a candidate unless he had friends in the House of Commons; and a man became a member because he was chosen, not by his constituents, but by his fellow-senators. The case could not be more pithily stated; but it reads oddly in a pamphlet[1] issued on behalf of a Cabinet which, by the brute force of partisan votes within the walls of Parliament, thrice unseated Wilkes, and ended by seating Luttrell.

These symptoms of nascent purity were not equally acceptable in a higher quarter. The King understood the inner working of his own system of government better than did the downright old Tory author who had taken up the cudgels to defend it. Little as George the Third loved Grenville when alive, he had still less liking for the well-meant and carefully devised statute which that statesman had left behind him as a legacy to his country. In February, 1774, the Commons had voted by more than two to one in favour of making the Act perpetual. No one argued against the proposal on its merits except Rigby, who, with a touch of genuine feeling, implored the House to think yet again before it forbade treating. But the King expressed to Lord North his regret that Parliament had been misled by a false love of popularity, and consoled himself with the reflection

[1] *The Patriot, Addressed to the Electors of Great Britain;* 1774.

that the mischief would some day be undone, because
" passion was a short madness."

Grenville's law had very seriously altered, for a time
at all events, the conditions under which his Majesty
practised the art wherein he was a master. The first
Dissolution which takes place under a new Corrupt
Practices Act is always a season of perturbation among
those more humble operators who now pull the hidden
strings of politics ; and the King and his coadjutors, in
the autumn of 1774, hesitated about doing many things
which they had done fearlessly at the general election
of 1768, and which, after the manner of their craft, they
had learned how to do safely before the general election
of 1780.[1] But, even in those early days, whenever they
were on firm ground, they acted broadly, promptly, and
decisively. Parliament had made it dangerous to bribe
the electors in the boroughs; but nothing, except the
limits of that Secret Service Fund which had been
extracted from the taxpayer on the pretext that it was
to be expended in securing the general interests of the
nation abroad and at home, stood in their way when it
was a question of bribing the patrons. " A note," (such
were Lord North's orders to Mr. John Robinson, the
Secretary of the Treasury,) " should be written to Lord
Falmouth in my name, and put into safe hands. His
Lordship must be told, in as polite terms as possible, that
I hope he will permit me to recommend to three of his
six seats in Cornwall. The terms he expects are 2500*l.*
a seat, to which I am ready to agree ; " and he had still
to agree when his noble friend, rather shabbily, (as he
complained,) made it guineas instead of pounds. " Mr.
Legge," wrote the Prime Minister on the sixth of Octo-

[1] The King and Rigby were not alone in their dislike of the Grenville
Act, as is indicated in Samuel Foote's play of *The Cozeners*, which was
put upon the stage in 1774.

" *Mrs. Fleec'em.* Have you advertised a seat to be sold ?

" *Flaw.* I never neglect business, you know ; but the perpetuating of
this damned Bribery Act has thrown such a rub in our way.

" *Mrs. Fleec'em.* New acts, like new brooms, make a little bustle at
first. But the dirt will return, never fear."

ber, "can only afford 400*l*. If he comes in for Lost-withiel he will cost the public 2000 guineas. Gascoign should have the refusal of Tregony if he will pay 1000*l*. ; but I do not see why we should bring him in cheaper than any other servant of the Crown. If he will not pay, he must give way to Mr. Best or Mr. Peachy." Six weeks afterwards, when the goods had all been delivered and the bills were coming in, some of the bargains had not yet been finally closed. " Let Cooper know whether you promised Masterman 2500*l*. or 3000*l*. for each of Lord Edgcumbe's seats. I was going to pay him twelve thousand five hundred pounds, but he demanded fifteen thousand." [1]

These delectable details had for George the Third the same fascination as the numbers and discipline of his soldiers had for Frederic the Great, and their height for Frederic's father. Determined to get his information from the fountain-head, if that phrase can be applied to such very muddy water, he wrote direct for news, and more news, to Mr. John Robinson, whose assiduity in keeping him informed of what was going forward, (so he graciously acknowledged,) he could not enough commend. He sent three letters to Lord North, in the course of five days, about the poll for Aldermen in the City of London, regarding it as an indication of the probable action which the Liverymen would take at the poll for their parliamentary members. He was careful to remind the Prime Minister of a report which had reached his ears, that bad votes were being tendered for the Opposition candidates at Westminster; and he gave personal orders that his household troops, horse and foot, should be canvassed on behalf of Lord Percy and Lord Thomas Clinton, who were standing in the Government interest. In one electoral department, more important then than now, he had a free hand, and he let its weight be felt. The mode of choosing Scottish representative peers was not affected by the

---

[1] *Abergavenny MSS.;* published by the Historical Manuscripts Commission, 1887.

Grenville Act; and the King arranged the list as sum-
marily as though he were nominating as many Lords
in Waiting.   His method of management called forth
on the present occasion a letter in refreshing contrast
to the waste of sycophancy and greediness by which it
is surrounded.   Lord Buchan informed Dartmouth, as
the only Minister with whom he cared to communicate
on a friendly footing, that Lord Suffolk, writing as Secretary of State, had thought proper to send him an
authoritative message on the subject of the sixteen
peers to be elected for Scotland.   "I returned his
Lordship an answer suitable to the affront he had ventured to offer; and I do most earnestly intreat your
Lordship, as an old acquaintance, and a person for
whom I have a singular good-will, that you will, when
an opportunity offers, suggest that, if I am to be
applied to for the future in that manner by any of the
King's servants I shall, notwithstanding my disposition
to rustication, make one more visit to the great city to
chastise the person who shall waste his ink and paper
in that manner." [1]

The consequences of the Grenville Act were not as
sudden, nor as sweeping, as Rigby apprehended.   It
may have seemed a dry election to those who, between
their twinges of gout, recollected the flood of liquor
which six years before had inundated the constituencies.
But there was as yet no lack of the rough conviviality
which long ere this had driven Horace Walpole from
Parliament.   It was a bad time for a member of the
Dilettanti Club who at that period of the year did not
care to leave London, and the great country houses
round London, for any point short of Italy ; especially
if his political interests required him to travel almost
as far as Italy, in exactly the opposite direction.   John
Crawford the younger of Auchinanes, — whose gratitude, (as has already been related,) Charles Fox acquired by coming chivalrously to the rescue when he

_____
[1] *Dartmouth MSS.;* vol. iii., p. 211.

was involved in rhetorical difficulties,[1] — has left a
record of what he went through in order to re-enter
a House of Commons where he was afraid to speak,
and did not greatly care to sit. No one can read without compassion, and few politicians without a pang of
sympathy, the letters which he addressed to those
members of the Fitzpatrick connection the necessities
of whose canvass took them no further afield than the
Home Counties. It had been serious enough when,
between one election and another, he had been doing no
more than nurse his popularity, and attempt painfully
to acquire in North British circles the reputation of a
good fellow. "I have at this moment," he wrote to
Lord Ossory, "three neighbours who are come to dine
with me. I dine at four, and they came at one, and I
am now making them my mortal enemies by not going
down to them. I had yesterday likewise three gentlemen to dine, whom I wished most to be well with ; but
I have heard that they were dissatisfied with me for not
giving them wine enough. My wine is the best, I suppose, in the world : my clarets of vintage fifty-nine ; my
Port, Sherry, Madeira, sweet wines, some of it forty
years old, and scarce any less than twenty." It is no
wonder that, when the Renfrewshire election came in
earnest, the owner of this cellar was paying his penalty
in bodily suffering for the glory of such a possession.
"This is a small county, and whenever I get upon my
feet, I shall be able to go through it in a few days.
The Duke of Hamilton has given me his interest, which
is very considerable. You may guess how I pass my
time between the gout, and the country gentlemen who
come flocking in upon me. I have passed two cruel
nights ; violent pain, abominable company, and no sleep.
Yesterday my antagonist came to see me. There were
eight besides myself, who only appeared for half an
hour. They sat from three to ten o'clock, and I had
the curiosity to inquire from the butler what they
drank. You can calculate better than I can, so divide

[1] *Early History of Charles Fox*, chapter x.

ten bottles of wine, and sixteen bowls of punch, each of which would hold four bottles. Can you conceive anything more beastly or more insupportable?"[1]

Meanwhile the leading member of Crawford's circle would have been well pleased to light upon a seat where the process of electioneering consisted in making himself agreeable to a duke, and drinking a sufficiency of fifty-nine claret with commoners. The purchase of boroughs was a cash transaction, and therefore outside the sphere of Charles Fox's financial operations; and the few which could be obtained as a favour were not for him. The most confiding of patrons would hesitate before he sacrificed a couple of thousand pounds for the honour of making a senator of a young gentleman whose shortcomings were historical, and whose public virtues might well be regarded as of too recent origin to stand the strain of a six years Parliament. Fox, said Walpole, like the Ghost in Hamlet, shifted to many quarters; but in most the cock crew, and he walked off. At last he found an asylum at Malmesbury, a delightful constituency with thirteen electors. It is possible that his success was the result of a compromise between the two parties; for his colleague was Mr. William Strahan, as estimable a man as supported the Government, which as King's Printer he could not very well help doing. To satisfy the current requirements of the Malmesbury burgesses he possessed that which

---

[1] Letters, in the Russell collection, from Crawford to Lord Ossory ; September, 1774. The *locus classicus* which determines what our ancestors regarded as an inadequate provision of liquor for a party of three may be found in a letter written to George Selwyn by a fast parson. "The whim took them of ordering their dinner, and a very good one they had: mackerel, a delicate neck of veal, a piece of Hamborough beef, cabbage and salad, and a gooseberry tart. When they had drunk the bottle of white wine, and of port, which accompanied the dinner, and after that the only double bottle of claret that I had left, I found in an old corner one of the two bottles of Burgundy which I took from your cellar when you gave me the key of it. By Jove, how they did abuse my modesty that instead of two I did not take two dozen ! But, having no more, we closed with a pint of Dantzic cherry brandy, and have just parted in a tolerable state of insensibility to the ills of human life."

Charles Fox wanted; for he had long been in a position to lay by a thousand pounds a year from the profits of his business.

The arrangement suited Strahan; for he was not one of those who carried public differences into personal relations. His two closest intimacies were with two men who had not a political view in common. He had done more than anybody else to help Samuel Johnson through his period of distress; and in later and happier days he acted as his banker, and such a banker as any literary man would rejoice to have. He found places for young people whom the great writer desired to assist; and franked his letters; and did his best to enable him to frank them himself by recommending him to the Secretary for the Treasury as a parliamentary candidate, on the ground that the King's friends would find him a lamb, and the King's enemies a lion. On the other hand Strahan came as near as the ordinary duration of human existence would allow to being a life-long friend of Franklin, whom in 1757 he already regarded as the most agreeable of men, and the most desirable of associates in the calling to which they had both been bred. In 1784, when even Franklin was too old for the offer of a partnership in a printing office, Strahan was still urging him to come as a guest to England, and to stay there for good and all. What Franklin thought of Strahan may be gathered from the fact that he forgave him his votes in favour of North's policy: a forgiveness which he conveyed in a letter of grim, and for him rather heavy-handed, raillery.[1] Charles

---

[1] "Philadelphia : 5th July, 1775.

"Mr. Strahan, — You are a member of Parliament, and one of that majority which has doomed my country to destruction. You have begun to burn our towns and murder our people. Look upon your hands. They are stained with the blood of your relations! You and I were long friends. You are now my enemy, and I am   Yours,
                                                        "B. Franklin."

There was some excuse for a French editor who took the letter in sad earnest.

Fox had every reason to be satisfied, for he had secured what in those facile days passed for an ideal parliamentary situation ; — the membership for a borough represented by two gentlemen of opposite opinions, of whom both were easy to live with, and one had plenty of money. The electoral calm in which he now basked was in striking contrast with all that awaited him from the moment when he set his foot on the Westminster hustings.

The dissolution found Burke, as well as Fox, at sea with regard to his electioneering prospects. The patron of his borough was tired of bringing into Parliament private friends, from whom he was loth to take a shilling, and who, not being local landowners, could do nothing towards helping forward his own election for the county. Burke, with his reverence for the British constitution as it existed, recognised the situation frankly, and almost sympathetically. " I am extremely anxious," he wrote to Lord Rockingham, " about the fate of Lord Verney and that borough. It is past all description, past all conception, the supineness, neglect, and blind security of my friend. He will be cheated, if he is not robbed." But none the less the blow was a heavy one. " Sometimes when I am alone," (Burke's letter proceeded,) " in spite of all my efforts I fall into a melancholy which is inexpressible. Whether I ought not totally to abandon this public station, for which I am so unfit, and have of course been so unfortunate, I know not. Most assuredly I never will put my feet within the door of St. Stephen's chapel without being as much my own master as hitherto I have been." Lord Rockingham hastened to relieve his friend's solicitude, and placed at his disposal one of his own seats at Malton. While travelling thither Burke learned that there were other public thieves busy at election time besides those who frequented the waiting-room at the Treasury, for he was stopped by two highwaymen on Finchley Common. In the same week the Prime Minister met the same fate. The perils of the road, at a season when the lot of a politician was already hard

enough without them, may be estimated by the circumstance that Lord North set out on his journey expecting
to be robbed, while Burke's feeling was surprise at his
good fortune in never having been robbed before.

A compliment was in store for Burke more valuable
even than the confidence and affection of a Rockingham.
Many of the citizens of Bristol had had enough of scandals and disorders at home and in the colonies, and were
desirous of lighting upon a representative who had studied business in its larger aspect, and who understood
the close connection between sound trade and good
government. They found their man in Burke; and he
had just been chaired at Malton when he received an
invitation to contest Bristol. He placed down no money.
He would give no pledges. Even about America he
promised nothing but impartial consideration of matters
deeply concerning the interests of a commercial community which still claimed to be the second port in the
kingdom. To borrow a phrase from the vocabulary of
transatlantic politics, he ran upon his record; and a
grand record it was, as he laid it before the people of
Bristol in the speech which he delivered at the moment
of his arrival amongst them. "When I first devoted
myself to the public service, I considered how I should
render myself fit for it; and this I did by endeavouring
to discover what it was that gave this country the rank
it holds in the world. I found that our prosperity and
dignity arose from our constitution and our commerce.
Both these I have spared no study to understand, and
no endeavour to support. I now appear before you to
make trial whether my earnest endeavours have been
so wholly oppressed by the weakness of my abilities as
to be rendered insignificant in the eyes of a great trading city. This is my trial to-day. My industry is not
on trial. Of my industry I am sure." He had not
slept, he said, from the time that he received their summons to the time that he was addressing them in their
Guildhall; and, if he was chosen their member, he
would be as far from slumbering and sleeping, when

their service required him to be awake, as he had been when coming to offer himself as a candidate for their favour.

It was a noble compact, and on his side it was nobly kept. He came victorious out of a struggle so protracted, and to his leading supporters so terribly expensive, that it might well have aroused, in a mind acute as his, some faint suspicion that the British constitution required not only defending but amending. His colleague, by one of those freaks of luck which so often allot to men, otherwise obscure, a conspicuous but uncomfortable niche in history, will pass to the end of time as the prototype of a political nonentity. But, in truth, he had both spirit and ability, and could explain himself with effect not only to a throng of triumphant partisans, but, as was afterwards shown on many occasions, to a hostile House of Commons. At the declaration of the poll, so far from saying "ditto to Mr. Burke," Mr. Cruger spoke first; and a good third of Mr. Burke's speech consisted in a statement of the points on which he differed from Mr. Cruger.

In many other constituencies besides Bristol there was plenty of independence, and little flagrant corruption. It was to an unusual degree a country gentleman's election. The King, so far back as August, had prophesied that a dissolution would fill the House with men of landed property, as the Nabobs, Planters, and other volunteers were not ready for the battle. There was less money forthcoming than on the last occasion; and, which was more to the purpose, people needed to be very cautious how they spent what they were prepared to part with. Mr. Grenville's Act (as Horace Walpole said) now hung out all its terrors. The rich Londoners had been taken by surprise, and did not venture at that eleventh hour to throw about their guineas and banknotes. The squires who lived close at hand, and who loved to entertain even where there was nothing to be got by it, had established a claim on the suffrages of rural boroughs by a course of hospitality which no laws, except those of health, could punish. It was not a crime for a host, who himself took his share, to give his friend a couple of bottles of wine and half a bowl of punch, and provide him with a bed in which to sleep them off. And again the large proprietors, who could afford to set aside a square mile of grass from the plough and the dairy farm, had at their disposal abundant material for sustaining their influence and popularity. A great family, which represented a great town, made little of keeping up a herd of five or six hundred deer for the express object of supplying the Corporation banquets, and the private tables of important citizens. The breaking-up of a deer-park was in those days regarded as an infallible symptom that the owner of it had done with electioneering. "Harry Mills was with me yesterday," (so runs a letter which is worth quoting,) "and says it now begins to be suspected by Sir John Trevylian's friends that he does not mean to offer himself again for Newcastle. It is affirmed that he is going to dispark Roadley, and lay it out in farms. All your Newcastle friends have been served with venison. And indeed I do not think there can be a more successful battery played off against a Corporation than one plentifully supplied with venison and claret." This letter was addressed in 1777 to Stoney Bowes, who had just been beaten in a bye-election for Newcastle-on-Tyne by the head of a family which had represented that city, with a few short intervals, for more than a century.[1]

Apart altogether from what he gave them, the freemen and freeholders preferred a neighbour for his own sake; and, whoever else had a chance against him, a courtier had none. Where bribery, (said Horace Walpole,) was out of the question, they would give their

[1] *Report of the Society of Antiquaries of Newcastle-on-Tyne* for 1857. Bowes was the original of Barry Lyndon, and a still greater scoundrel, with an even more extraordinary story. Thackeray, by a stroke of genius, turned him from a mean hound into a swaggering ruffian ; and such as Thackeray made him, he will remain.

votes to a man of birth who resided in their own district, or to a clever talking candidate from a distance who could show them a specimen of the style in which he would denounce sinecures if they sent him to Parliament. But from neither of those two classes did Walpole hope for any advantage to the nation. The country gentlemen were bitterly angry with the colonists; and, as for the bustling politicians, the King would still be able to buy the representatives themselves, though the representatives did not venture to buy the electors. And so his Majesty appeared to think; for, as soon as the first contests had been decided, he directed the Secretary of the Treasury to let him see the names of those who had been successful, tabulated under the heads of " Pro," " Con," and " Doubtful."

Walpole's belief that the new House of Commons would be no less compliant than the last were shared by even abler men who watched our politics from without. That was the sense in which the Prussian Minister wrote to Potsdam; and the old King replied that he never expected otherwise, as he had long known that money was the mainspring of the British Constitution.[1] Franklin, from what he saw of the elections, went so far as to doubt whether there was any use in having a House of Commons. " Since a Parliament," he wrote, " is always to do as a ministry would have it, why should we not be governed by the ministry in the first instance? They could afford to govern us much cheaper, the Parliament being a very expensive machine, that requires a great deal of oiling and greasing at the people's charge." But, dark as the future was, it contained an element of hope which escaped these sharp-sighted observers. They had reckoned without the country gentlemen who sate for their own boroughs, and the still greater country gentlemen who had been chosen by the Counties. Of the former sort there were many more than in the last Parliament. The price of seats was lower by from thirty to forty per cent., and was soon to be

[1] *Le Roi Frédéric au Comte de Maltzan;* 14 November, 1774.

lower still; for a membership of Parliament, like a commission in the army, ruled highest in time of assured
peace, and fell to next to nothing by the end of a long
war.   Gibbon, who was a country gentleman against
his will, and who remained one no longer than the first
moment when he could find a purchaser for the last of
his acres, was sent to Westminster by a Cornish kinsman at the general election of 1774.   For some time he
was left in ignorance whether his borough would be
Liskeard or St. Germans.   All that he knew was that
he would have to contribute the half of two thousand
four hundred pounds, and that Mr. Eliot would consent
to payment being postponed until his second son, who
was a lad of thirteen, had come of age.   Those terms,
even as between relatives, indicated a very different
state of the market from that which prevailed in 1798,
when George Selwyn got nine thousand for the double
seat at Ludgershall.   A bill for twelve hundred pounds,
or twelve thousand either, bearing no interest, and with
eight years to run, would have been within the compass
even of Charles Fox; and there is no wonder that, at
such prices, a patron with a fair share of public spirit
preferred to sit himself, or to keep his borough within
the family.   Indeed, a man who cared nothing for the
commonwealth, and had a single eye to the main chance,
might well take the same course; for there was every
prospect that a member, however cheaply he got into
Parliament, when once there would be able to sell himself for as much as ever.

The County members formed a class by themselves,
and a class to whom the nation owes an incalculable
debt.   They were great proprietors of long standing in
their neighbourhood, and true aristocrats, indifferent to
the frowns and favours of the central government;
while they were as proud of the confidence of their constituents as of the extent of their domains, the age of
their castles, and the running of their horses.   The
vast sums which leading families spent over a County
contest are already inconceivable to us who hear men

of property grumble at having to find twelve or fifteen hundred pounds where their ancestors coolly and complacently laid down twice as many thousands. The explanation is that, in the eighteenth century, the position of a County member was valued for itself, and not for what it might lead to. A rural potentate, who sate for the shire in which he lived, was thought as good as a lord, and was a great deal better liked, on his own countryside, in the London clubs, and especially within the walls of Parliament. The House of Commons took a domestic interest in a distinction which reflected credit on itself. Mr. Coke of Norfolk, with fifty thousand a year in his county, represented it for more than fifty years, and did not accept a peerage until long after his brother members had hailed him with an admiring cheer the first time that he walked down the floor after having had a son born to him at the age of seventy-six. The belief that the Upper and Lower Houses ought to be kept apart, and that their own was the finer institution of the two, was held not only by members of Parliament, but by the people who elected them. The freeholders of Somersetshire went so far as to pledge themselves not to vote for the brother or the son of a peer of the realm, or for any candidate whom a peer supported.[1] It was a sentiment not of recent, and certainly not of democratic, origin; for the feeling of Somersetshire had long ago been expressed, with a vigour that left nothing to be desired, by the most celebrated Tory who ever killed a fox within its confines. "It is true," said Squire Western, "there be larger estates in the kingdom, but not in this county. Besides, most o' zuch great estates be in the hands of lords, and I hate the very name of themmum."

The honour of representing a shire was neither conferred lightly, nor retained easily. A candidate, whether he presented himself, or whether he was put forward by a junta of local grandees, if his name was unfavourably

[1] *History of the Boroughs of Great Britain;* London, 1794, vol. ii., p. 44.

received by the freeholders in county-meeting assembled, would find at the declaration of the poll that he had lost his money and his labour. Those freeholders did not love a new man; and they interpreted the phrase in a manner creditable to themselves and to the object of their choice. "I cannot," Gibbon wrote to his friend Holroyd, "yet think you ripe for a County member. Five years are very little to remove the obvious objection of a *novus homo*, and of all objections it is perhaps the most formidable. Seven more years of an active life will spread your fame among the great body of the Freeholders, and to them you may one day offer yourself on the most honourable footing, that of a candidate whose real services to the County have deserved, and will repay, the favour which he then solicits."

The County electors proved a man before they took him; but none the less they were careful to see that the services which he promised were duly given. Confidence, with them, was not an empty word; and they permitted their representative an almost boundless latitude of action at Westminster, demanding only that he should not be inactive. They expected that he should attend diligently and faithfully to the business of the nation, all the more because they were ready to allow that he understood that business better than themselves. George Selwyn, as a borough member, soon found that his constituents troubled themselves very little about what he did, or left undone, so long as he refrained from cutting off their water supply, which came from a hill on his estate; and was at the pains of forwarding to the Prince of Wales, with the compliments of the Corporation, their annual offering of a lamprey pie. When he played truant during a political crisis, they were personal friends, and not electors, who appealed to his loyalty towards George the Third and, where that failed, to his self-interest. "You are now," wrote Lord Bolingbroke in 1767, "attending a sick friend; but I believe the Earls will think you have neglected the first of all duties, that of being ready to vote as they order.

In short, George, you who love your namesake, and
hate to see a poor helpless young man like himself oppressed by the obstinacy of such men as George Grenville and Lord Rockingham, must fly to his assistance.
Consider the obligations you have to him, and do not
let him be forced to give your place away to somebody
who will attend." When Selwyn was longer absent
from town than usual, his correspondents, writing with
quite sufficient breadth of detail, affected to believe that
he was detained by the attractions of a lady; — a sup-
position which, as applied to him, passed in that circle for the height of irony. But the movements of a
County representative were subjected to a much more
jealous scrutiny. "The member of St. Germans might
lurk in the country, but the Knight of Cornwall must
attend the House of Commons." So wrote Gibbon
about his cousin Mr. Eliot, with a lazy sense of superiority very consolatory to a man of letters who had
already discovered himself to be no debater, and was
beginning to suspect that he was not meant for a member of Parliament.

The great country gentlemen in the House of Commons entertained the prejudices of their order; and
some among them had their full allowance of faults as
individuals; but they felt that consciousness of responsibility which animates a race of men who, over and
over again, and time out of mind, have decided the fate
of a nation. They and their forerunners, for a century
and a half back, had borne their share in those successive political reactions which, in defiance of strict logic,
had saved England alternately from arbitrary power
and factious violence. Foresight was not their strong
point, particularly when it was a question of running
counter to the wishes of the sovereign. They never
had been very quick to detect and withstand the early
stages of a dangerous policy; but, in the last resort,
they were not going to see their country ruined. Moreover their hands were pure. Quiet folks in the villages,
who were well aware that their own part in a system

based upon profusion and venality was to get nothing
and pay for everything, never felt so comfortable as
when they were represented at St. Stephen's by a man
who desired to be no greater or richer than he was,
whether the motive of his contentment was personal
pride, or public spirit, or both of them together. Those
County magnates, who likewise were County members,
detested placemen as cordially as did their constituents.
The most important division, both in its moral and
political aspects, which took place between the adoption
of the Grand Remonstrance and the Second Reading
of the Great Reform Bill, was on the occasion when,
in April 1780, Parliament was called upon to declare
that the growing influence of the Crown was disastrous
to the nation. In that division sixty-two among the
English County members voted for the Resolution, and
only seven against it.

Holding their heads high, these men did not esteem
themselves as delegates, and still less as courtiers, but as
senators in the true sense of the term; and not even the
Roman senate, in its most powerful days, was more
supremely indifferent to the pressure of outside forces.
Party organisation, as we know it, was not then in existence. A man who asked nothing from the Government was free to take his own line. If he was not
himself a leader, he sought for direction from those of
his colleagues whose judgement he trusted, and who put
forward their views in a manner which pleased his taste
and persuaded his reason. The very last quarter to
which he would look for guidance was the daily press,
at a time when reporters were almost sure to be excluded
from a debate on any question by which opinion was
deeply stirred, and when editors were much too afraid
of the Speaker's Warrant to be formidable censors, or
frank and effective counsellors. The more sessions a
House of Commons had sat; the more good speeches
it had heard ; and the further it was removed from a
general election, with all the opportunity for the exertion
of illegitimate influence which at such a time a bad min-

istry enjoyed; — the better instrument it became for conducting the business of the country. That was the deliberate opinion of Burke; and he held it so strongly that he refused to support any proposal for shortening the duration of parliaments. So greatly, he said, were members affected by weighty arguments, cleverly put, that it was worth any man's while to take pains to speak well; and if, like Charles Fox, he spoke well whether he took pains or not, such a Parliament as that in which he now found himself was the very arena for an orator. He had fallen on days when rhetoric was at a premium, if only it was spontaneous; if it had good sense behind it; and if the quarter from which it came was favourably regarded by those for whose benefit it was produced. Aristocrats to the core, they lent their ears the more readily to one of themselves; and the titles of Fox to rank as an aristocrat, though abnormal, were generally and willingly recognised. His grandfather on the one side had been with Charles the First on the scaffold. His great-great-grandfather on the other side had stood to the same monarch in a much nearer relation; and the world had changed too little since the days of Monmouth and the Duke of Berwick for men of the world to trouble themselves greatly about the obliquity of the channel through which royal blood flowed in the veins of one whom they liked, and, to their surprise, were beginning even to respect. Charles had led his contemporaries, and only too many of his elders, in a career of fashion and folly; as he was now to lead them, with a pre-eminence equally undisputed, along more arduous and reputable paths. He sprang from a line of statesmen, conspicuous in place and long in years, though not in numbers; for Stephen Fox was serving the Crown four generations before ever his grandson entered public life. That grandson had now the authority of an old member in a fresh Parliament, which only knew his scrapes by hearsay, and, (whatever might be the case with its successor,) was not destined to witness a repetition of them. Eloquent and attractive, kindly and familiar with high and humble, he was inspired by a great cause with the new and needed qualities of patience, industry, and caution. In six years he acquired over his colleagues a mastery which, if the next dissolution had been deferred for another twelvemonth, would have made him, (what he soon afterwards became, and but for the unwisdom of a moment might have remained,) the master of the country. But that House of Commons, before it passed away, — teachable by events, and great in spite of errors, — had dealt a mortal blow to the famous system which the King and Bute, with the potent aid of Charles Fox's father, had constructed. It was a system which, as its one achievement of the first order, brought about the American war, and so made England sick, once and for all, of the very name of Personal Government.

But the lesson had not been learned when, late in November 1774, the Parliament met. For all that appeared on the surface, there was nothing to distinguish the occasion from others. Few signs were visible of serious dissatisfaction, or even of widespread interest. The King's speech began as usual with a tirade against the province of Massachusetts, and a guarded allusion to the spirit of disaffection prevalent in the other colonies; and the Opposition went to work in their desultory fashion. They confined themselves to asking for copies of the official correspondence relating to America, and for leave to defer making up their minds till further information had been given; but, small as was the demand which they made upon the courage of their party, they only succeeded in rallying seventy-three adherents. Even this paltry skirmish was as jealously guarded from the eyes of unprivileged spectators as the Potsdam manœuvres. The precincts were cleared of all strangers except members of the Irish Parliament, who were allowed what was for them the very superfluous opportunity of witnessing how smoothly things went in a Deliberative Assembly which was managed by bribery. Charles Fox gave the new House a first taste of his quality, and denounced the closing of the gallery as a mere trick to stifle inquiry; to shorten debate; and to enable ministers to maintain a convenient silence, and an air of unconcern which, alarming as they must have known the state of the nation to be, with characteristic effrontery they still professed to feel.

In spite of all precautions against publicity, one sentence got abroad which threw as much light on the intentions of the Government as many speeches; for Lord North contrived to say that the last Parliament had been a good one. He said it with Wilkes opposite him, whose presence in the existing House of Commons was an unspoken but unanswerable condemnation of the House which had preceded it. For six years the law had been strained and violated, popular rights had been trampled under foot, disorder had been provoked, and blood been shed; and all this had been done in order to establish the contention, — not that John Wilkes had been unduly elected, — but that he was unfit and unworthy then, or ever, to be a member of Parliament. And now he was visible on his bench, with his colleague for Middlesex, and three out of the four members for London City, round him; all of whom had signed a paper which virtually was an agreement to do as Wilkes bade them. There he sate, in secure anticipation of that popularity which, in the most good-natured of assemblies, awaits a man whom it has taken special and notorious pains to keep outside its doors. In order to prevent his election George the Third had been prepared copiously to administer those " gold pills " by which he thought it becoming for a King of England to influence public opinion. He had compassed town and country in vain to find Wilkes an opponent, and had urged the Secretary of the Treasury to set the Middlesex election "again on float," after Mr. Robinson himself had pronounced it as past praying, or paying, for. It was, indeed, a pill too bitter to be gilded. Wilkes could not be excluded from Parliament, and still less could he be ejected when once he had got there; for no candidate would face the crowd at Brentford, and no minister cared to have Wilkes and America on his hands at the same moment.   There was something heroic in the complacent dignity with which Johnson, (writing, it can hardly be doubted, on a hint from the Minister,) announced that the most awkward of customers was at last to be left with all the honours of victory.   " They," said the Doctor, " who are still filling our ears with Mr. Wilkes, lament a grievance that is now at an end.   Mr. Wilkes may be chosen, if any will choose him ; and the precedent of his exclusion makes not any honest or decent man think himself in danger." [1]   The warning which the situation contained, if George the Third had rightly interpreted it, would have been cheaply purchased at the price of even a deeper humiliation.   For the aspect of Wilkes among the crowd of members, cheerfully listening to the King's Speech at the bar of the House of Lords, was a foretaste of the scene eleven years later on when Mr. John Adams, the accredited Envoy from the United States, presented himself at St. James's as the first of all his fellow-citizens to stand before his Majesty in a diplomatic character.

On the earliest day that Parliament, and most of all a new Parliament, is assembled after a troubled and eventful recess, inexperienced politicians, who expect great things, are surprised to find that, instead of being very noisy and angry, everybody is very shy.   But in 1774 the deadness was of longer duration than a single evening ; for it was in the men and not in the moment.   The winter session ran its course.   Estimates were brought forward ; soldiers, sailors, and monies were voted ; and week after week of December slipped along as quietly as if the affairs of an empire, at peace with itself throughout its borders, were being administered by a cabinet of Solons.   The fact was that the principal members of the Opposition were engaged among themselves in one of their periodical discussions of a proposal which had

[1] *The Patriot,* 1774.

for them an extraordinary attraction, and on which they expended as much ink, in trying to convince each other, as would have covered every bookseller's counter in the kingdom with pamphlets showing up the policy of the Government. That proposal, to use their own favourite description, was a plan of non-attendance for Lord Rockingham's friends. The notion was that England would be brought to her senses by the contemplation of the empty benches. For very shame she would gird herself to the task of fighting her own political battles until such time as she could prevail on her leaders to leave their tent, and place themselves once more at the head of a resolute and repentant host of followers. The prospect was flattering ; and the Rockinghams would long ago have tried the experiment but for Burke, who told them that their secession must infallibly result in the Ministry being more free than ever for mischief, and in their being themselves forgotten by the public. Till the Christmas holidays, however, were over they could defend their inactivity by the excuse that they were waiting for Papers. On the nineteenth of January the Papers came. Lord North presented to the House a collection of letters, not from Massachusetts only, but from the governors of every colony, which proved beyond doubt or question that the whole continent of America, from New Hampshire to Georgia, had imitated, and in many instances outstripped, Boston in what the King's speech had described as violent and criminal resistance and disobedience to the law.

The case was presented in a style which might well arouse the envy of a modern politician whose vocation it has been to pick out the essential incidents in a long story from among the tiresome, and intricate, details with which the omnivorous appetite of Parliament has for many years past compelled the Foreign Office, and the Colonial Office, to load its table. With no official jargon, but in plain Eighteenth-century English, such as was spoken by the people whose deeds were being related, and by the members of Parliament who were to read the papers, the Governors and Deputy Governors set forth their budget of disastrous and ominous tidings. They told how the tea-ships had been turned away from every port where they showed themselves; how the farmers were drilling and arming, and were sinking the boats and overturning the carts which conveyed forage and provisions for the use of the army; how the Judges had cried off from their duties, and the King's writ had altogether ceased to run; and how the Governor of New Hampshire had just completed his admirable arrangements for supplying the wants of the garrison in Boston when the people of Portsmouth, his own principal trading-town, rose upon him, stormed his arsenal, and carried off a hundred barrels of powder. The one bright spot was in Virginia, where, when the House of Burgesses had turned themselves into a Convention, and met without leave from the Governor, the Headmaster of the Grammar-school had refused to preach them a sermon; but, as the Patriots were much better provided with eloquence than with ammunition, the news from Williamsburg did not counterbalance the serious character of the news from Portsmouth. Graver by far than any acted manifestations of discontent and estrangement were the Resolutions which had been passed at Philadelphia by that Congress in which Patrick Henry and the Adamses had been spokesmen, and Washington a guiding spirit. What purpose, human or divine, could be served by trying to dragoon such a population, so led and so minded, living along fifteen hundred miles of coast across three thousand miles of ocean, into paying a threepenny duty into the British Treasury?

It was a problem striking enough to impress the Poet Laureate. Whitehead thought the moment come for singing a word in season to the address of his Sovereign, and in 1775 he thus invoked the powers who guide the hearts of kings:—

> " Beyond the vast Atlantic tide
> Extend your healing influence wide
> Where millions claim your care.

> Inspire each just, each filial thought,
> And let the nations round be taught
> The British oak is there !"

The advice was well meant; but it fell as flat as the lines in which it was couched. Mason has commended Whitehead for insinuating sound counsel into the royal ear, in the shape of praise for wisdom and clemency which George the Third, unfortunately, had not the slightest intention of meriting. The Laureates of the eighteenth century were not of those to whom either kings or commoners looked for a contribution to the stock of political wisdom; nor, (except in the case of Warton,) for any other wisdom. Mason, a stout Whig, judged favourably of Whitehead's performances; but Samuel Johnson, who liked his politics even less than his poetry, called his odes "insupportable nonsense"; and posterity, irrespective of politics, has agreed with Johnson. Whitehead won his spurs, (if that phrase can be applied to the rider of such a Pegasus,) by a satire the title of which was "An Epistle on the Danger of Writing in Verse." It was his earliest serious performance; and it would have been well if the reflections which the theme suggested had warned him never to attempt another. So far as rhymes can throw light upon the relations of George the Third to the colonies, mankind will neglect Whitehead, and turn to the Birthday Ode of another bard who was not of the stuff out of which, in his day, a Poet Laureate was cut. What Robert Burns thought about the American war, and the policy of its royal author, may be seen in the fourth and fifth stanzas of "A Dream," — which he wrote, or professed to have written, on the Fourth of June, 1786. The poem is like the best Aristophanes, on those occasions when Aristophanes was writing with a serious political purpose underlying his humour and his fancy. There is nothing in the Choruses of the Old Greek Comedy more Attic, in every essential quality, than the admonition addressed to the Prince of Wales, the advice to the young Princesses, the compliments to

Lord Chatham and his famous son, the allusion to the loss of America, and the homely and downright judgment passed upon those Ministers whom, during the first two and twenty years of his reign, the king had delighted to honour.

> " 'Tis very true, my sovereign king,
>   My skill may weel be doubted :
> But facts are chiels that winna ding,
>   And downa be disputed.
> Your royal nest, beneath your wing,
>   Is e'en right reft and clouted;
> And now the third part o' the string,
>   An' less will gang about it
>   Than did ae day.
>
> " Far be't frae me that I aspire
>   To blame your legislation,
> Or say ye wisdom want, or fire
>   To rule this mighty nation!
> But, faith ! I muckle doubt, my Sire,
>   Ye've trusted ministration
> To chaps wha in a barn, or byre,
>   Wad better fill'd their station
>   Than courts yon day."

CHAPTER VII

THE KING AND LORD CHATHAM. FOX COMES TO THE
FRONT. THE AMERICAN FISHERIES

THE King had long ago settled his policy. "I am
clear," he announced to Lord North in the previous
September, "that there must always be one tax to keep
up the right; and, as such, I approve of the Tea Duty."
To secure this object he was prepared to fight, and was
in a hurry to begin. Ten days before Parliament met,
the first instalment of the American news had already
reached him. "I am not sorry," he wrote, "that the
line of conduct seems now chalked out, which the enclosed despatches thoroughly justify. The New England Governments are in a state of rebellion. Blows
must decide whether they are to be subject to this
country, or independent." He made no attempt to
conceal his satisfaction when he learned that the quarrel could not be patched up; and yet he did not, like
Napoleon, love war for its own sake; nor, like Louis
the Fourteenth, was he unscrupulously eager to make his
country great, and his own name great with it. Almost
as soon as he mounted the throne he had given a convincing proof of his indifference to personal glory and
national aggrandisement. At a time of life when the
desire of fame is a sign of virtue, or at worst a venial
fault, during the height of the most triumphant war in
which Britain has been engaged, he had thrust from
power the ablest war-minister whose deeds have been
recorded in her history; and he deserted the greatest ally
we ever possessed, at the exact moment of that ally's
greatest need. To the end of his days Frederic of Prussia
did not forget the pang of that appalling and unexpected

blow; and we were soon to learn that, when he remembered an injury, he was not of a nature to forgive it. The warlike promptings which actuated George the Third were neither ambitious nor patriotic, but political. He looked on the Americans not as foreign enemies arrayed against England, but as Englishmen who wanted more liberty than he thought was good for them; and he sent his fleets and his armies against them just as he would have ordered his Footguards to support the constables in clearing the street of a mob of Wilkites.

On one point, and one point alone, the King was in agreement with the great statesman out of whose control, as the first act of his reign, he had taken the destinies of the country. Chatham, like George the Third, regarded the colonists as compatriots. In his sight they were Englishmen, who did not choose to be taxed without being represented; Whigs, who had not abandoned the principles of the Great Revolution; fellow-citizens, who could not be subjugated without prospective, and even imminent, danger to the liberties of both our own islands. For Ireland had as much at stake as Great Britain, and Irishmen of all religions and classes were alive and awake to the consequences which would ensue at home if the cause ·of America was overborne and ruined. In such a contest, (so Chatham insisted,) every man had a right, or rather every man was under an obligation, to choose his side in accordance with the political faith which was in him. This was not a struggle against an external foe, but a dispute within our own family. "I trust," he wrote on the Christmas eve of 1774, "that it will be found impossible for freemen in England to wish to see three millions of Englishmen slaves in America." A month afterwards he had read the parliamentary papers, with the insight of one who had received and answered a thousand despatches from the same regions. "What a correspondence!" he exclaimed. "What a dialogue between Secretary of State and General in such a crisis! Could these bundles reach the shades below, the remarks of Ximenes and of Cortez upon them would be amusing." He need not have brought Ximenes in. When Chatham closed the volume, a yet stronger ruler than the Spaniard, and one who knew even better how to write to colonies and how to fight for them, had made himself master of the miserable narrative.

Already, before he knew the particulars, the heart of Chatham was too hot for silence. As the doom against America, (to use his own phraseology,) might at any hour be pronounced from the Treasury Bench, no time was to be lost in offering his poor thoughts to the public, for preventing a civil war before it was inevitably fixed. On the first day that the Lords met after Christmas he moved to address his Majesty to withdraw the troops from Boston, in order to open the way towards a happy settlement of the dangerous troubles in America. It was not a tactical success. Chatham had told Rockingham beforehand that he intended to pronounce himself against insisting on that theoretical right to tax America which Rockingham's own government had asserted in the Declaratory Act of 1766. Some of the Whigs were unwilling to throw over a Statute which, in its day, had formed part of a great compromise. Others were prepared to consider the question of repealing the Act, whenever that "proper time" arrived which in politics is always so very long upon its journey. The more prudent of them exerted themselves to suppress any public manifestation of the annoyance which their party felt. "My Lord," wrote the Duke of Manchester to his leader, "you must pardon my freedom. In the present situation of affairs nothing can be so advantageous to Administration, nothing so ruinous to opposition, nothing so fatal to American liberty, as a break with Lord Chatham and his friends. I do not mean to overrate his abilities, or to despair of our cause, though he no longer existed ; but, while the man treads this earth, his name, his successes, his eloquence, the cry of the many, must exalt him into a consequence perhaps far above his station." But the resentment of the Rockinghams was all the more bitter because they had to keep it among themselves. In their communications with each other they charged Chatham with the two unpardonable Parliamentary crimes of forcing their hand, and taking the wind out of their sails; and in the House they supported him reluctantly, and in small numbers.

But that was all of little moment compared with the fact that a famous and faithful servant of England had made known, to all and sundry, his view of the conduct which, at that complicated crisis, loyalty to England demanded. William Pitt, then in his sixteenth year, had helped his father to prepare for the debate; a process which, according to the experience of others who enjoyed the same privilege, consisted in hearing a grand speech delivered from an arm-chair, entirely different in arrangement, in wording, and in everything except the doctrine which it enforced, from the series of grand speeches which next day were declaimed in public when the orator had his audience around him.[1] "The matter and manner," (so the lad wrote to his mother on the morning after the discussion,) "were striking; far beyond what I can express. It was everything that was superior; and, though it had not the desired effect on an obdurate House of Lords, it must have had an infinite effect without doors, the bar being crowded with Americans. Lord Suffolk, I cannot say answered him, but spoke after him. My father has slept well, but is lame in one ankle from standing so long. No wonder he is lame. His first speech lasted over an hour, and the second half an hour; surely the two finest speeches that ever were made before, unless by himself." The most notable passage was that in which Chatham declared that the cause of America was the cause of all

[1] "I was at Hayes," (said Doctor Franklin,) "early on Tuesday, agreeable to my promise, when we entered into consideration of the plans; but, though I stayed near four hours, his Lordship, in the manner, I think, of all eloquent persons, was so full and diffuse in supporting every particular I questioned, that there was not time to go through half my memorandums. He is not easily interrupted; and I had such pleasure in hearing him that I found little occasion to interrupt him."

Irishmen, Catholic and Protestant alike, and of all true
Whigs in England; and in his mouth the name of Whig
included every man who was not a friend to arbitrary
power. The colonists were our countrymen; and, if
we persisted in treating them as aliens and foes, the
perils which awaited us were incalculable. Foreign
war, (so he told the House of Lords,) was at our door.
France and Spain were watching our conduct, and waiting for the maturity of our errors. The argument was
one not to be employed lightly; but if ever a statesman
was justified in referring to our neighbours across the
British Channel as our natural enemies it was at a period
when we had been at war with France for thirty years
out of the last eighty-five, and were still to be at war
with her for twenty-five years out of the next forty.
And if ever there was a man who might, without a sense
of abasement, refer to danger from abroad as an additional reason for dealing justly with our own people, it
was the minister who had fought France until he had
landed her in such a plight that no one, unless our
government was imprudent to madness, could foresee
the time when she would be in a position to fight us
again.

Any one who objected to Chatham's attitude on the
American question was at liberty to term him a poor
patriot and a bad citizen; and whatever reproach attached itself to his fame must be shared by those who
thought with him. Charles Fox was not easily abashed,
even when he was in worse company than Chatham's;
and at no time of his life did he care what names he
was called, as long as the course of action which earned
them was such that he could defend in the face of day.
He did not shrink from defining, as explicitly and clearly
as he stated everything, the governing motive by which
his conduct during those trying years was determined.
" I hope that it will be a point of honour among us all
to support the American pretensions in adversity as
much as we did in their prosperity, and that we shall
never desert those who have acted *unsuccessfully* from

Whig principles, while we continue to profess our admiration of those who succeeded in the same principles in 1688." That was how he wrote to his familiars in October 1776, when the colonists were on the edge of destruction, and when the liberties of England seemed worth but a very few years' purchase in the view of some who were neither fools nor cowards. Among them was Horace Walpole, who pronounced himself unable to conceive how a friend of British freedom could view with equanimity the subjection of America. Walpole little thought, (he said,) that he should have lived to see any single Englishman exulting over the defeat of our countrymen, when they were fighting for our liberty as well as for their own. Lord Chatham was not such an Englishman, nor Charles Fox either. They both of them looked upon the conflict as a civil war, in which no man was entitled, on any plea whatsoever, to rank himself against those whom in his conscience he believed to be in the right.

But when France stepped in, and our country was in danger, Fox took his place amongst the foremost, — nay, it may be said, *as* the foremost, — of Britain's defenders ; for no public man, out of office, has ever before or since played so energetic and effective a part in the management of a great war. "Attack France," he cried, "for she is your object. The war against America is against your own countrymen ; that against France is against your inveterate enemy and rival." In a series of speeches, replete with military instinct, he argued in favour of assuming the offensive against the fresh assailants who came crowding in upon a nation which already had been fighting until it had grown weary and disheartened. Aggressive action, (so he never ceased repeating,) was alike dictated by the necessities of the situation, and by the character, the spirit, and the traditions of our people. He urged the ministry, with marvellous force, knowledge, and pertinacity, to rescue the navy from the decay into which they had allowed it to sink. When the French and Spanish fleets rode the

Channel, with a superiority in ships of the line of two
to one, his anxiety carried him, and kept him, as close
to the scene of action as the most enterprising of lands-
men could penetrate.   He haunted the country houses
and garrison towns of the south-western coast, and lived
much on shipboard, where, as any one who knows sailors
could well believe, he was a general favourite.   He
shared the bitter mortification which his gallant friend,
the future Lord St. Vincent, felt when kept in harbour
at such a moment; and he went so far as to entertain
a hope of finding himself, a cheery and popular stowa-
way, in the thick of what promised to be the most desperate battle which, on her own element, England would
ever have fought.   He sympathised warmly with those
of his comrades and kinsmen who, having refused to
serve against America, were rejoiced at the prospect of
active employment when France entered the field; just
as a royalist, who would have cut off his right hand
rather than fire a pistol for the Parliament at Dunbar
or Worcester, might have been proud to do his share
among Cromwell's soldiers when they were driving the
Spanish pikemen across the sandhills at Dunkirk.   With
a steady grasp, and unerring clearness of vision, Fox
steered his course through intricate and tempestuous
waters; and he succeeded in reconciling, under difficulties as abstruse as ever beset a statesman, his fidelity
to a political creed with the duty which he owed to his
country.

At the commencement of 1775 Charles Fox was still
sadly behindhand in respect to the private virtues and
proprieties; but, as a statesman, he already was formidable by the virility of his powers and the fixity of
his purpose.   With his immediate object plain before
him, he went forth to take his place in a world too wise
to consider youth a drawback.   He was of the age at
which, ten years later on, Pitt superseded him in his
position as the first public man in Europe, and at which,
after another ten years, Napoleon in his turn superseded

Pitt.   Of the disadvantages which hampered others,
none existed for Fox. He was not, like the Rockinghams, bound by his antecedents to maintain against
America an abstract right of taxation, that could not be
enforced except by the sword which they thought it a
crime to draw. He was not, like Chatham, separated
from the majority of the Opposition by mutual dislike
and distrust. Fox was quite ready to pull with the
Whigs, if only they would do their share of work; and
he already was busy in the task of keeping them up to
the collar. "I am clear," he wrote to Burke, "that a
secession is now totally unadvisable, and that nothing
but some very firm and vigorous step will be at all
becoming."

By this time many people were looking about to see
where firmness and vigour could be found ; for the news
from America had begun to arouse the classes which
worked the hardest, and paid the most, to a perception
of the dangers towards which the country was being
hurried. "The landed interest," so Camden told Chatham before the middle of February, " is almost altogether anti-American, though the common people hold
the war in abhorrence, and the merchants and tradesmen for obvious reasons are likewise against it." Burke
complained to Mr. Champion, the constituent whom he
honoured with his confidence, that if men with business
interests had interfered decisively, when in the previous
winter the American question became acute, concilia-
tory measures would most certainly have been adopted.
Now, he said, they were beginning to stir because they
began to feel. It so happens that the exact date is
known when the true state of matters was first borne
in upon the public mind. A letter from London to a
gentleman in New York, dated the sixth of December,
1774, runs as follows : " This day there was a report
current that the Congress of the States of America had
adjourned, having fixed on stopping all imports into
America from Great Britain the first of this month.
From curiosity I strolled upon 'Change, and for the

first time saw concern and deep distress in the face of
every American merchant. This convinced me of the
truth of what I may have said before, that the merchants will never stir till they feel; and every one
knows that the manufacturers will never take the lead
of the merchants." [1]

The public despatches were alarming enough to those
who reflected that Governors and Lieutenant-Governors
would naturally have put the best face possible on a
situation which they themselves had done much to
create. But those despatches did not tell the worst.
Men could still write freely to each other across the
Atlantic; and the advices received by city merchants and
bankers were of a complexion to fill everybody, except
speculators for a fall, with a feeling nothing short of blank
dismay. No official papers from Maryland had been
printed, and it might have been supposed that no news
was good news as far as that colony was concerned;
but before December ended it came to be known that
a principal seaport of Maryland had placed itself in line
with Boston. When the brig Peggy Stewart of London, having on board two thousand pounds "of that
detestable weed tea," arrived at Annapolis, Messrs. William and Stewart, to whom the cargo was consigned,
put their hands to a paper acknowledging that they had
committed an act of most pernicious tendency to the
liberties of America. The same gentlemen then went
on board the said vessel, with her sails set and colours
flying, and voluntarily set fire to the tea. In a few
hours the whole freight, and the ship with it, had been
consumed by the flames in the presence of a great mul-

[1] The style of the letter to New York, with the curious similarity in certain expressions to those employed in the letter to Champion, renders it
more than possible that it was written by Burke, who, three years before,
had been appointed agent to the Assembly of New York with a salary of
500*l.* a year. It is true that he despatched a long and very famous epistle
from his home in Buckinghamshire on the fifth of December; but he was
speaking in the House of Commons that evening, and again on the sixth;
and he might well have gone on 'Change on the morning of the second of
those two days before writing the letter to the gentleman in New York.

titude of spectators. When the letter notifying this
transaction to the London correspondents of the unfortunate firm was passing up and down Threadneedle
Street, many a warm city man must have felt a shiver
go through him. In the same month a Whig nobleman received an account of the warlike preparations in
America, written at Philadelphia by General Lee, whose
reputation in fashionable military circles lent weight to
language which, like himself, was less soldierly than
soldatesque. "What devil of a nonsense can instigate
any man of General Gage's understanding to concur in
bringing about this delusion? I have lately, my Lord,
run through almost the whole colonies from the North
to the South. I should not be guilty of an exaggeration
in asserting that there are 200,000 strong-bodied active
yeomanry, ready to encounter all hazards. They are
not like the yeomanry of other countries, unarmed and
unused to arms. They want nothing but some arrangement, and this they are now bent on establishing. Even
this Quaker province is following the example. I was
present at a review at Providence in Rhode Island, and
really never saw anything more perfect. Unless the
banditti at Westminster speedily undo everything they
have done, their royal paymaster will hear of reviews
and manœuvres not quite so entertaining as those he is
presented with in Hyde Park and Wimbledon Common."
The time was too surely approaching when communications addressed from America to gentlemen and
noblemen in London would never get further than the
secret room in the Post Office; and colonists who wished
for peace hastened, while the avenues were open, to enlighten and admonish those English public men whom
they could hope to influence. At the end of 1774 a
member of the British Parliament was informed in two
letters from Pennsylvania that there were gunsmiths
enough in the Province to make one hundred thousand
stand of arms in one year, at twenty-eight shillings
sterling apiece; that the four New England colonies,
together with Virginia and Maryland, were completely

armed and disciplined; and that nothing but a total repeal of the Penal Acts could prevent a civil war in America.   The writer dealt as freely with large figures as General Lee; but he understood his countrymen better in a case where the merits of that officer were concerned; for the letters went on to explain that the colonies were not so wrapped up in the General's military accomplishments as to give him, when it came to choosing the Commander-in-Chief, a preference over Colonel Putnam and Colonel Washington, who had won the trust and admiration of the continent by their talents and achievements.   " There are several hundred thousand Americans who would face any danger with these illustrious heroes to lead them.   It is to no purpose to attempt to destroy the opposition to the omnipotence of Parliament by taking off our Hancocks, Adamses, and Dickinsons.   Ten thousand patriots of the same stamp stand ready to fill up their places."   Dickinson himself, writing not to England, but about England, summed up the view of the best and wisest men on his side of the controversy.   "I cannot but pity," he said, "a brave and generous nation thus plunged in misfortune by a few worthless persons.   Everything may be attributed to the misrepresentations and mistakes of Ministers; and universal peace can be established throughout the British world only by the acknowledgment of the truth that half a dozen men are fools or knaves.   If their character for ability and integrity is to be maintained by wrecking the whole empire, Monsieur Voltaire may write an addition to the chapter on the subject of ' Little things producing great events.' "[1]

From this time forwards there was a growing disposition in the House of Commons to take America seriously ; and there was a man in it determined never again to let the question sleep.   On the second of February, 1775, the Prime Minister moved an Address to the King, praying his Majesty to adopt effectual measures for

[1] The extracts given in this and the preceding paragraphs are all from the American Archives.

suppressing rebellion in the colonies. Later in the
evening a member rose, who, in the style of solemn cir-
cumlocution by which the chroniclers of proceedings in
Parliament appeared to think that they kept themselves
right with the law, was described as "a gentleman who
had not long before sat at the Treasury Board, from
whence he had been removed for a spirit not sufficiently
submissive, and whose abilities were as unquestioned as
the spirit for which he suffered." [1] Fox, (for Fox of
course it was,) proposed an amendment deploring that
the papers laid upon the table had served only to convince the House that the measures taken by his
Majesty's servants tended "rather to widen, than to
heal, the unhappy differences between Great Britain
and America." That was the turning point of his own
career, and the starting point for many others in a
hearty, fearless, and sustained opposition to the policy
of the Government. The effect of his oratory is established by various competent authorities; from the official
reporter, who broke off to remark that Mr. Charles Fox
spoke better than usual,[2] to Walpole, who records in his
journals that the young statesman entered into the whole
history and argument of the dispute with force and
temper, and made the finest figure he had done yet.

But the most lively and convincing testimony is found
in a letter written by a great man who on this occasion
learned, finally and resignedly, how hard it is even to
begin making a great speech. Gibbon had been getting
ready for the debate during the whole of the Christmas
holidays : studying the parliamentary papers as minutely
as if they had been the lost books of Dion Cassius ;
talking for four hours on end with one of the agents
from Massachusetts ; and "sucking Governor Hutchinson very dry," with as much probability of arriving at a
just conclusion as a Roman Senator who took his idea
of the Sicilian character from a private conversation with
Verres. But, when the hour came, he felt that he him-

---

[1] *The Annual Register* for 1775; chapter v.
[2] *The Parliamentary History of England*, vol. xviii., p. 227.

self was not the man for it. Throughout the Amendment on the Address, and the Report of the Address, he sate safe but inglorious, listening to the thunder which rolled around him. The principal antagonists on both days, he said, were Fox and Wedderburn ; of whom the elder displayed his usual talents, while the younger, embracing the whole vast compass of the question before the House, discovered powers for regular debate which neither his friends hoped, nor his enemies dreaded. On the first day, when Fox discoursed for an hour and twenty minutes, his contribution to the discussion is represented in the Parliamentary History by an abstract of five lines, and on the second day his name is not even mentioned ; while Wilkes obtained six columns, and Governor Johnston nine. It is evident, and indeed was sometimes as good as confessed in a foot-note, that, in those early and artless days of reporting, a speaker got back in print what he gave in manuscript. Fox would as soon have thought of writing down what he was going to say as of meeting a bill before it fell due ; and the rapid growth of his fame may be estimated by a comparison between the reports of 1775, and those of 1779 and 1780. Before the Parliament was dissolved, his more important speeches were reproduced without the omission of a topic, and, (so far as the existing resources of stenography admitted,) without the abbreviation of a sentence.

Fox took the sense of the House on his Amendment, and had reason to be satisfied with the result. He had been long enough a member of Parliament to have learned that, in politics, all's well that ends pretty well. The minority mustered over a hundred ; a number exceeding by forty the best division which, in the former Parliament, was obtained against the worst of the American measures. It would have been reckoned a most weighty protest on any occasion when any House of Commons has been invited to take steps which responsible ministers affirm to be necessary for vindicating the honour, and securing the predominance, of the country ;

but it was doubly significant in that age of intimidation and bribery. All who voted on the one side were perfectly well aware that, in so doing, they cut themselves off from the hope of their sovereign's favour, or even of his forgiveness. And meanwhile a full half of those who voted on the other side were drawing public salary, without rendering any public service except that of doing as they were bid; or were fingering money which had passed into their pockets from the Exchequer by methods that in our day would have been ruinous both to him who received, and to him who bestowed. The King pronounced the majority " very respectable "; as to him, in both senses of the word, it no doubt seemed. So pleased was he that he kindly condoled with his Minister on having been kept out of bed, (which in the case of Lord North was a very different thing from being kept awake,) till so late an hour as three o'clock in the morning.

That minister, however, was less easily satisfied. He now knew himself to be face to face with a very different opposition from anything which in the existing Parliament he had hitherto encountered; and he recognised the quarter from which vitality had been infused into the counsels and procedures of his adversaries. Before a fortnight had elapsed he came down to the House with a Resolution promising, in the name of the Commons, that any American colony, in which the Assembly consented to vote money for certain stated public purposes, should be exempted from the liability to be taxed by the British Parliament. Every man, in that Parliament and outside it, saw that the plan was specially and carefully framed to meet the argument on which, in his recent speeches, Charles Fox had founded the case that he had so brilliantly advocated. Governor Pownall, who immediately followed North, stated, in well-chosen words which no one ventured to contradict, that the Resolution was a peace offering to the young ex-minister.[1] Such a recognition would have been a

[1] "An honourable gentleman, in a late debate, certainly was the first, and the only one, to hit upon the real jet of the dispute between this coun-

high compliment from any man in office to any private member; but when paid by a First Lord of the Treasury to a former subordinate, who had left his Board within the twelvemonth, and had been attacking him ever since, it was a piece of practical adulation which put to a searching and unexpected proof both the strength of conviction, and the presence of mind, of him to whom it was addressed.

On neither of the two points was Fox unequal to the test. While Pownall was speaking, he had time to decide on his line of action, the importance of which he at once discerned. It was his first chance of showing that he possessed the qualities of a true parliamentary leader, who could make the most of a tactical situation without surrendering, in the smallest particular, his loyalty to a great cause. He commenced his remarks by congratulating the public on the change in the Prime Minister's attitude. The noble Lord, who had been all for violence and war, was treading back in his own footprints towards peace. Now was seen the effect which a firm and spirited opposition never failed to produce. The noble Lord had lent his ear to reason; and, if the minority in that House persevered in supporting the rights and liberties of the colonies, the process of his conversion would go on apace. He had spoken of the Americans with propriety and discrimination. He had refused to allow that they were rebels; and even to Massachusetts he would gladly open a door through which she might return to her allegiance. He had distinctly stated that Great Britain, dealing as one nation according to diplomatic usage deals with another, had at the outset demanded more than in the end she would insist on exacting; and, once that principle

---

try and America. He very ably stated that the reason why the colonies objected to the levying taxes, for the purposes of a revenue in America, was that such revenue took out of the hands of the people that control which every Englishman thinks he ought to have over that government to which his rights and interests are entrusted. The mode of appropriation specified in this Resolution takes away the ground of that opposition." — *The Parliamentary History of England;* Feb. 20, 1775.

admitted, the noble Lord would be as much inclined on
a future day to recede from what he proposed now, as
now he was ready to give up that which he had before
so strenuously defended.   But for the present the noble
Lord had not gone far enough.   He aimed at standing
well with the two sets of people whose views were irre-
concileable :— the colonists who were resolved, under
no conditions, to admit the right of Parliament to tax
them ; and the supporters of the Government who were
equally determined, in every contingency, to assert that
right and exercise it.   The noble Lord had wished
to content both parties, and he had contented neither.
On the countenances of gentlemen opposite, so far as
he was able to read them, the orator could descry no
symptoms of satisfaction ; and the Americans, it was
only too certain, must and would reject the offer with
disdain.

The speech was marked by the highest art, — that
of saying precisely what the speaker thought, in the
plainest language, and without a syllable over.   A
scene ensued when he resumed his place which was
long remembered within the House of Commons, and
has occupied a space in English and American histories
out of all proportion to its intrinsic consequence, except
so far as it discredited the Prime Minister, and established the position and authority of Fox.   It was one
of those rare moments when a great party, in a tumult
of indignant surprise, shakes off the control of those
to whom it is accustomed to look for guidance ; when
the Ministers sit on thorns, or jump up, each in his
turn only to confound confusion, and attract on to
his own head a share of the impertinences with which
the air is swarming ; and when an opposition feels itself
repaid in the wild joy of a single hour for long years
of disappointment and abstinence.   North, like much
greater men before and after him, experienced the in-
convenience of having sprung a policy on his followers,
and on not a few of his colleagues.   The mutiny began
at headquarters.   Welbore Ellis, a placeman who had

already turned his hundredth quarter-day, querulously
announced that, as a man of honour, he felt bound to
oppose the Minister; and though North could hardly
be called a sick lion, the House hailed with glee an
occurrence which bore a strong resemblance to a very
familiar fable. Rigby was seen taking notes, and could
with difficulty be persuaded to put them back into his
pocket; but he did not fail to make his views known
to that part of the audience which was the least likely
to be gratified by them. An aside from him was more
formidable than an oration from Welbore Ellis; and
every Right Honourable Gentleman within earshot on
the Treasury bench was obliged to hear how, in Rigby's
opinion, the proper persons to move and second Lord
North's Resolution were Mr. Otis and Mr. Hancock, of
whom the one had been the ringleader in the agitation
against the Stamp Act, and the other had superintended
the destruction of the tea. The most violent in the fray
was Captain Acland, a cousin by marriage of Charles
Fox. He was a young man of fierce manners and
dauntless courage, who now was always to the front
when sharp words were being exchanged; especially
where there was a prospect that on the next morning
recourse would be had to yet more pointed weapons.
Acland assailed the Government in a style which aroused
the wonder even of Chatham; whose standard of the
lengths to which a young military man might go, when
denouncing his elders in the House of Commons, had,
in the days when he himself was a cornet of horse, been
notably a generous one.[1]

The real danger to the Ministry lay in the sulkiness
of the King's Friends. These gentlemen, by an unac-
countable blunder, had been left without their orders.
Having to decide for themselves as to what their em-

[1] "Lord North was, in the beginning of the day, like a man *exploded*,
and the judgment of the House, during about two hours, was that his
Lordship was going to be in a considerable minority; Mr. Ellis and others,
young Acland in particular, having declared highly and roughly against
his desertion of the cause of cruelty." — Chatham to his wife; Feb. 21, 1775.

ployer expected of them, they naturally enough concluded that, as in the parallel case of Rockingham and
the repeal of the Stamp Act, their duty to the King
required them to stab his Minister in the back.   North
had been up five or six times, and matters were looking
very black for the Government, when, before it was too
late, a deft and able ally came to the rescue.   Sir Gilbert Elliot was a politician of account in his own generation, and had ere this been honoured by a message
from the King to the effect that he did not take so forward a part in the House of Commons as his abilities
warranted.   But he needed no one to tell him how to
make the most of his remarkable qualities ; and he reserved himself for emergencies when a King's Friend,
who could speak as well as vote, was of more value than
dozens or scores of silent courtiers.

Gilbert Elliot's political fortunes had gained much,
but his posthumous celebrity has suffered not a little,
from the unique distinction of his family; for he was
the midmost of five eminent men, with the same Christian name and surname, who succeeded each other as
father and son.   The world, glad to have anything by
which to identify him, has remembered him as the
writer of a pastoral song, admired by Sir Walter Scott.
It began with the line, perhaps better known than the
rest of the poem,

"My sheep I neglected, I broke my sheep-hook."

The author of the ditty now proved that he was skilled
in the use of that rustic implement.   Elliot bluntly
warned the official flock that it was high time to leave
off butting at each other, and scampering at large over
the country.   He contrived to convey something into
his manner which suggested to the King's Friends that
they were on the wrong scent ; as indeed was the case,
since the whole business had been arranged beforehand
between the Sovereign and the Minister.   The storm
abated ; and Fox, who saw that there had been sufficient of it for his purposes, moved that the Chairman

should leave the Chair. A division took place, and there was some cross-voting; for on both sides there were, as usual, certain of those ingenious senators who please themselves with thinking that they indicate their opinion on the main issue by the course they take on a technical point which is understood by no one outside Parliament, and by fewer within it than is generally believed. And so the business ended, with a twofold result. Fox, in his character of a champion of liberty, had shown himself not less prompt a warrior, and a much more judicious strategist, than in the days when he figured as Lord of Misrule in all the sham tournaments of the House of Commons. And North had been effectually frightened, for some long time to come, out of any inclination to try his hand at the conciliation of America.

The Prime Minister had no desire for a repetition of the lesson which that twentieth of February had taught him. He saw very plainly what his place would have been worth at noon on the twenty-first if the King's Friends had been correct in thinking that they had the King behind them. So long as North held his present employment there was no demand for the services of his better self; and he returned once more to plod the weary round of coercive legislation. The main occupation of Parliament during that session was a bill for excluding the New England colonies from the principal fishing grounds within their reach, and notably from the banks of Newfoundland. It was out of the cod fishery that the prosperity of those colonies had originally sprung; and by the same industry it was still largely maintained. A sea captain in the early years of the seventeenth century calculated that the charge of equipping a ship of a hundred tons, with eight boats of the sort now called "dories" on board, was four hundred pounds. "Eight boats with 22 men in a Summer doe usually kill 25,000 fish for every Boat. Sometimes they have taken above 35,000 for a Boat, so that they load not onely their owne Ship, but other spare ships which come thither onely to buy the overplus." This captain went on to explain that the cargo, if taken in the right season to the right market, (which was not "Touloune or Merselus," but England,) would sell for 2,250*l.* "At New Plimoth, in Aprill," the writer proceeded, "there is a fish much like a herring that comes up into the small brookes to spawne. After those the Cod also presseth in such plenty, even into the very harbours, that they have caught some in their arms, and hooke them so fast that three men oft loadeth a Boat of two tuns in two houres." [1]

James the First had conferred upon the settlers in New England the exclusive privilege of fishing in North American waters. That concession was justly resented by the English Parliament; but the colonists forbore from enforcing their uttermost rights, and indeed had no occasion for them. They lived and throve by fishing not because they were monopolists, but because they were on the spot; because the best boat-builders in the world, and very far from the worst ship-builders, had their yards at Boston ; and because, above all, they belonged to the right race for the work. And now, when it was proposed for political objects to drive them from the pursuit of their calling, the uneasiness which had begun to pervade the commercial world deepened into consternation. It was vain for the Ministry to hold forth the bait of the spoils of New England, and to evoke patriotic cupidity by the prospect of the three hundred thousand pounds, or the five hundred thousand pounds, which would be transferred yearly from the ship-owners of Salem and Providence to the ship-owners of Poole and Dartmouth. The trained leaders of commerce, who knew the open secrets of solid and profitable business, did not look for information from hack-writers whose statistics and

---

[1] The account may be found in " *The Generall Historie of Virginia, New England, and the Summer Isles,* by Captaine John Smith, London, 1624 "; under the head of " Master Dee, his opinion for the building of Ships."

arguments were dictated to them in Downing Street. The whole life of every English merchant and banker, and of his father and grandfather before him, had been one continuous course of instruction in the present and progressing value of the trade with America. The exports to Pennsylvania alone had increased fifty-fold in less than three-quarters of a century. New England was a large and regular customer, with an enormous current debt owing to British exporters and manufacturers. That custom would be a thing of the past, and those debts could never be recovered, if, with the loss of her fishing, she lost the means of providing herself with imported goods, and paying for those which she had received already. Nor was it only a question of New England. The colonies, one and all, were on honour to stand and fall together; and, when the cruel and insulting measure now before Parliament was once in the Statute-book, all hope that Congress would drop the non-importation agreement would have to be definitely abandoned.

This time there was little hesitation in the action of the mercantile classes throughout the English-speaking world ; and there could be no mistake as to their views, which found a voice in petitions, in deputations, and in evidence proffered at the bar of the Lords. The planters of the Sugar Islands, resident in London, entreated the House of Commons to stay its hand. As time went on, and the news of what was purposed reached the tropics, the Assembly of Jamaica, in the hurry of a well-grounded panic, drew up and despatched a petition explaining how in their case, with a vast slave population around and among them, the very existence of society would be endangered by the cessation of their traffic with the American colonies. The Society of Friends represented to Parliament the case of Nantucket, an island which lay off the coast of Massachusetts. The population subsisted on the whale fishery, and owned a fleet of one hundred and forty sail. The agricultural produce of Nantucket would hardly support twenty families ; but the island contained more than five thousand inhabitants.   Nine out of ten among them were Quakers, of whom none were disaffected politicians, and all drank tea to a man.   That was a sample of the extent to which the bill would involve opponents, well-wishers, and neutrals in one common destruction. The sentiments of the higher commerce, in its central haunt, found expression in an address laid by the Lord Mayor, the Aldermen, and the Liverymen at the foot of the Throne.   The occupant of that august seat received their remonstrance in public with marked coldness, and characterised it in private as a new dish of insolence from the shop which had fabricated so many.   It was a shop the proprietors of which could not fairly be charged with interfering in matters outside their own province ; for the debts due from New England amounted to eight hundred thousand pounds in the City of London alone.

The bill for restraining the trade and commerce of the New England colonies afforded Parliament one more opening to arrange by policy those difficulties which were rapidly tending towards a solution by the arbitrament of war.   That last opportunity was soon a lost one ; but the spokesmen of the minority comported themselves in a manner worthy of the supreme occasion, and of the great assembly to which they belonged. It was a question precisely suited to the genius of Burke.   The final series of appeals in which he exhorted the House of Commons to settle the American controversy by light and right, before it came to a contest of might, showed more than his usual power of mastering the details of trade and finance, and converting them into oratory for the instruction of his audience, and into literature for the admiration of posterity.   As member for Bristol he was bound to do his utmost in the interests of commerce ; and his constituents, the best of whom were not undeserving of such a representative, had supplied him with fresh stores of facts and calculations in addition to those which he possessed already.   His speaking had never been more rich in the fruit, and more sparing in the flowers; and he had his reward in the close and respect-ful attention of hearers uneasily conscious that the fate of the empire was slipping out of their grasp, and that an impulse had been given to it which might carry it far in the wrong direction.

Burke's exertions were supported and supplemented by Fox with an abundance, but no superfluity, of that straightforward and unlaboured declamation which, from his earliest to his latest speech, always commanded the ear, and never offended the taste, of the House of Commons. With headlong, but sure-handed, energy of delineation he sketched out the broad lines of states-manship, and filled them in with the special circum-stances of the situation. His warning against the folly of presenting all Americans, whatever might be their political sympathies, with the alternative of starvation or rebellion, impressed his listeners by its force and directness, and received striking confirmation at the critical moments of the war. On three several occasions the fate of a campaign was largely influenced by those very fishermen who had been driven wholesale from their employment into the ranks of Washington's army. The enthusiasm, the intrepidity, and the professional skill of the mariners, who served as soldiers in the New England regiments, enabled their general to deprive the British garrison of the supplies which abounded on the islands in Boston harbour; to accomplish the retirement from the lines of Brooklyn which averted what otherwise must have been a crowning disaster; and to effect that crossing of the Delaware on a mid-winter midnight which secured for him the most sorely wanted of all his successes. The loyalist poets amused themselves by describing how

> "Priests, tailors, and cobblers fill with heroes the camp,
> And sailors, like craw-fish, crawl out of each swamp."

But, as a matter of history, those sailors had walked ashore in a very dangerous temper from the fishing vessels which, in consequence of the action of Parliament, were lying useless alongside the quays of every town and village on the seaboard of New England.[1]

Fox's argument, roughly and insufficiently reported, has not come down to us in the shape for insertion in a handbook of oratorical extracts; but it has the stamp of a speech hot from the heart, and spoken by a man who thought only of convincing or confuting those who heard him, without caring how his words would read on the next morning, or in another century. "You have now," said Fox, "completed the system of your folly. You had some friends yet left in New England. You yourselves made a parade of the number you had there. But you have not treated them like friends. How must they feel, what must they think, when the people against whom they have stood out in support of your measures say to them: 'You see now what friends in England you have depended upon. They separated you from your real friends, while they hoped to ruin *us* by it; but since they cannot destroy *us* without mixing *you* in the common carnage, your merits to them will not now save you. You are to be starved indiscriminately with us. You are treated in common with us as rebels, whether you rebel or not. Your loyalty has ruined you. Rebellion alone, if resistance is rebellion, can save you from famine and ruin.' When these things are said to them, what can they answer?"

The opposite view to that held by Fox and Burke did not suffer for want of being boldly stated. A recent addition to the notabilities of Parliament had been made in the person of Henry Dundas, now Lord Advocate for Scotland, who very soon gave indication of those qualities which were to win for him his considerable future, and his unenviable fame. He entered on his career in the House of Commons with the advantage of having early in life played leading parts on a narrower stage. He had been Solicitor-General in the Court of Session of Edinburgh at four and twenty; and had

---

[1] The verse is quoted in Tyler's *Literary History*.

learned to debate, if he had learned nothing else there for his profit, in the General Assembly of the Church of Scotland. Tall and manly, — with a marked national accent of which, unlike Wedderburn, he had the good sense not to be ashamed, — his look and bearing betokened indefatigable powers and a dominant nature. His face showed evident marks of his having been a hearty fellow, for which a convivial generation liked him none the less; especially when they came to find that his speeches had other things in them which were broad besides their Scotch,[1] and that those who followed him closely might hope to carry away what passed for a good story after dinner, in circles which were not fastidious. Dundas now took upon himself to defend the ministerial proposal against the strictures of Charles Fox. The measure, he said, was not sanguinary; and, as for the famine which was so pathetically lamented, his only fear was that the Act would fail to produce it. Though prevented from fishing in the sea, the New Englanders had fish in their rivers; and though their country was not fit to grow wheat, they had a grain of their own, their Indian corn, on which they could subsist full as well as they deserved.

Such was the man who, when he was twenty years older, and neither more nor less unfeeling, had at his absolute disposal the liberties of Scotland, and the lives and fortunes of all who loved those liberties too ardently for their own safety. On the present occasion Dundas had gone further in his self-revelation than was pleasing to a House of Commons not yet accustomed to him and his ways. Lord John Cavendish, speaking amidst general sympathy, gravely rebuked the Minister who had uttered sentiments which would have been shocking even in the mouth of a parliamentary buffoon; and Burke followed

---

[1] Omond's *Lord Advocates of Scotland;* chapter xiv. Boswell, who had his personal jealousies, and his own political ambitions outside the Scotch Bar, was greatly exercised when Dundas began to play a part in London. He called the new Minister "a coarse dog." The specimen of Dundas's humour referred to by Mr. Omond, and reported in the 20th volume of the *Parliamentary History*, is not so much coarse as revolting.

up the attack in plain vernacular suited to the character of the offence which he was chastising. Nothing, he said, could be more foolish, more cruel, and more insulting than to hold out as a resource to the starving fishermen, ship-builders, and ship-carpenters, who would be ruined by the Act that, after the plenty of the Ocean, they might poke in the brooks, and rake in the puddles, and diet on what Englishmen considered as husks and draff for hogs. The friends of the Government who had been too apt, as Horace Walpole said, to treat the Americans in the spirit of a mob ducking a pickpocket, were ashamed at seeing their own worst features distorted in that brazen mirror. The Lord Advocate in vain attempted to extenuate, to explain, and, if possible, to excuse his conduct. Even the majority had had enough of him; and the only acceptable sentence of his second speech was that in which he announced that he should bow to the disposition of the House, and say no more.

It was time that an example should be made. Sandwich and Rigby were the two Ministers whose words went for most, because it was believed that they ruled the Government. As if by concert between themselves, they now adopted a tone of forced and studied insolence with reference to the colonists. One would think, Rigby said in the House of Commons, that the Americans were otters and ate nothing but fish. As to the notion, of which so much had been heard, that they might find courage in despair, it was an idea thrown out to frighten women and children. They had not amongst them the military prowess of a militia drummer. The Earl of Sandwich enlarged on the same theme in the House of Lords. What did it signify, he asked, if the colonies abounded in men, so long as they were raw, undisciplined, and cowardly? For his own part he wished that they would put into the field not forty thousand, but two hundred thousand, so-called soldiers; as the greater their numbers, the easier would be the conquest. And then he proceeded to tell the peers an anecdote which he professed to have got from

Sir Peter Warren. He related at considerable length, and with infinite gusto, how at the siege of Louisburg in 1745 the Americans had been placed in the front of the army; how they had shown much elation at the honour which had been conferred upon them, though they boasted that it was no more than their due; how they all ran away when the first shot was fired; how Sir Peter then posted them in the rear, and told them that it was the custom of generals to preserve their best troops to the last, especially among the ancient Romans, who were the only nation that ever resembled the Americans in courage and patriotism.

The story was a lie, on the face of it. No man with a grain of knowledge about military affairs would have believed it for a moment; and no man of honour would have repeated it without believing it, even if he were not a responsible Minister addressing Parliament. By putting it into the mouth of a British Admiral, Sandwich insulted not only the Americans, but the honest and generous service over which he unworthily presided. The speech was a poor compliment to the gratitude, or else to the information, of the peers; for it was known and acknowledged that the land force employed in those operations, which resulted in the first capture of Louisburg, had been levied in New England, and had behaved to admiration.[1] The Lords resented the language which

---

[1] Parkman says in the first chapter of his *Montcalm and Wolfe :* "New England had borne the heaviest brunt of the preceding wars. Having no trained officers, and no disciplined soldiers, and being too poor to maintain either, she borrowed her warriors from the workshop and the plough, and officered them with lawyers, merchants, mechanics, and farmers. To compare them with good regular troops would be folly ; but they did, on the whole, better than could have been expected, and in the last war achieved the brilliant success of the capture of Louisburg." The exploit, Parkman goes on to say, was owing partly to good luck, and partly to native hardihood.

Captain Mahan writes : "The most solid success, the capture of Cape Breton Island in 1745, was achieved by the colonial forces of New England, to which indeed the royal navy lent valuable aid ; for to troops so situated the fleet is the one line of communication." Lord Stanhope, in his History, attributes the taking of Louisburg to the people of New England. "For their commander they chose Mr. Pepperel, a private gentleman, in whom courage and sagacity supplied the place of military skill."

Sandwich had addressed to them.   The Earl of Suffolk, Secretary of State though he was, took his colleague of the Admiralty roundly to task ; and sixteen peers, in the Protest which they entered on the Journals, recorded their opinion that the topic so much insisted upon by a Lord high in office, namely the cowardice of his Majesty's American subjects, had no weight in itself as an argument for the bill, and was not at all agreeable to the dignity of sentiment which ought to characterise their House.

These taunts, directed against a people as high-mettled as our own, and more acutely alive to what was said and thought about them, exercised on the martial spirit of the colonists the same effect as Wedderburn's speech before the Privy Council had produced on their political sensibilities.   The records of America, during the next two years, indicate on every page how many recruits of the choicest sort were impelled into her armies by the determination that such a reproach should be proved a calumny.   Her national literature, throughout the next generation, shows that the memory rankled long after the veterans who survived the war had gone back to the stack-yard and the counting-house.   Unfortunately no one intervened in the debates who, with the authority of personal experience, could testify to the real value of the colonial militiamen.   Those great soldiers, who had served with them in the field, were in retirement or in the grave.   Chatham, who owed them so large a debt, was prevented by ill health from coming down to the House of Lords in order to abash their detractors.   From his sick-chamber he wistfully and critically watched all that was passing ; and he was not left without his consolations.   The Marquis of Granby, before he came of age, had been returned as member for the University of Cambridge for the sake of the hero whose noble portrait, as he stands by his charger, lights up the Great Combination Room of Trinity College with life and colour. The son was resolved that, as far as he could speak for his dead father, something should be heard, even at second hand, from one who had learned to be a judge of courage amid scenes very different from those with which the Bedfords were familiar. Breaking silence for the first time, he followed Rigby with a fine vindication of the colonists, and a happily expressed tribute to the Minister who had made use of their valour for the protection and enlargement of the Empire. His reward was a letter dictated by Chatham, exquisite in feeling, and containing words of praise which, coming from such a quarter, would do more than volumes of good advice to turn a young man into the right path.[1]

It may be observed with satisfaction that the chorus of calumny was swelled by no one with soldierly antecedents, or with the making of a soldier in him. Captain Acland, who was much too ready to inform Parliament how cordially he disliked the inhabitants of Massachusetts, always spoke of their martial qualities with decency, and even with respect. The time was not far distant when he learned the whole truth about the fighting value of New Englanders. After the last of a succession of hot engagements, in all of which he had shown daring and skill, he was picked up desperately wounded, well within the American lines; and, in the course of the ensuing year, his services to his country were cut short in a duel with a brother officer who had sneered in his presence at the military character of those colonists whom, brave as he was, Acland knew to be no less brave than himself.

[1] Chatham to Granby, April 7, 1775; from a draft in Lady Chatham's handwriting.

CHAPTER VIII

AMHERST AND GAGE. THE MASSACHUSETTS CONGRESS.
HOSTILITIES BECOME IMMINENT. LEXINGTON

RIGBY had told the House of Commons that, if the
Acts against which Congress protested were repealed,
the seat of the Empire would henceforward be at Philadelphia ; and he recommended gentlemen ambitious of
a career to transfer themselves to that capital, and enjoy
the honour of consorting with Dr. Franklin. For the
great American had now started on his way back across
the ocean ; though it was no fault of Rigby that he was
not still in London, and in very uncomfortable quarters.
If, by the publication of Hutchinson's letters, Franklin
contributed to embroil the relations between England
and the colonies, he had abundantly expiated his own
error, and had done his best to redeem the errors of
others. His existence during the last fourteen months
had been one long penance, which he endured manfully
and patiently, because he was conscious that he, and he
alone, possessed in combination the knowledge, position,
character, and capacity indispensable to any one who
aspired to bring the last faint chance of peace to a successful issue. On the day after the scene in the Privy
Council Office, he had been dismissed from his Postmastership; and, of his own accord, he dispensed himself
from all diplomatic ceremonies, keeping aloof from
levees, and abstaining from direct and ostensible intercourse with Cabinet Ministers, the most powerful among
whom made no secret of their opinion that the proper
residence for him was the inside of Newgate. Meanwhile his wife, to whom he had been happily married
forty-four years, and from whom he had been parted

for ten, was dying at home in Pennsylvania; and he never saw her again. But at no time in his life was his society so eagerly courted by such eminent men, for the promotion of such momentous objects. Chatham, (whom Franklin had once found unapproachable, but who, as is the case with strong and haughty, but generous, natures, had grown mild and mellow with years,) secured him as a guest in Kent, called on him at his lodgings in a street off the Strand, and took care to be seen paying him marked attention in public. In the House of Lords the old statesman, with characteristic ignorance of the non-essential, took Franklin to the space before the throne, which is reserved for Privy Councillors and the eldest sons of peers. On learning his mistake he limped back to the outer Bar, and commended his friend to the care of the door-keepers in accents which all might hear.

Lord Howe, now a Rear Admiral, who, if hostilities broke out, was sure of an important command, honoured himself by an endeavour to avert a war which could not fail to bring him wealth, however small might be the opportunity for acquiring glory. He commissioned his sister to challenge Franklin to a trial of skill at chess, and contrived to be within call on an evening when the invitation had been accepted.[1] Lord Howe, in the phrase of the day, opened himself freely to his new acquaintance on the alarming situation of affairs, and put him into communication with Lord Hyde, the Chancellor of the Duchy of Lancaster; and Lord Hyde, as was well understood all round, meant Lord Dartmouth. The Secretary for the Colonies would have given his salary, many times told, to prevent bloodshed; though in the last resort he could not induce himself to thwart, or even to contradict, a master towards whom he entertained a true attachment, and who esteemed him as he deserved. For George the Third was at his very best when exchanging ideas with Dartmouth for any

[1] Franklin's *Account of Negotiations in London for effecting a Reconciliation between Great Britain and the American Colonies.*

other purpose than that of harrying him into harrying the Americans. " If the first of duties," (so the Monarch wrote to the Minister in July, 1773,) " that to God, is not known, I fear no other can be expected; and as to the fashionable word 'honour,' that will never alone guide a man farther than to preserve appearance. I will not add more; for I know I am writing to a true believer; one who shows by his actions that he is not governed by the greatest of tyrants, Fashion." A slave of Fashion Dartmouth was not; but he was too subservient to Lord North, and most terribly afraid of Lord Sandwich.[1]

An unofficial negotiation for settling the difficulties between Great Britain and the colonies was set on foot forthwith. The details were conducted by Franklin in concert with two of those Englishmen of the middle class who, if a chance was given them, were able and willing to employ upon the business of the nation the same diligence and sagacity with which they had long managed their own. Mr. Barclay was a well-known member of the Society of Friends, as likewise was his colleague, Dr. Fothergill; a physician with a great London practice, and a Natural Historian of remarkable distinction. Their deliberations took shape in a document called by the modest name of a " Paper of Hints for Conversation." In truth it was the draft of a treaty which, if it had been approved, signed, and ratified, would have had a merit rare among the celebrated instruments in history; — that of terminating a sharp and extended controversy rationally, equitably, permanently, and without derogation to the self-esteem of either of the contracting parties. A copy of the proposed Articles had been in Dartmouth's hands, and he

---

[1] His Majesty, on one occasion, asked Dr. Beattie what he thought of Lord Dartmouth; and the author of the *Essay on Truth* responded with effusion which bordered on the fulsome. The King, who spoke and wrote a style greatly preferable to that of some among his subjects who most pleased the literary taste of the hour, smiled and said: " Doctor Beattie, you are perfectly right. I think precisely the same of him myself. He is certainly a most excellent man."

expressed himself about them hopefully and favourably in private. On the first of February, 1775, Chatham presented to Parliament a Bill for settling the troubles in America, and the Secretary for the Colonies begged their Lordships not to kill the measure by an immediate vote, but to let it lie on the Table until it had received their careful and respectful consideration. In his sincere desire to do his duty, according to the light of his own understanding, Dartmouth had for a moment forgotten the terrors of the Bedfords. Sandwich, who suspected that peace was in the crucible, knew only too well that premature publicity may be as discomforting to those who are planning good as to those who are plotting evil. He chose his moment with a sinister address, worthy of the orator who turned the debate in the Second Book of " Paradise Lost." Looking full and hard at Franklin, who was leaning over the Bar, Sandwich exclaimed that he had in his eye the person who drew up the proposals which were under discussion, — one of the bitterest and most mischievous enemies whom England had ever known. Chatham hastened to interpose the shield of his eloquence for the protection of one who might not speak for himself within those walls; but Franklin was not the quarry at whom Sandwich aimed. The shaft had gone home to the breast towards which it was really levelled. Dartmouth rose once more, and said that he could not press a course which evidently was unacceptable to their Lordships, and that he himself would give his voice for rejecting the Bill forthwith.

The scheme of reconciliation, which promised so fairly, had received its death-blow. Franklin, who was determined to leave no device untried, offered to pay the East India Company for their tea on the security of his private fortune, and, (he might have added,) at the risk of his popularity among his own countrymen. Mr. Barclay on the other hand, in his honest eagerness to save the irretrievable, hinted that, if the representative of America would show himself sufficiently easy to deal with, he might expect not only to be reinstated in the Postmastership which he had lost, but to get any place under Government that he cared to ask for. Franklin, more offended than he chose to show, replied that the only place the Ministry would willingly give him was a place in a cart to Tyburn ; but that he would do his utmost without any other inducement than the wish to be serviceable. The proceedings of the conference trickled on for a few weeks, and then ended in a marsh ; as must always be the case where the agents on either of the two sides are not their own masters, but have those behind them who intend the negotiations to fail. By the middle of March Dr. Fothergill sadly admitted that the pretence of an accommodation was specious, but altogether hollow ; and that the great folks, whom he was in the habit of attending as patients, had all along regarded the colonies as nothing better than " a larger field on which to fatten a herd of worthless parasites." Some days afterwards Franklin sailed for Philadelphia, and beguiled a protracted voyage by drawing up an account of the doleful transactions on which he had been recently engaged, and by the more profitable and congenial occupation of testing with his thermometer the breadth and the direction of the Gulf Stream.

After a short interval he was followed across the Atlantic by emissaries the colour of whose coats showed that the day of grace was passed. The affairs of America were in a tangle which the King, and his Ministers, had neither the will nor the wit to unravel. The knot was now for the sword to cut, and they looked around them for a man who had the skill of his weapon. Clive, and his old chief Lawrence, had died within the last few months. Granby had fought in the best British fashion at the head of a British contingent as large as a formidable army ; and Wolfe had done miracles with smaller numbers. But they both had gone, leaving nothing except their example. Lord Albemarle too was dead, who as General of the land forces in the West

Indies had shared with the navy in the undoubted honour, and the vast profit, which accrued from the conquest of Havanna. As an officer who had been tried in a supreme command there remained Sir Jeffrey Amherst. He had won his laurels in America, where he had gained the character of a cautious and sound strategist. His name stood high among the colonists, who had formed half of the very considerable body of troops which he was careful to gather around him before he opened a campaign ; whom he had treated handsomely ; and to whose co-operation he gratefully attributed an ample portion of the credit of his victory.

The judgement of new Englanders on their rulers, when newspapers were few and cautious, was to be found in their sermons, which never flattered those whom the preacher and his hearers did not love. When Montreal was taken in the autumn of 1760, the pulpits rang with praises of "the intrepid, the serene, the successful Amherst." The pastor of Brookfield, who had been a chaplain in a Massachusetts regiment, (for American military chaplains generally contrived to smell whatever powder was being burned,) after hailing the downfall of the Canadian Babylon, broke out into praises of Amherst, the renowned general, worthy of that most honourable of all titles, the Christian hero ; who loved his enemies, and while he subdued them, made them happy. Amherst had indeed endeavoured to infuse some chivalry and humanity into the rude, and often horrible, warfare of the backwoods ; and his severities, sharp enough on occasion, were necessitated by the hideous cruelties which the Indian allies of France inflicted upon the farming population of the English border.

Amherst had proved himself a stout warrior elsewhere than in the field. In the year 1768 he had been in collision with the King over a matter about which neither was in the right ; and the General had come off with flying colours and abundance of spoil. A Court favourite had been nominated to a post which Amherst held, but the work of which he did not do.   In his wrath he threw up all his functions and appointments, and aroused such a commotion in the political and military world that he had to be coaxed back at any sacrifice.   He returned to the official ranks stronger, and better endowed with public money, than ever ; and neither minister nor monarch ventured to disturb him again.   By January 1775 George the Third had reconsidered the favourable opinion which he had formed of General Gage, and now declared him wanting in activity and decision.   He proposed to confer upon Amherst the command of the troops in America, together with a commission to use his well-known influence and popularity among the colonists for the purpose of inducing them to make their peace before recourse was had to arms.   Gage meanwhile, by an arrangement in which the tax-payer was the last person thought of, was to continue Governor of Massachusetts, and to draw his pay as Commander-in-Chief.   George the Third undertook in person the task of appealing to Amherst's loyalty, which he endeavoured further to stimulate by the offer of a peerage.   In the disagreeable and disastrous war which was now at hand, titles were of use rather for the purpose of tempting men into active service, than of rewarding them when they returned from it.   The veteran stated very plainly that he could not bring himself to serve against the Americans, " to whom he had been so much obliged."   The King, with sincere regret, informed Dartmouth that Amherst could not be persuaded.   It only remained, he said, to do the next best ; to leave the command with Gage, and send to his assistance the ablest generals that could be thought of.

The choice of those generals was not an act of favouritism.   George the Third, as long as he continued to transact public business, looked closely into all high military appointments which involved grave military responsibilities.   His judgement was excellent save when, as in the case of the Duke of York, it was misled by considerations of family interest and of strong affection.   Determined to have his armies well commanded, he set aside his personal inclinations, and overcame his political prejudices. In time of peace and war alike, even when he was told that the salvation of the country depended on it, no importunity from a Cabinet which required strengthening could prevail on him to employ a statesman whom he regarded as an opponent; and between one war and another he was far from overlooking political considerations in his treatment of the army and the navy. Whenever a veteran, scarred with wounds and honoured throughout the whole service, ventured to give a vote displeasing to the King, he was harshly received at Court, and ruthlessly deprived of the rewards which his valour had earned. But when hostilities broke out, if a famous soldier or sailor, who had been wronged and slighted, had any fight left in him, George the Third did not fail to display what moralists class as the rarest form of magnanimity, — that of overlooking the injuries which he himself had inflicted.

Ingratitude during peace, alternating with a tardy recognition of merit under the pressure of war, up to the very last marked George the Third's dealings with great soldiers whose politics displeased him. Sir John Moore complained that he was treated as a "bad subject" by the King, for whom he had been wounded five times, and the discipline and efficiency of whose army he had done more than any living man to restore. At length, when he was wanted for the chief command in Spain, George the Third "very graciously," — and, it must be owned, very candidly, — said that a stop should be put to persecution, and that Sir John Moore "must not be plagued any more." Lord Lynedoch had been nothing but a Whig country gentleman till he was five and forty; and a Whig country gentleman he remained until he died at ninety-five with a military reputation second only to that of Wellington. He was even worse used than his friend and patron Sir John Moore; for the King angrily refused to give him army-rank. His Majesty quarrelled even with Lord Melville when that statesman protested against the treatment to which so distinguished an officer was exposed, and was quite prepared to quarrel over the same matter with Pitt.   After Corunna, when such a sword as Graham's could not be suffered to remain idle, he at length received his due, and was sent as Wellington's right-hand man to the Peninsula, where he won Barossa and helped to win Vittoria.[1]

Chief among the three Major-Generals selected to serve in America in the spring of 1775 was William Howe, brother of the Admiral, and of the Lord Howe who fell at Ticonderoga in the year 1758.   That nobleman, who was an Irish viscount, had been member for Nottingham.   When the news of his death reached England, his mother in pathetic terms urged the people of the city, which her son had represented, to replace him by his younger brother, who himself was then at the front with his regiment.   So William Howe was nominated and chosen, and had sat for Nottingham ever since.   At the general election of 1774 he told his constituents that the whole British army together would not be numerous enough to conquer America, and assured them that, if he were offered a command against the colonists, he would not scruple to refuse it.   The King, who knew him as a splendid officer, the discipline of whose battalion had been a model, and whose gallantry was a proverb, himself was courageous enough to take the risk of a rebuff from his valiant subject. Invited to sail for America, Howe inquired whether he was to consider the message as a request or an order; and, on being informed that it was an order, he obeyed it.   He came back before the end of the Parliament, with a reputation for every military quality, except that of coolness under fire, sadly impaired, — to find at the next election that the freemen of Nottingham had good memories, and a different view of his personal obligations from that which he himself had held.

The next of the three was John Burgoyne.   He had gone through the usual experiences of a distinguished

[1] Delavoye's *Life of Lord Lynedoch*, pp. 269, 262, 249, 250.

military man who was likewise a politician. He had
been thanked in his seat in Parliament; he had received
the Governorship of a fortress in marked and special
recognition of his brilliant valour; and he had been the
subject of a letter in which the King told the Prime
Minister that, if Colonel Burgoyne had not been prudent enough to vote for the Royal Marriage Bill, his
Majesty would certainly have taken that Governorship
away. Burgoyne's sentiments towards the colonists
were friendly, but his view of the legal and constitutional aspect of the controversy was not favourable to
their claims. He agreed to serve against them without
compunction, though he missed that sense of exhilaration which he had hitherto felt whenever he had gone
to meet the enemy. He confessed his lack of enthusiasm to his Sovereign in a letter not unbecoming a
soldier, but too long and too laboured, like all which Burgoyne ever wrote even under circumstances calculated
to prune and chasten the most copious and flowery style.
  The third Major-General was Henry Clinton, who had
learned his trade under Prince Ferdinand during the
Seven Years' War, and who now was member for
Newark, and a supporter of the Ministry. The dash
and dexterity with which these officers, one and all,
had seized their opportunities, in America, in Portugal,
or in Germany, fully justified the King in his hope that
they would be equal to larger enterprises; and the public opinion of the army confirmed his choice. The connection between war and politics, in the aristocratic
England of four generations ago, was not less close
than in the great days of ancient Rome. Then the
scion of a consular family courted the suffrages of the
people in order that he might go forth to command
their legions; and returned to the senate from Spain,
or Gaul, or Pontus, to be congratulated if he had triumphed, or to defend himself in case things had gone
badly with him in the field. The three Major-Generals
were all members of Parliament, and all remained members while year after year they were campaigning and

administrating thousands of miles away from Westminster.   After the frightful miscarriages which befell them
personally, or which had taken place under their auspices,
they all resumed their seats on their accustomed bench
in the House of Commons as naturally and quietly as if
they had come back from a week of partridge shooting.
   The expedient adopted was singularly unfortunate.
If any one of the three had been invested with the
command in chief, he would, for the sake of his own
reputation, have applied to the War Office for as many
regiments as could be spared from home duties ; and,
being on the spot in London, he would have made his
representations felt.   But no Ministry will press upon
an absent general larger means and appliances than
those which he insists on having.   Gage was the author
of the pleasant theory that the military side of the difficulty would prove to be a very small matter.   He now
had begun to be alarmed, and wrote in vague terms
about the necessity of being provided with a "very respectable force " ; but during his recent visit to England,
speaking as a soldier who knew the colonies and who
was responsible for keeping them, he had set going a
notion that the Americans were unwarlike as a community, and pusillanimous as individuals.   That agreeable and convenient idea had been eagerly caught up
by the noisiest members of the Government, and had
been employed by them in public as an argument against
those who condemned their policy as hazardous.   They
had assured Parliament that a course of coercion would
be effective, safe, and the very reverse of costly ; and
this they had done on Gage's authority.   He had named
a limited number of additional battalions as the outside
which he would require in order to complete the business ; and those battalions he should have, and not a
musket more.   The reinforcements which accompanied
Howe and Burgoyne across the sea brought up the
garrison at Boston to ten thousand men.   It was an
army powerful enough to inspire all the colonies with
alarm for their independence, and so burdensome as

to irritate Massachusetts beyond endurance; but it was utterly inadequate to the task of holding down New England, and ludicrously insufficient for the enterprise of conquering, and afterwards controlling, America. When the war had endured a twelvemonth David Hume, — who had lived through an eventful period of our history, and had written almost all the rest of it, — pronounced that the show of statesmen in power, and generals and admirals in command, had up to that point been the poorest ever known in the annals of the country. Of those generals Gage was the first, and perhaps the worst; and in his combined quality of civil administrator, military leader, and above all of adviser to the Government in London, he played, for a very small man, a material and prominent part in the preparation of an immense catastrophe.

A Governor who was bound by statute to destroy the liberties of his province, and ruin the prosperity of its capital, had a very narrow margin within which he could display himself as a beneficent ruler; but there were two ways of discharging even such a commission. Obliged to punish, Gage should have avoided the appearance of enjoying the work on which he was employed, unless he was prepared to abandon the hope of ultimately playing the peacemaker; and that function was one among the many which he was called upon to fulfil. He had been confidentially instructed by the King to "insinuate to New York and such other colonies as were not guided by the madness of the times," proposals which might entice them back to due obedience, without putting "the dagger to their throats."[1] The General had already tried his hand at pacification. In October 1774 he wrote to the President of the Congress at Philadelphia congratulating him on his endeavours after a cordial reconciliation with the mother-country, and promising his own services as a mediator.[2]

[1] George the Third to Dartmouth; Jan. 31, 1775.
[2] *Historical Manuscripts Commission.* Fourteenth Report, Appendix, Part X.

He might have spared his fine phrases. He was the last man whose arbitration or intervention would have been accepted by any New Englander endowed with a grain of local patriotism; for by making public reference to a hackneyed and offensive taunt he had done that which private persons seldom forgive, and communities never. To be called a saint by the unsaint-like is a form of canonisation which nowhere is held to be a compliment; and just now there was something too much of it in Boston. "The inhabitants of this colony," wrote an officer, "with the most austere show of devotion are void of every principle of religion or common honesty, and reckoned the most arrant cheats and hypocrites in America." That was the creed of the barracks; and Gage paid it the homage of a joke such as a parcel of subalterns might have concocted after mess, and been ashamed of long before the eldest of them had got his company. When Massachusetts, threatened in her liberties and her commerce, bowed her head, (though not in fear,) and set aside a day for prayer and fasting, he inflicted a deliberate and official insult on the people whom he governed by issuing a proclamation against Hypocrisy. Having thus paralysed, for ever and a day, his power of acting as an intercessor between the Crown and the colony, he informed the Cabinet that, public feeling in America being what it was, the penal Acts could not be enforced, and had much better be suspended.

Such a recommendation, from the very man whose sanguine assurances had decoyed the Government into what he himself now confessed to be a Slough of Despond, was described by the King, with pardonable impatience, as "the most absurd course that could possibly be suggested." But whatever might be the quarter whence it emanated, the advice came on the top of tidings which foretokened that a river of blood would be set flowing unless it was acted upon without delay. The cannon and stores of the Massachusetts Militia were kept at and near Cambridge. Gage now learned

the ominous circumstance that the several Townships of
the province had begun quietly to withdraw their share
of the ammunition. Before sunrise, on the first of September 1774, he despatched an expedition from Boston
by road and river, which took possession of a couple of
field pieces and two hundred and fifty kegs of powder,
and lodged them securely behind the ramparts of the
Castle. The performance was smart, and the most was
made of it, not so much by the vanity of the author as
by the apprehensions of those against whom it had
been projected. The truth was spread all over Middlesex County in a few hours. It ran through the New
England colonies with the speed and the growing di-
mensions of a rumour ; and, by the time it got to New
York and Philadelphia, good patriots professed to know
for certain that a British man-of-war had fired on the
people and had killed six of them at the first shot. In
some such shape the news reached London ; and all
the friends, and all the foes, of America believed that
Gage had made good his boasts and his promises, and
that the colonists, at the first glint of a bayonet, had
indeed proved themselves such as Rigby and Sandwich
had represented them.

Charles Fox expressed his thoughts to Edmund
Burke in a letter which has been quoted ere now in
condemnation of them both, but which proves nothing
worse than that the patriotism of the two statesmen
embraced their fellow-countrymen on both sides of the
Atlantic. " Though your opinions," Fox wrote, " have
turned out to be but too true, I am sure you will be far
enough from triumphing in your foresight. What a
melancholy consideration for all thinking men that no
people, animated by what principle soever, can make a
successful resistance to military discipline ! I do not
know that I was ever so affected with any public event,
either in history or life. The introduction of great
standing armies into Europe has then made all mankind
irrevocably slaves ! " The consideration which most
depressed him was " the sad figure which *men* made

against *soldiers*." Fox's remarks, however, were based on a curious and total misapprehension of the facts. As fast as the report of the seizure of the powder travelled up and down the coast, and among the inland villages, the neighbours flocked to each centre of resort, and remained together throughout the night. Next morning many thousand people converged on Cambridge. They arrived with staves and without fire-arms; as citizens, and not as militia; under the command of a Selectman of their Township, or a member of their Committee of Correspondence. The General had taken a step implying war; and they, as civilians, had come for the grave purpose of doing that which meant revolution. Oliver, the Lieutenant-Governor of the province, who resided at Cambridge, had gone into Boston for the purpose of entreating Gage to keep his troops within their barracks. The distance to and fro between the two towns was only what a sophomore of Harvard College would cover for his daily exercise between lecture and chapel; but Oliver who knew his countrymen as one who feared them, and Joseph Warren as one who loved and led them, were agreed in their opinion that, if a detachment marched, it would never find its way back to Boston.

It was Oliver whom the people sought, and they waited with full knowledge of the purpose for which they wanted him. They kept their hand in, during his absence, by taking pledges of renunciation of office from a High Sheriff and two Mandamus Councillors. When the Lieutenant-Governor came back, with what he intended to be the welcome announcement that no armed force was on the road from Boston, they requested him formally to resign his post; and after some gasconading on his part, which they endured very stolidly, he acceded to their desire. Then, standing closely packed beneath the rays of the hottest sun which had shone during that summer, they began like true Americans to pass Resolutions; acknowledging that Gage, when he removed the powder, had not violated the constitution; and voting unanimously their abhorrence of mobs and

riots, and of the destruction of private property. The
British General, in anxious self-defence, wrote to the
Ministry at home that they were no town rabble, but
the freeholders and farmers of the county. Guided by
their own good sense, and by the advisers on whom
they had been accustomed to rely in the ordinary transaction of civil business, they exhibited a firmness combined with moderation which reassured those who, with
Charles Fox, expected little from the behaviour of *men*
when placed in opposition to *soldiers*. Soldiers, however, within a few days, and not many hours, they
might have had in abundance; for the contingents
from the more distant regions, where the alarm was
greater, and the exasperation not less, came armed and
in martial array. Israel Putnam, his deeper feelings
touched to the quick by the loss of the material for so
many good cartridges, took upon himself to call out the
militia of Connecticut, and sent the fiery cross far and
wide over the continent. Twenty thousand musketeers
were already on foot, with their faces towards the mouth
of the Charles River, when they were turned back by
expresses from Boston bearing the intelligence that, for
the present, everything was well over. Putnam, proud
of the result, if only half pleased at the ease with which
it had been attained, replied by an assurance that, but
for the counter orders, double the force would have been
on the move in another twenty-four hours; and he took
the opportunity of giving the people of Massachusetts
an admonition, (the more mundane part of which he
evidently thought that they needed,) to put their trust
in God, and mind to keep their powder safe.[1]

The Boston patriots were never again caught nap-
ping; and they very soon commenced a system of re-
prisals, or rather of depredations on their own property,
which kept both the garrison and the squadron awake.
One night, within hearing of the nearest man-of-war, if

[1] "We much desire you to keep a strict guard over the remainder of
your powder; for that must be the great means, under God, of the salvation of our country."

only the officer of the watch had known what they were about, they withdrew the cannon from a battery at Charlestown, which commanded the entrance of the inner harbour. Another night they removed four pieces which were stored in the neighbourhood of the Common. Their audacity and ubiquity were so bewildering that Admiral Graves, who now was conducting the blockade, could think of no better expedient than that of spiking the guns which, from the North point of the city, bore upon the roadstead where his ships were lying. At other seaports, to which the Royal navy was only an occasional visitor, the inhabitants were still more free to act ; and in laying hands on what belonged to their colony they felt that they had on their side the moral law, or at any rate as much of it as sufficed for their simple needs. At Portsmouth, in New Hampshire, the Sons of Liberty entered the fort in broad daylight, to the sound of music ; and, disregarding the remonstrances of half a dozen invalids who were quartered in the precincts, they carried off sixteen cannon, and a hundred barrels of powder with which to load them.

Outside the glacis of the earthworks, which General Gage in hot haste was now constructing across Boston Neck, British rule was dead. The condition of New England then, and throughout the winter, has no parallel in history. Elsewhere provinces and nations, while in open and declared revolt against their former rulers, have been under the control of an organised and established government of their own. But by the end of the year 1774, throughout the Northern Colonies, the old machinery of administration had ceased to work, and it had not been replaced by new. Elsewhere, as in provincial France after the fall of the Bastile, and in rural Ireland more than once in the course of more than one century, the written law lost its terrors, and was not obeyed. But in New England, though the tribunals were void and silent, crime was repressed and private rights were secure, because the people were a law to themselves. It was as if in a quiet English county there were no assizes, no quarter and petty sessions, and no official personage above the rank of a parish overseer. The Selectmen of the townships were the most exalted functionaries who continued to perform their duties; power rested in each locality with the Committees of Correspondence; and the central authority was the revolutionary Convention, or, (as it called itself,) the Congress, of the colony.

In Massachusetts that Congress had even less than a legal title; for it sate, deliberated, and even existed in defiance of the Constitution. Gage had appointed the Assembly to meet at Salem at the commencement of October; but before that date arrived he thought better of it, and issued a proclamation declining to be present as Governor, and discharging the elected representatives from the obligation of attendance. The document was unusual in form, but perfectly clear in meaning. If the members of the Assembly took the course enjoined upon them, all hope of continuing the struggle was over, and they would have nothing to do except to sit by their firesides, with hands folded, till their fate overtook them. True indeed it was that the Congress of all the provinces was still in session at the capital of Pennsylvania; but the popular leaders of Massachusetts would look in vain to that quarter for protection. It was a far cry to Philadelphia, and the danger was knocking at their own door. The Continental Congress was nothing more than an aggregation of delegates, provided only with general instructions, of varying fulness and tenor, from the colonies by which they were severally commissioned. Those delegates, in their corporate capacity, were not inclined to usurp executive functions; and they did not as yet think fit to go beyond the stage of presenting to the world, in a precise and forcible shape, the case against the British Government. To make good that case by arms, — and to arms it was plain that the decision must speedily come, — it was essential that there should be an authority fur-

nished with powers which, whether constitutional or
not, were recognised and respected by the people in
whose name they were exercised; an authority planted
on the scene of action, and inspired by that sort of unanimity and energy which actuates men who know that,
if they do not pursue their forward march together and
to the end, they have already gone much too far for
their personal safety.

The Massachusetts Assembly met. After waiting
two days for the Governor who never came, the members constituted themselves into a Congress and adjourned from Salem to the more remote and inaccessible
retreat of Concord. Hebrew or English, the names of
the two places had little in common with the mood in
which these men set forth upon their up-country journey.[1] True to their national origin, they took some
pains to define their constitutional position, and to defend it by adducing precedents and quoting charters.
But they had attention to spare for more pressing business. They commenced by ordering "that all the
matters that come before the Congress be kept secret,
and not be disclosed to any but the members thereof
until further order of this body." Then, on the twenty-
fourth of October, they appointed a Committee to consider the proper time for laying in warlike stores; and
on the same day the Committee reported that the
proper time was now. And therefore without delay
they voted the purchase of twenty field pieces and four
mortars; twenty tons of grape and round-shot; five
thousand muskets and bayonets, and seventy-five thousand flints. They made an agreement to pay no more
taxes into the royal Treasury. They arranged a system
of assessment for the purposes of provincial defence,
and made a first appropriation of ninety thousand dollars. They then proceeded to elect by ballot three generals. They appointed a Committee of Public Safety,
of which John Hancock was the most notable, and
Joseph Warren the most active, member. They in-

[1] "Being King of Salem, which is, King of Peace."—Hebrews vii. 2.

vested that Committee with authority to call out the militia, every fourth man of whom was expected to hold himself ready to march at a minute's notice; a condition of service that suggested the name of Minute-men by which the earlier soldiers of the Revolution were called. And, having done the best they knew, they adjourned until the fourth Wednesday in November; by which time the Committee of Public Safety, disbursing their funds thriftily, had bought, in addition to the prescribed amount of ordnance, three hundred and fifty spades and pickaxes, a thousand wooden mess-bowls, and some pease and flour. That was their stock of material wherewith to fight the empire which recently, with hardly any sense of distress, had maintained a long war against France and Spain, and had left them humbled and half ruined at the end of it.

Whether on a large or small scale, the irrevocable step was taken. The Massachusetts congressmen were fully aware that, with the first dollar which passed into the coffers of their own Receiver-General, the game of armed resistance had begun, and nothing remained except to play it out. Men in power had called them rebels rudely and prematurely; and rebels they now were in fierce earnest. In a series of Resolutions every one of which the most indulgent Attorney-General, without thinking twice about it, would pronounce to be flat treason, they gave consistence and direction to the seething excitement of the province. They recommended to the inhabitants of the several towns and districts that any person who supplied intrenching tools, boards for gun platforms, or draught oxen and horses, to the troops in Boston, ought to be deemed an inveterate enemy to America and held in the highest detestation. The methods of expressing that detestation they left, as they safely might, to local effort and initiative; for ten years of almost unintermittent agitation had perfected New Englanders in the science of making themselves unpleasant to those whom they regarded as bad friends of the cause. They most solemnly exhorted "the

Militia in general, as well as the detached part of it in Minute-men, in obedience to the great law of self-preservation," to spare neither trouble nor expense over the task of perfecting themselves in their exercises; and in April 1775, taking more upon them as time went on and perils thickened, they framed and issued a paper of Rules and Regulations for the Massachusetts army. They were not afraid to notify that whatever officer or soldier shamefully abandoned a post committed to his charge, or induced others to do the like when under fire, should suffer death immediately. Nor were they ashamed to lay down what, according to the tradition of their colony, was the right preparation for that frame of mind in which homely and half-trained men may best meet the stress of danger. All officers and soldiers who, not having just impediment, failed diligently to frequent divine service and to behave decently and reverently when present at it, were to be fined for the benefit of sick poor comrades; and the same penalty was imposed upon any who were guilty of profane cursing and swearing.

Their statement of the circumstances, on which they grounded the necessity for tightening the bonds of military discipline, differed widely from the preamble of the Mutiny Act which annually was placed on the Statute-Book at Westminster. That statement consisted in an outspoken vindication of religious and political convictions, ennobled and elevated by the pride of ancestry. "Whereas the lust of power," such was the wording of the recital, "which of old persecuted and exiled our pious and virtuous ancestors from their fair possessions in Britain, now pursues with tenfold severity their guiltless children; and being deeply impressed with a sense of the almost incredible fatigues and hardships our venerable progenitors encountered, who fled from oppression for the sake of civil and religious liberty for themselves and their offspring; and having seriously considered the duty we owe to God, to the memory of such invincible worthies, to the King, to Great Britain, our country, ourselves, and our posterity, we do think it our indispensable duty to recover, maintain, defend, and preserve the free exercise of all those rights and liberties for which many of our forefathers bled and died. And whereas we are frequently told by the tools of the Administration that Great Britain will not relax in her measures until we acknowledge her right of making laws binding upon us in all cases whatever, and that if we persist in our denial of her claim the dispute must be decided by arms, in which it is said we shall have no chance, being undisciplined, cowards, disobedient, impatient of control;" — and so the passage continued to run in phrases clearly showing that its authors had got hold of some sentences which English ministers had recently spoken in Parliament, and were putting their discovery to a telling, but quite legitimate, use.

Having invested themselves with the responsibility of dictating the policy of the colony, and of equipping it for self-defence, the representatives of Massachusetts remained together either at Cambridge or at Concord, (as the chance of interruption by the armed hand of authority was less or more present to their minds,) through the rigours of a New England winter. In consideration of the coldness of the season, and that the Congress met in a room without a fire, it was resolved that the members who inclined thereto might keep on their hats. Resembling in that respect, but in few others, the British House of Commons, they sate almost continuously; although they adjourned for some days in order to observe a Thanksgiving appointed in acknowledgement of the special protection which Heaven had extended to the colony of Massachusetts. Determined to be thankful, they detected a mark of Divine favour in the unanimity with which their province had faced the crisis. By their fervent recognition of a blessing that, after all, was mainly due to themselves, they gave Providence, on the eve of a doubtful war, a significant indication of the gratitude which they were prepared to feel for such greater mercies as it might have in store for them.

These proceedings, whatever figure they might eventually make in history, were not of a nature to be contemplated with equanimity by the British garrison. Our troops had hitherto behaved, on the whole, quite as well as could be expected from men who were planted down in such a place for such a purpose; but, by the time the winter was over, their patience had reached its limit. In the first week of March the townspeople assembled to hear the annual address in celebration of the event which was popularly known as the Boston Massacre. The scene has been described by an eye-witness, whose point of view is not disguised by his narrative. "The military were determined not to suffer the least expression that had a tendency to reflect on the King, or Royal Family, to pass with impunity. In the pulpit were Warren, the orator of the day, Hancock, Adams,[1] Church, and others. Some of the gentlemen of the Army had placed themselves on the top of the pulpit stairs. Officers frequently interrupted Warren by laughing loudly at the most ludicrous parts, and coughing and hemming at the most seditious, to the great discontent of the devoted citizens. The oration however was finished, and it was moved by Adams that an orator should be named for the ensuing fifth of March, to commemorate the bloody and horrid massacre perpetrated by a party of soldiers under the command of Captain Preston. At this the officers could

[1] This was Samuel Adams. John Adams in a former year declined to take the principal part in the ceremony, on the ground that he had acted as Captain Preston's advocate. "Though the subject of the Oration," he said, "was compatible with the verdict of the Jury, and indeed even with the absolute innocence of the soldiers, yet I found the world in general were not capable, or not willing, to make the distinction; and therefore I should only expose myself to the lash of ignorant and malicious tongues on both sides of the question." In 1774 he attended the meeting, and heard with admiration John Hancock, who might be trusted not to fall below the topmost altitude of the occasion; and he would certainly have agreed with every syllable which in 1775 came from the lips of Warren.

no longer contain themselves, but called ' Fie ! Shame !'
and ' Fie ! Shame !' was echoed by all the Navy and
Military in the place.   This caused a violent confusion ;
and in an instant the windows were thrown open and
the affrighted Yankees jumped out by fifties."

The ludicrous parts of Warren's speech were, it may
be presumed, his references to the Bible ; and the
promise, (which he kept,) to give his life in case his life
was wanted.   And, as a matter of fact, they were women
who escaped by the windows.[1]   In the spring of 1775
it took something more than a loud noise to make New
England men leave a spot where their duty called on
them to stay.   The commotion grew from bad to worse
until an officer, "dressed in gold lace regimentals, with
blue lapels," thought fit to put a gross affront upon the
Chairman of the meeting.   In the course of the next
fortnight the army broke loose from restraint, or rather
from self-restraint ; for those who ought to have kept
others in order were the prime actors in every successive manifestation of partisanship.   The day of prayer
and fasting ordained by Congress for the whole colony
was observed with marked solemnity by the townsmen
of Boston.   On that day the members of a corps, which
was bent on deserving its title of The King's Own,
pitched two "marquee tents" within ten yards of the
church at the West End of the city, and played their
drums and fifes as long as the service lasted, while their
Colonel looked approvingly on.   Real or reputed patriots
of all grades in society became the objects of insult and,
where a plausible excuse could be found, of personal
violence.   A party of officers broke Hancock's windows,
and hacked the railing of his lawn with their swords.
A country fellow who, as his friends asserted, had been
entrapped into buying a gun from a soldier, was tarred
and feathered in the guardhouse of the regiment and
paraded about the streets on a truck, escorted by a crowd
of all ranks from the commanding officer downwards,
and preceded by a band playing " Yankee Doodle."

[1] *American Archives;* March 8, 1775.

Those strains were not agreeable hearing for the crowd before whose pinched and anxious faces the procession passed. In and about the town there was plenty of employment to be had which would have kept Boston children plump, and Boston cottages warm and garnished; but for six months past all the mechanics had struck work on the Barracks, and the roughest labourer refused to turn a sod at the fortifications. They hung outside the shops where bricklayers and carpenters, fetched from Nova Scotia, or, (a reflection more bitter still,) even from New York, were freely spending the excellent wages which in such a strait the Government was only too glad to pay. They stood in line at the doors of the Donation Committee, waiting for their allowance of meal, and rice, and salt fish, the further supply of which was at that very moment in the act of being cut off by the legislation of the British Parliament. They took their turn of labour on municipal industries extemporised under the superintendence of the Selectmen, and paid for out of the savings of that middle-class which, as the artisans had the good sense to foresee and the neighbourly feeling to regret, would soon be as poor as themselves.

It was a cheerless season; but for those who looked in the right quarter there still were smiling visages to be seen. "My spirits were very good," a lady said, "until one Saturday riding into town I found the Neck beset with soldiers; the cannon hoisted; and many Tories on the Neck, and many more going up to see the encampment with the greatest pleasure in their countenances, which gave a damp that I had not before felt." The inner thoughts of these people may be read in a letter from Dr. Samuel Peters, of Hebron in Connecticut. That divine had taken sanctuary in Boston after having been rabbled at home by fellow-townsmen whom he had sorely provoked, if any provocation could excuse outrage. "I am in high spirits," he wrote. "Six regiments are now coming from England, and sundry men-of-war. So soon as they come, hanging work will go on, and destruction will first attend the seaport towns. The lintel sprinkled on the side-posts will preserve the faithful." Years afterwards, when Peters had long been resident in England, his old parishioners learned with interest that the style of preaching which had given displeasure at Hebron was too strong meat even for a congregation of Londoners. A brother exile, who heard Peters deliver a sermon in an English metropolitan pulpit, said that "it was hard to conceive how he got there." [1]

On week-days, when the Episcopal churches were closed, the Boston Tories could draw comfort from the periodical effusions of a vigorous writer, the style of whose prophecies and invectives proved that neither side in the great American controversy had a monopoly of grandiloquence. According to "Massachusettensis," the Boston Committee of Correspondence was the foulest, subtlest, and most venomous thing that had ever issued from the eggs of the serpent of sedition ; — a knot of demagogues, who did for their dupes no more solid service than that of inducing them to swallow a chimera for breakfast. The point of the observation was all the sharper at a time when the families of citizens, who followed Hancock and Warren, were in a fair way to have very little indeed that was more substantial for breakfast, dinner, or supper either. Such was the condition of mutual charity and good-will to which George the Third had reduced the inhabitants of a colony into whose local elections, at a date so recent as ten years before, the element of political partisanship had not as yet entered. 1766 was the first year in which the Selectmen of even so considerable a place as Braintree were chosen for their politics. The waters of strife had then been first stirred by a violent Tory sermon ; and on the next Sunday a Whig clergyman replied by preaching from the text, "Render unto Cæsar the things that are Cæsar's"; from which things he specially excepted the price of stamps bearing Cæsar's head.

[1] Sabine's *Loyalists;* vol. ii.

The royalists in Boston, as they watched the reviews on the Common, and listened to the professional opinions which were freely delivered around them, never doubted of a rapid and triumphant issue. Reinforcements continued to arrive from England, and a large body of marines was landed from the squadron. By the end of the year there were eleven battalions in garrison ; weak, for the most part, in numbers ; but well housed, splendidly equipped, and brimming over with confidence. The British officers set a high value on the fighting quality of their own men, which indeed it was not easy to overrate. But the estimation in which they held the colonists was not creditable to their habits of observation or to their knowledge of military history, and said very little indeed for the worth of oral military tradition. " As to what you hear of their taking arms, it is mere bullying, and will go no further than words. Whenever it comes to blows, he that can run fastest will think himself best off. Any two regiments here ought to be decimated if they did not beat in the field the whole force of the Massachusetts province ; for though they are numerous, they are but a mere mob without order or discipline, and very awkward in handling their arms."

That was the view of the regimental officers, who were unaware of the fact that colonists, so far from being awkward with their weapons, were as a rule marksmen before they became soldiers. The familiar conversation of the staff, which ought to have been better informed, was in the same strain. The Quartermaster-General wrote home that Congress had appointed three scoundrels to command the militia. It was the very reverse of the real case. The first commanders of the American forces had indeed, as always happens at the commencement of a civil war, the defects of leaders chosen on account of exploits performed many years before ; but they were of blameless, and even rigid, character. In the days of their early renown, they had gone forth against the power of France in the stern conviction that they themselves were the champions of Protestantism. Seth Pomeroy, a good man, but no better than his colleagues, had seen the hardest service of the three. In September 1755 he was colonel of a Massachusetts regiment at the action of Lake George, fought by a colonial officer at the head of sixteen or seventeen hundred rustics, very few of whom had been under fire before, against an army largely composed of regulars. The general of the French, in the lightness of his heart, encouraged his soldiers with the assurance that American Militiamen were the worst troops on the face of the earth. After the battle, a prisoner with three bullets in him, he pronounced that in the morning the New Englanders had fought like good boys, at noon like men, and in the afternoon like devils; and at all times of the day their aim was such that their adversaries "dropped like pigeons." Pomeroy, who was employed to bury the slain, took measures to preserve the French dead from the indignities of the Indian scalping-knife. He had lost a brother in the battle. " Dear Sister," he wrote, "this brings heavy tidings : but let not your heart sink at the news, though it be your loss of a dear husband. Monday was a memorable day ; and truly you may say, had not the Lord been on our side, we must all have been swallowed up." It was not the letter of a scoundrel.[1] But the deeds of the colonists in former battles, though well remembered in Paris, were forgotten at British mess-tables. In all ranks of our army there unhappily prevailed that contempt of the enemy before the event which is the only bad omen in war ; — quite another sentiment from the invaluable consciousness of superiority arising from the experience of victory.

The latest comers had some excuse for their ignorance of the country; for between them and the outer world an impenetrable veil was spread. Inside Boston there was little to be learned. Whenever a scarlet coat was in the company, Whigs kept their own counsel; and

[1] Parkman's *Montcalm and Wolfe ;* vol. i., chapter 9.

Tories spoke only pleasant things which, human nature being what it was, they had honestly taught themselves to believe. Beyond the fortifications, over a breadth of many score of miles, lay a zone of peril and mystery. Officers could not venture to leave the precincts of the garrison unless they were accompanied by a strong force in military array ; and, in the case even of such a force, its reception depended upon the character of its errand. When the General was contented to march his people out in order to march them back again, — without attempting to impound military stores, or arrest political leaders, — the expedition encountered nothing more formidable than black looks and closed shutters. In January 1775 a party of infantry proceeded to Marshfield, with the object of protecting the formation of a Loyal Militia, and took with them fire-arms in greater numbers than there were loyalists in the neighbourhood to carry them. The troops preserved exact discipline. They molested no one, and no one molested them. As long as they stayed in the town, (so a Government newspaper in New York boasted,) every faithful subject there residing dared freely to utter his thoughts and drink his tea. But when they left Marshfield, and returned to Boston, the Loyal Militia disappeared from history, and General Gage would have felt more easy if he had been certain that their muskets had disappeared with them.

A month afterwards Colonel Leslie sailed to Marblehead, for the purpose of seizing some artillery which the provincials had deposited at Salem as a place of comparative security. He landed his detachment successfully on a Sunday morning ; but, when the alarm reached the nearest meeting-house, the congregation turned out and took up a position upon some water which barred his route. They refused to lower the draw-bridge, on the plea that there was no public right of way across it ; and, when Leslie attempted to lay hands on a couple of barges, the owners proceeded to scuttle them. The soldiers drew their bayonets, and inflicted some wounds not so wide as the church-door from which the patriots had issued, and only just deep enough to allow Salem to claim the honour of the first drops of blood which were shed in the Revolution. A loyalist clergyman intervened. The people agreed to lower the bridge, and Leslie pledged his honour not to advance thirty rods beyond it. Brave to imprudence when duty as well as danger lay clear before him, he was not prepared, without specific orders from a high quarter, to light the match which would set the thirteen colonies in a blaze. He recalled his men, and re-embarked them empty-handed just as the company of minute-men from the next township, with plenty more of their like to follow, came marching in to the help of Salem.

A countryside, in this state of effervescence, presented few attractions even to the most adventurous officers of the garrison; whether they were sportsmen, or students of manners, or explorers of the picturesque. But nevertheless one of their number has left a narrative which affords a glimpse of New England in the February of 1775. Gage despatched a captain and an ensign through the counties of Suffolk and Worcester, with a commission to sketch the roads, to observe and report upon the defiles, and to obtain information about forage and provisions. They dressed themselves as countrymen, in "brown clothes, and reddish handkerchiefs." Their disguise was so far artistic that, on their return, the General and his staff mistook them for what they pretended to be; though during their expedition no one, either friend or foe, looked at them twice without detecting what they were. They stopped at a tavern for their dinner, which was brought them by a black woman. " At first she was very civil, but afterwards began to eye us very attentively. We observed to her that it was a very fine country, upon which she answered, ' So it is, and we have got brave fellows to defend it.' " Downstairs she told the soldier-servant, who looked still less of a ploughman than his masters, that, if his party went any higher up, they would meet with very bad usage. Towards the close of the day they came to a village where they had a more hearty, but a not less alarming, welcome. "We stopped at the sign of the Golden Ball, with the intention to take a drink, and so proceed. But the landlord pleased us so much, as he was not inquisitive, that we resolved to lie there that night; so we ordered some fire to be made, and to get us some coffee. He told us we might have what we pleased, either Tea or Coffee." Their relief on hearing the Shibboleth of loyalty was more than balanced by the reflection that this landlord was not inquisitive only because he had seen all he wanted without needing to ask a single question.

Another stage of their journey brought them to Worcester. "The next day being Sunday we could not think of travelling, as it was not the custom of the country. Nor dare we stir out until the evening, because nobody is allowed to walk the street during divine service without being taken up and examined: so that we thought it prudent to stay at home, where we wrote and corrected our sketches. On our asking what the landlord could give us for breakfast, he told us Tea or anything else we chose. That was an open confession what he was : but for fear he might be imprudent, we did not tell him who we were, though we were certain he knew it. At Shrewsbury we were overtaken by a horseman who examined us very attentively, and especially me, whom he looked at from head to foot as if he wanted to know me again, and then rode off pretty hard." They got their meal at an inn, and had an opportunity of watching from the window a company of militia at drill. "The commander made a very eloquent speech, recommending patience, coolness, and bravery, (which indeed they much wanted ;) quoted Cæsar, Pompey, and Brigadiers Putnam and Ward ; recommended them to wait for the English fire, and told them they would always conquer if they did not break ; put them in mind of Cape Breton, and observed that the Regulars in the last war must have been ruined but for them. After a learned and spirited harangue he dismissed the parade, and the whole company drank until nine o'clock, and then returned to their homes full of pot-valour." The allusion to Cape Breton showed that the rank and file of the colonial militia were familiar with the true history of that first siege of Louisburg which Sandwich had so woefully garbled for the amusement of the Peers.

On their way to Marlborough the two officers were accosted by riders, who asked them point-blank whether they were in the army, and then passed on towards the town. They arrived after nightfall, in what now would be called a blizzard; but the street was alive and buzzing. They were waylaid and interrogated by a baker who, as they afterwards learned, had a deserter from their own regiment harboured on his premises. They had hardly entered the dwelling of Mr. Barnes, a well-to-do loyalist, when the town-doctor, who had not been inside their host's door for two years past, invited himself to supper and fell to cross-examining the children about their father's guests. They were sent off again into the darkness at once, and not a minute too soon; for immediately after their departure the Committee of Correspondence invaded the house, searched it from garret to cellar, and told the owner that, if they had caught his visitors under his roof, they would have pulled it down about his ears.[1] It was not until the travellers had completed a march of two and thirty miles through wind and snow that they reached a friendly refuge, and were comforted with a bottle of mulled Madeira, and a bed where they could rest in safety. Next morning they walked back to Boston, having enjoyed the rare privilege of being in contact with an Anglo-Saxon population as highly charged with electricity as any among the Latin races at the most exciting junctures of their history.

---

[1] *American Archives;* Feb. 22, 1775. The entertainer of these officers paid dearly for his opinions. An important Whig, whose goods were within the British lines at Boston, was allowed by way of compensation to use the furniture of the Marlborough loyalist for his own so long as the siege lasted. Mr. Barnes was subsequently proscribed and banished. He died in London.

At last the thunder-cloud broke, and flash after flash lit up the gloom which overhung the land. Gage, rather because he was expected to take some forward step, than because he saw clearly where to go, conceived the idea of destroying the stores which had been collected at Concord. The force told off for this service, according to a faulty practice of those times, consisted of detachments from many regiments; and the officer in charge of the whole was incompetent. The troops started before midnight. At four in the morning, just as an April day was breaking, they reached the village of Lexington, and found sixty or seventy of the local militia waiting for them on the common. Firing ensued, and the Americans were dispersed, leaving seven of their number dead or dying. It was a chilly and a depressing prologue to a mighty drama. The British advanced to Concord, where they spoiled some flour, knocked the trunnions off three iron guns, burned a heap of wooden spoons and trenchers, and cut down a Liberty pole. In order to cover these trumpery operations a party of a hundred infantry had been stationed at a bridge over the neighbouring river, and towards ten o'clock they were attacked by about thrice as many provincials, who came resolutely on. After two or three had fallen on either side, the regulars gave way and retreated in confusion upon their main body in the centre of the town.

Pages and pages have been written about the history of each ten minutes in that day, and the name of every colonist who played a leading part is a household word in America. The main outlines of the affair are beyond dispute. When Colonel Smith discovered that there was nothing for him to do at Concord, and made up his mind to return to Boston, he should have returned forthwith. As it was, he delayed till noon ; and those two hours were his ruin. The provincials who had been engaged at the bridge did not push their advantage. They hesitated to act as if war had been openly declared against England ; and they were not in a vin-

dictive frame of mind, as they had heard nothing
beyond a vague report of the affair at Lexington. But
by the time the British commander had completed his
arrangements for withdrawing from his position the
whole country was up, in front, around, and behind
him. Those who came from the direction of the sea
knew what had taken place that day at early dawn;
and, where they had got the story wrong, it was in a
shape which made them only the more angry. From
every quarter of the compass over thirty miles square
the Ezras, and Abners, and Silases were trooping in.
The rural township of Woburn "turned out extraordinary," and marched into action a hundred and
eighty strong. The minute-men of Dedham, encouraged
by the presence of a company of veterans who had
fought in the French wars, spent, but did not waste,
the time that was required to hear a prayer from their
clergyman as they stood on the green in front of the
church steps. Then they started on their way, " leaving the town almost literally without a male inhabitant
before the age of seventy, and above that of sixteen."
Carrying guns which had been used in old Indian
battles, and headed by drums which had beat at Louisburg, they covered the hillsides, and swarmed among
the enclosures and the coppices, in such numbers that
it seemed to their adversaries "as if men had dropped
from the clouds." It was a calamity for the British
that the first encounter of the war took place under
circumstances which made their success a military
impossibility. When a force, no larger than the rear-
guard of an army, is obliged to retreat, and to continue
retreating, the extent of the disaster is only a question
of the amount of ground that has to be traversed, and of
the activity and audacity which the enemy display. The
colonists well knew the distance at which their fire was
effective, and were determined, at any personal risk, to
get and to remain within that range. The English
regimental officers, whenever one of them could collect
a few privates of his own corps, made a good fight dur-

ing the earlier stage of the retreat. But, before they emerged from the woods which lined most of the six miles between Concord and Lexington, ammunition began to fail; the steadier men were largely employed in helping the wounded along; many of the soldiers rather ran than marched in order; and the column passed through Lexington a beaten and, unless speedy help should come, a doomed force.

They had still before them twice as much road as they had travelled already. But the very worst was over; because a few furlongs beyond the town they were met by the reserves from Boston. The supporting body was better composed than their own, for it was made up of whole regiments; and it was much better commanded. Lord Percy, owing to stupid blunders which were no fault of his, should have been at Concord by eleven in the morning instead of being near Lexington at two in the afternoon; but, now that he was on the ground, he proved that he knew his business. He disposed the field pieces which he had brought with him in such a manner as to check the provincials, and give a welcome respite to Colonel Smith's exhausted soldiers. When the homeward march recommenced, he fought strongly and skilfully from point to point. The hottest work of the whole day was as far along the line of retreat as West Cambridge. It was there that an example was made of some minute-men who had covered sixteen miles in four hours in order to occupy a post of vantage, and who were too busy towards their front to notice that there was danger behind them in the shape of a British flanking party. But the Americans were in great heart, and they were briskly and gallantly led. The senior officer present was General Heath, a brave and honest man, who had learned war from books, but who did well enough on a day when the most essential quality in a commander was indifference to bullets; and Warren had hurried up from Boston, eager to show that his oration of the month before was not a string of empty words. "They have begun it," he said, as he was waiting to cross the Ferry. " That either party could do.   And we will end it.   That only one can do."   From the moment that he came under fire at Lexington he was as conspicuous on the one side as Lord Percy on the other : and there was not much to choose between the narrowness of their escapes, for the New Englander had the hair-pin shot out of a curl, and the Northumbrian had a button shot off his waistcoat.

No courage or generalship on the part of the British commander could turn a rearward march into a winning battle.   As the afternoon wore on, his men had ex-pended nearly all their cartridges; and they had noth-ing to eat, for the waggons containing their supplies had been captured by the exertions of a parish minister. " I never broke my fast," so a soldier related, " for forty-eight hours, for we carried no provisions.   I had my hat shot off my head three times.   Two balls went through my coat, and carried away my bayonet from my side." [1]   The provincials had surmounted their re-spect for the cannon, and kept at closer quarters than ever.   As the tumult rolled eastwards into the thickly inhabited districts near the coast, the militia came up in more numerous and stronger companies, fresh and with full pouches.   When the sun was setting the re-tiring troops, half starved and almost mad with thirst, came to a halt on the English side of the causeway over which the Cambridge highway entered the peninsula of Charlestown.   They were only just in time.   " From the best accounts I have been able to collect," Wash-ington wrote six weeks later on, " I believe the fact, stripped of all colouring, to be plainly this : that if the retreat had not been as precipitate as it was, (and God knows it could not well have been more so,) the minis-terial troops must have surrendered, or been totally cut off.   For they had not arrived in Charlestown, under cover of their ships, half an hour before a powerful body of men from Marblehead and Salem was at their

[1] *American Archives;* Letter of April 28, 1775.

heels, and must, if they had happened to be up one hour sooner, inevitably have intercepted their retreat to Charlestown." That was the conclusion at which Washington arrived; and his view, then or since, has never been disputed.[1]

The Americans lost from ninety to a hundred men, of whom more than half were killed outright; and the British about three times as many. The strategic results of the affair were out of all proportion to the numbers engaged in it; for it settled the character and direction of the first campaign in the Revolutionary war. For fifteen months to come the British army did not again take the open field. Bunker's Hill was but a sortie on a large scale, and ranks only as a terrible and glorious episode in the operations of a siege which, by the time the battle was fought, had already lasted for the space of eight weeks. For when Lord Percy crossed Charlestown Neck, and General Heath halted on Charlestown Common, the invasion of Massachusetts by the English was over, and the blockade of Boston by the Americans had begun. In the previous December the Secretary at War had confided his anticipations to the Secretary for the Colonies. "I doubt," so his letter ran, "whether all the troops in North America, though probably enow for a pitched battle with the strength of the Province, are enow to subdue it: being of great extent, and full of men accustomed to fire-arms. It is true they have not been thought brave, but enthusiasm gives vigour of mind and body unknown before."[2] As Lord Barrington had turned his attention to the subject of courage, it was a pity that he could not find enough of it to tell his views to the King and the Bedfords, instead of writing them to Dartmouth, who knew them already. But at sundown on the nineteenth of April the event had spoken; and it mattered little now what the English ministers said, or left unsaid, among themselves.

[1] Washington to George William Fairfax in England; May 31, 1775.
[2] *The Political Life of Viscount Barrington;* Section viii.

CHAPTER IX

MASSACHUSETTS, from the nature of the case, had fought the first engagement single-handed; but consequences were sure to ensue which would be too much for her unassisted strength. Next morning her Committee of Safety reported the condition of affairs to the rest of the New England provinces, and urged them to send help, and to send it promptly. "We shall be glad," they said, "that our brethren who come to our aid may be supplied with military stores and provisions, as we have none of either, more than is absolutely necessary for ourselves." These words were written as soon as it was light; but the people to whom they were addressed did not generally wait for a summons. The news of Lexington found Israel Putnam, in leather frock and apron, busy among his hired men over the labours of his farm. He started off on a round of visits to the nearest towns of Connecticut; called out the militia; and ordered them to follow him as fast as they were mustered. Then he set out for Cambridge, and arrived there at daybreak on the twenty-first of April, having ridden the same horse a hundred miles within the eighteen hours. By noon on the twentieth the word had got across the Merrimac, and the boats on their return journey were crowded with New Hampshire minute-men. "At dusk," Mr. Bancroft writes, "they reached Haverhill ferry, a distance of twenty-seven miles, having run rather than marched. They halted at Andover only for refreshments, and, traversing fifty-five miles in less than twenty hours, by sunrise on the twenty-first paraded on Cambridge Common."

Rhode Island was somewhat more deliberate and, as befitted its size, more heedful of its dignity. On the twenty-fifth of April the Assembly of the little community voted to raise an army of observation which should co-operate with the forces of the neighbouring colonies, but with a separate Ordnance department and a Commander-in-Chief of its own. If they were bent on a policy of isolation and punctiliousness, they had chosen the wrong man to have charge of their troops in the field. Nathanael Greene was a born soldier, and had in him the material for making the sort of general under whom other born soldiers desire to fight. For years past he would leave his ordinary occupations, if for nothing else, in order to be present at any review where a score of militia companies were being put through their exercises together. He had been seen, in a coat and hat of Quaker fashion, watching the regulars on the Common at Boston, and buying treatises on the Military Art at the booksellers'. When he arrived in camp he found his troops lukewarm for the cause, and in a state of discipline demanding on his part capabilities of a higher order than could be acquired out of a drill book. But before many weeks were over he had them thoroughly in hand, and he showed himself as eager to obey as he was competent to command. When Washington was placed by Congress at the head of the Continental army, the Assembly of Rhode Island got the better of their passion for independent action; and Greene had the satisfaction of placing himself and his contingent at the disposal of one who, as the captain of a citizen army, would have stood a comparison after the manner of Plutarch with any of those heroes of antiquity whose histories Greene had so long and so lovingly studied.

The army of New England, — for such it was, and such, by whatever title it might be called, it remained until the fate of New England was finally and irrevocably decided, — soon attained a strength of sixteen thousand men. Of these Connecticut furnished two thousand three hundred, New Hampshire and Rhode Island between them about as many, and Massachusetts the rest. On the morning after the fight General Heath, before he handed over the command, took measures to provide a first meal for the assembled multitude. " All the eatables in the town of Cambridge, which could be spared, were collected for breakfast, and the college kitchen and utensils procured for cooking. Some carcasses of beef and pork, prepared for the Boston market, were obtained; and a large quantity of ship-bread, said to belong to the British Navy, was taken." [1] Such were the foundations of a commissariat system which, as long as Boston was the seat of war, kept itself on a level with the reputation of that well-fed neighbourhood. The organisation of the army, in all other departments, was loose and primitive, but, until the British garrison should become numerous enough again to take the offensive, not inefficient. The Congress of Massachusetts had nominated General Artemas Ward to command their forces; and the superior officers from the other colonies copied his orders of the day, and yielded him as much obedience as he cared to exact, which was very little. He was old and ill; unable to get on horseback; and quite willing to leave to his energetic and enthusiastic brigadiers the responsibility of guarding their own front, when once he had allotted to them their posts in the line of investment.

Elementary as were their warlike arrangements, the Americans presented a formidable appearance when viewed from behind the intrenchments opposite. Many of them were dressed in the working clothes which they had been wearing when the alarm reached them in their fields and villages; and they were officered by tradesmen, and mechanics, and graziers who differed little from those of their own class in Europe, except that they esteemed themselves as good as people who had been brought up to do nothing. But that levy of civilians had already vindicated their claim to be treated in

[1] *Heath's Memoirs;* April, 1775.

as strict conformity to the laws, and even the courtesies, of war, as if they had been so many thousand white-coated Frenchmen, with a Marshal to command them, and with Dukes and Marquises for their colonels. Gage soon discovered that, when he wanted anything from the colonists, he would have to ask for it civilly. After a long negotiation with the authorities of the popular party he concluded an agreement under which all inhabitants of Boston who, when the siege commenced, found themselves on what they considered the wrong side of the wall, might pass from town to country, (or, as the case might be, from country to town,) and take their chattels with them. Early in June the Americans obtained a practical recognition of their rights as combatants in the shape of an exchange of prisoners; and the occasion was lacking in none of the compliments and hospitalities with which the chivalry of warfare has, time out of mind, invested that ceremony. The event was the more grateful to men of honour in both camps because it led to the final extinction of a singularly discreditable calumny. The London Gazette, in an official account of the affair of the nineteenth of April, informed the world that the provincials had scalped the wounded. When the English who had been captured were restored to their regiments, they all, officers and men, were warm in their expressions of gratitude for the kindness they had met with, and the tenderness with which they had been nursed; for very few of them had been taken unhurt.[1]   From that day forward nothing more was heard

---

[1] An antidote to the calumny was not long in reaching England. In the June number of the *Gentleman's Magazine* there appeared a statement by a Lieutenant of the King's own regiment. " I was wounded," he says, " at the attack of the bridge, and am now treated with the greatest humanity, and taken all possible care of, by the Provincials at Medford." Gage was expressly told that his own surgeons might come out and dress the wounded ; but there was no need of it, for they were admirably doctored. A soldier's wife wrote home on the 2nd of May: " My husband was wounded and taken prisoner ; but they use him well, and I am striving to get to him, as he is very dangerous. My husband is now lying in one of their hospitals, at a place called Cambridge. I hear my husband's leg is broke, and my heart is broke."

of a fable very unlike anything which, before or since, has appeared in a military despatch written in our language. The Americans, if they had been on the watch for a grievance, might with some plausibility have put forward countercharges; because, when a force loses more killed than wounded, there is ground for supposing that rough things were done by the enemy. But they knew that hand-to-hand fighting is a rude and blind business; they were satisfied by having so quickly conquered the respect of their redoubtable adversary; and their complacency was not diminished by the indignation which these mutual amenities excited in the Boston Tories, who had devoutly believed in all the vaunts that Gage had ever uttered about his fixed determination never to treat with rebels.

The hour was at hand when the title of the Americans to rank as belligerents was to be severely tested. In the early summer reinforcements from home raised the British garrison to seventeen battalions of infantry, and five companies of artillery. Gage had now at his disposition a force half as large again as the army which triumphed at Culloden, and four times more numerous than the regular troops who crushed the rising of our Western counties at Sedgemoor. On the twenty-fifth of May the Cerberus arrived with the Major-Generals on board. They disembarked under a fire of epigrams which their number, taken in conjunction with the name of the three-headed monster after whom their ship was called, suggested to those Boston wits who had read Virgil, or at any rate a classical dictionary. It was an evil day for Gage when Burgoyne landed; for the faults and the merits of that officer combined to make him as dangerous a subordinate as ever a commander was afflicted with. Inventive and enterprising, and undeniably gallant, he had obtained just enough military celebrity to turn his head, and to tempt him, through discontent, into disloyalty towards his chief. Before leaving London he had been admitted, among other guests, to the weekly dinner of the Cabinet. He was impressed by the absurdity of pretending to do the secret business of the State in " so numerous and motley a company ; " but he had made excellent use of his opportunities for his own personal advantage. He had succeeded in establishing relations with great men, and men on the way to greatness, no one of whom was fully aware how intimate Burgoyne was with the others. As soon as he was ashore at Boston he began a correspondence with Lord Rochford, who was a Secretary of State, and Lord George Germaine, who seemed likely to become one ; with Lord Dartmouth, with the Military Secretary of the Horseguards, and, above all, with the Prime Minister. Burgoyne's voluminous, but always vivid and interesting, letters, the burden of which was a searching exposure of Gage's mistakes, ruined that officer in the judgement of his employers, and remain on record to destroy his chance of passing in the eyes of posterity as an unfortunate, rather than an incapable, commander. But, however full Burgoyne's sheet might be with comments upon his chief's blundering strategy, there always was a corner kept for the demands of self-interest. When addressing a Minister, or any one who had the ear of a Minister, the persuasive Major-General never failed to insist on the paltry nature of his own present functions as compared with his abilities and antecedents ; and implored that he might be recalled to England for the purpose of giving the Cabinet, by word of mouth, information and advice which he could not venture to set down in writing.

That which was reported about Gage to Downing Street was a grave matter for him ; but his fame suffered still more from the compositions which his eloquent subordinate prepared for publication, at his request, and in his name. Proud of his soldiership, Burgoyne rated himself higher yet in his character as an author. His most ambitious literary efforts belonged to the leisure of a later period in his life, when there was no further demand for the services of his unlucky sword. Up to 1775 he had achieved nothing more durable than prologues and epilogues; and, as his highest flight, he had prepared an operatic version of "As You Like It." One quatrain will suffice as a specimen of the adaptation.

> "Who was the man that struck the deer ?
> The badge of triumph let him wear.
> Round the haunch of the noble prey
> Hail him, hail him, lord of the day !"

But Burgoyne was as much in love with his pen as if he had written the original comedy; and that pen he now placed at the disposal of his superior in command. His style, excellent in a letter, became artificial in a State-paper, and had in it a touch of rhodomontade fatally unsuited to documents which dealt with burning questions at a time of almost unexampled seriousness. On the twelfth of June General Gage issued a proclamation denouncing the rebels who, "with a preposterous parade of military arrangement, affected to hold the royal army besieged;" assuring "the infatuated multitude" that he did not bear the sword in vain; declaring martial law; offering pardon to such as would lay down their arms and "stand distinct and separate from the parricides of the constitution;" but excepting from that pardon, under any condition whatsoever, Samuel Adams and John Hancock. No manifesto was ever worse adapted to the taste of its intended readers, except perhaps the celebrated address to the French nation, in the year 1792, which earned for the Duke of Brunswick a place in literature as the most unsuccessful of royal authors. The minute and affectionate care, which evidently had been bestowed on the task of polishing each of the bloodthirsty sentences in Gage's proclamation, suggested to the patriots that it had been prompted by the devil; but as a matter of fact it was drafted by Burgoyne, who, except on paper, was as humane a man as lived. And so it came to pass that Gage, after all the disasters which overtook him on account of his being exceedingly dull, contrived to saddle himself with the

additional curse of a reputation for pretentious and misplaced cleverness.

Burgoyne was on surer ground when he was exposing to Cabinet Ministers the defects and dangers of the
military situation. He and his two colleagues were
filled with surprise and shame by the state of matters
which they found at Boston. These paladins of the
great war, accustomed to drive the enemy whenever
and wherever they met him, were greeted by the news
that a British force, as large as any which had ever
taken the field in America, was blockaded in its quarters
by an army of whose existence they had never even
heard until that moment. The town on the land side,
Burgoyne wrote, was invested by a rabble in arms
flushed with success and insolence, who had advanced
their sentries within pistol shot of the royal outposts.
The servants of the Crown, and their well-wishers
among the civil population, were lost in a stupefaction
of anger, bewilderment, and despondency. All passes
which led to the mainland were closely beleaguered ;
and, even if the hostile lines were forced, the British
were not in a condition to make a forward movement.
Bread waggons, hospital carriages, sumpter-horses, and
artillery horses were wanting. The magazines had been
left unfurnished ; the military chest was empty ; and
there was no money in the town. Our troops were unpaid, and our officers could not get their bills cashed at
any sacrifice. Even the five hundred pounds apiece,
which his Majesty promised that his Major-Generals
should receive on their arrival, were not forthcoming ;
and all this at a time when, (so Burgoyne declared
with a pathos which soared above statistics,) a pound of
fresh mutton could only be bought for its weight in
gold. For the apathy and dejection which prevailed
among military people had gained the sister service.
The Royal ships lay idle and helpless, expecting from
day to day to be cannonaded at their moorings. The
crews of the rebel whale-boats had cleared off the sheep

and cattle from the neighbouring islands; had burned a British schooner under the very eyes of the Admiral; and had carried away the cannons to arm their own batteries. When those batteries opened fire, there would be witnessed the most singular and shameful event in the history of the world, — a paltry skirmish, (for Lexington was nothing more,) "inducing results as rapid and decisive as the battle of Pharsalia; and the colours of the fleet and army of Great Britain, without a conflict, kicked out of America."

The style of writing was after the model of Junius, rather than of Julius Cæsar. But the sentiments were those of a soldier; and Burgoyne took no pains to hide them in any company. He exclaimed to the first colonist whom he met, and in the course of a talk which served the purpose of the modern interview of disembarkation: "Let us get in, and we will soon find elbow-room." The saying caught the popular ear, and the time was not far distant when its author learned to his cost that it is more easy to coin a phrase than to recall it from circulation. The lie of the country was such that Burgoyne's expression exactly represented the necessities of the hour. To North and South of the peninsula of Boston, separated from the town in each case by some five hundred yards of salt water, two headlands, of the same conformation and size as the peninsula itself, ran out into the bay.[1] If Gage made play with his elbows, he would sweep the heights of Dorchester on his left hand, and the heights above Charlestown on his right. His subordinates insisted that he should exert himself. As soon as there was a prospect of fighting under leaders whom it was an honour to follow, the army recovered its spirits, and, of all the disagreeable sensations which had affected it, retained none except resentment. " I wish the Ameri-

[1] All localities mentioned in the text may be identified in the map of " Boston and its Environs " at the end of this volume, reproduced from the Atlas accompanying Marshall's *Life of Washington*, published at Philadelphia in 1807. The map has been partially coloured, and a certain number of additional places marked, for purposes of elucidation.

cans may be brought to a sense of their duty. One good drubbing, which I long to give them, might have a good effect towards it." That was how Captain Harris of the Fifth Foot, a young man of spirit, with a great future before him, (for he died Lord Harris of Seringapatam,) wrote home on the twelfth of June; and by every packet which sailed for England such letters were being posted by the score.[1]

Gage and his advisers, with sound judgement, determined to begin by occupying the heights of Dorchester. The promontory which lay to the South was of the two the more accessible to the Americans; and, if they succeeded in establishing themselves there, it would be a more tenable post and a more formidable menace to the garrison of Boston. But the earlier operations in a civil war are dictated rather by human nature than by strategic principles; and the clash of battle, when it arose, broke out in an unexpected quarter. The moral forces at work in the Colonial, and in the British, camps were not dissimilar. General Ward, like General Gage, and with much better reason, would have preferred to strengthen his defences and stay quiet behind them; but he too had brigadiers who were bent upon action. An American council of war debated the proposal to seize and fortify the heights of Charlestown. Ward was against the plan, and Warren also; for it

---

[1] The letters which Captain Harris sent home from Boston agreeably portray the feelings of the best among our regimental officers. He joined the garrison in August 1774, and arrived at his destination ready to be pleased, and very willing to make himself pleasant to the civilians among whom he was quartered. "The Harbour," he wrote, "and the view of Boston is the most charming thing I ever saw: far superior to the Bay of Naples, and having the advantage of being wooded by nature as picturesquely as if art had superintended her operation." The herbage on the Common was richer than he had ever seen elsewhere ; and he was at much pains to protect the cows of the citizens, as they ate the sacred grass, from any interference on the part of British sentries. "Though I confess," said the keen young soldier, "that I should like to try what stuff I am made of, yet I would rather the trial should be with others than these poor fellows of kindred blood." But he could not avoid his fate; and in the retreat from Lexington, where he commanded the rear-guard, he lost his Lieutenant, and half his company.

was a question of policy, and not of valour ; but Putnam
took the other side, on grounds which were characteristic of the man. The operation in his view was so
critical, and the position so exposed, that the British
would be irresistibly tempted to attack under circumstances which might be trusted to bring out the strongest points of the colonists. "The Americans," he said,
"are not afraid of their heads, though very much afraid
of their legs. If you cover these, they will fight for
ever." Even such a qualified species of courage was
a great deal to demand from men who had never been
drilled to hold up their heads, and whose legs had
hitherto been chiefly employed in walking between the
plough handles ; but Putnam, if any one, knew both the
best and the worst which could be expected from his
countrymen at the stage of military discipline to which
they had then attained. His opinion carried weight
in a quarter where, at that period of the Revolution,
the ultimate decision lay. On the fifteenth of June the
Committee of Safety of the Massachusetts Congress
unanimously resolved to advise the Council of War that
possession of the hill called Bunker's Hill in Charlestown
should be securely kept, and defended by sufficient
forces.

Next evening twelve hundred New Englanders were
paraded on Cambridge Common, and listened to the
President of Harvard College while he invoked the
divine blessing on an enterprise the nature of which was
still a secret for almost all his hearers. They were
under the command of Colonel Prescott, who was old
enough to have served at Cape Breton, where he had
exhibited qualities which procured him the offer from
the British military authorities of a commission in the
regular army. When night fell the expedition started ;
the Colonel in front, and carts filled with intrenching
tools following in the rear. The men had their weapons,
their blankets, and one day's rations ; loose powder in
their horns, but not very much of it ; and in their
pouches bullets which they had cast themselves. Even

so they had plenty to carry. Their equipment was described by a lieutenant of the Royal Marines; a corps which, after its usual custom, contrived next day to get a very near view of the enemy. Both officers and soldiers, this gentleman wrote, wore their own clothes ; nor did he see any colours to their regiments. Their firelocks seemed unwieldy, and some were of quite extraordinary length ; but the men, (he remarked,) were mostly robust and larger than the English. It must be remembered, too, that the clumsy gun was an old friend, with whose good and bad qualities they were intimately acquainted; and which they preferred even to an elegant Tower musket, weighing only fifteen pounds without the bayonet, so long as there was something in front of them on which to rest their barrel.[1]

Prescott made his way by the aid of dark lanterns over Bunker's Hill, which at the highest point rose but a hundred and ten feet above the level of the sea. He halted his men, further to the eastward, on a still lower spur of the same upland. They looked straight down on the lights of Charlestown ; and they stood within twelve hundred yards of the Boston batteries, and nearer yet to the men-of-war which lay in the channel. Lines of fortification were marked out ; arms were stacked ; and spades and pickaxes distributed. Farmers and farm-hands wanted no teaching for that part of the business ; and every one except the sentries, officers and soldiers alike, fell to work in silence, and with extraordinary speed. When day broke, — and, on the seventeenth of June, it was not long in appearing, — the morning watch on the British vessels discovered an intrenchment six feet high where overnight there had been a smooth pasture. The ships, and the guns ashore, concentrated

[1] Lieutenant Clarke relates that some of the guns, which his men picked up in the captured redoubt, were near seven feet long ; but the statement, though proceeding from a credible eye-witness, appeared to require confirmation before it could be inserted in the narrative. That confirmation is given by an American colonel, who wrote : "The arms are most of them good fowling-pieces, but unfit for war, some of them being no less than seven feet." Robert Livingston to Lord Stirling ; June 11, 1776.

their fire upon the little redoubt, which measured fifty yards on its longest face. The noise was terrific, for the part of the squadron which was engaged carried eighty cannon on a broadside; and, as the forenoon went on, the flood-tide brought with it several floating batteries which took up their position within easy range. The Americans, who had not the means of replying, liked it little at first; but Prescott, on the pretence that he wanted a better point of view from which to superintend his people as they worked inside the wall, sauntered round the top of the parapet, giving directions where to place the gun-platforms, and bantering those who were not as handy with the saw as they had been with the shovel. A Royal general noticed him in his blue coat and three-cornered hat, and asked whether he would fight. The person to whom, as it happened, the Englishman applied for his information was Prescott's own brother-in-law; who asseverated with a great oath that on that point he would answer in the affirmative for his kinsman. More quietly worded, but sincere and eager, testimony with regard to the part played by Prescott was given in much later years by David How of Haverhill in Massachusetts. How had been currying leather in a small way before he joined the American army in 1775, and was still currying leather on a large scale in 1842. A few months before his death the old man was asked about his experiences inside the redoubt. "I tell ye," he cried, "that if it had not been for Colonel Prescott there would have been no fight. He was all night, and all the morning, talking to the soldiers, and moving about with his sword among them in such a way that they all felt like fight."

If the cannonade had driven the Americans from their works, there would have been bitter disappointment in the British garrison. Something was said at head-quarters about landing a force on Charlestown Neck, and so taking the colonists in the rear. Something was said about starving them into surrender by stationing gunboats on either flank of the isthmus, which was only

a hundred yards in breadth, and had no protection
against a cross-fire. One or the other of the two courses
would have been tactically correct, and our officers owed
it to their military conscience to make a pretence of dis-
cussing them; but neither the generals nor the army
were in a mood to wait. To win without fighting had
no attraction for men who on the last occasion had
fought without winning. Our troops were eager to
try conclusions at the earliest moment, and under difficulties which would enable them to show their mettle.
As soon as it was known that there were fortifications
to attack, the resolution to approach them in front was
automatic, and all but unanimous. By one o'clock of
the day four entire regiments, and twenty companies of
grenadiers and light infantry, had landed on the extreme
East of the peninsula, to the North of Charlestown.
Howe, who was in command, after carefully inspecting
the ground in face of him, sent back the barges for reinforcements, and ordered his men to take their dinner.
In a couple of hours the flotilla returned with two more
battalions. The assaulting force was now between two
thousand, and twenty-five hundred, strong; and soldiers
more full of heart, and in more gallant trim, had never
stepped over the gunwale of a boat on to soil which they
meant to make their own.

It was high time for the Americans also to demand
help from their main army. Some of the officers in the
redoubt thought it their duty to go even further, and
urged Prescott to claim that those companies which had
borne the labour of the night, and the strain of the
bombardment, should be relieved by other troops. Not
a few of the minute-men, as inexperienced soldiers will,
had left their bread and meat behind them; there was
no water to be had; and the heat was stifling. But
Prescott would have none of it. The men might be
hungry and thirsty, and had already done a double turn
of duty; but they had become accustomed to cannon-
balls; and, when it came to bullets, they might be
trusted better than any newcomers to defend the fortifi-

cations which their own hands had raised. Those fortifications consisted of the redoubt, and a breastwork extending a hundred yards towards the left of the position. From the end of the breastwork to the North shore of the peninsula the country was open. On that side the British overlapped and threatened Prescott's flank; and he accordingly told off a detachment of Connecticut militia to occupy the vacant interval. They were soon joined there by a fine New Hampshire regiment, which came fresh from camp; and the combined force stationed themselves along the foot of Bunker's Hill, well to the rear of the redoubt. They were covered by a low fence, stone below and rails above, the interstices of which they had stuffed with piles of hay. A poor defence against musketry, and none whatever against cannon, at all events it marked the line which they meant to hold. It was a bulwark much of the same character as that behind which their descendants stood on the Cemetery hill at Gettysburg.

When the fight began, the colonists mustered fifteen hundred men; quite as many, if all present stood their ground, as could be effectively employed along a front of less than seven hundred paces. They had six cannon; and generals in plenty, though none to spare; for it was a day on which good example could not be too abundant. The military etiquette prevailing in the American lines was not yet rigid enough to prohibit an officer of rank from taking part in an operation outside the precincts of his own command. Seth Pomeroy had borrowed a mount from the Commander-in-Chief; but the cannon-fire which raked Charlestown Neck was so hot that he did not conceive himself justified in risking an animal not his own property. His person, however, belonged to himself; so he walked across the isthmus, and up to the rail-fence, where he was received with cheers, and provided with a musket. Putnam, who had horses of his own and never spared them, was seen during the course of the afternoon in every corner of the field. Wherever he might be, he took his share of the danger, and a great deal more than his share of the responsibility which was going a begging. Warren, the evening before, had been in the Chair of the Massachusetts Congress ; and he now came on to the ground with a bad headache, which was soon to be cured. Like everybody else on that day, he fell in with Putnam, and asked him where would be the crisis of the battle. Putnam directed him to the redoubt ; and, when he showed himself within the enclosure, Prescott greeted him warmly and offered him the command. But Warren refused to take over a trust which had hitherto been so admirably discharged, and assured those who were within hearing of him that he was only one of two thousand who were marching to their assistance. And thereupon, as a first instalment of the promised reinforcements, he placed himself, gun in hand, among the marksmen who lined the wall.

He was just in time. At three o'clock the second British detachment landed, and Howe at once proceeded to the business of the afternoon. He briefly and frankly explained to his men the situation of the army, which nothing would save except a victory. " I shall not," he told them, " desire one of you to go a step further than where I go myself:" and, whatever the case might have been where it was a promise to his constituents, when Howe spoke as a soldier he acted up to what he said. He then marched straight at the rail-fence, with the grenadiers and the light infantry behind him. The Marines and the Forty-seventh Regiment advanced upon the redoubt ; while the breastwork was assaulted by the Forty-third and the Fifty-second, numbers which are indissolubly linked in the memory of those who have studied on Napier's pages the story of the Light Division in the Peninsular War. Such military rhetoric as was employed by the American leaders was of the most practical character : and up to the very last moment they were exhorting their people to aim low, to fire at the handsome coats, and, above all, to wait so long that there could be no mistake between one uniform and another.

The American artillery was badly served, for reasons
which it subsequently required a couple of court-martials to explain for the benefit of those who exacted too
much from the scientific department of a raw army.
On the other hand, the round-shot which had been
brought across the bay did not fit the British field
pieces ; and the officer in charge pronounced the ground
in his front so soft that they could not be driven up
within range for grape. The Royal troops moved forward steadily, but all too slowly. They were burdened
with full knapsacks ; the hay rose above their knees ;
they had fence after fence to cross ; and they were
allowed to open fire too soon. The colonists would
have followed the example ; but their commanders were
on the alert. Putnam, at the rail-fence, threatened to
cut down the next man who let his gun off without
orders ; and Prescott's officers ran round the top of the
parapet, and kicked up the muzzles of the firelocks.
When the discharge came at last, the execution done
was very great. The British volleys, delivered with
the regularity of a full-dress review, were almost disregarded by the colonists, who were loading under cover,
talking among themselves, and arranging to shoot, two
or three together, at the same officer. " Before the intrenchments were forced," wrote Lieutenant Clarke of
the Marines, " a man whom the Americans called a
Marksman, or Rifleman, was seen standing upon something near three feet higher than the rest of the troops,
as their hats were not visible. This man had no sooner
discharged one musket than another was handed to him,
and continued firing in that manner for ten or twelve
minutes. In that small space of time it is supposed that
he could not kill or wound less than twenty officers. But
he soon paid his tribute ; for, upon being noticed he was
killed by the Grenadiers of the Royal Welsh Fuzileers."
The attack fared badly in every quarter of the field.
" Our light infantry," another army letter relates, "were
served up in companies against the grass fence. Most
of our grenadiers and light infantry, the moment of pre-

X 2

senting themselves, lost three-fourths, and many nine-tenths, of their men. Some had only eight and nine men a company left; some only three, four, and five."[1] Ten minutes, or it might be fifteen, of such work, (for no one present had the curiosity to take the time,) showed the British leaders that the position could not be carried then; and the less resolute among them already doubted whether it could be carried at all. The assaulting force retreated; and Howe, with the composure of a man who had more than once been in affairs which began ill and ended to his satisfaction, rallied and re-formed his troops as soon as he had withdrawn them out of gunshot.

The British advanced a second time in the same style as before. The men were still overloaded. Again they came on firing. Their opponents noticed, and admired, the deliberation with which they stepped over the bodies of their fallen comrades; for the acclivity leading up to the American lines, (as was said of the face of the hill between Hougoumont and La Haye Sainte by one who had been at Badajos,[2]) already resembled rather a breach after an assault than a portion of a field of battle. The colonists this time did not pull a trigger until the British van was within forty yards, and then aimed at the waist-belts. A continuous stream of flashes poured forth along the whole extent of the intrenchments, from the instant that the word was given to fire, until the ground in front was cleared of all except the dead and wounded. The British officers, utterly regardless of everything but their duty, urged the men forward with voice and sword-hilt; and, where no officers were left, the oldest privates placed themselves in charge of the half-sections which represented what once had been companies. Howe, on the morning of Quebec, had stood with twenty-four others in a forlorn hope on the heights of Abraham; but he was more alone now. He

[1] These companies are stated to have averaged thirty-nine men at the commencement of the battle. *Clarke's Narrative*, p. 15.

[2] *Diary of a Cavalry Officer* (Lieutenant Colonel Tomkinson); p. 317.

had twelve officers, naval and military, in his personal staff at Bunker's Hill; and, soon or late, they were all shot down. Outside the works no one could live; and it was evident, almost from the first, that, on this occasion likewise, no one could penetrate within them. The British regiments once more fell back to the landing-place: a repulsed and disordered, but, (to their honour be it spoken,) not a disorganised or a routed army.

For they had that in them which raised them to the level of a feat of arms to which it is not easy, and perhaps not even possible, to recall a parallel. Awful as was the slaughter of Albuera, the contest was eventually decided by a body, however scanty, of fresh troops. The cavalry which pierced the French centre at Blenheim, though it had been hotly engaged, for the most part had not been worsted. But at Bunker's Hill every corps had been broken; every corps had been decimated several times over; and yet the same battalions, or what was left of them, a third time mounted that fatal slope with the intention of staying on the summit.[1] Howe had learned his lesson, and perceived that he was dealing with adversaries whom it required something besides the manœuvres of the parade ground to conquer. And to conquer, then and there, he was steadfastly resolved, in spite of the opposition which respectfully indeed, but quite openly, made itself heard around him. He ordered the men to unbuckle and lay down their knapsacks, to press forward without shooting, and to rely on the bayonet alone until they were on the inner side of the wall. He confined himself to a mere demonstration against the retired angle within which the rail-fence was situated, and instructed all his columns to converge upon the breastwork and the redoubt. He insisted that the artillery, swamp or no swamp, should be planted where they could sweep the fortification with an enfilading fire. Howe was loyally obeyed, and ably

[1] Howe was reinforced by four hundred additional Marines in the course of the engagement; but, so far as is known, every regiment which took part in the earlier attacks went forward the third time also.

seconded. The officers who had remonstrated with him for proposing to send the troops to what they described as downright butchery, when they were informed of his decision returned quietly to their posts, and showed by their behaviour that, in protesting against any further bloodshed, they had been speaking for the sake of their soldiers, and not of themselves. General Clinton had assumed the command of the left wing, and was prepared to lead it into action. From across the water he had perceived two regiments standing about in confusion on the beach. He threw himself into a boat, revived their courage, re-arranged their ranks, and placed himself far enough in their front for every one to see how an old aide-de-camp of the fighting Prince of Brunswick stepped up a glacis.

It detracted nothing from the merit of the British that their undertaking was less desperate than they were aware of. They advanced for the third time in the stern belief that the position was held by a force superior in numbers to their own, and amply provided with everything which the defence required. But the case was otherwise. Behind the intrenchments few had bayonets ; and, what was a much more serious matter, the powder horns were empty. On the very eve of the last assault, by opening some cannon cartridges, Prescott contrived to supply his garrison with a couple of rounds a man, and bade them not to waste a kernel of it. Now was the moment for the arrival of those thousands whom Warren had announced to be on the way ; but they were on the way still, and not very many ever reached their destination. The result was largely due to the absence of a military system, which it remained for a younger brain than General Ward's to create, and a stronger hand than his to impose upon that civilian army. The Commander-in-Chief never left his house ; he had not the staff officers to convey his orders ; and those orders were given too late.[1]   Plenty of troops

[1] In Colonel Stark's regiment, when the word came to turn out from their quarters, " each man received a gill cup full of powder, fifteen balls,

marched, but they did not start betimes. When they reached the skirts of the battle they found no one with full powers to tell them where to go, and to see that they got there; — a circumstance the more serious because the conditions of the conflict were such that undisputed authority, and responsible supervision, were as much needed in the rear of the army as on the fighting front.

Burgoyne had watched the track of Clinton's boat with much the same feelings as those of Fitz Eustace when he saw Blount plunge into the mêlée at Flodden. " For my part," (thus he grumbled to one of his eminent correspondents,) " the inferiority of my station left me an almost useless spectator, for my whole business lay in presiding during part of the action over a cannonade." But, in truth, he could not have been more usefully occupied. The fire of his batteries, though too distant to be very murderous, had a more decisive influence on the fate of the day than if he had been mowing down whole columns of infantry with grape discharged at point-blank range. To march through a tornado of round-shot, across a narrow causeway and over a bare hill, into a torrent of British bullets which had flowed over the heads of those for whom they were intended, would have tried old and well-led troops. The spectators, who crowded every coign of vantage and safety, averred that Charlestown, whose wooden houses were going up to the sky in smoke and flame, added to the grandeur of the panorama; but that spectacle did not increase the attractions of the East end of the peninsula to those who approached it in the character of actors in the scene. Prescott had shown his good sense, when he pronounced that a hungry and weary man, who had endured a cannonade, was worth more than any

and one flint. After this the cartridges were to be made up, and this occasioned much delay." And yet they were the first to arrive of all the reinforcements.

The ammunition was prepared in camp by the soldiers. David How of Haverhill has left a military diary curiously attractive by its meagre simplicity. " I have been a Running Ball all day ; " he says on one occasion. " I went to prospeck hill after I had done my Stint Running Ball."

newcomer, however well he might have slept and break-
fasted. Some of the regimental leaders missed their
way. Others showed hesitation, and heard of it afterwards to their disadvantage. Many of the privates
sought shelter after the undignified fashion, or an excuse for retiring in the disingenuous pretexts, which
have been known even among professional armies on
some of the most famous days in history. They
straggled, and dispersed themselves behind rocks, hay-
cocks, and apple-trees; or they went back in large
groups around any of their comrades who happened to
be wounded. A captain of Connecticut militia noticed
that, when he crossed the top of the hill, there was not
one company except his own in any kind of order,
although three battalions had started from camp at or
about the same moment. Those battalions might have
behaved very differently if the familiar figure of their
own General of Brigade, or Division, had been there to
conduct them through the zone of panic into the less intolerable ordeal of actual combat. Putnam, in the short
intervals between the attacks, galloped back to do what
he could. His exertions, however, were necessarily in-
termittent, and his title to command in some cases was
disputed and denied. Part of the reserves advanced as
far as the rail-fence, and did the good service which
might be expected of men who found themselves at
their posts because they wanted to be there, and not because they were told to go; but the brunt of the last
onset mainly fell upon those who had been on the spot
from the very first. Sooner or later, and for the most
part all too late, four thousand of the colonial troops
passed over Charlestown Neck; but, in the opinion of
Washington, the Americans actually engaged at any
one period of the day did not exceed fifteen hundred.

The injunctions both of Prescott and of Howe were
observed to the letter. Our people came on without discharging a shot; and it is hardly too much to say that
every American bullet told. The front rank of the British went down close to the wall; and those who came next

behind them were not long in going over it. In another moment the whole South side of the redoubt was bristling with bayonets; while, with their backs set against the opposite parapet, those colonists, who had a pinch of powder remaining, fired it off at the closest quarters. And then all was over. Without lead or steel, resistance would have been impossible even against soldiers of a very inferior sort to those who now were scrambling across the earthworks by hundreds. It was at this point of the battle that the Fifth Fusiliers were pronounced by a high authority to have " behaved the best, and suffered the most; " which was already an old story with that glorious regiment. Captain Harris, the young fellow who had been so keen to fight, was one of them ; and when he was carried off the field to be trepanned, Lord Rawdon, no bad substitute, succeeded him in the command of his company. Among the foremost was Major Pitcairn, — the officer who at sunrise on the nineteenth of April had given the word to fire on Lexington Common, and whose noble and amiable disposition has been scrupulously recognised by American historians. He had been wounded twice before in the course of the afternoon ; and he now died with four balls in his body, having spent his latest breath in calling on his men to show what the Marines could do.[1] Other gallant leaders at Bunker's Hill, after seeing the battle through, fell in the very moment of success. Colonel Abercrombie, who had charge of the Grenadiers, was taken down to the boats mortally hurt, and feverishly entreating his comrades not to hang his old friend Putnam, because he was a brave fellow.

Whatever foolish and wrong things had been written

---

[1] A youth named Oldfield, who had attached himself to Pitcairn, also received two wounds; but he lived to fight again, and often again, by sea and land as an officer in the famous corps with which at Bunker's Hill he had served as a volunteer. Fourteen years afterwards, at St. Jean d'Acre, he was interred in the trenches by the French, with his sword upon him, as a mark of esteem and admiration; and Napoleon, when a prisoner on board the *Northumberland*, spoke to the Marine officers of his extraordinary valour.

or spoken before the event, there was no cruelty, and
no want of chivalry, between adversaries who had looked
so close in each other's eyes.   Within the circuit of the
rampart the garrison left more dead than wounded upon
the ground.   But the first few minutes after an escalade
cannot be regulated by the laws of a tournament; and
determined men, who resist to the last, do so with the
knowledge that they must take their chance of what
will happen while blood is hot, and the issue still doubtful.   The wonder was that so many of the defenders
went off alive and free; but the dry loose earth rose in
clouds of dust, and in rear of the redoubt the inter-
mingled throng of friends and foes was so dense that
the British did not venture to fire.   Prescott walked
quietly through the tumult, parrying thrusts with his
sword, much as his grandson's narrative describes Her-
nando Cortés on a certain day in the Great Square of
Mexico.   Thirty of his people were picked up by the
British, badly injured though still living, and were not
claimed as prisoners in the despatches.   On no occasion has it been more signally proved than at Bunker's
Hill how all but impossible it is to capture those who do
not wish to surrender.[1]

It would have gone harder with the men from the
fortification if the men at the rail-fence had behaved
less stoutly.   They stood until the retiring garrison had
passed beyond the right of their line.   Then they gave
ground with a coolness and deliberation most creditable
to young troops whose flank had been turned, and who
were now learning that the first ten minutes of a retreat
are sometimes more dangerous than the whole of a
battle.   For when the American array had disentangled
itself from the mass of enemies, and presented a clear
and safe mark, the worst moment of the day began.
The volleys of the British infantry, and the salvoes from

---

[1] Gage, in his official letter, speaks of "thirty found wounded in the
field, three of which are since dead."   Some months afterwards special
account was taken of ten among their number ; and seven of the ten were
no longer alive.

ship and battery in flank and rear, were not soon forgotten by those who were exposed to them. "The
brow of Bunker's Hill," we are told, "was a place of
great slaughter." It was there that Putnam, in language which came perilously near a breach of the rule
against swearing in the Military Regulations of Massachusetts, adjured the colonists to make a stand and give
them one shot more. Pomeroy, without a sword, but
with a broken musket in his hand which did as well,
took upon himself to see that his younger countrymen
marched steadily past the point of danger. Warren
never left the redoubt; for he fell where he had fought,
and he was buried where he had fallen : a bright figure,
passing out of an early chapter of the great story as un-
expectedly and irrevocably as Mercutio from the play.[1]
Pomeroy lamented that on a day when Warren, — ardent, hopeful, and eloquent, — had fallen, he himself,
"old and useless," escaped unhurt. He had not long
to wait. Having resigned his post of Brigadier-General,
for which he no longer felt himself fit, Pomeroy became
a regimental officer and, with his seventy years upon
him, went campaigning in the Jerseys. A course of
bivouacs brought him a pleurisy ; and he died for America just as certainly as if, like his young friend, he had
been shot through the head at Bunker's Hill.

A hundred and fifteen Americans lay dead across the
threshold of their country. Their wounded numbered
three hundred. Of six American cannon one was with
difficulty dragged back to Cambridge ; and under the
circumstances even that was much. The British gave
their own loss at a thousand and forty, of whom ninety-
two bore the King's commission. That striking dispro-
portion between leaders and followers was due to the
gallantry of our officers, and the fatally discriminating
aim of the minute-men. It reflected nothing whatever

---

[1] Massachusetts Congress, June 19, 1775 : "That three o'clock be
assigned for the choice of a President of this Congress in the room of the
Honourable Joseph Warren, supposed to be killed at the battle of Bunker's
Hill."

upon the conduct of the soldiers. Burgoyne indeed, in the first moment of surprise and pity, wrote home that the zeal and intrepidity of the commanders was ill seconded by the private men, among whom "discipline, not to say courage, was wanting;" but in after days, when something of the same kind was alleged in the House of Commons, he indignantly refuted the charge. It may be presumed that, on thinking it over, he arrived at the conclusion that troops who, after losing three men out of every seven, walked up to the hostile intrenchments without breaking step or snapping a flint, had earned their day's pay honestly, if ever soldiers did.

Our officers had looked for an easy victory, and had given much too free an expression to their anticipations. When the hour came they did not fight like braggarts; and they now manfully admitted that they had an adversary with whom it was an honour to measure themselves. "Damn the rebels, they would not flinch," was a form of words in which the most prejudiced subaltern paid his tribute to the colonists; and veterans of the royal army unanimously agreed that the affair had been more serious than anything which they had seen at Minden, or had been told about Fontenoy.[1] A string of chaises and chariots, sent down to the water-side by the Loyalists of the City, filed slowly back through the streets. "In the first carriage was Major Williams, bleeding and dying, and three dead captains of the Fifty-second Regiment. The second contained four dead officers; and this scene continued until Sunday morning, before all the wounded private men could be brought to Boston."[2] But the result of the engagement was small in comparison to the slaughter. General Gage was still on the wrong side of Charlestown Neck, looking across it at a range of heights stronger by nature, and much more elaborately fortified, than that grass-grown upland which

---

[1] *American Archives*, from June 18, 1775, onward through July. It is noticeable, there and elsewhere, how habitually Minden was quoted as the standard of desperate fighting.

[2] *Lieutenant Clarke's Narrative.*

was strewn so thickly with the flower of his army. It was a poor consolation to know that, as Nathanael Greene put it, the colonists were always ready to sell him another hill at the same price. Burgoyne told the Ministry, plainly and at once, that the main position held by the enemy could not be carried by assault, and that, if the British garrison was ever to leave Boston, it must go by water; and Howe, who had been deeper in the carnage than either Gage or Burgoyne, and whose memory contained a larger repertory of similar battles to compare it with, was never the same man again as when, standing on Charlestown beach among his picked companies, he gave the signal for the first onset. "The sad and impressive experience," (so we are told,) "of this murderous day sank deep into his mind." After Howe had succeeded to the supreme command, it exercised a permanent and most potent influence on the operations of the war. That joyous confidence, and that eagerness to bring matters to an immediate issue, which had been his most valuable military endowments, thenceforward were apt to fail him at the very moment when they were especially wanted. Careless as ever of his personal safety, he was destined to lose more than one opportunity of decisive victory by unwillingness to risk his men's lives, and his own fame, against an intrenchment with American riflemen behind it.

CHAPTER X

DEPRESSION reigned in the beleaguered city; but
there was no exultation in the camp of the besiegers.
In war as in politics, the morrow of an epoch-making
event is not always a season of exhilaration. There is
weariness and disappointment, and a consciousness that
the thing has been incompletely done, and an uneasy
suspicion that it had better never have been attempted.
Bunker's Hill, next morning and for years to come, presented to the colonists who had taken a share in it the
aspect of something very much short of a Marathon.
Contemporary accounts of the action, it has been justly
said, were in a tone of apology or even of censure.[1]
The affair produced a whole sheaf of court-martials; no
one stepped forward to claim the credit of it; and, (what
in New England was a more significant omission,)
more than one Seventeenth of June came and went
without a proposal being made to keep the day as an
anniversary. The patriots had expected from the enterprise tactical advantages which it was not capable of
yielding; and they did not yet perceive that, in its
indirect results, it had been the making of their cause.
The importance of what had happened was detected by
their adversaries, and the most accurately by those who
knew the country best. A gallant Loyalist of Massachusetts, who fought so well for King George that he
rose to be a full General in the British army, regarded
Bunker's Hill as a transaction which controlled everything that followed. " You could not," he would say to

---

[1] This is one of the many points acutely perceived, and powerfully illustrated, by Mr. Frothingham in his *Siege of Boston.*

his friends on the other side, "have succeeded without it. Something in the then state of parties was indispensable to fix men somewhere, and to show the planters of the South that Northern people were in earnest. That, *that* did the business for you." [1] "The rebels," Gage wrote a week after the battle, "are shown not to be the disorderly rabble too many have supposed. In all their wars against the French they have showed no such conduct and perseverance as they do now. They do not see that they have exchanged liberty for tyranny. No people were ever governed more absolutely than the American provinces now are; and no reason can be given for their submission but that it is a tyranny which they have erected themselves." [2]

There was justice in these conclusions, though they were not expressed in friendly words. Bunker's Hill had exhibited the Americans to all the world as a people to be courted by allies, and counted with by foes; and it had done them the yet more notable service of teaching them some home-truths. It was a marvel that so many armed citizens had been got together so quickly, and a still greater marvel that they had stayed together so long. Even a Cabinet Minister could not now deny that as individuals they possessed the old courage of their race. They had displayed, moreover, certain military qualities of a new and special type, such as were naturally developed by the local and historical conditions under which they had been born and bred. But no one who passed the early hours of that summer afternoon on the hill over Charlestown, and still more no one who witnessed the state of things in rear of the position and among the headquarters staff at Cambridge, could be blind to the conviction that a great deal would have to be done, and undone, before the colonies were able to hold the field throughout the protracted struggle which was now inevitable. The material was there, — excellent, abundant, and ductile, — of a national army with

[1] The account of General John Coffin in Sabine's *Loyalists;* vol. ii., p. 325.
[2] Gage to Dartmouth; *Dartmouth MSS.*, vol. ii., p. 320.

features of its own deeply marked; but to mould that material into shape was a task which would have to be pursued under difficulties of unusual complexity. The artificer was already found. A second Continental Congress had assembled at Philadelphia on the tenth of May; and Colonel Washington, who from that day forward attended the sittings in his uniform, was Chairman of all the Committees appointed to deal with military questions. Just before the battle took place, John Adams, — resolved to show that New Englanders would welcome a Virginian as their general, if a Virginian was the right man, — proposed that the assemblage of troops then besieging Boston should be adopted by Congress as a Continental Army, and indicated Colonel Washington as the officer best fitted to command it.

The suggestion was very generally approved, and in the end unanimously accepted. Washington was nominated as chief " of all the forces then raised, or that should be raised thereafter, in the United Colonies, or that should voluntarily offer their service for the defence of American liberty." There was no stint in the terms of his commission; and he assumed the trust in a spirit that was a pledge of the manner in which he would fulfil it. He did not make a pretence of begging off; but once for all, and in simple and solemn terms, he desired his colleagues to note that he thought himself unequal to the charge with which he was honoured. He refused a salary, but agreed to take his actual personal expenses; and the accounts which he thenceforward kept for the information of Congress are a model for gentlemen who have nothing in the world to do except to post up their household and stable books. It was a fine example, and one which, as the war progressed and brought corruption in its train, was every year more sorely needed. But Washington, according to his own views of what made life best worth having, surrendered that for which he would not have been compensated by the emoluments of a Marlborough. " I am now," he said to his brother, " to bid adieu to you, and to every kind of domestic ease, for a while. I am embarked on a wide ocean, boundless in its prospect, and in which perhaps no safe harbour is to be found." Mrs. Washington, like a true wife, took care to destroy before her death whatever written matter her husband had intended for her eyes alone; but she made an exception in the case of the letter announcing the news of his appointment. The world can read that letter as a whole, and it should never be read otherwise.[1]

Washington was the prototype of those great American generals in the War of Secession who, after receiving a thorough military education, retired into civil life because they loved it, or because the army in time of peace did not afford scope for their energies. Grant, Thomas, and Sherman had all been trained at West Point, had all served long enough to make themselves into practical soldiers, and had all left soldiering in order to seek more congenial or profitable work in other callings. Sheridan, alone among the Federal commanders of the first order, had a continuous military career; but he was too young to have gone from the army before the Civil War broke out. There had been no West Point for Washington; but the school which he had attended was not lax nor luxurious. Carrying his own knapsack; steering through floating ice a raft of logs which he had hewn with his own hatchet; outwitting murderous Indians whom he was too humane to shoot when he had them at his mercy; and then, after he had penetrated the secrets of the wilderness, applying his knowledge to the demands of active service against the French enemy, — he learned as much as his famous successors ever gathered in the classes of their Academy, or in their Mexican campaigns. Like them, he laid aside his sword, after he had proved it. Like them he resumed it at the call of duty. Like them he was not less of a soldier, and much more of a statesman and administrator, than if he had spent the whole of his early manhood in the superintendence of a provincial arsenal, or in the blockhouse of a frontier fort.

[1] *The Writings of George Washington*, by Jared Sparks; vol. iii., p. 2.

When Washington entered the boundaries of Massachusetts it became evident that the confidence evinced towards him by the representatives of New England at Philadelphia was shared by the great majority of their countrymen. The Provincial Assembly presented him with a congratulatory Address, and did not hesitate to admit, in the most uncompromising language, the arduous nature of the work which he had before him. Their troops, they confessed, were inexperienced and untrained, and required to be instructed in the most elementary obligations of the soldier. "The youth of the army," they said, "are not impressed with the absolute necessity of cleanliness in their dress and lodging, of continual exercise and strict temperance, to preserve them from diseases frequently prevailing in camps, especially among those who from their childhood have been used to a laborious life." On arriving at Cambridge the Commander-in-Chief discovered a condition of matters for which his recollections of early colonial warfare had only in part prepared him. "I found," he said, " a mixed multitude of people under very little discipline, order, or government." It was true that they knew how to shoot; but, taking the force round, they had only nine cartridges a man. One other military accomplishment they possessed, and they had exercised it to good purpose. From the brigadiers downward they all could dig; and in a marvellously short space of time they had thrown up a semi-circle of forts, extending over a front of ten miles, which effectually enclosed the garrison of Boston on the side of the mainland. Their industry in this department took no account of Sundays, and had something to do with that want of external smartness which attracted the unfavourable attention of their provincial Congress. General Putnam for instance, who held that every virtue, even the second on the list, had its times and seasons, was toiling at the intrenchments of Prospect Hill on the morning of the eighteenth of June in the same clothes as he had worn on the sixteenth, and through the dust and smoke of the battle of the seven-

teenth. In answer to a sympathetic inquirer he allowed
that he had not washed for eight and forty hours.

But by the end of June the immediate danger was over.
The works had been so aptly planned, and so vigorously
prosecuted, that the steady labour of another week
rendered them as good as impregnable. Towards the
North, the key of the position was Prospect Hill; or
Mount Pisgah, as these sons of Puritans preferred to
call it when they surveyed from its commanding summit that which they now, in all the confidence of victory,
regarded as the Promised City. At Roxbury to the South,
opposite Boston Neck, the ground was rocky, and the
American engineers had made the most of their advantages. "Roxbury," an observer wrote, "is amazingly
strong. It would puzzle ten thousand troops to go through
it." Washington was able to muster fifteen thousand soldiers fit for duty; too few, and too new, for an attempt
upon the British lines; but, as long as he could keep his
numbers undiminished, amply sufficient to guard his own.
There was a breathing space, and he turned it to profit.
In his first General Order he reminded the troops that
they were now a national army. "It is to be hoped,"
he wrote, "that all distinctions of colonies will be laid
aside, so that one and the same spirit may animate the
whole, and the only contest be who shall render the most
essential service to the great common cause in which
we are all engaged." He distributed the regiments into
brigades and divisions, under the best commanders
whom he could obtain; or at all events under the least
bad of those whom he was obliged to take. Some generals were imposed upon him by the very circumstances
which made them unsuitable, or intractable. He could
not get quit of Ward, who was strong in the universal
respect acquired by his all too ancient services. Charles
Lee, whose pretensions and plausibilities, not yet brought
to the proof, gained him an undeserved reputation in
that homely civilian army, had usurped, and for many
months continued to occupy, the secure ground of a man
supposed to be indispensable. But in Greene and Putnam,

Sullivan and Thomas, Washington had coadjutors of whom the first became, ere very long, equal to any responsibility which could be imposed upon him, and the others were thoroughly at home in every position below the highest.

The motley host, all alive with independence and individuality, was housed in appropriate fashion. A pleasing representation of what he saw on the hillsides to the West of Boston has been left by the Reverend William Emerson, of Concord: the member of a family where good writing was hereditary, and in which, two generations after, it became united to lofty thought and a teeming imagination. "It is very diverting," the minister said, "to walk among the camps. They are as different in their form as the owners are in their dress; and every tent is a portraiture of the temper and taste of the persons who encamp in it. Some are made of boards, and some of sailcloth. Again, others are made of stone and turf, brick or brush. Some are thrown up in a hurry; others curiously wrought with doors and windows, done with wreaths and withes, in the manner of a basket. Some are your proper tents and marquees, looking like the regular camp of the enemy. I think this great variety is rather a beauty than a blemish in the army."

In the eyes of the Commander-in-Chief, however, there was a limit to the advantages of the picturesque. The troops might lodge themselves according to their fancy; but he was determined that their superiors should have a voice in settling how they were to be clothed. The men provided their own raiment; and they were perpetually trading and swapping their habiliments, and even their accoutrements, or they would not have been New Englanders.[1] Those who possessed a uniform

[1] All through the siege, and for some time afterwards, David How's Diary gives a minute account of the traffic which went on in the cantonments.

"Feb. 3, 1776. I drawd a pare of Breaches out of the Stores price 27ˢ 6ᵈ."

had not yet learned to take a pride in it, as was shown
on the seventeenth of June by some Connecticut troops
who behaved very creditably in the battle. "We
marched," their commander wrote, "with our frocks
and trowsers on over our other clothes, (for our company is in blue, turned up with red,) for we were loath
to expose ourselves by our dress." Washington reported to Congress that the provision of some sort of
Regulation costume was an urgent necessity. "A number of hunting shirts, not less than ten thousand, would
remove this difficulty in the cheapest and quickest manner. I know nothing in a speculative view more trivial,
yet which if put in practice would have a happier tendency to unite the men, and abolish those provincial
distinctions which lead to jealousy and dissatisfaction."
Meanwhile he did his best, with the store of finery which
was at his disposal, to establish the outward signs of a
military hierarchy. Under a General Order, Serjeants
were to carry a stripe of red cloth on the right shoulder,
and Corporals one of green. A field officer mounted a
red cockade, and a Captain a yellow cockade. Generals
were desired to wear a pink riband, and Aides-de-camp
a green riband; while the person of the Commander-in-
Chief was marked by a light blue sash worn across his
breast between coat and waistcoat. As long as the head
of the army was Washington, he needed no insignia to
distinguish him. Whether on foot or in the saddle,
wherever his blue coat with buff facings was seen, — on
a Sunday parade, or as he galloped through the bullets
to meet, and lead back into the fire, a retreating regi-

"Feb. 6. I let David Chandler have my Breaches that I drawd out of
the Stores.
"Feb. 26. I sold my Cateridge box for 4ˢ 6ᵈ Lawfull money.
"March 12. William Parker made me a pair of Half Boots. I sold
William Parker my old Half Boots for Two Shillings and 3ᵈ.
"May 27. William Parker made me a pare of Shoes." It may be
mentioned that Parker was a private in the same company as the writer.
"June 29. I went to for teag" (fatigue) "this Day. I bought a pare
of trouses of Sergᵗ· Camble price 9 s. I sold A pare of Trouses To Nathan
Peabody price 10 s."

ment, — he looked, every one of his many inches, the king of men that nature had made him. Those on whom his countenance was turned in battle, in council, or in friendly intercourse, never doubted that the mind within was worthy of that stately presence. " I was struck with General Washington," wrote Mrs. Adams to her husband. " You had prepared me, but I thought the half was not told me. Dignity, with ease and complacency, the gentleman and the soldier, look agreeably blended in him. Modesty marks every line and feature of his face."

On grounds of policy, and from the bent of his disposition, the Commander-in-Chief missed no opportunity for such spectacles and pageants as the exigencies of the time allowed. "There is great overturning in the camp," Emerson wrote, " as to order and regularity. New Lords, new laws. The Generals Washington and Lee are upon the lines every day. New orders from his Excellency are read to the respective regiments every morning after prayers." One of those Orders required and expected of all officers and soldiers, not engaged on actual duty, a punctual attendance at Divine Service, to implore the blessings of Heaven upon the means used for the public safety and defence. These religious gatherings were occasionally enlivened by a touch of genial enthusiasm. On the eighteenth of July a message from Congress was read to the troops on Prospect Hill ; "after which an animated and pathetic address was made by the Chaplain to General Putnam's regiment, and was succeeded by a pertinent prayer. General Putnam gave the signal, and the whole army shouted their loud Amen by three cheers ; immediately on which a cannon was fired from the fort, and the standard lately sent to General Putnam flourished in the air." On the banner was inscribed a short and telling Latin phrase, implying that He who had brought the fathers across the ocean would not forget the children.[1] Against one ceremony which, it is to be feared,

[1] " Qui Transtulit Sustinet."

was more popular among New England troops than any
other, Washington set his face resolutely; for he would
not permit them to burn the Pope.   There were so few
Catholics in the army that the General did not refer to
their presence as a reason for disappointing his soldiers
of a treat which they had so often relished in their native villages.   He based his decision on the importance
to the colonies of doing nothing to alienate the French
Canadians, whose friendship and alliance the statesmen
at Philadelphia had not yet despaired of securing.

Washington knew that something more than sermons
and celebrations was required to make an aggregation
of human beings into an obedient army.   " The strictest
government," said Mr. Emerson, "is taking place, and
great distinction is made between officers and soldiers.
Every one is made to know his place, and keep in it."
Discipline and morality were maintained and vindicated
with less of indulgence and connivance, but with a far
smaller amount of cruelty, than prevailed in European
camps.   Loose women were expelled from the lines,
marauding was severely checked, and corporal punish-
ments were inflicted; though, (in a community where
everything was regulated on Scriptural precedents,) the
number of lashes appears never to have exceeded thirty-
nine.[1]   Rogues were in terror, and laggards found it
their interest to bestir themselves; but honest fellows
who did not shirk their duty enjoyed life as it never has
been enjoyed in any campaign, the familiar details of

---

[1] " Feb. 7.   This Day two men In Cambridge got a bantering who
would Drink the most, and they Drinkd so much That one of them Died
In About one houre or two after.

" Feb. 10.   There was two women Drumd out of Camp this fore noon.
That man was Buried that killed himself drinking.

" March 27.   There was four of Capt. Willey's men Whept, the first fifteen stripes for denying his Deuty: the 2^d 39 stripes for Stealing and deserting: 3^d 10 lashes for getting Drunk and Denying Duty: 4^d 20 lashes
Denying his Duty and geting Drunk.

" May 1.   One of Capt· Pharinton's men Was whipt 20 lashes for being
absent at rool Call without Leave.

" May 26.   This Night Mical Bary was whipt 39 Stripes for being
absent at rool Call."

which have been noted with equal minuteness. All
arrangements which bore upon the health and the comforts of the private men were diligently taken in hand
by their commander. Regimental officers were made
answerable for seeing that every dwelling, where soldiers
lived, was cleaned every morning. Camp kitchens were
built; very great care was given to the cookery; and
there was plenty to cook. "I doubt not," King George
wrote to Lord Dartmouth, "but the twenty thousand
provincials are a magnified force occasioned by the fears
of the correspondent. Should the numbers prove true
it would be highly fortunate, as so large a corps must
soon retire to their respective homes for want of sub-
sistence." But there was very little prospect of such
a termination to the war; for the Provincial Assembly
was determined that the defenders of the colony should
be well on the right side of starvation. The Massachusetts soldier received every day a pound of bread, half
a pound of beef, and half a pound of pork, together
with a pint of milk, a quart of "good spruce or malt
beer," and a gill of peas or beans. A pound and a
quarter of salt fish was substituted for the meat on one
day in the seven. Every week there were served out
half a dozen ounces of butter, and half a pint of vinegar,
(if vinegar was to be had,) to each of the men, and one
pound of good common soap among six of them. Nor
was that all. Supplies poured into the camp; and the
soldiers bought largely and judiciously, eating and drinking freely of what they could not sell again at a profit.
In the course of eight days the caterer of a single mess
purchased three barrels of cider; seven bushels of chest-
nuts; four of apples, at twelve shillings a bushel; and
a wild turkey for supper, which weighed over seventeen pounds.[1] It may safely be said that his Majesty,
who set a praiseworthy example of abstinence in the
midst of a gouty generation, would as soon have thought
of consuming the whole of the daily ration which was

[1] *David How's Diary;* January 24 to 31, 1776.

placed before his rebellious subjects as of adopting their political tenets.

Within the city good eating was almost a thing of the past. Before the end of July Washington had learned that the British troops were insufficiently and badly fed, and that their health suffered. Captain Stanley, who as a son of Lord Derby would command the best which might be had for money, mentioned in a letter that he had only tasted fresh meat twice since his arrival in Boston.[1] The wounded men, he said, recovered very slowly indeed upon a diet which, even if no battle had taken place, would soon have filled the hospitals. A local merchant, — writing to his brother with a latitude of virulence which, in times of danger and discord, civilian partisans too often allow themselves, — stated positively that, when the ammunition in the pouches of the rebels on Bunker's Hill was examined, the balls were found to be poisoned; but no military man either believed, or repeated, a slander quite superfluous for the purpose of explaining the high rate of mortality which prevailed in the garrison. Our soldiers took what came as the fortune of war; and the fortune of war was very hard. Sick or well, whole or hurt, they had nothing to eat but salt pork and peas, with an occasional meal of fish. "An egg was a rarity," and their wretched diet was never mended by so much as a vegetable or a drop of milk. What fresh beef there was in the town had been obtained by slaughtering milch cows which could not have been kept alive in the increasing dearth of forage. The daily deaths never sank below ten, and sometimes rose to thirty. From July onwards, to prevent discouragement, no bells were allowed to toll. As summer changed to autumn, and autumn to winter, the distress, sharp everywhere, became extreme in private

[1] According to the American satirists the Commander-in-Chief himself was no better off than his regimental officers. In a contemporary poem Gage is represented as exclaiming : —

"Three weeks; — Ye Gods! nay, three long years it seems
Since roast beef I have touched, except in dreams."

families; and those were not few, for between six and seven thousand of the population had remained in the town.   Fresh meat in July cost fifteen pence a pound; and by the middle of December that price had to be paid for salt provisions.[1]   The King's stores ran so very short that no flour or pulse could be spared for the use of non-combatants.   It was bitterly cold, and all the fuel had been burned away.   That want was met by an expedient which excited painful feelings among the Loyalist exiles across the ocean,[2] and was a cruel sight indeed for people who were still in their native city because they loved it so that they could not bear to leave it.   All of Charlestown which had survived the conflagration was first pulled down, and issued to the regiments for firewood; and then the troops proceeded to help themselves from the fences of the Boston gardens, and the doors and rafters of the Boston houses.   The British General sent the Provost Marshal on his rounds, accompanied by an executioner, and armed with powers to hang on the spot any man who was caught in the act of wrecking a dwelling house; but the authorities continued to do on a system that which the soldiers had begun under the spur of necessity.   A hundred wooden buildings were marked for demolition; and hatchet and crow-bar were steadily plied, until the arrival of a fleet of colliers from the Northern English ports spared Boston any further taste of the destiny which had overtaken her humble neighbour beyond the ferry.

It was sad work at the best; and all the more hate-

---

[1] After the investment of the town commenced, Captain Harris, "as good a beef-eater as any belonging to His Majesty," sorely resented the want of fresh meat; and he made himself a garden in order to provide the mess with vegetables. "Such salad! Such excellent greens the young turnip-tops make! Then the spinach, and radishes, with the cucumbers, beans and peas promised so well," as a future relish to the salt provisions. Before ever his garden-produce came to maturity, Harris was seriously wounded at Bunker's Hill. "As a sick person," he then wrote, "I am confined to broth alone; but broth of salt pork! We ourselves get a piece of an old ox, or cow, at the rate of fourteen times as much as we paid last summer."

[2] *Curwen's Journal;* Feb. 15, 1776.

ful to Bostonians because it afforded a pretext for
mortifying the richer members of the popular party
whose circumstances had enabled them to leave the
town, and those poorer patriots who had no choice but
to stay there.   A fine old elm, which went by the name
of Liberty Tree, had during ten years served the public
as a rallying place for political gatherings.   Fourteen
cords of firewood were now obtained from the venerable trunk.   Sons of Liberty, all the continent over,
consoled themselves by knowing, or at all events by
believing, that a soldier had met his death in falling
from the branches while engaged upon what they regarded as an act of sacrilege.[1]   It was perhaps too much
to expect that the noteworthy tree would be spared
in the hour of retribution by redcoats who had so
often been roundly abused beneath its spreading foliage; but far worse things were done with much less excuse.   The old North Church had stood for a hundred
years, and, relatively to the duration of the city, was as
much a piece of antiquity as St. Albans Abbey or
Beverley Minster.   It was now taken down and sent in
smoke, with all its memories and associations, up the
chimneys of a hundred barrack-rooms.   The steeple

[1] The catastrophe was celebrated in the kind of verses which somebody at all times can be found to write, and which, during a period of
national excitement, even sensible men contrive to read.

> "Each, axe in hand, attacked the honoured tree,
> Swearing eternal war with Liberty.
> But e'er it fell, not mindless of its wrong,
> Avenged it took one destined head along.
> A Tory soldier on its topmost limb, —
> The genius of the shade looked stern at him,
> And marked him out that self-same hour to dine
> Where unsnuffed lamps burn low at Pluto's shrine."

There were smaller Liberty Trees in other quarters of the city.   On
May 4, 1766, John Adams wrote : —
"Sunday.   Returning from meeting this morning I saw for the first time
a likely young button-wood tree, lately planted on a triangle made by
three roads.   The tree is well set, well guarded, and has on it an inscription,
       'The tree of Liberty, and cursed is he who cuts this tree !'
What will be the consequences of this thought?   I hear that some persons
grumble, and threaten to girdle it."

of the West Church, built of large timbers, underwent the same fate.

Little love was lost between the British authorities and the minister and deacons of the old South Church, which had been frequently lent to the patriots for town-meetings. The parsonage was destroyed, mercifully and at once; but the church was treated as too bad for burning. The nave was made over to the cavalry as a place in which to exercise recruits on horse-back. Pulpit and seats were cut in pieces. Earth and gravel were spread over the floor; a leaping-bar was set up; the gallery was fitted as a refreshment room for spectators; and the stoves were fed with the contents of a library, the pride of the connection to whom the chapel belonged. The responsibility for this desecration, justly or unjustly, was laid at the doors of General Burgoyne. He had offended a people with quick tongues, and long memories. Two years afterwards, when he entered Boston as a prisoner, he called the attention of his staff to a public building beneath which they were passing, as having been formerly the residence of the Governor; and a voice in the crowd quietly observed that, when they got round the next corner, they would see the Riding-school. Burgoyne took that remark like a man who loved a jest; but he subsequently confessed that at another point of his route, he had been for a moment disconcerted by learning that the first sentence which he was known to have uttered after reaching America had not yet been forgotten. As the procession filed with difficulty through the ranks of a populace, good-humoured, but obtrusively curious, an old lady called out from the top of a shed: "Make way! Make way! Give the General elbow-room!"

It was a miserable life inside Boston for troops who had sailed from England in the belief that they were to take part in a triumphant, and leisurely, progress through a series of rich and repentant provinces. The horses soon became useless from want of food; a circumstance always predominant among the material causes which

destroy the efficiency of a blockaded army. Moral
deterioration began to be observed among the soldiers,
whose spring and energy were slowly and stealthily un-
dermined by the depressing character of the existence
which they were condemned to lead. No one could
show himself outside the earthworks without having a
bullet through him; and the men on guard within them
carried their lives in their hand at every moment.
Generals bred in the traditions of European warfare
complained of the proceedings of the colonists as un-
generous and unprofessional. In July and August the
Southern riflemen marched into Washington's camp, —
stout hardy men, in white frocks and round hats, — who
had trudged four, five, or even seven hundred miles to
have a shot at the regulars; and who were determined
not to be baulked of it however much Prince Ferdinand
and Marshal de Contades, many years back and thousands of miles away, would have been shocked at such
a departure from the honourable amenities of a campaign. On the way North they had shown off their
skill at a review. One of their companies, while ad-
vancing in skirmishing order, had put a good proportion of balls into a mark seven inches broad at a
distance of two hundred and fifty yards. They now
posted themselves in ambush, five or six of them behind
as many neighbouring trees, and watched for a favourable chance at a British sentry as they had been accustomed to wait upon the movements of a deer in the
forests of South Carolina.

Cooped up within two promontories, which were like
small islands without the security of an insular position,
our soldiers lost their health and spirits, and after a
while something of their self-respect. Scurvy showed
itself; the smallpox raged in the streets and cantonments;
and the British commanders were of opinion that Washington, on that ground alone, even if he had not still
better reasons, would think twice and thrice before he
should assault the town. When winter was half over
the rank and file no longer retained the smart appear-

ance which was then, even more than now, the delight of regimental officers. Hats without binding, and shirts without frills; unpowdered hair, unwashed linen, and unbuttoned gaiters, formed the subjects of denunciation in General Orders; and, that nothing might be wanting, some of the privates went so far as to borrow from the enemy that habit which was the least worthy of imitation, and chewed tobacco when they came on duty. The British Commander-in-Chief was far from indifferent to these deviations from the recognised standard of military perfection ; and he was stern and inflexible when the demoralisation, of which they were the symptoms, took the shape of violence and spoliation directed against the inhabitants of the city. Subordination was preserved, and crime kept in check, by that form of punishment which had become so much of an institution in our fighting services that officers, who otherwise were neither unjust nor unkindly, altogether lost sight of the distinction between severity and barbarity. Sentences were passed, and carried out, of four hundred, six hundred, one thousand lashes.

There was one General in Boston who viewed these excesses of rigour with disapprobation. Burgoyne held that harshness was seldom required for the government of men who were habitually treated by their superiors with discrimination and sympathy. He hated flogging. Wherever he commanded, he exercised his artistic ingenuity in order to find a substitute for that penalty ; and when, according to the ideas of the time, it could not be dispensed with, he took care that it was inflicted in a measure carefully regulated by the gravity of the offence. A splendid disciplinarian of the right sort, he kept his officers in order, and they liked him all the better for it. He had learned by experience that that was the surest method of keeping order among the privates. According to Burgoyne, the captain and the subalterns between them should be acquainted with the disposition and the merits of every man in the company, and were not to be contented with noting down his height, the girth of his chest, and the number of times his name had appeared on the defaulters' list. "To succeed," he said, "where minds are to be wrought upon requires both discernment and labour. Admitting that English soldiers are to be treated as thinking beings, the reason will appear of getting insight into the character of each particular man, and proportioning accordingly the degrees of punishment and encouragement." [1]

Burgoyne now did his best to divert the monotony of the siege, and to show the troops that, since good victuals had run short, their superiors were all the more anxious to cater for their amusement. Faneuil Hall, where the people had assembled both after the Boston Massacre, and before the destruction of the tea, was converted into a theatre. The idea of turning the cradle of liberty to such a use did not escape censorious comment; but it must be remembered that Boston was a city where it was not easy to find any capacious building, sacred or profane, in which a political meeting had never been held. The company gave the tragedy of Tamerlane; some modern comedies; and a piece of occasion entitled the Blockade, in which the person of Washington was caricatured with a flippancy which the course of events soon rendered unfashionable even among his adversaries. Burgoyne contributed a prologue, spoken by a very young nobleman who had distinguished himself on the seventeenth of June. "Lord Rawdon," said Burgoyne, "behaved to a charm. His name is established for life." That life was long, and so varied and stirring that it reads like the story of as many separate men as the three names by which he, who lived it, was successively called. Always to the front in a fight, and the last in a retreat, Lord Rawdon proved himself a brilliant and successful partisan leader

[1] Burgoyne, in the fulness of time, had an able biographer in the late Mr. Edward Barrington de Fonblanque. Mr. de Fonblanque was in our own days a wise, perfectly informed, and, (for he was a permanent official in the War Department,) a singularly courageous, military reformer. He wrote quite as well as might be expected from a nephew of the famous editor of the "Examiner."

in the war which now was opening. As Lord Moira he was an orator for many a long year at Westminster, and in the House of Peers of Ireland, as long as Ireland had one; a prominent and a popular statesman; and a good friend of Fox and of liberty, at a time when they both wanted friends badly. And far into the next century, as a Governor-General too old to lead his own armies, Lord Hastings organised conquest on a scale which dazzled his fellow-countrymen, and terrified his employers on the board of the East India Company. After he had taught a lesson to Nepaul, and had finally and effectually broken the power of the Mahrattas, — perhaps the greatest single service which our rule has conferred on our Eastern dependency, — it may well be believed that he but dimly remembered what his sensations were when he found himself on the right side of the breastwork at Bunker's Hill, with two bullet holes in his hat, and his reputation made.

George the Third was not long in showing what he considered to be the practical value of the victory which his troops had gained. As soon as the news reached Kew he at once desired that General Gage should turn over the command to Howe, and sail for England in order to inform the Ministry as to what supplies and reinforcements the army wanted for carrying on the next campaign. It was a kindly pretext, devised to spare the feelings of an unprofitable, but a faithful and a brave, servant.[1] In recalling that ill-starred commander, the King acted on his own first, and most just, impressions. He made up his mind without waiting to read a letter containing Burgoyne's enumeration of the points wherein Gage failed to resemble Julius Cæsar, especially in the wise munificence with which the great Roman dispensed public money to his deserving lieutenants. Burgoyne himself went home in November, having been summoned back by royal command because his advice was really wanted. Before, however, the two

[1] Not very long ago a gold medal, presented to Gage by the Duke of Cumberland after Culloden, was sold at auction for 230*l.*

Generals departed from Boston they were engaged on one more joint literary undertaking. Washington had addressed to the British Commander-in-Chief a remonstrance against the denial to American officers, who had been taken prisoners, of the privileges and alleviations due to their rank. Gage's reply was worded by Burgoyne. "Britons," he wrote, "ever pre-eminent in mercy, have overlooked the criminal in the captive. Your prisoners, whose lives by the law of the land are destined to the cord, have hitherto been treated with care and kindness; — indiscriminately, it is true, for I acknowledge no rank that is not derived from the King." The author might well have stopped here; but the opportunity was irresistible, and he proceeded to inflict upon Washington, as a person only too likely to need it, a lecture on the obligation of scrupulous truthfulness. When the rough copy had been fairly written out, the letter was addressed to George Washington, Esquire; and the notoriety obtained by this superscription is the cause that the effusion itself, unfortunately for Burgoyne, has been more read than all his dramas and epilogues together.

The authorities in England had not foreseen the privations which our troops in Boston were so early called upon to endure. It was difficult to understand that the army of a great sea-power, strongly established in a seaport town, would at the very commencement of hostilities be faring no better than the sailors on board an ill-found East Indiaman in the last days of a long voyage. The crops and live-stock, on the islands alone, might have been counted upon to stave off scurvy until such time as the harbour was crowded with provision-ships attracted from far and near by the prospect of a splendid market. But, upon her own element, Great Britain was poorly served; and, in a species of warfare where personal qualities went for everything, the skill, the energy, and the daring were to a preponderating degree on the side of the insurgents. On the fifteenth of July the colonels of American regiments were directed to report the names of men in their respective corps who were expert in the management of whaleboats.[1]   The House of Commons which, in spite of all that Charles Fox could say, had insisted on driving New England fishermen from the prosecution of their calling, had made it certain that the list of the volunteers would in every case be a long one. A large fleet of these boats had already been brought overland from Cape Cod, and from the towns lying between that point and Boston.   The vessels were fitted out in the Cambridge, and the Mystic, rivers, and before another week was over they were busy in the bay. Thenceforward the men in the garrison got no fresh food, and the horses neither fresh nor dry.   The colonists seized what remained of the flocks and herds. They cut the standing grass, and loaded up their barges from the hay-ricks.   They came off the best in their encounters with the British soldier, who could do himself little justice in operations for which he had not been trained ; and in which, as he complained, assistance and guidance did not come from the quarter where he had a right to look for them.   " The Admiral," so a General wrote, " must take to himself a great share of our inactivity, our disgrace, and our distress.   The glaring facts are not to be concealed ; that many vessels have been taken, officers killed, men made prisoners ; that large numbers of swift boats have been supplied to the enemy, in which they have insulted and plundered islands immediately under the protection of our ships, and at noonday landed in force and set fire to the light-house almost under the guns of two or three men of war." [2]

For the British squadron was not efficient.   It had been put in commission, and despatched to America,

[1] *American Archives.   Writings of George Washington ;* vol. iii., Appendix X.

[2] When Judge Curwen, the Massachusetts Loyalist, was travelling in the West of England, they pointed out to him " the seat of the well-known Admiral Graves, whose base unworthy conduct in America has justly brought the curses of the people on his head, displeased his sovereign and the Ministry, and rendered himself the contempt of all." *Samuel Curwen's Journal ;* October 18, 1776.

under an impression that its duties would be confined to warning merchantmen not to enter the harbour of Boston, and to intimidating the idle and famished mariners who crowded her quays by the rows of cannon which protruded from its portholes. Too few sloops and gun-boats had been provided; and the crews both of large ships and small were on a peace establishment which, (before the days of Continuous Service,) fell much below the complements carried in time of war. The belief that America would take her punishment submissively was an article of the Ministerial creed which no one at the Board of Admiralty ventured to dispute. As one very serious consequence of that delusion, the fleet, and not a few of the vessels composing it, were indifferently commanded. Unaware that he had already to deal with an active and amphibious rebellion, and that several great wars were in the near future, the Earl of Sandwich gave full scope to private and political favouritism in his management of the Service for whose condition, and in no small degree for whose honour, he was responsible. Clever and industrious, he had the Navy List by heart; and he knew the opinions, and the family and social connections, of his Admirals and Post-Captains as familiarly and thoroughly as ever Mr. John Robinson knew his Members of Parliament. Eminent officers, who held with Rockingham, were not in request at Whitehall; and there was a still blacker mark against the names of those veterans who had illustrated by their achievements the Ministry of Lord Chatham, and who repaid his gratitude and esteem with a personal loyalty which cost them dear.[1]

Their place was taken by men of a much lower order; among whom the two flag officers successively appointed to the American station were conspicuous, the one by his insolence and indiscretion, and the other by his

[1] Captain Mahan, in his account of the operations at sea between 1775 and 1783, remarks that, with the notable exception of Rodney, almost all the distinguished admirals of the time were Whigs; — " a fact unfortunate for the naval power of England."

incompetency. Admiral Montagu had done a great deal
to provoke the rebellion, and Admiral Graves did nothing whatever to quell it. " It may be asked in England,"
said Burgoyne, " what is the admiral doing ? I wish I
were able to answer that question satisfactorily; but I
can only say what he is *not* doing." The array of instances by which charges of procrastination, want of
spirit, and professional incapacity were supported would
have been formidable in the hands of any accuser ; and,
as unfolded by Burgoyne, the indictment was as portentous in length as it was damning in force and accuracy.[1]
But nothing that was done or neglected in American
waters had escaped the eye of a master who never pardoned slackness in himself or others. " I do think the
Admiral's removal as necessary, if what is reported is
founded, as the mild General's." So the King wrote
to Lord North in the summer; and, before the winter
was through, Graves had been deprived of his command. He was preceded to England by the news, or
it may be the rumour, of the only bit of fighting in which
he was personally engaged, — a scuffle in the streets of
Boston with an official of the revenue. He considered
himself to have been badly treated by the Government,
and evinced his resentment in a manner which was
honourable to him. Having refused a lucrative post on
shore, he passed the short remainder of his days in a retirement which he made it to be understood that nothing
except a call to active service would induce him to quit.[2]

Before the Admiral received his letter of recall the
mischief was already done. The colonists had not been

[1] *Life and Correspondence of Burgoyne*, by E. B. de Fonblanque ; pp.
197, 198.
[2] Popular report made out Graves to be absurd as well as unsuccessful;
for the opposite of a hero, like a hero, is usually something of a mythical
personage. It has been related in print how, on his elevation to the peerage, he chose a Latin motto to the effect that an eagle does not stoop to
flies; and how the wags translated it as meaning that a Vice Admiral need
not concern himself with whaleboats. As a matter of fact, the peerage was
bestowed not on Samuel Graves, but on Thomas Graves, who earned it
gloriously on the First of June, and who was always ready for anything
which came in his way, from a longboat to a couple of three-deckers.

slow to catch at an opportunity when the interests of
Great Britain were entrusted to a squadron which was
ill provided, and worse commanded; and the American
navy came into being during the second half of the
year 1775. The first vessels sailed beneath the pine-tree
flag. The emblem was appropriately chosen; because
the service, which fought its earliest battles under that
ensign, struck its own roots and grew up of itself.
In every colony, (since all touched the ocean somewhere,) there were shipowners whose whalers and
coasters were laid up in harbour, merchants whose
capital was producing nothing, and whole villages of
sea-faring people with their occupation gone. Rhode
Island had two cruisers afloat in July; and on the first
of the same month the Assembly of Connecticut author-
ised the equipment of two others. The Congressmen
of Massachusetts had been the first to recognise the
necessity of a fleet; but Bunker's Hill diverted their
attention to the war on land, and the subject was allowed
to sleep. Soon, however, the hand of the Provincial
authorities was forced by individuals who put to sea
without letters of marque; and who, while the enemy
classed them as pirates, had not the status of privateers
even in the eyes of their own Government. Moved by
the danger to their necks which these adventurous
patriots had cheerfully incurred, the Assembly at Concord hastened to legalise the employment of armed ships,
and proceeded to establish a Court for the trial and condemnation of prizes.

The prime mover in the creation of a national marine
was the man most intimately acquainted with the broad
aspects of the military position, and most deeply concerned in the issue. Washington, outstepping the attributes of his office in substance, but careful to observe
them in form, directed " a captain in the army of the
united colonies of North America to take command of
a detachment of the said army, and proceed on board
the schooner Hannah at Beverley." [1] The Congress at

---

[1] *The Writings of George Washington ;* vol. iii., Appendix X.

Philadelphia was not in a mood to get up a quarrel with
their General for exceeding his powers. Urged by his
importunity, and fired by his example, they armed and
manned six schooners, which by the end of October
were chasing, and being chased, in and about Massachusetts Bay. A permanent Committee, with John Adams
upon it, was appointed for the supervision of naval
affairs; a code of regulations was drawn up and issued
to the squadron ; and skippers and mates in sufficient
number were duly commissioned as Captains, and Lieutenants, of the Continental Navy. Washington, however, to all intents and purposes continued to act as
Admiral; until Captain Manly of the Lee by the audacity of his enterprises was marked out to the judgement
of America for her first Commodore.

It was evident from a very early date that the new
sea-power had an instinctive grasp of the good old
methods. The American commanders were fully alive
to the truth of the famous proverb which passes as the
last word of military wisdom, though it is not certain to
which of the world's great warriors the original inven-
tion of it should be attributed. They knew that, in
order to make omelettes, eggs must be broken ; and
that a captain cannot hope to bring his adversary's ship
into port unless he will run the risk of losing his own.
A rapid series of successes, chequered by disaster, formed
a worthy commencement to the history of a navy which
has always done an amount of fighting quite extraordinary in proportion to the national money that has been
spent upon it. The public in London, when it cared to
visit the Admiralty, was very soon treated to a look at a
captured pine-tree flag ; and, on the other hand, Manly
alone, to say nothing of his consorts, in the course of
four months intercepted stores sufficient to have vict-
ualled his squadron many times over, and almost enough
liquor to float his little flagship. A vessel laden with a
hundred butts of porter ; a brigantine whose cargo included a hundred and thirty-nine hogsheads of rum, and
a hundred cases of right Geneva ; a sloop with Indian

corn, potatoes, and oats; two Whitehaven ships with coal and potatoes; two large merchantmen carrying provisions for the British garrison, — these were some, and by no means the most valuable, of the Commodore's prizes.

When the condition of the besieged troops became known in England, the Ministry endeavoured to supply their wants by means of a profuse expenditure. Five thousand oxen, (so it was computed by a very well-informed writer,) fourteen thousand of the largest and fattest sheep, and a huge consignment of hogs were purchased, and sent out alive. Vegetables of all kinds were cured by a new process, and stowed away in the holds. Five thousand chaldrons of coal were shipped, along with the very faggots required to kindle them; oats, beans, and hay for the horses; and near half a million of money in Spanish and Portuguese coinage. The employment given in many and diverse quarters by this feverish activity; the shares in lucrative contracts allotted to men of rank and fashion, ignorant of business, who had never before in their lives sold anything except their votes in Parliament; the fervent, and expectant, gratitude of brewers who supplied ten thousand butts of strong beer, and of merchants who provided shipping at a fourth above the usual rate for tonnage; — all these circumstances added political strength to the Government. But at that point the public advantage stopped. The transports sailed too late in the season, and contrary gales kept them long near our own shores. The preserved vegetables fermented and were thrown overboard. The waves were so tempestuous that the greater part of the animals perished, and the tides carried their carcasses in thousands up and down the Channel. As the vessels neared their destination, the periodical winds set in and blew full in their teeth. Some were driven off to the West Indian Islands. Others drifted towards the American coasts, and were boarded and plundered in the creeks to which they resorted for shelter. Those which survived, after beating the seas for three or four months, found them-selves, with leaking sides and rotten cordage, on the cruising ground of a hostile navy the first notice of whose existence reached them through a shot fired across their own bows. Time, and no very long time, had brought about the due revenges; and Boston had become a closed port in a sense which Parliament never contemplated or intended.[1]

The supineness of the British naval commanders during the first period of the war was less detrimental to the royal cause than their occasional ebullitions of sinister energy. On the fifteenth of October, 1775, George the Third assured Lord North, in a sentence never yet forgotten beyond the Atlantic, that he would concur in any plan which could be devised with the object of "distressing America." A week afterwards a despatch went from Downing Street recommending that the rebels should be annoyed by sudden and un-expected attacks of their seaboard towns during the winter; and directing the total destruction of any place, large or small, in which the people assembled in arms, or held meetings of committees or congresses. Charles the First, who has sometimes been called a tyrant, but who fought his civil war as became an English King, would on these grounds have been justified in utterly demolishing Bristol and Leicester, and, (if he once could have got inside them,) Norwich, Gloucester, Cambridge, and London itself.

Already something had been done in anticipation of the Ministerial policy. On the middle day of October Captain Mowatt had sailed into the port of Falmouth, in that part of Massachusetts which afterwards became the state of Maine, and had poured a shower of gre-nades and shells upon the unprotected streets of the little community. Some wooden houses were soon in a blaze, and Marines were landed to prevent the fire from being extinguished. The church, the public buildings, and three-fourths of the dwellings perished; all the vessels

[1] *Annual Register* for 1776; chapter ii. of the *History of Europe.*

in the harbour were sunk or carried off; and the inhabitants were left, homeless and without the means of escape, to the approaching rigours of a Northern winter in that remote, and, (when the sea was blockaded,) all but inaccessible region. The members of the Continental Congress were then waiting for a reply to the Address in which they had appealed to the King to stand their friend, in spite of the prejudice and animosity entertained by Parliament against his subjects in America. The tidings from Falmouth reached Philadelphia on the same day as the news that the British Government was raising an army of German mercenaries to be employed against the revolted colonies. These two pieces of intelligence, by their simultaneous effect, killed outright all hope, or even desire, of reconciliation. "Brother rebel," said a Southern delegate to one of his New England colleagues, "I am ready to declare ourselves independent. We have now got a sufficient answer to our petition."

The doom of Falmouth was a foretaste of what the Northern colonies had to expect; and the lesson was next taught in another quarter. Norfolk, at the mouth of the James River, had for many years been the seat of a brisk, and mutually profitable, trade with the West of Scotland in the staple commodity of Virginia. Near sixty thousand hogsheads of tobacco were annually brought into the Clyde; and most of them were shipped from the estuary of the James. The town was largely owned by merchants whose warehouses lined Virginia Street in Glasgow. Their clerks and factors formed that part of the population of Norfolk which was most in evidence; especially since the troubles began, and the partisans of the Revolution had retired into the interior of the country. These good Scotchmen, if left to themselves, would have lived peaceably. When forced to show colours, they very tardily took up arms for the Crown, and formed themselves into a Loyal Militia. Before long, a force of native Virginians came down from the upper districts, and re-entered Norfolk after a sharp encounter with a small garrison of regu-lars. The Loyal Militia, who during the action had con-trived to post themselves where the fighting was not, sought refuge among the ships of a squadron which lay in the river, with Lord Dunmore, the Governor of the province, on board. That nobleman, and the captain of the largest man of war, laid their heads together over the paper of Instructions which had been issued by the Government at home. They came to the conclusion that Norfolk was " a town in actual rebellion, accessible to the King's ships," and that they had no choice except to carry out the King's order. Accordingly on the afternoon of New Year's day, 1776, the bombard-ment commenced. The pinewood structures, coated with paint, were soon alight ; and, favoured by the wind, the conflagration spread fast. Wherever the Ameri-cans were not on the look-out, a boat's crew pushed off, and set a match to the sheds where the Scotch factors kept their stores of an article which they intended eventually to be burned, but not by so wholesale and unremunerative a process. Sixty cannon, deliberately trained upon the points where the flames were advanc-ing, defeated every effort to save the town ; and the fire raged until four-fifths of the houses were in ashes.

That lamentable occurrence stirred the calm temper of the most famous of Virginians, and animated his pre-cise and severe style ; for the Commander-in-Chief of the American army wrote from his headquarters at Cambridge that a few more of such flaming arguments as those which were exhibited at Falmouth and Norfolk would secure a majority in favour of a separation be-tween England and her colonies. Franklin, when Charlestown was shelled and destroyed, had pronounced himself unable to discern how such proceedings could favourably affect those commercial claims on the part of the mother-country which had been the ostensible origin of the war. " Britain," he said, " must certainly be distracted. No tradesman out of Bedlam ever thought of increasing the numbers of his customers by

knocking them on the head, or of enabling them to pay
their debts by burning their houses." This specimen of
Franklin's habitual humour was fraught with as grim a
purpose as that which inspired Washington's unwonted
rhetoric. The glare thrown upon the future by these
acts of official arson lighted them both to the same conclusion. "It has been with difficulty," Franklin wrote,
"that we have carried another humble Petition to the
Crown, to give Britain one more chance of recovering
the friendship of the colonies: which however she has
not sense enough to embrace; and so she has lost them
for ever."

CHAPTER XI

WASHINGTON, meanwhile, was struggling against difficulties, less hopeless indeed than those which beset the British General, but of a character more unusual in modern warfare, and demanding more exceptional qualities in the man whose duty it was to deal with them. The royal garrison was dwindling from disease and privation; but it seemed as if the American army would melt away of itself. Within a week after Bunker's Hill there were many honest militiamen who thought it an eminently suitable occasion to go back to their farms, and get in the hay, and possibly the corn, before the next battle. One captain appears to have been left with a single file of soldiers. During the last ten days of June the Massachusetts Committee of Safety informed the Selectmen of Bradford that "the whole of a company of fifty men, save two, have scandalously deserted the cause of their country, and stained their own honour by leaving the camp, and returning home." The circumstances under which the troops had originally assembled in that camp were such as to render it unlikely that they would be induced to remain there through the winter. They had turned out on the morning of Lexington to try their weapons against the British, and to run their chance of getting a bullet back; but the idea had never crossed the minds of most of them that they were mortgaging their services for a whole campaign, and still less for an interminable war. They had taken up arms for liberty; and it was a poor beginning, as far as their own share of that blessing was concerned, to

348

find themselves converted from free citizens into the rank and file of a standing army before their leave had been asked, and without a single shilling of bounty. A British recruit entered on the military career with a handsome sum in his pocket, however short a time it might remain in that receptacle. Even a Hessian, when he put on the red-coat, had the satisfaction of reflecting that his beloved Landgrave was the richer by seven guineas a head for himself and each of his comrades; but the American minute-man had nothing but his ration, and a suit of clothes made of wool which his sisters had spun. It was no wonder that an invitation to subscribe the Articles of War, as laid down by the Continental Congress, met with scanty response. Both officers and men preferred to keep within the terms under which they had enlisted in the military establishments of their several Provinces. The regiments of Connecticut and Rhode Island stood engaged up to the first of December, and for not a day longer; and no one portion of the entire force was bound to serve into the coming year. On the first of January, 1776, everybody was free to go; and the lines, which required fifteen thousand men to defend them, would thenceforward be manned by a handful of such volunteers as did not care to survive their cause, and were ashamed to abandon their general.

Washington had been born and trained for precisely such a crisis. He had an aversion to arbitrary methods, a keen sense of what was due to others, and a quiet but comprehensive sympathy with their feelings. He knew that his countrymen did not love to be bullied, and were the worst people in the world to entrap or to overreach. It was in vain, (he said,) to attempt to reason away the prejudices of a whole army.[1] Instead of trying to force the Articles of War on a reluctant and, in some cases, a vigorously recalcitrant militia, he resolved to form a regular establishment composed of men who had accepted those Articles by choice, and with their eyes

[1] Washington to the President of Congress; Sept. 21, 1775.

open. A Committee of Congress three in number, of whom Franklin was one, repaired to Cambridge in order to confer with delegates chosen by the New England colonies. They found Washington ready with a scheme for raising twenty-six regiments, of soldiers who should engage themselves for a twelvemonth certain. He asked for twenty thousand infantry; and the representatives of New England assured him that he might draw thirty thousand from the Northern provinces alone.

It was a striking instance of that too sanguine American temper which the delays and rebuffs of war convert, not into disgust or despair, but into patience and perseverance, and an unalterable determination to win. The enrolment of the new force began in the last week of October. At first the results were most discouraging. No privates would enlist in any corps until they knew the names of the whole regimental hierarchy from the colonel downwards; and, when it came to the distribution of commissions, the aspirants were exceedingly difficult to please. Where an officer was too patriotic to be exacting, his colony was jealous for him. At one time Washington expected that half of his captains and lieutenants would leave him. His confidential letters were couched in scathing terms. " Such a dearth of public spirit," he wrote, " and such want of virtue; such stock-jobbing, and fertility in all the low arts to obtain advantages of one kind or another in this great change of military arrangement, I never saw before, and I pray God's mercy that I may never see again." In that atmosphere of intrigue recruiting was sometimes at a standstill, and then for a while moved slowly on. The call of duty, and the hope of distinction, were there for whatever they were worth in each man's estimation; but, over and above those inducements, the temptations which the Continental Treasury was able to hold forth were pitifully, and almost pathetically, small. The donative offered to the prætorian guards of American liberty consisted in the prospect of a month's pay in advance, as soon as there was anything in the military chest, and a promise that at some period in the distant future they would be allowed to buy their uniforms at cost price.[1] During the first three weeks, out of a group of eleven battalions of militia, less than a thousand men had given in their names. Four thousand at the most joined, in and before November; and, when another month had elapsed, the whole number on the new establishment was still below ten thousand, of whom one in every ten was off home on a furlough which he had claimed as a condition of re-enlistment.

That was the strength of the new army at the end of the year; and by that date the old army had been dissolved. "We have found it," said Washington, "as practicable to stop a torrent as these people, when their time is up;" and, even before their time was up, the rank and file of the Connecticut Militia, when they ascertained that a bounty was not forthcoming, planned to march away in a body. That purpose was defeated by the firmness of the General, and the exertions of their own officers, and not least by a spirited and well-timed sermon from the military chaplain of the colony; but no amount of exhortation or supervision could prevent many of the privates belonging to the corps from deserting singly, or in small parties. Washington showed a tranquil countenance to the outside world; but beneath the seal of a letter he begged his most intimate correspondent to imagine, since he himself was unwilling to describe, the situation of his mind during that trying interval. It was no light burden, (so he assured his friend,) to maintain a post against the flower

---

[1] A General Order of October 28, 1775, (quoted by Mr. Frothingham in his *Siege of Boston*,) recommended to the non-commissioned officers and soldiers at next pay day to procure themselves underclothing, and not coats and waistcoats, as it was intended that the new army should be dressed in uniform. "To effect which the Congress will lay in goods upon the best terms they can be bought anywhere for ready money, and will sell them to the soldiers without any profit ; by which means a uniform will come cheaper to them than any other clothing that can be bought. A number of tailors will be immediately set to work to make regimentals for those brave men who are willing at all hazards to defend their invaluable rights and privileges."

of the British troops for six months together, and then to have one army disbanded, and another to be raised, in the presence of the enemy. " Search," he wrote, " the volumes of history through, and I much question whether a case similiar to ours is to be found."[1]

The depletion of his ranks was only one, and not the most painful, of Washington's manifold perplexities. He was engaged on a siege, and the whole camp did not furnish him with a single engineer. With no money in hand he was making an army at a distance of three hundred miles by road from the seat of government, and the treasury; and, in spite of his eager remonstrances, no regular system of communication had as yet been established between Cambridge and Philadelphia. Except plenty to eat, his troops had little or nothing that soldiers wanted. Winter was coming on fast, and they were not provided with blankets or firewood. The Pennsylvanian mechanics, who were to have turned out muskets at the rate of eight or nine thousand a month, fell very far short of the anticipations which ardent patriots had formed in the hopeful days before muskets had begun to be fired. A sentry in the trenches still shouldered the fowling piece which he had taken down from above the mantel-shelf on the morning of Lexington. Privates who left for home on furlough, and still more those who went away for good, could not bear to be parted from their guns. The military authorities at Cambridge would gladly have bought in those guns on credit; but they were not in a position to use compulsion against men who still had owing to them the whole of the pay which they had earned. New recruits for the most part came in without arms; and, while the regiments were as yet only half complete, there were not a hundred muskets in store.

The moment seemed close at hand when it would no longer matter whether the soldier carried a gun or a pitchfork. On the third of August account was taken of the stock of ammunition; and the magazine was so

[1] Washington to Reed; Cambridge, Jan. 4, 1776.

bare that Washington wrote off at once to beg for powder from the neighbouring colonies, assuring them that
no quantity, however small, would be beneath notice.
Three weeks afterwards he detected a mistake in the
return, and pronounced the situation nothing short of
terrible. He had reckoned, he said, upon three hundred
quarter casks, and had but thirty-two barrels. The rains
had been heavy and continuous, and the cartridges
which had already been served out were spoiling in the
pouches. From that time forwards, under whatever
provocation, the American batteries were silent; and
the powder was reserved for firing musket balls at pistol distance in an emergency which nothing could postpone if once the plight of the besiegers became known
to the British General.[1] Under these circumstances
clever men, who had seen something of warfare, began
to discuss the advisability of having recourse to very
primitive instruments of destruction. General Charles
Lee wrote to Franklin in favour of enlisting pikemen,
and received a reply urging him not to despise even
bows and arrows. Franklin's arguments in favour of
that form of artillery are excellent reading, and on paper
unanswerable; but Washington was proof against them.
Bows and arrows were used with effect on the side
of the besiegers by some Indian warriors, who had been
trained into Christians and agriculturists at Dartmouth
College without having forgotten how to lay an ambush;
but it is not on record that any pale-face went into battle armed with a weapon more antiquated than his grandfather's firelock. Pikes, indeed, which had not gone
altogether out of fashion among European military
theorists, were manufactured by hundreds with a view
to tide the American cause over that period of destitu-
tion in all the articles that made up the equipment of a
soldier.[2] It was a cruel time for George Washington.

---

[1] Washington to the President of Congress, 11 November, 1775; and
the retrospective letter of March 31, 1776.

[2] " The people employed to make spears are desired by the general to
make them thirteen feet in length, and the wood part a good deal more

" The reflection," he wrote, " on my situation, and that
of this army, produces many an unhappy hour when all
around me are wrapt in sleep. I have often thought
how much happier I should have been if I had taken a
musket on my shoulder, and entered the ranks; or, (if I
could have justified the measure to posterity and my
own conscience,) had retired to the back-country, and
lived in a wigwam."

In this mood, and in such straits, he was tasting the
full bitterness of the treatment which every great commander, other than an absolute sovereign, is in his first
campaign called upon to endure.   Patriots, all the continent over, were wondering and questioning why Boston
had not long ago been stormed; and the mouth of the
one man who could tell them the reason was closed in
public by considerations of which, in his familiar correspondence, he made no secret.   " I cannot stand justified
to the world," so Washington wrote, " without exposing
my own weakness, and injuring the cause by declaring
my wants, which I am determined not to do, farther
than unavoidable necessity brings every man acquainted
with them.   If I did not consult the public good more
than my own tranquillity, I should long ere this have put
everything on the cast of a die."   The chimney-corner
heroes, as he styled them, urged him to begin by recapt-
uring Charlestown.   But long before Christmas Bunker's
Hill was an Ehrenbreitstein, or a Gibraltar, by comparison with what it had been in the month of June.   According to Washington's own description it was, both in
rear and in front, " by odds the strongest fortress" of
the British; which one thousand men, made of the stuff

substantial than those already made.   Those in the New Hampshire lines
are ridiculously short and light." — *American Archives*, July 23, 1775.
In an early General Order Washington desired that pikes should be kept
clean and greased.

Major-General Lloyd served several campaigns against Frederic the
Great, and, (a matter more arduous still,) succeeded in pleasing Mr. Carlyle, who pronounced him a writer of great natural sagacity. Lloyd, in
that section of his *History of the Seven Years' War* which treats of the
Ordering of a Modern Army, recommended that one infantry soldier, out
of every four, should have a pike in place of a musket.

that was behind those ramparts, could keep against any twenty thousand. And in the American camp there were not half that number, all told, under arms; — if such an expression could be fairly applied to troops who had nothing with which to load their cannon, and whom the first half-hour's fight would leave without a cartridge for their muskets.

Criticism was severe upon Washington in Congress, in the newspapers, and above all in the taverns ; but he already had secured the confidence and the loyalty of those who immediately surrounded his person. On the eighteenth of October he summoned his major-generals and brigadiers to a conference. The delegates from Philadelphia, who answered pretty closely to the cele-brated Representatives on Mission to the Armies during the early wars of the French Revolution, had invited Washington to say why an assault should not forthwith be ordered. His own decision had been made ; and he was well able to express it, and to stand by it. And yet, for the satisfaction of his employers, he was not sorry to fortify that decision by the concurrence, (if such could be obtained,) of his ardent and, in some cases, very capa-ble subordinates. Charles Lee would not commit him-self to the support of one whom he had the presumption to regard as an overrated rival, and spoke in guarded phrases, like a man not sufficiently behind the scenes to judge. But Ward, Greene, and Putnam, and their other colleagues, one and all, roundly declared that an attack on Boston by open force, until things changed greatly for the better, could not even be contemplated as a prac-ticable operation. Washington, in addition to every-thing else, had his special troubles with the provincial assemblies ; whose good-will, in an army composed like his, imported at least as much to him as that of the cen-tral government. Massachusetts and Connecticut had desired him to send them back strong detachments from their own militia regiments in order to protect the towns on their coasts from the armed vessels of the enemy. To this requisition the Commander-in-Chief replied that the threatened districts would have to take measures for defending themselves ; and that, if it came to the worst, they must patiently endure calamities against which he could not effectually guard them without sacrificing the general interests of the cause.[1]   He quietly but explicitly gave it to be understood that not a man could be spared from that neighbourhood where the great game was being played out which would fix the fate, not of Boston only, but of every fishing hamlet along the seaboard of all the colonies.

His constancy was rewarded. At last he began to reap the advantage which accrues to a strategist who, amidst perils and anxieties the full extent of which is known only to himself, steadfastly maintains at least the appearance of an aggressive attitude. New England felt proud of having an army which could keep the field. The spirit of her people was high and buoyant, and they were ready to perform their duty, when that duty was told them by a man whom they believed. To fill the gaps in his line, while recruitment for the Continental army was in progress, Washington invited Massachusetts and New Hampshire to call out five thousand min- ute-men on temporary service. They came in great numbers, and their behaviour in camp left nothing to be desired. It soon was evident that the action of the Connecticut militia was not to the taste of their fellow- citizens. The men, as they straggled home in twos and threes, met with a reception which convinced them that, unless they returned straight away to their regiment before the public opinion of their village took shape in action, they would have to travel at least the first stage of their journey to Cambridge by a mode of conveyance neither easy nor dignified, and in a costume not unsuited to people who had chosen to display the white feather. The next time that the battalion was paraded, and the roll called, only eighty of the delinquents were missing.

[1] Washington to the Speaker of the General Assembly of Massachusetts Bay ; 31 July, 1775.

But the gallant colony, after having played so vigorous a part in the scenes of political disturbance which ushered in the war, was not now contented with seeing that a parcel of unwilling soldiers were sent back to their quarters. A touch of shame and compunction, at the thought of the vexation inflicted by her unworthy sons on their uncomplaining General, gave such an impulse to the patriotism of Connecticut that the force which she contributed to Washington's army, from that moment onwards, and throughout the whole course of the struggle, exceeded the contingent furnished by any province, except Massachusetts only.[1] The alacrity of the New Hampshire minute-men, and the splendid repentance of Connecticut, afforded examples which were not wasted. The tide had turned, and ran in fast. Companies filled up with recruits. Older soldiers came promptly from furlough. By the middle of February, 1776, Washington reckoned his strength at the full number of seventeen thousand fighting men; and the best intelligence which he could obtain from inside Boston led him to conjecture that the losses and privations of the siege had reduced the British to a little over five thousand effective infantry.

The informants on whom the General relied had put the hostile force at too low a figure; but for them, and for him as well, it was the hour of hope. He had worked and waited long with less than no encouragement; and now everything seemed to be on the mend at once. The first gleam of success had been the capture of the Nancy, a royal ordnance brig which Captain Manly brought into shore at Cape Ann, the northern point of Massachusetts Bay. Washington, who knew the value of the prize better than did the British admiral, hurried off a strong party of minute-men to protect the unlading of her cargo. It was well worth the trouble; for among the items were two thousand muskets, a hundred thou-

---

[1] In 1776 Massachusetts sent 13,372 men to the army, Connecticut 6,390, Virginia 6,181, and Pennsylvania 5,519. During the remaining years of the war Massachusetts sent 38,091, Connecticut 21,142, Virginia 20,491, and Pennsylvania 19,689.

sand flints, thirty thousand round-shot, and thirty tons of bullets. When the trophies arrived in camp the most popular, if not the most useful, was a monster mortar, which Putnam, amidst universal hilarity, baptized with a bottle of rum; but which enjoyed a very short life under its new name of the "Congress." [1] There was no fear that the old General would be accused of wasting good liquor, for immense and increasing abundance reigned throughout the cantonments. The only difference in the ration, as months went on, was that the men got another half-pound of meat daily, and that their allowance of vegetables was doubled. Means had been discovered to remedy the scarcity of fuel; and the soldiers secured enough of the illimitable forests that clothed the land to cook their generous meals, and to keep them warm in weather which, even under less comfortable circumstances, would have had no great terrors for a New Englander. For the winter, which had promised badly, became first endurable, and then unusually mild. "The Bay is open," a colonial officer wrote in January. "Everything thaws here, except old Put. He is still as hard as ever, crying out for powder, powder, ye Gods give us powder!" And at last the powder came. Washington, who would stoop and traffic for nothing else, had begged, bought, or borrowed a modest but well-husbanded stock of that precious commodity; and, in the very same letter which recommended the use of bows and arrows, Franklin reported the welcome intelligence that the Secret Committee of Congress, appointed to provide the material of war, — a Committee of which he himself was the life and soul, — had contrived to lay its hands on a hundred and fifty tons of saltpetre.

Whether the supply of powder in the Cambridge magazine was small or large, the news from England was of a nature to make it go off of itself. On the first of January, 1776, a flag of thirteen stripes, one for each colony, was hoisted for the first time over the American

[1] "Our people splet the Congress the third time that they fired it." *How's Diary;* March 4, 1776.

headquarters ; and on the same day copies of the speech made by the King at the opening of Parliament were distributed broadcast among the besiegers by the exertions of the Boston Tories. Those gentlemen anticipated that the august document would strike panic, and implant penitence, in the hardiest breast; but the blockade had already endured long enough for them to have lost touch with the mass of their countrymen. They were woefully out in their calculations. "We are favoured," wrote Washington, "with a sight of his Majesty's most gracious speech, breathing sentiments of tenderness and compassion for his deluded American subjects. We now know the ultimatum of British justice." The tone of the royal manifesto was haughty and confident ; the threats were formidable ; and the Ministry was labouring with zeal, and spending with prodigality, in order to make those menaces good.

Ordinary men, whether in their own corner of a battle, or from their particular post in the wider operations of a war, discern that which is immediately to the front of them, and do not trouble themselves about what is in the distance or the future. The Americans who, from Prospect Hill and Roxbury Fort, saw Howe and his regiments cooped up within an acreage which would not support the dignity of a small British squire, laughed at King George's assurances that a speedy retribution was to fall "on the author and promoters of a desperate conspiracy." Horace Walpole descanted to his friend Mason on the absurdity of the idea that the Congress at Philadelphia would be so frightened at the British army being besieged in Boston that it would sue for peace. The thought which struck a man of letters, writing in his study at Twickenham, was still more forcibly brought home to a Continental soldier, already something of a veteran, as he stood behind the parapet of an impregnable redoubt, and fingered the lock of a new Tower musket which was his share in the spoils of the store-ship Nancy. The conclusion at which Walpole arrived by intuition, Franklin reached by a process of reckoning. "Britain," he said, "at the expense of three millions has killed one hundred and fifty Yankees this campaign, which is twenty thousand pounds a head; and at Bunker's Hill she gained a mile of ground, half of which she lost again by our taking post on Ploughed Hill. During the same time sixty thousand children have been born in America." From these data, (the Doctor argued,) a mathematical head might easily compute the time and expense necessary to kill all American rebels, and to conquer their whole territory.

Congress had already voted a Resolution which reads like a decree of the Roman Senate in the sternest days of the Republic. It was to the effect that, if General Washington and his council should be of opinion that he could make a successful attack on the troops in Boston, the attack should be made, notwithstanding that the town, and the property in it, might thereby be destroyed. The President of the assembly, who had large possessions in the devoted city, communicated the Resolution to the General, and added on his own part a prayer that God would crown the undertaking with victory. Half way through February, when a spell of hard weather came, and the channels between the town and the mainland were choked with ice, Washington was ready, and even persuaded himself that he was eager, to assault the British lines. But his military advisers were almost unanimous in the opposite sense. They warned the Commander-in-Chief that he greatly underestimated the strength of the garrison; and a very recent event had indicated what would be the chances of an advance in broad daylight, across an ice-field swept by grape, against works held by British infantry, and plenty of it. The patriots had already made an attempt upon Canada. An American storming party had assaulted Quebec in the darkest hour of the last night of the old year, 1775. The enterprise was a complete and costly failure, though it had been heroically led by Richard Montgomery, who was killed, and by Benedict Arnold, who was badly wounded, but, for his misfortune, was borne away alive. The slaughter and discomfiture which marked the operation against Quebec would in all human probability be repeated at Boston on a far larger scale, and with most damaging consequences to the cause of the Revolution. Congress might be willing to sacrifice Boston; but the generals of the only army which Congress had would not expend their people without reasonable hope of an adequate return. As men of tried and admitted courage, they had no qualms about speaking out on the side of caution; and their sturdy frankness did Washington a service which he himself before long came very near to acknowledging. When he had slept twice on their counsel, with such sleep as during that winter visited his pillow, he allowed that the intolerable irksomeness of his personal situation might possibly have inclined him to put more to the hazard than prudence would have sanctioned.[1]

He had refused to move forward at the dictation of public clamour; and he had been restrained by those around him from obeying the momentary promptings of his own impatience. At length he took action, at the due time, and in the right way. General Howe had arrived at the conclusion that Boston was useless as a base of operations against the continent of America, and most assuredly could not be regarded in the light of desirable quarters for the ensuing summer. Fully intending sooner or later to evacuate the city, he had preferred to wait for additional transports, a fresh supply of provisions, and a season more suited to a voyage which at the best would be uncomfortable and distressing, and fearfully dangerous in a gale. It was no light matter to conduct along four hundred miles of hostile coast, in the northern seas, a fleet into which would be crowded a whole army, the staff of a civil government, and all the Loyalists of a great province, together with their families and furniture. Some Whigs inside Boston, always quick to detect any symptoms favourable to their cause, apprised the American commander that the Brit-

---

[1] Washington to the President of Congress; 18 Feb., 1776.

ish garrison would not be long with them; and his telescope confirmed the story. Heavy cannon were seen to be withdrawn from the fortifications, and carried on board the ships. The square-rigged vessels in the harbour had been taken into the royal service; their sails were bent, and their water-casks sent ashore to be filled. All this show, Washington opined, might only be a feint;[1] and he resolved to make sure that it should become a reality. He devised a scheme which would oblige the British either to surrender the capital of Massachusetts, or come forth and attack him on his own ground with no probability of success, and all but the certainty of a frightful disaster. But at one end of the city or the other, in fair weather or in foul, with or without bloodshed, from Boston he was determined that they should go.

Howe reposed in the belief that he might choose his own moment for the step which he had in contemplation. An attempt from the rebels, (he informed Lord Dartmouth,) whether by surprise or otherwise, was not in the least to be apprehended. Nothing, he said, was so much to be wished as that they would have the rashness to quit those strong intrenchments to which alone they owed their safety. Howe was so far in the right that for either Washington, or himself, to assault was to court defeat; inasmuch as the English and the American positions were equally strong, and manned by troops who, when fighting under cover, were equally good. But, where two armies are so situated that the defence is more formidable than the attack, special attention must be paid to any commanding post which one or another of the parties can seize and fortify without a contest. Just such a post was the promontory of Dorchester, which covered and dominated Boston on the South. Two miles long, and two-thirds of a mile broad, it was dotted with heights of sufficient elevation for military purposes, planted exactly where they were most useful to the besiegers. A battery placed on the Eastern

---

[1] Washington to Major-General Lee; Cambridge, 26 Feb., 1776.

extremity would carry its shot across the deep-water approach to the harbour; and a battery on the Western horn could annihilate the town.

Howe had neglected to secure the peninsula; and he was not without his excuse. The ground, open on the quarter towards the enemy, required a larger force to hold it than he could spare from his widely extended and ever-threatened lines. He had no hope of being reinforced from across the ocean. Lord Barrington, in January 1776, laid a paper before the King stating that the strength of the army at home fell short of fourteen thousand, counting in the officers, who in the higher grades were in prodigious excess with reference to the men. "North Britain," he wrote, "never was so bare, having only one battalion of foot, and one regiment of dragoons, besides invalids." Such scanty detachments as were sent sailed months behind time, in bad ships, for the worst of reasons. Frederic the Great did not profess an intimate acquaintance with naval matters; and indeed his solitary experience of navigation had been an inland voyage in a Dutch canal-boat; but he understood as thoroughly as any man in Christendom that reinforcements should be brought on to the field before the event, instead of after it. He learned with astonishment from his envoy in London that, at a crisis when every day was of consequence, men of war were not employed for the conveyance of troops because people high in place would not surrender their commission of three per cent. on the hire of trading vessels.[1]

Bad as it was, that was not the worst of the story. In the course of January, General Clinton, under express orders from home, started for the Carolinas with a detachment which was withdrawn from the already inadequate garrison of Boston. Lord Barrington was opposed to the expedition; but his dislike of the project had been overborne by other Ministers who, because inside the Cabinet they were ruder fighters than the Secretary at

---

[1] Le Roi Frédéric au Comte de Maltzan; Potsdam, 8 Avril, 1776. Le Comte de Maltzan au Roi Frédéric; Londres, 23 Avril, 1776.

War, thought themselves sounder judges of a military operation. The unhappy nobleman, who was supposed to wield the sword of England, surrendered his view the more easily because the raid on the Southern colonies of America soon became a pet scheme of his royal master. The King himself, with his customary minuteness and precision, named the regiments which were to sail from the Home ports; and his zeal was so great that, while the army in Ireland had been reduced too low for safety, and Scotland had been stripped almost bare, only three battalions of regular infantry remained available for the protection of the whole of England. Clinton was joined off Charleston by Lord Cornwallis, who brought at least two thousand more soldiers, and by Sir Peter Parker with some fifty-gun-ships and frigates. But the force which, if it had been left with Howe, might have enabled him to hold his own in New England, was all too weak for independent action. The outworks protecting the approach to Charleston were feebly attacked, and stoutly defended; and the affair resulted in a failure for Clinton, and in nothing short of a calamity for Parker and his squadron.

Washington, on the other hand, had men enough not only for the indispensable requirements, but also for the profitable risks, of war. There had been a deficiency of heavy guns; but at last that want was supplied. Immediately after Lexington a handful of American volunteers, — with Benedict Arnold, and better men than he, among them, though braver there could not be, — captured Ticonderoga by a stroke of well-timed and audacious inspiration. Ethan Allen, who led the band, in default of a more regular commission under which to act, took possession of the place in the name of the great Jehovah and the Continental Congress. The fortress contained a great store of cannon, which had formerly been transported into those distant wilds by Anglo-Saxon energy. The stock of that latter article had not run out. Colonel Knox, a deft and enterprising officer high in Washington's confidence, built sledges, and in the dead of winter hauled the priceless freight Southward along frozen lakes, and over forest roads which had been barely passable during the droughts of summer. When the first and worst stage of the journey had been overcome, and nothing more serious than fifty leagues of snowdrift and mire lay between himself and the goal towards which he was travelling, the Colonel gaily wrote that he hoped to present his Excellency with a whole train of artillery. Before March he handed over to his chief forty large guns, and half as many mortars; and Washington in the meanwhile, by his own exertions, had scraped together the wherewithal at least to open fire. He had ammunition enough to go once round the army; but, when the cartridge boxes of the infantry were replenished, and the magazines in the batteries had been filled up, only a hundred barrels of powder remained in reserve. Other military stores had been provided in plenty; rude of design, although suited for rough and temporary work in the hands of dexterous and hardy men. As material for breastworks there were vast piles of faggots, and of grass ropes such as a pair of New England haymakers could twist at the rate of a fathom a minute. There were empty casks, to hold the earth from the ditches; stacks of shovels and pickaxes; and two thousand bandages for broken limbs, which by the grace of Heaven, or the good sense of man, never came to be needed. Out of sight from the British lines, if not from the British spies, there lay in Charles River two floating batteries, and barges with room to carry ten battalions across a stretch of smooth water. They had been constructed hastily and slightly, but by people the occupation of whose lives had taught them to know whether or not a boat would swim. And, at the last moment, the militia of all the neighbouring townships repaired to camp, with a pledge from Washington that he would not keep them long, and a belief on their part that this time the General purposed to see the business through.

They were correct in their anticipations. On those rare occasions when Washington had the means to assume the offensive, his action was as swift, as direct, as continuous, and, (for its special characteristic,) as unexpected as that of any captain in history. He had not fought Red Indians in his youth for nothing. But, secret and silent as he was in regard to the direction and the details of his future movements, Washington was too much of a citizen not to place himself in close mental relation with his soldiers before he called upon them for unusual efforts and sacrifices. On the eve of the final struggle he issued an appeal to the army. Except in its perfect suitability to the tastes and aspirations of those whom he addressed, it was a composition very unlike those bulletins by which under the Directory, and the First Empire, the French were incited to the conquest and plunder of Europe. His General Order of February the twenty-sixth began by forbidding officers, non-commissioned officers, or privates to play at cards or other games of chance; inasmuch as, at a time of distress, men might find enough to do in the service of God and their country without abandoning themselves to vice and immorality. As the season was now fast approaching, (so the proclamation went on,) when every man might expect to be drawn into the field of action, it was highly important that he should prepare his mind for what lay before him. They were engaged in a noble cause. Freedom or slavery would be the result of their conduct. Every temporal advantage, to them and their posterity, would depend upon the vigour of their exertions.

These words were still being quoted and commented on throughout the camp when they were drowned by the roar of cannon, but not forgotten. On the second of March, and again on the fourth, the American batteries commenced to play. The noise was tremendous, but the slaughter small. A distant bombardment, with the ordnance of the eighteenth century, produced few of the horrors of war except only to the taxpayer. Up to Christmas, 1775, the British garrison had discharged two thousand rounds, and had killed less than twenty of the enemy ; and the moral effect, as it is called, had been so much the reverse of what was intended that the commanding officer of artillery advised General Howe to discontinue the cannonade, as the only perceptible result was to inure the colonists to danger. In March, however, when Washington's cannon began to speak, the British gunners could not refuse the challenge. They replied lustily ; but they shot next to no one, and dismounted nothing, although the besiegers contrived to burst five of their own mortars.[1]

The Americans hit a regimental guard-house, which they could not very well miss, and not many human beings. Nevertheless, on their side, it was no waste of powder. On Monday the fourth of March the besiegers maintained a heavy fire far into the night. The soldiers in Boston were kept busy extinguishing flames, and removing goods, from beneath falling roofs ; and they had neither eyes nor ears for what was passing to the Southward of them. Soon after dark General Thomas led a strong brigade over Dorchester Neck, followed by three hundred carts laden with fascines and coils of twisted hay. With these materials a parapet was rapidly built along the causeway, under cover of which fresh loads of stuff travelled to and fro throughout the night. Meanwhile on each of the twin heights in the centre of the peninsula, which were the keys of the position, the colonial soldiers were digging, and ramming, and plastering the earth, like so many peasants of Holland strengthening an embankment to save their village from

---

[1] General Heath relates in his Diary how, on December 18, 1775, the Americans broke grounds on Lechmere Point, the most exposed spot in their lines. Their working party numbered three hundred. An expectation prevailed that it would be " a bloody day "; and Washington personally superintended the conduct of the operation. The British batteries, until the afternoon, thundered away, both with shot and shell; and the American surgeon, who was at hand throughout, never once drew his instruments from their case, or a roll of lint from his dressing-box. A plain man, who has fired a charge of slugs at an object in the water a hundred yards off, may estimate the value of a remote cannonade from old-fashioned twenty-four pounders, even if he has never looked into a treatise on the law of projectiles.

an inundation. At dawn of day two forts were already in existence, and in a condition to protect their inmates from grape-shot and musket-balls. A British officer of a sentimental turn compared the result of the night's labour with the wonders wrought by the lamp of Aladdin. In less flowery, but fatally unpractical, words General Howe told Lord Dartmouth that at least twelve thousand men must have been employed on the fortification. The rebels, he remarked, had done more between evening and morning than the whole of his own army would have accomplished in an entire month. He had made an error of a thousand per cent.; for the American working party did not exceed twelve hundred pairs of arms. It would have been well for Howe if his professional education had included a course of land-surveying in company with Washington, or even of building fences with Putnam. The royal forces were embarked on a war of such a character, and in such a country, that the hatchet and the spade ranked high among military weapons. A general who knew something about homely industries, and their application to strategical purposes, would have been of great service to an army where guidance and teaching in that department were peculiarly needed. The behaviour of the British soldier in the labours of the trench and the field-work was his weakest point then, and forty years afterwards; as was sorrowfully admitted by the best judges, who in other respects were his warm admirers.[1]

Howe was unskilled in appraising the amount which any given number of sappers or artificers could get done in a given number of hours; but he had seen too

[1] On this subject Sir John Burgoyne, in his account of the Siege of Burgos, has made some observations which are most interesting, but, (even after this lapse of time,) not altogether agreeable reading. "I had," he says in the course of his remarks, "an opportunity of pointing out to Lord Wellington, one day, a French and an English working party, each excavating a trench. While the French shovels were going on as merrily as possible, we saw in an equal space, at long intervals, a single English shovelful make its appearance." *Life and Correspondence of Field Marshal Sir John Burgoyne,* pp. 232 and 233 of the edition of 1873.

many battles and sieges for him to have any doubt as
to the plight in which the latest move of his adversaries
had landed him. He was not the player to accept
checkmate when it was first offered. Between two and
three thousand of his infantry were at once shipped on
transports to Castle Island, with the design that they
should thence attack the promontory of Dorchester.
For their commander Howe had only to choose among
the men of headlong courage at his disposal; and he
chose Lord Percy, who had no objection, on his own
account, to face whatever might await him across the
southern arm of the harbour. The forces under Thomas
had been doubled by a reinforcement of two thousand
men. The works, formidable at daybreak, before noon
had received a finishing touch. Orchards had been cut
down to form an abattis. Rows of barrels filled with
earth were placed along the edge of the hill, which was
bare and steep, with the design of rolling them down
upon the ascending columns. The Americans everywhere seemed cheery and resolute, and those ensconced
behind the earthworks on Dorchester Heights were even
exhilarated. They looked forward to another battle of
Bunker's Hill in a position twice as strong, with a force
more than twice as large, and under the immediate eye
of the General-in-Chief; for Washington was on the
spot full of fight, and, for him, full of talk, and as hopeful of victory as the youngest of his followers.

Hopeful, that is, in the quarter where he commanded
in person; for he was far from easy about the fate of
the operation to which his left wing stood committed.
Putnam had four thousand selected troops on the
parade ground at Cambridge, ready at a signal from
Dorchester Heights to enter the flotilla which lay in the
river, and advance by water against the western face
of Boston under cover of the new floating batteries.
Washington disapproved the project; but his judgement
had been overridden, and it only remained for him loyally to make the best of a plan the wisdom of which he
gravely and sadly doubted. At this period of the war

the command in chief of the American army was rathei a limited monarchy than the benevolent despotism into which it was gradually converted by the pressure of his strong character, and the lustre of his first great success. Congress began by being keenly inquisitive into the movements of the army, and was much too anxious about the event to refrain from advising, and even from meddling. The delegates at Philadelphia were sufficiently afraid of Washington to abstain from giving him a direct order. They transmitted their views to the headquarters at Cambridge in the shape of proposals which they requested him to have debated and decided in a council of war. Such a council had recently been convoked, in which Washington was outvoted; and so it came about that the Americans were to deliver, and to sustain, an attack on one and the same day. That day was the anniversary of what was called the Boston Massacre, and this time there would have been a massacre indeed. It was odds, and large odds, that neither of the two assaults could succeed; and the assailants in both cases were of such tough fibre, and their leaders so fiery and determined, that failure would not have taken place until after a prolonged slaughter. If the fighting had once begun, the history of the Revolutionary war would have been disfigured by a more deeply crimsoned page than any which can now be found in the volume.

But it was not so to be. The wind blew a gale. Sashes were forced in, sheds were wrecked and overthrown, and vessels torn from their moorings and driven against the quays. Percy's transports could not cross the water in such a hurricane; and, until the British took the initiative, Washington refused to give the signal for Putnam's forward movement. He was blamed for want of firmness; but the old officer whom he had superseded in the command of the army generously and indignantly defended one who never was at the pains to defend himself. The prudence of Washington, so General Heath declared, was applauded by military men of several nations after they had made an inspection of the land and water which was to have been the scene of action. And the veteran was mindful to direct his gratitude higher still, and to aver that Providence, kind not for the first time, must have interposed to save his countrymen when they were bent on self-destruction.[1]

The storm raged through the afternoon and night of the fifth of March; and the next day the wind was still boisterous, and the rain came down in torrents. Before the weather grew calm and dry it had been brought home to the British General that the Americans could not be expelled from their redoubts, and that, so long as they stayed in their redoubts, they were masters of the whole promontory. Immediately to their front, and at their disposal when they thought fit to occupy it, was a mound known as Nook's Hill, from which, at the distance of half a mile, they could enfilade the British earthworks on Boston Neck, and would not be much further from Griffin's Wharf where the immortal tea was spilt. Admiral Shuldham, who had succeeded Graves in command of the fleet, warned the military authorities that, if Washington retained his hold on the Dorchester Heights, he himself could not keep a ship in the harbour. When the prospect of a battle had vanished, the disappointment of the British soon took the form of despondency. Right or wrong, the belief was general that, for the space of several months, no despatches had been received from the Government in London. It looked, (such was the burden of the private letters written by the garrison during that anxious fortnight,) as if the men in the post of danger, now that it was fast becoming an abode of despair, had been left to get out of a bad scrape as best they could. "The fleet and the army," it was said, "complain of each other, and both of the people at home." With that suspicion in their minds the superior officers repaired to a council which Howe convened, and learned from him, without surprise or dissatisfaction, that he was fully determined at whatever cost to save the army.

[1] *Heath's Memoirs;* Feb. 15th and March 5th, 1776.

2B 2

The danger was pressing. After dark on the ninth of March the New Englanders were already busy on Nook's Hill. They laboured undiscovered and unmolested till some stupid fellows kindled a fire in rear of the knoll, and soon found the place even warmer than they wished or intended. Four of them were killed by one cannon-ball, and the detachment was withdrawn to await a more convenient opportunity.[1] But the incident gave Howe food for reflection. The Americans, it was evident, might choose their own moment for erecting batteries at a range within which round-shot could be aimed with effect at a knot of men, and much more against ships and houses, the tilt of a powder waggon, or the flank of a line of cannon planted along the curtain of a fortification. Next day he began to push forward his arrangements for the evacuation of the town ; and, wherever Howe exerted himself, he worked fast. But he was not quick enough to please Washington, who gave him a significant hint that the patience of the besiegers was near to exhaustion. The colonists returned to Nook's Hill, and crowned the eminence with a redoubt, from which this time they refused to be driven. That was the notice to quit. It was handed in on the sixteenth of March ; and on the seventeenth General Howe embarked his army, and Washington was a figure in history. It was exactly the operation which, repeated half a generation afterwards in the port of Toulon, laid the founda-

---

[1] In 1899, after the first publication of this volume, the author was honoured by a letter from the late Mr. E. J. Phelps, who so effectively, and so acceptably to Londoners, discharged the office of American Ambassador at the Court of St. James's. "You mention," (wrote Mr. Phelps,) "that, while the New Englanders were engaged in fortifying Nook's Hill, ' some stupid fellows' kindled a fire, and soon found the place warmer than they intended ; and that four of them were killed by one British cannon-ball. Well ; my maternal grandfather, a soldier in the American army, was one of those to whom you allude in such complimentary terms ; and he was sitting by the fire when the cannon-ball came in. He was not hurt ; but lived to tell me the story in my boyhood. To that small extent I can corroborate by hearsay evidence the truth of your account." It is pleasant to think of the old fellow relating his adventures at a more secure fireside than that by which he sate on Nook's Hill half a century back.

tion of a fame less desirable, and a life's work far less durable, than his.[1]

Unfortunately there was more than a tactical and topographical resemblance between the recapture of Toulon and the capture of Boston. Those two great events are marked by the same melancholy, and even tragic, circumstance. In both cases the retirement of a fleet and an army was accompanied by a wholesale and enforced emigration of non-combatants. The announcement that the city was to be surrendered fell as a thunderbolt on the Loyalists whose home it was, and not less on those who had repaired thither as a place of temporary refuge. The last trump, (so Washington wrote,) could not have struck them with greater consternation. A fixed and ardent faith in the overwhelming and omnipresent power of Britain was the first article in the creed of the American Tories ; — for that term was universally applied to them by themselves and their fellow-colonists ; although, among those politicians at Westminster whom they had trusted and followed to their ruin, many still laid claim to the name of Whigs. When Howe departed from Boston there were eleven hundred people who dared not stay behind, or one for every ten of his soldiers

---

[1] For the two previous paragraphs see *Heath's Memoirs ;* March 9, 1776. Washington to the President of Congress; March 7, 9, 13, and 16. Frothingham's *Siege of Boston ;* chapter xii.

David How's Diary shows how a great event struck a humble contemporary, who had played a man's part in helping to bring it about.

"March 3. Last night there was Firing Almost all night on both sides. Two of our mortars splet in pices at Litchmor's point.

"March 4. Last night there was A fiering all night with cannon and Morters on both sides. Three Regments went from Cambridge to Roxbury and carried Some Field Pieces with them. The Milisher from Several towns are called In to stay 3 days.

"March 5. Our people went to Dodgster hill Last Night and built a fort there. They have ben firing at Dogester amost All Day.

"March 10. Last night our people went to Dodesther neck And there was a hot fire from Boston which Killed 4 men with one ball. I went to meting all Day ; Mr. Lennard preached.

"March 12. Last night there was brisk fireing all Night From boston. William Parker made me a pair of Half Boots for Two Shilling and 8d."

and sailors. They formed the aristocracy of the province by virtue of their official rank; of their dignified
callings and professions ; of their hereditary wealth ; and
of their culture, except so far as it partook of that self-
education which was open to all.

Eighteen were clergymen, for the most part Episco-
palians, as true to what they believed to be their political obligations as any English Nonjuror who went out
from his parsonage or his palace in the summer of 1689.
Among the exiles many were landowners and substantial
men of business, and a greater number still were public
servants. Good places, whether lay or legal, were reserved for people who regarded themselves as belonging
to good families. The same names, and those not many,
occur over and over again as Judges of the Superior
Court; Receivers General, and Cashiers, of his Majesty's
Customs ; Commissioners, Inspectors, Treasurers, and
Registrars and Clerks of Probate. Hutchinsons and
Olivers, Leonards, Chandlers, and Coffins, —patronymics
which to a Bostonian of those days denoted the very
quintessence of exclusiveness, —divided among themselves salaries and honours, perquisites and privileges.
They honestly believed that the fitness of things required
the established method of distribution to last for ever.
Their best feelings were hurt when a new man, with
newfangled political opinions, put in his claim to a
share. The inspiring motive, according to their story,
of every Revolutionary leader was the need and greed
for office ; and their posterity across the Canadian frontier continued, in filial good faith, to repeat the same tale
for the benefit of our own generation.

In their view Congressmen and Committee-men were
" a set of rascals, who only sought to feather their own
nests, and not to serve their country." An unlucky
Loyalist who happened to use those expressions in ill-
chosen company got himself inside a jail; and the words
have a natural, and almost elemental, ring about them
which irresistibly suggests that it was not the first time,
by a hundred, that they had been uttered with emphasis

in Tory circles. According to the theory accepted by
those circles, Otis started the agitation, which started
everything, because his father had missed a judgeship.
Joseph Warren was a broken man, and sought to mend
his fortunes by upsetting those of others. John Hancock,
too rich to want a place, suffered from wounded vanity
when walking behind his betters in the order of prece-
dence. Richard Henry Lee had been baulked of an
appointment as Distributor of Stamps under the Act
which then, and only then, he came forward to denounce.
John Adams turned rebel because he was refused a Commission of the Peace ; and Washington himself never
forgave the British War Office for having treated him
with the neglect which was the natural portion of Provincial military officers. It was an argument with two
edges ; and there is now little doubt which of the two
cut the sharpest. What claim to perpetuity, (it has been
finely asked,) had those institutions under which John
Adams could not be a magistrate, and any stripling who
had purchased a pair of colours took rank of George
Washington ? [1] Disappointed men perhaps they had
been ; but their day arrived ; and, if they could not be
justices or majors in a marching regiment, they both
obtained a post for which they were not less competent,
and became each in his turn the chief governor of a
nation.

The Loyalists were a prosperous and enjoying set,
free with their cash ; hearty with their fellows ; just, and
something more, towards those who had a claim on them ;
and very indulgent to their negro slaves. They were
not ascetics ; and, if they had stayed in the country, it
is possible that the march of Temperance legislation
would have been seriously delayed in some of the New
England districts. The breaking of his punch-bowl was
the worst damage to his property which Doctor Peters
of Hebron had to deplore, when his angry parishioners
came to search his house for arms. An epitaph com-

[1] Sabine's *Historical Essay ;* p. 57 in the Boston edition of 1864.

posed for himself by an Episcopalian clergyman, commencing with the lines,

> " Here lies a priest of English blood
> Who living liked whate'er was good,"

would not have been misplaced on the tombstones of
many among his reverend brethren. Clerics, men of
business, and country gentlemen, they dressed ceremoni-
ously and expensively ; and they had manners, and
those not merely skin-deep, in harmony with their external appearance. Dr. Walter of Boston "was a re-
markably handsome man, tall and well-proportioned.
When in the street he wore a long blue cloth cloak over
his cassock and gown ; a full-bottomed wig, black silk
hose, and square-quartered shoes with silver buckles.
Happy himself, he communicated happiness to all around
him. In the desk he read the glorious service like one
inspired ; and his heart, his house, his purse was ever open
to the needy." The Governor of Rhode Island, who was
a native of the colony and a resident at the pleasant town
of Newport, in the matter of a wig was satisfied with
nothing less than one made in England of the pattern
and size worn by the Speaker in the House of Commons.
Green and gold, or purple and gold, formed the daily
costume of a wealthy Tory merchant.[1] It was not all
outside show. The more notable members of the British
party were given to polite learning, and spared neither
care nor money over the education of their sons. In
that numerous contingent of emigrants which left the
province when Boston fell, one out of every five was a
Harvard man. The colonies, if we may trust a comparison which occurred to a lady who knew them before the
war, suffered as much, and in the same way, by the ex-
pulsion of the Loyalists as France, under Louis the
Fourteenth and ever after, suffered by the expatriation
of the Huguenots. The remark went too far, and not
exactly in the right direction ; but it cannot be questioned

---

[1] The Articles on the Rev. William Walter, Joseph Wanton, and Nathan
Rogers in Sabine's *Loyalists*.

that the Revolution made America the poorer by some elements which, during the next half-century, that country could ill afford to lose.[1]

The Loyalists were fully persuaded that they were more estimable than the majority of their fellow-subjects; and they attributed their superiority, whether real or fancied, to themselves and not to their circumstances. They spoke and wrote of their opponents in a tone of class arrogance which, when once the rift came, made reconciliation impossible. In the rhymed satires and political catechisms which issued from the Tory press the most respected members of the popular party were held up to scorn as the refuse of mankind. The delegates to the Congress were described as pettifogging attorneys, disbarred advocates, outlawed smugglers, bankrupt shopkeepers; and, at the best, as innkeepers and horsedealers who had not as yet gone through the Court. The world was told how a bricklayer or carpenter would lie down at night, and awake in the morning a Lycurgus or a Solon. As each demagogue in turn, by rope or otherwise, went to his appointed place, he would be hailed as a brother by Catiline, Jack Cade, and Cromwell; an ill-assorted trio, it must be allowed, who would have found some difficulty in establishing fraternity among themselves. History, — or what in the days before Niebuhr and Mommsen passed for history, — was ransacked for humiliating parallels to the statesmen of the American Revolution.

> " Imperial Rome from scoundrels rose:
> Her grandeur's hailed in verse and prose:
> Venice the dregs of sea compose.
> So sprung the mighty Congress.
> When insects vile emerge to light
> They take their short inglorious flight,
> Then sink again to native night;
> An emblem of the Congress."

[1] Mrs. Grant of Laggan. She left America in 1786 at the age of thirteen or fourteen; but she was a very precocious child, and grew into a thoughtful woman.

The loyalist poets and pamphleteers might have mal-
treated the politicians with comparative impunity to
themselves and their cause if they had left the soldiers
alone.   Men accustomed to the give and take of controversy fail to recognise what it is, for quiet obscure people,
to have those near and dear to them ridiculed and vili-
fied in print.   A farmer's family, with an empty chair
reminding them of some one who was digging in the
trenches amidst the cannon-balls, or lying three feet
below the grass on Bunker's Hill, with his face to the
daisies, did not see the joke when they read how the
American militia were awkward cowardly bumpkins,
and their officers scheming upstarts.

> " With loud peals of laughter your sides, sirs, would crack
>   To see General Convict, and Colonel Shoe-black,
>   All strutting the standard of Satan beside,
>   And honest names using their black deeds to hide."

That was how a Tyrtæus of the messroom burlesqued
the manly, unpretending figures of Greene and Thomas,
and the antique worth of Heath and Pomeroy.   Those
must have been far gone in political fanaticism who
could detect either truth or humour in such couplets.
It may be that, amidst the distractions of the period,
the authors of these effusions had not leisure to write
better; but it is strange that descendants of the Pilgrim
Fathers should have borrowed their controversial weapons from one or another Cavalier libeller in the middle
of the seventeenth century.   New Englanders, if any
people, should have remembered that the reproach of
having earned their bread by manual labour, or by trade,
was habitually levelled at Roundheads, and that the
sturdy warriors against whom the imputation was directed cared nothing for it; nor, when the battle was
joined, was it much consolation to those among the
scoffers who had to face them in the field.   Seldom, if
ever, have two assemblages of men, — divided from
each other by four generations, and a thousand leagues,
— had so much in common as the army which fought
against Charles the First, and the army which followed

⚠︎

Washington.   Lampoons and pasquinades, on one side
of the question or the other, were composed for the
amusement of partisans who were prudent enough never
to quit their own chimney corner; but the hymns which
comforted the starving shoeless groups around the camp-
fires at Valley Forge might have been sung in one of
Massey's guard-rooms at Gloucester, or by a party of
troopers returning from the pursuit after Naseby.[1]

Those sorry scribblers, who constituted themselves
exponents of loyalist sentiment, vulgarised, and possibly
exaggerated, the intolerance and the prejudices of their
patrons.   But caste-feeling, intense, aggressive, and almost universal, beyond any doubt prevailed in the Tory
society of America; and it was terribly and quite dis-
proportionately punished.   There are benighted parts
of the world where injustice and oppression, in cruel
and practical forms, have survived through the ages un-
assailed and unquestioned; but in a civilised and high-
spirited community the far, or near, future never fails to
exact retribution from those who have caught the trick
of disdaining and disparaging the mass of their countrymen.   When once the British flag had been hauled
down from the roof of Province House, Boston would
be no place for those who had hitherto walked the
streets as favourites of the Government and hereditary
tenants of the public offices.   The moment had come
when they must resign credit, and power, and salary,
and all that constituted "the life that late they led,"
to men whom they disliked and tried hard to think that
they despised.   They abandoned their pulpits and count-

[1] " Lessons of war from Him we take
    And manly weapons learn to wield.
    Strong bows of steel with ease we break,
    Forced by our stronger arms to yield.

    " 'Tis God that still supports our right.
    His just revenge our foes pursues.
    'Tis He that with resistless might
    Fierce nations to His power subdues."

The "American Soldier's Hymn," quoted by Professor Tyler in his 31st
Chapter.

ing-houses, their pleasant gardens in the English style, and their mansions shaded with tall poplars ; and the land knew them no more by sight, nor, after a while, by name.   So far as the memory of them, even in their own neighbourhood, was concerned, it was much if a later generation pointed out their old home as a house which was haunted by Tory ghosts.[1]

The last days which the Loyalists of Massachusetts passed on their native soil were disturbed by the menace of an appalling catastrophe.   The artillerymen of the besiegers now had Boston at their mercy ; and General Howe allowed a rumour to get abroad that, if his troops were harassed during their embarkation, he should destroy the town.   The Selectmen of the municipality sent a flag of truce across the lines, and implored the American Commander-in-Chief, since the garrison was unquestionably on the eve of departure, to take no steps which could afford an excuse for the consummation of so dreadful a threat.   From an official point of view there was only one reply to such an appeal.   His Excellency, (the answer ran,) could take no notice of an unauthenticated paper, containing assurances which, if accepted at the American headquarters, did not in any way bind the British General.   But none the less Washington kept his guns silent, and his soldiers within their intrenchments ; and the preparations for the removal of the British army went steadily and securely on.   It may well be believed that, even in the last extremity, Howe would not have been as bad as his word.   It might be argued that a servant of the Crown was under an obligation to carry out his Sovereign's expressed wish, and use "every means of distressing America." To set the city on fire, rather than it should be the seat of Congresses and Committees, and a rallying centre for armed insurgents, was presumably within the letter of the Ministerial instructions, and most assuredly in strict accordance with their spirit.   Boston was only waiting

[1] Sabine's *Loyalists ;* vol. ii., p. 357.

until the red-coats were gone in order to behave quite
as rebelliously as Norfolk or Falmouth; but it did not
share their fate. In the opinion of Howe, enough
American towns had been offered as burnt sacrifices
upon the altar of personal loyalty. To give the capital
of Massachusetts to the flames would excite horror
throughout Europe, and most of all among the people
who had been his own political associates and familiar
friends. He could not stay in America for ever; and,
if he returned to London with such a deed on his fame
and conscience, however gracious might be his reception at the Palace, he would only need to walk half-way
up Saint James Street, and enter Brooks's Club, in
order to discover that not one of the men, whose respect
and good-will he most valued, would ever take his hand
again.

Howe, before the war was over, had done some cruel
things, and from carelessness or misplaced good-nature
had excused still more barbarous conduct in others;
but, when he obeyed his better instincts, he was ever a
good-natured English gentleman. Lord Dartmouth, who
was something much better than good-natured, had
long ago written to desire that, if Boston fell, all
should be done to save the friends of the Government
from the worst consequences of their fidelity. Howe
addressed himself strenuously to the task of mitigating
the hard destiny of the fugitives. He had transports
barely enough for the conveyance of the army; and it
required not a little unselfishness on the part of those
responsible for the conduct of the embarkation to find
room for the Loyalists, their families, and their possessions. In order to provide storage for the effects of
those unfortunate civilians, the military left behind and
lost much property of their own which they could not
pack into the ships, and which, it is needless to say, no
patriot could just then be found to buy. The exigencies
of duty, on a front of battle lying within a few hundred
yards of an enterprising and elated adversary, were unusually heavy and anxious; the soldiers, as the moment

of departure approached, were with difficulty restrained
from drink and riot; and it is to the honour of the
British officers that all the time which could be spared
from keeping the besiegers in respect, and preserving
discipline in barracks, was devoted to helping those who
were more to be pitied than themselves.

The Loyalists were by no means in all cases a feeble
folk. Many of them knew the water-side of old, and
had secured for the transportation of their goods the
pick of such labour as there was to be hired. Some
of them, indeed, understood very well how to help themselves, in every acceptation which the words would bear.
A certain Crean Brush had been noisy and noticeable
among the Tories who remained in Boston during the
siege. He was not a native of the city, nor of the
colonies. Born in Dublin, he settled himself in New
York, and was appointed to official posts which, (being
before his age,) he contrived to make very lucrative. In
an unguarded hour Sir William Howe had given him
a commission to impound, and to place on board the
fleet, all the linen and woollen in the town. Brush, at
the head of some violent and dishonest partisans, proceeded to break open stores, shops, and dwelling-houses.
Without observing any distinction in the nature of his
spoils, he loaded a brigantine with a cargo of stolen
property worth a hundred thousand dollars. The example was followed by gangs of seamen from the royal
fleet, ill-watched, and sometimes encouraged, by their
officers. The soldiers could not always be kept from
emulating the sailors; and for some days and nights
the city presented frequent scenes of violence and
pillage. It was high time to go. Vast quantities of
public stores were abandoned to the enemy, after having
been damaged as effectually as could be done by people
who had begun to count their stay at Boston by half-
hours. The British officers sacrificed all except the
most portable of their private baggage. They themselves, huddled up amidst a miserable throng of both
sexes and all ages, with top-heavy decks and encum-

bered gangways, put to sea praying for a quick passage. The scene, according to the Historical writer in the "Annual Register," resembled the emigration of a nation rather than the breaking up of a garrison. In Benjamin Hallowell's cabin "there were thirty-seven persons, — men, women, and children; servants, masters, and mistresses; obliged to pig together on the floor, there being no berths." Mr. Hallowell, nine months previously, had been hunted into Boston by a cavalcade of patriots; and this was how he left it. Such are the lesser miseries of a Revolution.

The fleet was bound for Canada, as was reported both in the city and in the American camp; but Washington thought it possible that the British staff had disseminated the story for a blind. He apprehended that the real destination might be New York, and made his dispositions accordingly. But, when the leading ships had finally threaded the islands and gained the open sea, they steered for Halifax in Nova Scotia, a small town on an inhospitable coast, where the passengers, armed and unarmed, would find themselves hardly less crowded and uncomfortable than on board the transports. The reputation of the quarters towards which they were moving was expressed vigorously and compactly throughout the convoy by means of the proverb, "Hell, Hull, and Halifax." [1] Some of the Royal battle-ships were left behind when their consorts sailed; but the captains did not venture to remain at their moorings within the harbour. The vessels dropped down to Nantasket Road, well out of harm's way, where they lay off and on for some while to come, much to the annoyance of the inhabitants of Boston.

That was the only cross in their lot. Every Patriot

[1] It was an old Yorkshire saying, dating from our Civil War, which the British officers applied on the present occasion to the Halifax of Nova Scotia. "A cursed cold wintry place, even yet;" said one of them on the 17th March. "Nothing to eat; less to drink. Bad times, my dear friend. The displeasure I feel from the very small share I have in our present insignificancy is so great that I do not know the thing so desperate I would not undertake in order to change our situation."

who had remained within the walls was his own man once again; and the Patriots in the camp without were impatient to learn how their besieged brethren looked after ten months of hardship, and, (what to people of their nature was perhaps as trying,) of taciturnity, and enforced abstinence from public affairs and from commercial business. While Howe's rearguard were pushing off their boats at one extremity of the town, General Putnam, at the head of a thousand men who had had the smallpox, entered it at the other. Three days afterwards, when it was ascertained that the danger of infection was less than had been feared, the main body of the American army marched through the streets amidst cheers and smiles; although it was observed that the faces which filled the windows bore marks of hunger, and of the gloom which had so long oppressed the city.

But joy had returned, and abundance with it; and both the one and the other had come as permanent residents, and not as passing guests. On the twenty-second of March a great concourse of people thronged into Boston. They came home by thousands, to find most, but not all, of those whom they had left there; and we are told, though we do not require to be told, that on that day the whole place was in tears and laughter. They were glad once more to roam about their beloved town, — their Carthage which, in spite of the Latin quoted at Westminster, after all was not to be destroyed. When they surveyed and reckoned up their losses, they enjoyed the surprise of finding that the waste and wreck of their property was not so extensive as seriously to spoil their pleasure. John Hancock's fine well-decorated mansion seemed very slightly the worse for a hostile occupation. "The town," Washington wrote to him, "although it has suffered greatly, is not in so bad a state as I expected to find it; and I have a particular pleasure in being able to inform you, Sir, that your house has received no damage worth mentioning. Your furniture is in tolerable order, and the family pictures are all left entire and untouched." When the

President of Congress came off so easily, it may be believed that little was missing out of habitations which presented fewer temptations to the marauder, and whose owners exercised less prominent and invidious functions. Even those ancient wooden dwellings which had been pulled down for fuel were pronounced to be well away for reasons connected with the future health and beauty of the town. Everything, to the eyes of a true Bostonian, was thenceforward to be for the best in the best possible of cities. A visit prompted by eager curiosity, and attended by well-founded satisfaction, was that which was paid to the British fortifications.[1] Soldiers, and yet more the parents and wives of soldiers, gazed with shuddering thankfulness on those formidable works which it had cost so much labour to erect, and so little bloodshed to capture. Doctor John Warren, who had repaired to the spot where he could stand as close to his brother as was now possible for him, has left a description of the fortress which Howe's engineers had erected on the peninsula of Charlestown. "When I came," he wrote, "to Bunker's Hill I found it exceedingly strong; the front parapet about thirteen feet high composed of earth contained in plank supported by huge timber." The same care and skill had been bestowed wherever they were required; and Washington reported that every avenue to Boston had been fortified in such a manner that the town was almost impregnable. And yet, — by dint of endurance, and self-control, and rigid reticence, followed by strong decision, and sudden action, when the proper moment came, — he had made that

[1] "March 17. This morning about Nine aclock there was A Larem and our people went into the boats for to go to Boston. General Sulliven With a party of men Went to Bunker Hill and took posesien of it.
"This afternoon I went Down to charlestown neck in order to go over to Bunker hill. But the Sentinals Stopt me.
"March 18. This morning I went to Bunker Hill and Charlestown For to see the Ruens of the Town.
"March 25. I cooked this day. I have ben up bacon Hill this day."
And so at last David How got into Boston, and saw the view from Beacon Hill on the North of the Common, — the site where the State House now stands.

stronghold his own at an expenditure of less than a score of New England lives.

The prizes which fell into the hands of the victors were well worth securing. Great numbers of fine cannon lay about in the batteries. They had been spiked, and otherwise mutilated; but their repair was within the resources of an army containing excellent blacksmiths, among the best of whom was Nathanael Greene, the second best of the generals. There were huge piles of shot and shells, and a great quantity of miscellaneous stores. Washington's quartermaster-general estimated the contents of the magazines at something between twenty-five, and thirty, thousand pounds in value.[1] But all that the Americans found on land was insignificant as compared with what they captured at sea. Even while the men of war lingered in Nantasket Road, an armed schooner hailing from Marblehead had already picked up a store-ship from Cork, which carried fifteen hundred barrels of powder in her hold. After the lapse of two months, in consequence of a hostile demonstration by the Continental army assisted by provincial militia, the royal squadron took its departure from the scene. An imaginative population, on the look-out for anniversaries, pleased itself by remembering that, according to the provisions of the Act devised by the British Ministry for the ruin of Boston, the fourteenth of June, 1774, had been the latest date for trading vessels to leave or enter the condemned harbour. And now the fourteenth of June, 1776, was the last day on which the last of the Ministerial war-ships was seen in Boston waters. Then began an uninterrupted harvest for the colonial privateers. They made an easy prey of the crazy merchantmen which, as a substitute for swift frigates, were bringing the reinforcements for Howe's army. When these belated and ill-adapted vessels at length reached the coast of Massachusetts, the royal fleet had gone for good, and the whole bay between headland and headland was alive with American cruisers.

[1] Washington to the President of Congress; March 19, 1776.

Four transports were captured; and the Highland soldiers on board at last reached their destination, but reached it as prisoners of war.[1] The Patriots learned, with a satisfaction which few will grudge them, that the brigantine chartered by Crean Brush was taken, with himself and all his booty on board of her. From that time forward his life was one series of misfortunes, until it came to a bad end.[2]

In their relief and exultation the inhabitants of the rescued city were not heedless of the dangers which the future might have in store for them. As soon as the royal sails were over the horizon, Boston began to take precautions against the possible contingency of their reappearance. The British, on the eve of their retirement, had demolished those works on Castle Island which commanded the main entrance to the harbour; and the municipal authorities now applied themselves vigorously and expeditiously to the task of restoring the ramparts. Every able-bodied townsman gave two days a week of voluntary labour,[3] working as Themistocles, at a famous crisis, made the Athenians work on the Long Walls which led from their city to the Piræus. Boston, (to use a good old military term,) was soon safe from insult. A hostile squadron, whose commander was not prepared to sacrifice some of his masts and a large proportion of his crews, could not thenceforward penetrate except in a thick fog; and even then only

---

[1] "June 16. This morning our Privitesters Spy a large Brig Bound from Scotland to Boston and they chased Them all Day and at Night they had a Smart fight and took them.
"June 17. This day the Prisoners Ware brought to Boston. There being upwards of 200 Hilanders besides other valuable loading :
"June 19. This morning our Priviteteres took a Ship. She had on board 112 Hilanders with a Cuterments all fixed for war." *David How's Diary* for 1776.

[2] After a detention of more than a year and a half, Crean Brush escaped from prison, and made his way into New York. He applied to the British Commander-in-Chief to compensate his losses, but was told by Sir Henry Clinton that his "conduct merited them, and more." Brush soon afterwards committed suicide.

[3] *Travels through the Interior Parts of America, in a Series of Letters by an Officer.* London, 1791. Letter XLVIII.

with much better pilots than the class of New England mariners who would consent to hire out their services for such a purpose. No admiral, — and least of all one of those political admirals whom Sandwich was in the habit of appointing, — would feel comfortable when he opened a sealed order directing him to place his ships within cannon-shot of the wharves of Boston.

Making reference to the proceedings of the English Ministry, Frederic of Prussia, as was not unusual with him, employed the language of a book which he loved better to quote than to read. "When I reflect," he said, "on the conduct of that Government in the war with their colonies, I am almost tempted to say what the theologians maintain with regard to Providence, that their ways are not ours." And indeed they were not. North and Sandwich resembled Frederic as war-ministers even less than Gage resembled him as a general, or George the Third as a monarch. Bunker's Hill had been a soldier's battle; but the responsibility for the campaign of which it formed an episode lay with the placemen and their Royal master. They had contrived among them to bring about the discomfiture of a valiant army, responsive to discipline, and containing more than a due proportion of distinguished or promising officers. They had involved it in almost every calamity which could befall a military force, except disgrace. They had so managed matters that, in a region overflowing with plenty, their troops had been fed from Leadenhall Market, as an orator of the Opposition cleverly and not untruly put it.[1] Burke was reported to have said that, though two hundred pounds a man had been spent on salt beef and sour crout, our garrison could not have remained ten days longer in Boston unless the heavens had rained down quails and manna. And yet, much as the English had suffered during the course of the siege from the scarcity and badness of their food, in the last resort they were refused the com-

[1] The phrase was Lord Effingham's. *Parliamentary History;* vol. viii., p. 1350.

parative satisfaction of having yielded to famine, and not to force. The Government despatched three thousand British infantry to the Carolinas, on an ill-considered and ill-conducted expedition, at the moment when Howe most needed to be strong. The reinforcements which were sent to him from home arrived two months too late; and so it came to pass that the neglected General was, in the end, not starved but manœuvred out of his positions. The acts of aggressive warfare sanctioned or condoned by the Ministers were as futile as their defensive arrangements, and had consequences most disastrous to the national interests. They had not occupied a single square furlong of soil, fortified or open, in any of the colonies; but they had shelled three towns, had sent into the Gazette a score of loyal merchants, and had rendered a few hundred families homeless. They had alienated all the neutral opinion in America, and had lighted a flame of resentment against Great Britain which they continued to feed with fresh fuel until it grew so hot that it did not burn itself out for a couple of lifetimes.

England had never reaped so little glory or advantage from so great an expenditure of money, and after so much preliminary swagger on the part, not of the people who were to pay or the soldiers who were to fight, but of the statesmen who had already begun to blunder. Colonel Barré, in a speech rich with traditional knowledge, and personal observation, of war, declared that this unsuccessful effort to keep our ground in one small corner of our own empire had cost the Treasury half as much again as the operations of the year 1704, in which our armies were conquering all over Europe from Blenheim to Gibraltar. Barré, however, had not occasion to go outside the memory of the youngest of his audience. No long interval had elapsed since Warburg and Plassey, — since the defeat of Montcalm, the conquest of Havanna, and Hawke's victory off the coast of Brittany; but during that interval a process had been going forward the effects of which were now manifest. George the Third had at length accomplished his purpose. He had rooted out frankness, courage, and independence from the councils of the State; but he had pulled up along with them other qualities which his policy, when brought to a trial, could not afford to dispense with. His Cabinet was now exclusively composed of men, willing to pursue ends which he dictated, but incapable of discerning, or rightly directing, the means by which alone those ends could be attained.

APPENDICES

APPENDIX I

(See page 33)

Eton in the Days of Fox

THE muniment-rooms of our old families are rich in curious notices of the educational conditions under which British statesmen of that day formed their earliest ideas of the habitual relations that ought to exist between man and man. Among them is a typical story dating from the time when the memory of Charles Fox was still fresh at Eton. One George Harlow, in January, 1779, thus wrote from the Queen's Palace to Sir Michael de Fleming. "Give me leave to call to your remembrance an adventure which happened about 13 or 14 years ago at Windsor. Myself and a friend went from Richmond lodge to Windsor to see the Castle. We dined at the Swan Inn, and looking out of the window we saw a number of Eton scholars coming over the bridge, and, as they passed the window, you, Sir Michael, was pleased peremptory to demand my name; and I not being acquainted with the manners of Eton scholars, and likewise stranger to your quality, refused to satisfy your curiosity; on which you, and I believe a score of your schoolfellows, jumped in at the window, and threatened destruction to us, if we did not resolve you. My friend told you his name; but before I had time to reflect you took up my whip, and with the butt end of it levelled a blow at my head, the marks of which I now carry, which stunned me for some minutes. When I recovered you was standing before me, and told me I was not hurt but that I bled damnably. However, you obliged me to tell my name, which done you swore I was a good fellow, and offered me any recompense for my broken head, and said you was sorry for what had happened. I was lately telling this story to a friend who advised me to make myself known, not doubting but you would use your interest to remove me to a place of less confinement than I have at present in his Majesty's household. If I should be so happy as to meet your favour, and succeed, I shall for ever remember you and the adventure at Windsor with pleasure, and consider my scar as the promoter of my happiness."

How agreeably a youth, who had a tolerant tutor and an obliging dame, might pass the later years of his school life is narrated in a letter written in the summer quarter of 1767. "I believe Mr. Roberts is fixed upon to be my tutor, who is the only man in the place I have any regard for. I sincerely think him the most sensible man I ever came near in my life, and has behaved himself so good natured to me all through the Remove that I shall always have a very great regard for him. Mrs. Sturgess is very good natured to the boys, and behaves herself very freely amongst us ; now and then gives a bottle of wine or a bowl of punch which she makes very good. I always wish your company to partake. In short we are very happy. I take no other amusement here but tennis, never enter the billiard rooms. Hulse is our best player. He was to play a set with a gentleman last week for twenty guineas, but the gentleman was afraid to play him."

APPENDIX II

(See page 146)

Fox's letters to his Mother

"My dear Mother," (Charles Fox wrote in the winter of 1773–4,) " in regard to what you say of my father's feelings, I am sure if you could have known how very miserable you have made me you would not have said it. To be loved by you and him has always been, (indeed I am no Hypocrite, whatever I may be,) the first desire of my life. The reflection that I have behaved in many respects ill to you is almost the only painful one I have ever experienced. That my extreme imprudence and dissipation has given both of you uneasiness is what I have long known, and I am sure I may call those who really know

me to witness how much that thought has embittered my life.
I own I lately began to flatter myself that, particularly with
you, and in a great degree with my father, I had regained that
sort of confidence which was once the greatest pride of my
life; and I am sure I don't exaggerate when I say that, since I
formed these flattering hopes, I have been the happiest being
in the universe. I hate to make professions, and yet I think I
may venture to say that my conduct in the future shall be such
as to satisfy you more than my past. Indeed, indeed, my dear
Mother, no son ever loved a father and mother as I do. Pray,
my dear mother, consider how very miserable you have made
me, and pity me. I do not know what to write or how to
leave off writing, but you may be assured that no son ever felt
more duty, respect, gratitude, or love than I do for both of you,
and that it is in your power, by restoring me your usual confidence and affection, or depriving me of it, to make me the
most unhappy or contented of men."

In a subsequent letter to his mother, Charles excused himself for not having come to see his father at Bath on account
of having spent the morning at the Treasury, and being engaged in the afternoon to dine, and talk business, with the
Attorney-General; — a line of defence which must have appeared most valid in the eyes of Lord Holland. "If it is any
comfort to him," the son goes on to write, "to think that his
unexampled kindness has delivered me from certain and absolute ruin, and given me as fair a prospect as Man can desire, I
am sure that is a satisfaction he may enjoy very completely. If
it turns out as I am confident it will, only consider the situation
I may now be in, and that which must have inevitably and
almost immediately been my lot if nothing had been done; and
I am sure you will reflect upon it with pleasure. Adieu, my
dear mother, and Believe me, that, as there never was a man so
obliged as I have been, so there never was one more sensible
of his obligations."

APPENDIX III

(See page 162)

Franklin, and the Signing of the Treaty with France

THE appearance of this volume brought me frequent private communications from America; and the work was the subject of many articles both there, and on this side the water. There were those who differed from my conclusions, and who thought that some considerations had been neglected, while others were placed in undue prominence; but in only one case was I charged with inaccuracy in facts. Blackwood's Magazine, of March 1899, contained a paper on my book, not of a laudatory character, in which the following passage occurs. "The author," (so the reviewer writes,) "gives us the old story that Franklin wore at Versailles, on signing the Declaration of Independence, the very coat which he wore when he was insulted regarding those letters by Wedderburne in the Privy Council. Mr. Wharton, in his Appendix to his 'Digest of American International Law,' has long ago, it seems to us, disposed of that story. It ought so to die."

To a man at my time of life, not unacquainted with literary history, the haphazard slap-dash vigour, with which Blackwood still belabours one whom it regards as a Whig writer, gives a pleasing impression of the continuity of human affairs. I made no reference whatsoever to the story of Franklin having worn his spotted velvet coat when he signed the treaty establishing the Independence of America in September 1783. That story, of course, has been amply disproved by Mr. Caleb Whiteford, the official secretary to the Commission, in a letter of July the 11th, 1785. I spoke expressly of Franklin having worn the suit when signing the treaty of amity and commerce with France, at Paris, in February 1778. That circumstance rests on the authority of an eye-witness, Doctor Edward Bancroft, a Fellow of the Royal Society, and an intimate friend of Franklin. Doctor Bancroft was present when Wedderburne addressed the Privy Council in January 1774; and he saw Franklin daily at Paris in February 1778. Bancroft's account may be found in the works of Franklin, as edited by Jared Sparks, in Volume IV, page 451.

LORD MACAULAY'S WORKS AND LIFE

THE COMPLETE WORKS OF LORD MACAULAY.
"Albany" Edition. 12 vols., with 12 portraits. Large cr. 8vo.

CRITICAL AND HISTORICAL ESSAYS, WITH LAYS OF ANCIENT ROME. Complete in one volume.
Popular Edition. Cr. 8vo.
"Silver Library" Edition. With Portrait and Illustrations to the "Lays" by J. R. WEGUELIN. Cr. 8vo.

HISTORY OF ENGLAND FROM THE ACCESSION OF JAMES THE SECOND.
Popular Edition. 2 vols., cr. 8vo.
Cabinet Edition. 8 vols., post 8vo.

LAYS OF ANCIENT ROME.
Popular Edition. Fcp. 4to. Sewed,   ; cloth,
Illustrated by J. R. Weguelin. Cr. 8vo, cloth extra, gilt edges.

MISCELLANEOUS WRITINGS AND SPEECHES.
Popular Edition. Cr. 8vo.

LONGMANS, GREEN, & CO.,
New York, London, Bombay, Calcutta, and Madras.

SELECTIONS FROM THE WRITINGS OF LORD MACAULAY.
Edited, with Occasional Notes by the Right Hon. Sir G. O. TREVELYAN, Bart. 8vo.

THE LIFE AND LETTERS OF LORD MACAULAY.
By the Right Hon. Sir G. O. TREVELYAN, Bart.
Library Edition. 2 vols., 8vo.
Popular Edition. 1 vol., 12mo.